MIAMI

Also by T. D. Allman

UNMANIFEST DESTINY

T. D. Allman

MIAMI

City of the Future

The Atlantic Monthly Press   New York

For permission to reprint excerpts, the author is grateful to the following:

Florida Department of Public Instruction, for *Florida, A Guide to the Southernmost State*, Copyright © 1939, by the Florida Department of Public Instruction.

Alfred A. Knopf, Inc., for "Exquisite Nomad," and "O Florida, Venereal Soil," from *The Collected Poems of Wallace Stevens*, Copyright © 1954 by Wallace Stevens.

Jimmy Buffet, for "Changes in Latitudes, Changes in Attitudes," Copyright © 1977 by Outer Banks Music, Coral Reefer Music, and BMI.

First Edition

Library of Congress Cataloging-in-Publication Data

Allman, T. D.
  Miami, city of the future.

  Bibliography: p.
  1. Miami (Fla.) 2. Miami (Fla.)—Social conditions.
I. Title.
F319.M6A45 1987 975.9'381 86-28848
ISBN 0-87113-102-1

Published simultaneously in Canada

Printed and bound in the United States of America

Design by Laura Hough

First printing, March 1987

IN MEMORY OF MY FATHER,

PAUL J. ALLMAN,

MASTER MARINER, SAVANT, POET, ADVENTURER
AND ACCIDENTAL FLORIDIAN, TOO

Contents

CONTENTS

MIAMI

Prologue: An Aleph of a Metropolis

Miami has no beginning. It has no middle. But it does have an end
—if you're willing to drive far enough to find it.

Start by turning your back on that palm-fringed picture-postcard
view of Miami. Head away from the ocean, across the white, hard
sand beach, toward the soft blue-and-white towers of the Fontainebleau hotel. Walk past the Beach Broiler, Coconut Willie's, the
Lagoon Saloon and the 18,000-square-foot, 368,000-gallon, free-
form swimming pool. When you reach the ground-floor arcade,
make your way through the crowds of teenagers in yarmulkes
playing video games and the women in Bermuda shorts eating
chocolate sundaes in Chez Bon Bon. Take the escalator up into the
main lobby. Walk under the twenty-two-foot glass dome past the
Poodle Lounge, then beyond the elevators into the reception
lobby, and thread your way through the lines of South American
tourists cashing traveler's checks. Now walk outside, onto the entrance facing Collins Avenue, and give the Cuban in the uniform
a five-dollar bill.

When he brings you your car, head south past the shabby vacan-
cy-sign hotels, past the vacant-faced old people sitting out in front
of them. Turn right onto Arthur Godfrey Road, and as you do,
consider this: from the honeymoon suite of the Fontainebleau you

can see the geriatric ward of Mount Sinai Hospital. Miami's exuberant escapism is next-door neighbor to intimations that, even here in this brilliant sunshine, beneath these swaying palms, buildings decay and so does flesh. By the time Arthur Godfrey Road reaches Biscayne Bay, though, turning into a divided highway called Julia Tuttle Causeway, a new intimation—of irrepressible growth, of dawning grandeur—looms up through the windshield of your car. Beyond that tropical blue bay shimmer the new skyscrapers of Miami.

The locals love to compare their skyline to the one in Manhattan, but comparisons to older, bigger, more "established" cities miss the point. Miami's not just its own invention. It's its own point of reference. That shimmering skyline couldn't be Manhattan, because the skyline of Manhattan is angular, sharp—like the scratch of a steel stylus on a granite slate. As you head across Tuttle Causeway, you can see those buildings vibrating, oscillating—see the angularity vaporizing in the heat. Strange new shapes emerge under that sky as you get closer, beckoning like promises in a foreign language you'd like to learn.

That sky those buildings scrape is another reason this could only be Miami. Here the light is too hard and the air is too soft. The creeping green foliage is too implacable. So every night when the big hot fuzzy orange Miami sun sinks behind that skyline and sets the Everglades on fire you don't just see flames. You find yourself "Beholding all these green sides / And gold sides of green sides." You find yourself sensing "The big-finned palm / And green vine angering for life." You see what Wallace Stevens once described in his poem "Nomad Exquisite," because right at you "come flinging / Forms, flames, and the flakes of flames." New York is granite; New York is about cold. Miami is very different because Miami is vegetal and Miami is about fire, and that is the first paradox of Miami, photosynthesis and fire together.

It's all the same highway, but once on the mainland Julia Tuttle Causeway changes its name to Robert Frost Expressway. A strange name for a Florida freeway—stranger still when you consider you've now reached another Miami landmark famous as the Fon-

4

tainebleau. You're now traversing Liberty City, where the weeds flourish like arson, and not only the green vine angers for life. Actually you're not so much traveling through, as over, Liberty City, because in Miami even the freeways are practitioners of public relations. As if to spare the visitor any inkling that the tourist brochures may not be entirely correct, that even here life is not always about stepping on the gas and going where you want, the freeways elevate you above the surrounding squalor on giant, thirty-foot-high concrete pillars. So you—up on your soaring roadway, in your air-conditioned car, with the windows up, doors locked, the tape deck playing Jimmy Buffett—go your way. And down in those urine-soaked projects, on those hot, garbage-strewn streets where you can find crack and angel dust and dirty syringes, they go theirs. You can't see them; the freeway takes care of that. But they can see you, they can see your car.

When it reaches the big old jai alai fronton, the road that started out honoring Arthur Godfrey ends its homage to the poet laureate of New England and dissolves into asphalt linguine. Here you must follow the signs carefully and make sure you wind up on LeJeune Road going south. On your right is Miami International Airport, sometimes called MIA (as in Miami In Action). Cocaine from Colombia, marijuana from Jamaica, flight capital from Venezuela; machine guns, cluster bombs and "interrogation devices" exported by the Miami munitions merchants, to say nothing of all kinds of legitimate, peaceful, tax-paying commerce: everything and anything that can be fitted into an airplane, then flown somewhere and sold for a profit, you can find at MIA. Many people know Miami airport is the great nexus of North and Latin America. What most people don't know is that MIA is rather lovely—certainly a lot prettier than the surrounding jungle of neon bars and cut-rate rent-a-car places.

The terminals are efficient and pleasant; surprisingly enough, they're also one of Miami's cultural resources. There's Mexican mariachi one day, Jamaican reggae the next, an ongoing celebration of all the international rhythms that converge there. They also hold food festivals at MIA—wine and cheese flown in from France, lobster from Maine, Argentine beef from the pampas. At MIA you can bathe in a Jacuzzi, eat crepes suzette, sell gold, buy land, hold a cocktail party, do aerobics, get married and, if need be, give birth or go to jail.

It's not only these amenities that make MIA much more attractive than you'd expect. It's the sense of nature you find in this jet-age, $6 billion operation, which covers more than five square miles of land and provides sixty-eight thousand people with jobs. MIA is set in a tropical jungle; big-finned palms, vines, flowering shrubs and trees are everywhere.

As you drive south on LeJeune you might wonder why, in a city of denatured tropical islands and concrete-covered swamps, the airport should be so leafy, so pleasant—the focus of so much care and pride. An answer suggested itself one time back in New York, when I was at the Oyster Bar in Grand Central station: for lots of New Yorkers, Grand Central's not just a rail terminus. It's a living celebration of all the convergences that make their city unique, and, when I first visited southern California, I noticed the same thing about the freeways. People in L.A. loved their freeways, and what impressed me most wasn't that there were so many of them, or that they were so broad and smooth and kept in such good repair. It was that the median strips were as carefully mowed as suburban lawns, the embankments all planted with shrubs and flowers—no one would ever dream of littering a freeway in southern California. It's the same way with Miami and its airport, which is only fitting because Miami's not a city of iron or even asphalt.

It's a city built on air, and maybe that's why every evening hundreds of cars converge on MIA, even though the people in them don't have tickets or reservations. They park along the perimeter roads, and they watch the dark spiky palms silhouette the pastel sky and watch the big planes breathe fire. The planes descend, immense and slow, like bright-tailed griffins into a primeval swamp. Then they take flight again, this time fast and fire-eyed, as though they'd fed on primordial vegetation.

If you get the directions right, you're now coming into the junction where LeJeune Road intersects with the East-West Expressway.

If you get on the East-West Expressway, you'll reach the end of Miami a little sooner, but don't. Continue south another mile or so, then turn right on Southwest Eighth Street. In south Florida the cocaine cowboys aren't the only ones with multiple aliases. Southwest Eighth Street is also known as Calle Ocho, U.S. 41 and the Tamiami Trail.

This thoroughfare has another alias. It's often called the "Main Street of Little Havana," although Calle Ocho doesn't look like Main Street and Little Havana in no way resembles Havana unless your idea of both is gas stations, used-furniture stores, porn shops, gun shops, fast-food franchises, big Winn-Dixies and little motels with plaster flamingos out front.

Of course there are many Cuban restaurants along Calle Ocho, too, but most of them look like diners and the most famous Cuban one of all, Versailles, is in fact a converted diner. Most people do speak Spanish in Little Havana—though if you stopped and asked directions, it would be hard to find someone who couldn't answer you in English. According to lots of people in Miami, to drive down Calle Ocho is to leave America. Actually, it's to rediscover an America where most of us or our ancestors started out. In Little Havana it isn't the foreign touches that surprise you—the signs in Spanish, the old men in *guayaberas* playing dominoes in Antonio Maceo Park, the spicy food. It's the girls in Jordache jeans, the kids on skateboards, the Reagan-Bush bumper stickers, the ketchup on the table—the fact that these immigrants have become so American so fast.

Driving out Southwest Eighth Street is like making *café con leche*. It starts out black, quickly turns brown, and, as you add more and more milk, winds up white as any "real" American with a Florida suntan. Not that this part of the city is totally devoid of the exotic. Just after you pass Fifty-fifth Avenue, look left. You'll see a part of Miami that really does look like a foreign country.

It's a real Latin-style thoroughfare, lined with handsome old mansions with red-tiled roofs, elegant gardens and gracious patios; down the middle of this boulevard runs a delightful park, planted with ornamental shrubbery and dotted with classical sculpture. The side streets have names like Venetia and Alhambra. But this isn't Little Havana, and this lovely avenue, which might be in Barcelona or Buenos Aires, wasn't laid out by Latins.

This is Coral Gables, Miami's Beverly Hills, and this grand *avenida* was built by the son of a Congregational minister named George Merrick nearly forty years before the Cubans arrived and Little Havana was founded. Merrick called this foreign-looking street Country Club Prado—one of the most wonderfully revealing names on the whole map of Miami.

Resist the temptation to turn left on Country Club Prado—at least resist it if you want to get back by dark. Keep heading due west out Southwest Eighth. True, nothing much changes for the first couple hundred blocks. Whether the signs are in Spanish or English, whether the people are white, black or brown, Miami still looks like a used-car lot of a metropolis.

Be patient. Eventually the subdivisions will thin out. The sky will open up. You will find yourself in an immense swamp. A little later the signs will tell you you're in an Indian reservation. Don't believe them. You're still in Miami because in this Indian reservation they charge you five bucks to watch some Seminole wrestle an alligator. Don't stop; in fact speed up. There are still miles to go. Keep a lookout for the American flag on the flagpole, and when you see it, make a sharp left. Stop at the parking lot; get out of the car and walk a quarter mile down the trail into the swamp.

You will know you have reached the end of Miami because you are face to face with a ten-foot alligator—and this is not one of those alligators that wrestles Seminoles for a living.

Every day this monstrous fusion of all that is innocent, all that is savage, lumbers half out of the water, half onto the trail. So the rangers of Everglades National Park have done what the Miami cops do when some drug dealer fire-bombs another drug dealer's car or when there's a riot in Liberty City.

They have cordoned off the alligator with those red plastic cones used to divert traffic when there is danger up ahead. Even the visiting school kids from Little Havana and Liberty City know what the cones mean, whether they understand what the alligator means or not: Don't come closer; you might get your arm ripped off.

The alligator comes there every day. It lies there listening to something, and it is as though that reptilian brain is trying to comprehend what it hears. What does it hear?

Even if you slip beyond the red cones, and in a friendly, conversational, nonthreatening manner ask the alligator, the alligator won't tell you. Instead that tiny mind will cause that immense tail not so much to move as to convey the slightest hint of a quiver: Don't come closer, this alligator's tail says; don't come closer.

If you put your ear to the ground, you nonetheless can hear what the alligator hears, even in the midst of this swamp. It is a distant roar, a kind of faint rumble, a little like breaking waves, a lot more like the hum of a freeway.

The alligator is listening to the sound of quicksand being metamorphosed into concrete, of swamp and scrubland transforming itself, almost overnight, into a test case of America's future.

The alligator may not know it, but it is listening to Miami.

Even people who have lived in Miami most of their lives are like that alligator when it comes to all the events that have overtaken their city. The changes have come so fast and been so big the human brain can hardly encompass them all.

Is Miami race riots and drowning boat people? Is it the drug and crime capital of the United States? Is Miami the crisis of the elderly or some Sun Belt fountain of perpetual youth? The glamour of "Miami Vice"—or just a bad remake of *Scarface*? Or is it the world's newest great city, as the local boosters like to say?

"The most charming thing about Miami," John Keasler, a *Miami News* columnist, told me during one of my first visits there, "is that no one knows what it is."

In recent years the confusion has become national. For a long time people in the rest of America had little doubt about Miami's identity. It was a place where middle-class, middle-brow folks went for some winter sun—and where the elderly went to cash Social Security checks, play shuffleboard and die.

Later, Miami acquired another dimension. It was the place where Cubans went when they wanted to escape Communism, Castro-style. Even then, Miami seemed off the beaten track so far as most Americans were concerned. It had too many old folks, too many Hispanics—and far too much sunshine to be relevant to our national condition.

In 1980 Miami's image changed forever, and not for the better, when it was struck by a triple disaster that might have crippled a less resilient place. First, Liberty City and many of its other black neighborhoods exploded into some of the most frenzied civil disorders ever seen in this country. Then Miami fell prey to a veritable foreign invasion as more than 100,000 people fleeing Castro's Cuba poured into the city. Finally, scores of Haitian boat people drowned in the waters off south Florida, and, in full view of visiting tourists, their bodies washed ashore on the beaches.

The Liberty City riots had turned Miami into a city of race hatred and fear; soon thousands of Marielitos, as the newly arrived Cubans were called, were inflicting what amounted to a permanent crime wave—a kind of chronic, slow-motion, law-and-order riot—on the city, too. But it was those drowning Haitians who seemed to provide the rebuke to the old pretension that here in the Miami sunshine you could escape all the cold realities of life. Even the area's most attractive asset, its beaches, no longer was immune to the contagion of foreign infiltration, and death.

Liberty City, the Marielitos and the Haitians weren't Miami's only claims to fame by then. The city also had the highest murder rate in America. This was partly because Miami, like the rest of Florida, has always had lax gun laws and high homicide rates. But it was also because drug smugglers were finding Miami just as attractive as illegal aliens did. By the beginning of 1981, federal officials estimated that 70 percent of all cocaine and marijuana smuggled into the United States passed through the Miami area. One detail, among all others, seemed to exemplify Miami's fall from grace. The municipal morgue, it was widely reported, was so overcrowded that the bodies of murder victims now had to be stored in refrigerated trucks.

Suddenly, so far as many people in other parts of the country were concerned, and for many people in south Florida, too, it was clear what Miami was—the place where the American dream had turned into a nightmare.

That wasn't the end of the story, however. In the early 1980s, Miami underwent the biggest building boom in its history. Within sight of the burned-out storefronts of Liberty City, those new sky-scrapers—some of them of stunning beauty and idiosyncratic originality—arose in downtown Miami and along the boulevards flanking Biscayne Bay. Miami's new artificial harbor, almost overnight, turned into the biggest cruise ship port in the world. MIA became the second busiest international air terminus in the United States, offering more international flights than any other airport in the world. Hundreds of multinational corporations, banks and insurance firms opened offices. A futuresque, billion-dollar Metrorail system sprang up.

Suddenly Miami wasn't just booming; it was fashionable. Wealthy Venezuelans, glitzy Europeans and Arab oil sheikhs flocked in. Almost overnight the Miami look became the hottest thing in everything from rock videos to sports clothes. Miami had staked out a whole new niche for itself in the world's imagination.

Today migrants—both American and foreign, both legal and illegal—continue to flock to south Florida. It is principally their hard work and savvy that make Miami the commercial and intellectual capital of the Caribbean, and much of Latin America as well. But businessmen, merchants, foreign investors and professionals— along with painters, writers and sculptors—aren't the only ones who come when Miami beckons.

At the luxury residential clubs of Miami it is not unusual, on any given weekend, to encounter Hollywood stars, New York celebrities and the superrich from all over the United States, Europe and

Latin America. There are other places, to be sure, where in the course of a few nights out on the town, you can run into Sophia Loren, James Caan, Mikhail Baryshnikov, Martina Navratilova, Julio Iglesias and the Bee Gees. But what beckons such people—to say nothing of yachtfuls of Levantine princelings, planeloads of stylish Europeans and American "socialites"—to Miami?

For all its dark notoriety, Miami offers more pleasures and excitements than most major cities anywhere. Miami is paella and ballet, and the exuberant Calle Ocho festival in Little Havana; it is also country music and crab cakes at Alabama Jack's, caviar canapés at the Indian Creek Country Club and hot pastrami at the Omni center downtown. Miami is the *dolce vita* of Coconut Grove, the Art Deco bohemianism of South Miami Beach and the WASP gentility of the Bath Club. It's jai alai and the Orange Bowl, also racing and flamingos at Hialeah, sailing on Biscayne Bay and landing marlins in the Atlantic Ocean. Miami is Thai curry along the South Dixie Highway and the best sushi I've had outside Japan—to say nothing of succulent stone crabs at Joe's, one of those Miami institutions where you find proof of the city's capacity, in both good times and bad times, not just to survive, but to prevail.

In the United States only New York and Los Angeles clearly exceed Miami in sheer cosmopolitan, urban excitement. Yet the richest "cultural" experience I had there was one you can't find in any concert hall. At Sunday morning mass in Little Haiti, thousands of worshipers sang "Vini, Jouinn Jezi" (Come, Find Jesus). As this Creole hymn of hope and affirmation vibrated out into the surrounding slums, one could sense what people who come to remake their lives in Miami have always believed, for all the city's problems. Miami is a place where even the most impossible dreams—to say nothing of the most baroque fantasies—can, and do, come true.

In fact, where Miami once frightened people, it now intrigues them. What once was denounced as Miami depravity is now considered Miami chic. Like New York before it, Miami has become one of those places where "real" Americans may not want to live, or even visit very often, but which nonetheless has become a code word for the kind of life in the fast lane many people secretly envy, and others quite openly aspire to copy.

The transformation of Miami's image began when the embers of Liberty City were barely cool.

"Bustling Town: Builders, Banks, Ports Thrive in Miami as City Becomes Trade Center," the *Wall Street Journal* reported in 1982. By 1983 no less an authority than *House & Garden* was calling Miami "one of those magical American places."

The next year *Vogue* ran a celebration of the city that made Miami seem like a fusion of Monte Carlo, Manhattan and pre-Castro Havana. The article was remarkable for its upbeat treatment. But it was even more remarkable, many Miamians noted, for the fact that crime, drugs, illegal immigration, the Haitians and Liberty City —as well as Miami's status as one of the AIDS capitals of the United States—weren't mentioned at all.

In the space of a year, noted the local Department of Tourism, which pays obsessive attention to such matters, 298 favorable articles written about Miami had appeared in newspapers and magazines around the world. Only twenty-six derogatory articles had been published, according to the same survey. In the same article that proclaimed these glad tidings, the *Miami Herald* reported another sign of the Miami renaissance: "Playboy's new Playmate of the Year, Karen Velez, is from Miami."

"Miami," the paper concluded, "is no longer Paradise Lost."

It was true the city hadn't been doomed back in 1980, when most of the rest of the nation had written it off. But no subsequent amount of purple prose and media gushing could transform it into a place where there was only bright sunshine, no dark shadows.

Indeed, just as outsiders decided it was safe to go back into the water, Miami itself was passing through one of its dry spells. The crime rate was rising again, and far from booming, the economy was in the doldrums. Thanks to the oil glut and the debt crisis— to say nothing of Miami's own chronic tendency to oversell and overhype—the real estate market had collapsed. The Haitians, of course, kept coming, even after Baby Doc was overthrown. But more and more Venezuelans and Saudis, along with their flight capital, were staying home.

It was true there hadn't been a major race riot for more than three whole years, but affluent whites, whether they happened to speak English or Spanish, still feared to drive, with their windows closed and their doors locked, through poor black neighborhoods. Even when they confined their transits of Liberty City to the freeways, however, it was impossible to pretend the "underclass" had disappeared. Black youths had taken to scaling those thirty-foot-high concrete pillars, and scattering nails and broken glass on the freeway. Then, when Honkie got a flat tire, they'd attack the BMW like it was a covered wagon and they were Seminoles. They didn't take scalps. But they sure took watches, luggage, cash and jewelry.

In July 1985—even as Miami basked in the bright sunshine of favorable publicity—the FBI reconfirmed the city's foremost claim to fame. In Miami you were three times more likely to be killed as in Seattle, nearly twice as likely to be done in as in Washington, D.C. Only Atlantic City, home of casino gambling and the mob, had a higher homicide rate than metropolitan Miami. Within the city limits, you were more likely to be murdered than in all other American cities except for Detroit and Gary, Indiana. But all this didn't stop Miami from being the "real" America in still another way, namely its genius for finding silver linings in even the darkest clouds.

"We're No Longer Number One!" Thus a local headline celebrated Miami's latest triumph. Thanks to the help of killers in Detroit, Gary and Atlantic City, Miami was no longer first in homicide. It was only number two or three, depending on which figures you preferred. There was only one drawback to this happy news. Killing more people elsewhere didn't make Miami any safer. "We are literally on the ragged edge of anarchy," warned one federal judge.

Murder was only a short-term problem. If you weren't blown away by that handgun anyone could buy in any shopping mall, there was, geologists revealed, the long-term possibility that—along with the rest of Miami—you might be blown away quite literally, by a killer hurricane.

This latest portent of Miami doom emerged almost jocularly when Senator William Proxmire of Wisconsin presented one of his Golden Fleece Awards to the U.S. Army Corps of Engineers for its "costly, never-ending and futile effort" to keep the beach at Miami Beach from being washed away by the Atlantic Ocean. The ten-year, $80 million project, Proxmire proclaimed, was a "wasteful, ridiculous and ironic" misuse of the taxpayers' money, and not merely "because one storm could easily sweep away all this sand." The massive land-fill project, Proxmire asserted, actually increased the likelihood of environmental, and human, catastrophe.

Local boosters made dismissive comments about federal subsidies for Wisconsin cheese, but the experts agreed with the senator: "Shoreline engineering destroys the beach it was intended to save," and so actually increases the danger of massive destruction onshore and of catastrophic flooding further inland. The next time a truly major hurricane hits south Florida, the experts added, a dome of water up to fifty miles wide and eighteen feet high would surge over Miami Beach, then sweep across Biscayne Bay into the city, where the average elevation is only six feet. Skyscraper hotels and apartment houses built on sand, and designed to withstand 120-mile-an-hour winds, would be lashed by 200-mile-an-hour winds as the sand beneath them washed away. The lives of 300,000 people would be directly imperiled, and the question wasn't whether all this would happen. As Laura Misch pointed out in the *Miami Herald,* "The only question is when." The only real solution, according to participants at the Second Skidaway Institute of Ocean-ography Conference on America's Eroding Shoreline, was a planned retreat from the coast.

Would it be drowning by blood—or only water?

One thing was certain. As *Vogue* put it, Miami always could be counted on to be "trying something exciting."

*

Paradoxically enough, these contradictory images all proved the same thing. Miami, for both better and worse, has captured the imagination of America.

People may love Miami or love to hate it. But one emotion Miami no longer arouses is indifference. It is the most fascinating city in America right now precisely because everything everyone says about it is true. It's the unique Miami combination of good and bad, gorgeousness and ugliness, boundless promise and crushed hope—Miami's capacity both to repel and to attract—that makes it such an intriguing place to visit, and such a worthwhile place to try to understand.

The travails of recent years have given Miami a lot of pain. But they've also given it something else—a strength of character, a gritty resourcefulness and an ability to rebound from the worst kinds of crises, which is one of the city's most attractive qualities.

Without the grit Miami would only be a large-scale, down-scale Palm Beach. And without the glitter Miami would be what it was until so recently—just another Sun Belt city on the make.

It's the combination of both grit and glitter that makes Miami both irresistible and important to the rest of America.

It's a rock video of a city—one of those astonishing inventions, like computer graphics and laser discos, that only today's America could have produced. One can't imagine Caracas or Bangkok or even Paris attracting quite such a polyglot, heterodox crew of victims and victimizers, high rollers and petty operators, survivers and prevailers—let alone developing such a quintessentially American capacity to arrange them into a chaotic yet functioning whole.

Ninety years ago Miami didn't exist. Yet in less than the lifetimes of some of the old people playing shuffleboard there, the Miami experience has recapitulated the experience of America. It was built on the bedrock of illusion—the dream that if only people pushed far enough, fast enough, into the uncharted vastness, they could escape the cold and corruption of the past, and build for themselves a sunny and virtuous New World. Miami's destiny—like America's

—has turned out to be far less simple, and much more interesting, than that.

Every major national transformation the United States is undergoing—from the postindustrial revolution to the aging of America, and from the third great wave of immigration into the United States to the redefinition of American sexual relationships—has converged on Miami. How Miami solves, or fails to solve, those problems cannot but provide clues as to how the whole country will cope with the massive changes—full of both peril and opportunity—that are transforming the lives of us all.

Appropriately enough it was a foreigner and, even more appropriately, a Latin American who—without knowing it—best defined the essential quality of this quintessentially American city.

"An Aleph is one of the points in space containing all points," that blind Argentinian seer, Jorge Luis Borges, wrote, long before the great Miami convergence started. Borges also explained why an Aleph as dark as Miami contains so much illumination: "If all the places on earth are in the Aleph, the Aleph must also contain all the illuminations, all the lights, all the sources of light."

When Borges finally finds the Aleph, in his story of the same name, he might well have found a convergence of alligators and skyscrapers, where millionaires catch marlins while Marielitos steal their Porsches. He might simultaneously have seen impoverished old people lining up for baloney sandwiches in South Miami Beach while, a few miles up Collins Avenue, a real estate magnate orders a zebra steak and a four-hundred-dollar bottle of claret at Dominique's. He might have seen a black, unwed, teenaged mother shooting heroin in Liberty City, at the same moment a wealthy Cuban girl tries on a diamond-studded Rolex in a boutique on Miracle Mile in Coral Gables.

He would surely have seen the hunger that drives Haitians to swim to Miami, seen the utter weariness of life that others find when they get there as well. Borges might have been seeing Miami when he saw the Aleph, for in his words:

> In that gigantic instant I saw millions of delightful and
> atrocious acts; none astonished me more than the fact that
> all of them together occupied the same point, without
> superposition and without transparency. What my eyes
> saw was simultaneous: what I shall transcribe is succes-
> sive, because language is successive.

There are true Alephs and false Alephs, Borges explains. But in
the city of the true Aleph there are to be found, engraved in stone,
the following words:

> *"In republics founded by nomads, the assistance of foreigners is
> indispensable in all that concerns masonry."*

Who, looking at the Miami we American nomads have conjured
up, and considering the assistance Miami's many foreigners, both
legal and illegal, have given us in constructing it, could doubt that
Miami is a true Aleph—one of those bright, dark, infinite points
where, if we look closely enough, we can see everything and anything, including ourselves?

Part I

"Miami Vice"

Prime Time

Gunfire crackled down the dark, sultry-hot streets. Sirens blared; lights flashed. You could smell smoke, see fire. It was a city built on dreams; maybe that was why, when the nightmare struck, the city was sleeping. Now Miami rubbed its eyes and awoke: people were being dragged from their cars and burned alive.

It was a sultry Sunday night, May 18, 1980; the violence was everywhere. Overtown, once considered Miami's model black community, was aflame. There was looting up in suburban Carol City. There was arson down in Homestead, where Miami's exurban sprawl petered out into a morass of trailer parks, citrus groves and swamps; gunfire on Rickenbacker Causeway, the toll road leading out to Key Biscayne, Florida home of President Nixon.

The sky above Opa-locka glowed like an all-night sunset. Black mobs were assaulting whites in Perrine; they were stoning whites in Coconut Grove, which liked to call itself the most liberal part of the city. Of all Miami's amenities, escape had always been the sweetest. But now there was no escape, not even when you got on I-95 and fled the city. Even when you pressed the accelerator to the floor, the smoke, the rage, the terror pursued you. It was as though the darkest fantasies of the American soul had come true.

*

The riots had begun Saturday at sunset. For three days marauding blacks burned white-owned buildings, looted white-owned businesses, stoned and beat white pedestrians, dragged white motorists from their cars and killed them. Not until Tuesday were the roadblocks removed and whites permitted to drive through black areas of the city. It wasn't until Wednesday that the schools reopened. Not until Friday, six days after the first killings occurred, was the citywide curfew lifted. The hatred and terror the "Liberty City" riot aroused would endure for years and cost Miami more, both humanly and financially, than anyone could calculate. But even if the long-term costs weren't counted, the immediate casualty count was appalling: eleven hundred people arrested; property damage estimated as high as $200 million. Hundreds were injured; eighteen dead.

The greatest casualty, however, was the comfortable assumption that new, Sun Belt Miami, with its beach resorts and suburban-style shopping malls, was immune to the catastrophes that had stricken older, northern cities. As the smoke of countless arsons hung over the city, Miami faced an awesome reality: it had been the scene of the worst racial paroxysm in modern American history.

As Bruce Porter and Marvin Dunn later pointed out in their book on the upheaval, earlier disorders in other cities "could be regarded as 'property riots,' wherein blacks directed their anger largely against buildings. The deaths that did occur . . . were overwhelmingly those of blacks killed by white policemen and National Guardsmen. The few white deaths . . . occurred as a byproduct of the disorder."

Things were very different in Miami, because "attacking and killing white people was the main object of the riot." What accounted for these dreadful assaults, which Porter and Dunn didn't hesitate to compare "to the Nat Turner–style slave rebellions before the Civil War, when blacks rose and killed the whites at hand"?

Afterward blacks and whites, liberals and conservatives, southerners and northerners, all drew their habitual conclusions. But there was total agreement on one thing. Everyone knew what spark had first set Liberty City, then much of the rest of the city, ablaze. Five months earlier white policemen had brutally murdered a respected black businessman named Arthur McDuffie. McDuffie, thirty-three, was an insurance agent, an ex–Marine corporal and the father of two young daughters. He had no criminal record, no previous history of encounters with the police. Not even his killers claimed that McDuffie had been carrying a weapon or that he had attacked them.

Yet early on the morning of Monday, December 17, as many as a dozen white policemen vandalized the motorcycle McDuffie was riding, broke the glasses he was wearing and stomped on them, grabbed his watch, threw it down on the pavement, then shot at the watch. McDuffie was kicked to the ground. The police kicked him repeatedly in the head; "in three minutes, it was all over: McDuffie lay immobile, his head split open and his brain swelling uncontrollably." He was buried a few days before Christmas in his Marine corporal's uniform, his casket covered with an American flag. A well-documented police cover-up followed.

The McDuffie murder was only the latest in a long series of assaults by white police on unarmed blacks, including an unprovoked attack on a junior high school teacher and his family, and the sexual molestation of an eleven-year-old girl. No policemen had been imprisoned for these actions; some had been promoted. Yet even after McDuffie's death, Liberty City and Miami's other black neighborhoods remained calm as four of the policemen were indicted on murder charges, then brought to trial on the other side of the state in Tampa.

The proceedings lasted nearly a month, and at 2:42 P.M. on May 17, many Miami radio stations broke into their regular programs with a news flash. After only two hours and forty-five minutes of deliberation, an all-white Florida jury had found all four policemen not guilty.

The court over in Tampa had rendered its verdict, but McDuffie's mother delivered Miami's: "They're guilty in God's sight and they have to live with this."

If anyone in Miami disagreed, I never found them. "The cops were guilty as hell," Miami mayor Maurice Ferre told me after he left office. "They kicked McDuffie's brains out; then the court said white cops can kill insurance agents with impunity so long as they're black." Speaking privately, senior police officials said the same thing, sometimes with considerably more bitterness.

Liberty City still remained calm. Then, around six that evening, a rumor swept through the ghetto that a white motorist had shot a black child. By 6:15 hundreds of people were pouring out onto the streets. By 6:20 the crowd had attacked its first white victim.

In a typically gruesome incident, rumor produced its own fulfillment. A terrorized white motorist ran down an eleven-year-old black girl named Shanreka Perry, "crushing her pelvis, severing her right leg and smearing the wall with a wide swath of blood." Enraged neighbors pulled two men from the car and viciously beat them. The driver later died. His companion was permanently disabled. Yet even in the midst of this savagery, there were instances of chivalry and courage. While some blacks attacked the two men in the car, others helped their white woman passenger to escape. Elsewhere black motorists picked up injured whites and drove them to hospitals. Some blacks, notably a retired social worker named Georgia Ayers, made heroic efforts to calm the crowds.

Chivalry, however, was exceptional. Other whites were dragged from their cars, doused with kerosene and burned alive. Even fair-skinned blacks weren't safe: one man was so grotesquely mutilated his body later could only be identified by his boots and eyebrows.

The McDuffie riot deeply traumatized Miami. But it also had another very important consequence. It had been a long time since the rest of the country had paid much attention to Miami—and on those occasions when Americans did, they thought mostly of palm trees, beaches and sunshine. Now, for the first time in years, Miami galvanized the nation's attention, and what America saw now certainly wasn't some sunny vacationland.

In catastrophe, Miami nonetheless could count one small public relations victory. The networks all called them the "Liberty City" riots, not the Miami riots. And to viewers all over the country, that at least conveyed the impression this rampage of hate was limited to one relatively isolated part of the city.

Geographically inaccurate as it was, naming this upheaval after Liberty City turned out to be curiously appropriate. The name of the ghetto where McDuffie had been killed now seemed an ironic rebuke to the notion that America was a land of freedom and justice for all.

The United States, of course, is not the only country where people sometimes become so outraged at the system under which they live that they resort to violent action. Even as the McDuffie drama unfolded, Cuban president Fidel Castro found himself facing widespread discontent. Increasing numbers of Cuban dissidents were seeking refuge inside Latin American embassies in Havana. Other Cubans—as disenchanted with Castro's brand of "justice" as Miami blacks were with the American version—were hijacking boats and fleeing to the United States. How should the United States react?

When Americans had hijacked airplanes to Havana, the U.S. government called them criminals, urged the Cubans to prosecute them—and Castro complied. Now Castro turned the tables. He called on the American government to prosecute Cuban hijackers with the same vigor with which Cuba prosecuted American hijackers.

A judicial decision over in Tampa had provoked one of the most traumatic upheavals in Miami history. Now a political decision up in Washington proved just as fateful. The Carter administration totally rejected Castro's arguments. Far from prosecuting the newly arrived Cubans, it welcomed the hijackers as heroic freedom fighters.

In early March 1980, following another hijacking, Castro issued a public warning: if the Americans went on giving Cuban criminals a "hero's welcome," he would be delighted to send them other lawbreakers as well. A month later Cuban guards were withdrawn from the Peruvian embassy in Havana, which also had followed a policy of granting indiscriminate asylum to all Cubans who asked for it. Within three days nearly eleven thousand Cubans had invaded the embassy compound. If the Peruvians were so determined to take in political dissidents, Cuban officials said, then let them deal with the consequences.

This was only the dress rehearsal for a much bigger drama. At the end of April, the Cuban government opened the little fishing port of Mariel, just outside Havana, to unrestricted navigation between Cuba and the United States. For years Americans had accused Castro of turning his country into a jail, his people into prisoners. Now Castro called the Americans' bluff: anyone who wanted to leave Cuba could leave. But would the Americans accept them?

Within days, the Straits of Florida were the scene of a Dunkirk in reverse, as tens of thousands of Cubans invaded the United States in small boats. These newcomers had no passports, no visas—no more legal right to enter the United States than any of the other illegal aliens U.S. forces constantly intercepted, arrested and deported. Yet the Navy, Coast Guard and Immigration and Naturalization Service did nothing to stop them. Castro not only had sprung his trap, he had baited it well. U.S. officials had no choice but to let wave after wave of undocumented Cubans land in Florida: to turn them back would have proven Castro's claims that the United States was applying a double standard, and given him an even greater propaganda victory.

Officials in Washington tried to conceal their embarrassment. Officials in Havana made no effort to hide their glee. "This was a very erroneous policy of the Carter administration—to consider everyone who wanted to leave Cuba for the United States as a heroic dissident," Cuban vice-president Carlos Rafael Rodríguez told reporters. "The United States is now paying the consequences."

Washington may have made the mistake, but it was Miami that paid the price. Over the next five months, more than 120,000 Cubans sailed north to Florida from Mariel. After landing at Key West, they headed straight for Miami. But these "heroic dissidents" didn't consist only of Castro's political opponents. Good as his word, he was also getting rid of Cuba's misfits and most hardened criminals.

Soon the Orange Bowl was packed with penniless refugees all sleeping on bleachers, and with no possessions other than the clothes they wore and a seemingly inexhaustible supply of weapons. Tent City, a collection of leaky canvas shelters and portable toilets that sprang up beneath I-95, the city's main freeway, housed thousands more Marielitos.

One of the most persistent characteristics of Miami is a naïveté you seldom find in the boondocks. One reason the city had been so unprepared for the initial crisis was that it simply never occurred to all those Miami sophisticates that a jury over in Tampa would acquit McDuffie's killers. It was the same with the Marielitos. They'd fled Castro's Cuba, hadn't they? What more proof did you need that they were all law-abiding friends of freedom?

So Miamians, initially at least, were more ashamed than frightened to find tens of thousands of jobless, homeless, rootless foreigners camping out under their freeway. Cesar Odio, who at the time was in charge of Tent City and later became Miami city manager, summed up this first reaction to the Marielitos: "They came to the United States of America to find the good life, and found a tent under an expressway. At the end of the rainbow, it was not gold they found, but I-95." How to show the Marielitos that America really was a land of opportunity?

Odio, who had himself fled Cuba back in the sixties, thought he had a good idea. "It seems ridiculous now," he later told me. "But

27

I thought, why should they have to stay in their tents all the time? Why not show them the good side of Miami?" So he ordered dozens of buses, filled them up with Marielitos, and sent the buses rattling across MacArthur Causeway to Miami Beach. "I thought they'd enjoy the sun, the sand, the water," he said. "It sure was no fun being cooped up under the freeway all the time."

This version of a Fresh Air Fund for Marielitos was surely a success in one way. A certain number of them took to Miami Beach the way certain species of fish, notably barracudas and pirhanas, take to water. Soon Marielitos were invading South Miami Beach's welfare hotels, mugging its elderly Jewish retirees, robbing its delicatessens, staging cockfights in erstwhile kosher dining rooms. Young male prostitutes now patrolled Lummus Park, where, hitherto, elderly men in yarmulkes and beards had read the Talmud aloud. Taking to the free-enterprise system with a vengeance, other Marielitos turned the Deco district into a drug peddlers' paradise. Still others quickly mastered the intricacies of the food stamp and welfare programs.

Not all Marielitos found Miami so congenial. Dozens, disenchanted with life in America, hijacked planes back to Cuba, giving Castro new support for his assertions that the promise of America was false. Of the twenty-seven U.S. airliners hijacked to Cuba between the beginning of 1981 and the end of 1983, twenty-four were seized by Cuban "refugees" so eager to escape the United States they didn't care if returning home meant going to prison: Cuban officials pointedly informed the U.S. government that twenty-six persons had been tried, and convicted, for such offenses.

The Marielito invasion and Liberty City riots had something else in common besides the fact that both transformed Miami, in the eyes of the nation, from a winter resort into a year-round war zone. Even at the height of the riot's fury, only a small minority of Miami's blacks had engaged in criminal activities. Most blacks, like most whites, had simply lain low, waiting for the fire storm to abate. The same was true of these Cuban newcomers. The majority were poor and unskilled. Almost none were the valiant "freedom fighters" both officials in Washington and people in Miami had imagined all those who wished to leave Castro's Cuba, by definition, had to be. But more than 100,000 out of the 125,000 were basically law-abiding folk. Thousands more—drug addicts, prostitutes, drifters, flagrant homosexuals, unruly teenagers—were "criminals" only by Castro's socialist-puritan standards.

That, however, couldn't change the fact that many were criminals. Even though more than a thousand convicted felons were arrested upon arrival in the United States, Odio himself estimated that of those who got through to Miami, ten thousand were "violent types" and two thousand more were hard-core criminals. This was an estimate subsequent events amply bore out. Following the arrival of these "refugees," crime in the neighborhoods abutting Tent City increased 400 percent. As the Marielitos learned to find their way around the city, crime statistics—in every category from rape and murder to petty larceny and auto theft—soared everywhere else as well.

U.S. officials had granted the Cuban boat people free entry on the grounds they were seeking freedom, even though a substantial minority of them were criminals. But when thousands of Haitian boat people faced terrible dangers to find liberty in the United States, they were turned back at sea or imprisoned without trial at the Krome Detention Center on the fringes of the Everglades— even though they were fleeing a regime that was as corrupt and cruel as any in the world.

If you fled a dictatorship the U.S. disliked, you were welcome in America. But if you fled a dictatorship the U.S. supported, you either went to jail or were handed back to the Tontons Macoutes. Immigration officials denied it, but many people in Miami believed another double standard was also at work: most of the Cuban boat people were white or of mixed race; all the Haitians were black.

Few Americans gave any more consideration to these thorny moral and legal issues than they had to the miscarriage of justice that had led to the Liberty City explosion. Instead, as in the past, Miami provided a vivid spectacle to the nation. In place of those orange sunrises over Miami Beach, there were now orange fireballs over Liberty City; marauding Marielitos replaced the bathing beauties of yore. For months at a time, it seemed all Haitians did was drown, then wash up on Florida beaches.

On the morning of May 17, 1980, the day the riots began, Miami may not have been the paradise the tourist brochures pretended. But most people thought of it as a pleasant-enough place—the city where your great-aunt or mother-in-law had a condo, and where you could go sailing or swimming when people in the rest of the country were stuck with skis and snowmobiles. Now that comfortable, sunny view of Miami had been destroyed forever.

Miami, almost overnight, had been transformed into the most feared city in America—"Paradise Lost" as a celebrated *Time* cover story of the period put it. But the drama wasn't over; these telegenic catastrophes were only the prologue to an even more astonishing transformation.

In the months following the Liberty City riots, the city's zoning and planning authorities suddenly found themselves at wit's end. How to cope with the new construction boom throughout the city?

In the downtown area alone, more than $3 billion was spent on nineteen major projects in the early eighties. These included office buildings, hotels, shopping and convention centers, luxury condominiums and yacht marinas. A quarter-billion dollars in new construction doubled the capacity of Miami's artificial seaport, and Miami International Airport embarked on a $1 billion expansion.

"Real" Americans may have written off Miami, but wealthy Europeans and South Americans were converging on the city. Although these "boat people" arrived in yachts, they still had one thing in common with the Haitians and Marielitos. So far as they were concerned, Miami was nothing less than "Paradise Found." In 1981 British tourists spent more money in Miami than tourists from Ohio and Texas. Wealthy Latins went on a $1.5 billion shopping spree—spending more than twice as much as visiting New Yorkers, Miami's traditional main source of tourist revenue.

The truth was that by then tourism itself was no longer Miami's mainstay, which was why the city's new notoriousness hurt it so little. Though people in the rest of the country had scarcely noticed, the erstwhile resort town had been transforming itself into a major world metropolis with stunning speed.

As late as 1964, when its artificial seaport opened, for example, Miami might as well have been landlocked; there was almost no foreign trade. But by the time the Marielitos arrived, the port was already handling $9 billion a year in foreign business. Even more recently than that, Miami airport had no transatlantic flights at all; it had been merely the place where a lot of tourists got off. Yet by 1981 MIA had become the place where the air routes of North America, Europe and Latin America all converged. It was handling twenty million passengers and about $4 billion in foreign trade a year.

As late as 1977, there had been no foreign banks in Miami. By the early eighties, more than 130 banks in Greater Miami were engaged in international operations, and more than 250 multinational corporations had opened offices. At the end of 1982, the Insurance Exchange of the Americas, modeled on Lloyd's of London, began operation in Miami as well.

This was a rise to international preeminence as stunning as Miami's simultaneous fall from American grace. The south Florida area was handling more than half of all U.S. trade with the Caribbean and about 40 percent of all U.S. trade with Central America. Finance, banking and international trade accounted for two-thirds of all income and jobs. Directly and indirectly, this influx of foreign money was pumping more than $35 billion a year into the area's economy—and this translated itself into dramatic growth not just in the city center, but everywhere else as well.

Out on the far periphery of Miami—where the Palmetto Expressway had once been the boundary between city and scrubland—dozens of new shopping malls, commercial parks and residential subdivisions were springing up. To the south and southwest, citrus groves were turning into cities as the suburbs sprawled toward the Florida Keys. To the north, suburban Broward County was turning into part of metropolitan Miami as skyscrapers arose in Fort Lauderdale, too.

Even in Miami's black neighborhoods, there proved to be life after death. Following the riots, city, state and federal officials applied the habitual Band-Aids. Miami's banks launched a major ghetto redevelopment project. But the most striking examples of the city's resiliency occurred spontaneously. A vast warren of old warehouses on the fringes of Liberty City suddenly transformed itself into a thriving, and ultrachic, garment district. In the very part of the city where abandonment had once seemed inevitable, fashion-conscious people of all races now congregated to mingle and shop and—when these labors made restoration of their energies necessary—to wine and dine in expensive restaurants with names like Food Among the Flowers. Such "redevelopment" was more than mere philanthropy. Investors had begun to realize that places like Overtown and Liberty City had something else to offer besides poor people and slums—proximity to one of the fastest-growing centers of international trade in the world.

By 1983 the city was issuing nearly ten thousand building permits a year, and this represented only a fraction of the hurricane of new construction that was sweeping across the whole of Greater Miami. Miami wasn't being "revitalized" like many other American cities. An entirely new city was being built.

Other Sun Belt cities also had lots of new skyscrapers, but the best of the new Miami buildings were very different from what you'd see in Atlanta or Houston. There was something new and gripping, something beautiful and exciting—also something exotic and fun—about them.

One of the most striking of them was begun just as Liberty City erupted and the Marielitos arrived, and, like the burning buildings and people clinging to leaky boats, this idiosyncratic Miami masterpiece—with its red triangle "roof," its yellow triangle balconies, its metallic blue gridwork—seemed ready-made for TV.

Its designers, members of a new local firm called Arquitectonica, called it the Atlantis—a most appropriate name for a city that seemed sure to sink. Most people in Miami, however, called it "the condo with the big hole cut out of the middle," after its most eye-catching feature. Up where the tenth-to-fourteenth stories should have been, there was nothing but a thirty-seven-foot-square hole. Perched inside it was a palm tree. Its designers called the big square hole with the big-finned palm in it a "sky court," and besides the tree there were yellow, undulating walls, a big blue Jacuzzi and a bright red corkscrew staircase. Whatever its utility, the "sky court" was a visual sensation. That surreal juxtaposition of bright blue sky, tropical green foliage and state-of-the-art technology seemed to sum up all the surreal anomalies of Miami itself.

The Atlantis wasn't Arquitectonica's only tour de force. The firm was peppering the city with stunning new houses, apartment blocks and office buildings. Probably the most influential, and certainly one of the most striking of these projects, was a private residence called Spear House.

Outside, this exotic, postmodern villa was basically nothing but a bright pink slab of reinforced concrete. But inside, you entered a world of soft shadows and shimmering pastels where, just as in the rest of Miami, nothing was quite as you expected it to be. There was a swimming pool where, in most houses, you'd find the living room. Beyond that turquoise pool, through hundreds of separate glass panes, the kitchen, study and dining room looked out on the turquoise waters of Biscayne Bay.

Spear House was ultramodern and romantic, unrestrained and disciplined, shocking and pleasing, inviting and challenging all at the same time. Like the Atlantis, it became an instant landmark. Again people ignored the official title, and gave it their own name, Pink House. In Arquitectonica's hands, under the bright Florida sun, its shocking-pink façade, bright as it was, didn't seem garish. As the shadows of royal palms played across it, as passing clouds modulated the cobalt sky, that pastel façade constantly changed. Sometimes it was harsh, violent. Other times it was subtle, playful —almost philosophical. Arquitectonica's buildings were like Miami: you had to see them to believe them. They were, quite literally, unlike anything else in America.

Where had this fascinating new style come from? To some, the firm's foreign-sounding name seemed to indicate that even architecturally Miami had fallen prey to a foreign invasion. Miami's cultural Old Guard certainly reacted as though these talented young designers were aesthetic Marielitos. "Wet T-shirt architecture" was one city planner's pained reaction. "Shock for shock's sake," sniffed the *Miami Herald,* which in cultural matters seems to know only the missionary position.

One of the firm's two most innovative designers was indeed a Latin immigrant, a Harvard-educated Peruvian named Bernardo Fort-Brescia. But the real originator of Arquitectonica's unique sensibility was as American as American can be—a young graduate of Brown and Columbia named Laurinda Spear, who had been born and bred in south Florida. Spear had built Pink House for her parents, and it was in the pursuit of that old American tradition— a young architect designing a dream house for the family—that she and Fort-Brescia had started working together, and Arquitectonica's revolutionary new style had been born.

Far from representing some foreign "takeover," Arquitectonica was a stunningly successful example of Miami's ability to attract foreign talent, and to arouse in it possibilities that couldn't exist anywhere else.

Exemplifying another Miami trend, this Anglo-Latin partnership wasn't limited to the drawing board. Spear and Fort-Brescia were later married and now have three children. Their lives, like their work, can't be labeled, but, if anything, Spear seems the exotic Latin dreamer, Fort-Brescia the one with the American know-how. "My father was a developer," he explained once. "We know better than to fool around with production schedules." As for his American wife, she talks about architecture as though she were one of those South American surrealist novelists; she describes it as the actualization of "dreams without limit."

Whenever I visit Miami, I try to catch up with Bernardo and Laurinda because, like some other people you'll meet in this book, they have a gift not just for knowing, but also for being what Miami is. This isn't always easy because they, like Miami, seem constantly in a state both of perpetual motion and of ceaseless self-reinvention. On one visit I asked them if the strangeness of their buildings—like the striking originality of so much else in Miami these days—indicated that Miami was now really a foreign city.

"It's the opposite," Bernardo said. "We only could have done what we've done here in America."

The locals may have had their doubts. (The Spears had to go to court while Pink House was being built to fight off suits claiming it would "ruin" the neighborhood.) But Arquitectonica's work created an international sensation and turned Laurinda Spear and her husband, overnight, into architectural legends. Jazzy, intriguing, romantic, classic and playful, "luxuriously surreal"—those were only a few of the phrases delighted architecture critics used to describe their work.

Out in Los Angeles two television producers named Anthony Yerkovich and Michael Mann had caught, like most Americans, fleeting glimpses of the Miami that formed the backdrop to the televised melodramas of Liberty City, the Marielitos and the Haitians. Both young men were tired of that transported-midwesterner, middle-American blandness that always seemed to turn adventure shows into sitcoms when you filmed them in southern California. Yerkovich had what was, by Los Angeles standards, a very strange idea: why not make Miami the locale for a new TV series? Earlier, Yerkovich had won an Emmy for setting a kind of "general hospital" melodrama in Boston, of all places. Now he proposed to do for "Surfside Six" what "St. Elsewhere" had done for "Ben Casey"—infuse new color and character into a tired Hollywood formula by getting it out of Hollywood.

Yerkovich was attracted by the human complexity of Miami—the drama of all those Cubans, rednecks, Jews, blacks and other uprooted newcomers trying to survive with each other, even to work with each other, in an instant America that, for most practical purposes, wasn't much older than network TV.

Mann had a significantly different reaction—one that would prove to have incalculable impact on the outside world's vision of the city, indeed on Miami's view of itself.

He found himself intrigued by the *decor* of Miami—by Miami's seemingly inexhaustible supply of exciting visual situations.

By then the Atlantis wasn't the only eye-catching skyscraper in Miami. In fact the city was becoming an extraordinary collage of all the best, and some of the worst, in eighties architecture and design. Both award-winning condominiums and shlocky rip-offs were rising along Biscayne Boulevard. Big-name architects like I. M. Pei, Philip Johnson and Skidmore Owings and Merrill had converged on the downtown area as though it were a playpen and they were kids who'd just got Erector Sets for Christmas. But it was along Brickell Avenue, site of the Atlantis and some other of Arquitectonica's most striking constructions, that developments intrigued Mann most.

Well into the seventies, Brickell Avenue had remained to Miami what, generations earlier, Park Avenue had been to New York— a quiet boulevard lined with the mansions of the rich. By the early eighties, however, Brickell Avenue had come, thanks to the city's booming foreign trade, to resemble Park Avenue in quite a different way. Big new office and apartment buildings were replacing the old mansions, and Brickell Avenue was being transformed from a residential area into an international commercial and banking center. That was as far as the parallel went because there was nothing staid, nothing predictable, nothing "tasteful" about these new buildings. The best were instant classics of iconoclasm. The worst were simply garish. But taken together, they comprised an assemblage of unpredictable shapes and dazzling colors as wild, as zany as Miami itself.

" 'Wow, what fabulous locations!' was my first reaction," Mann later told me. "My second reaction was, 'That can't be Miami.' My third reaction was, 'If that really is Miami, let me see more.' "

Everywhere he looked, Mann found exciting video images—the flamingos at the Hialeah racetrack, the exotic human plumage of Little Havana's Calle Ocho festival, or the high-speed, $250,000 "cigarette" (or more accurately "marijuana") boats etching white waves in the blue waters of Biscayne Bay. Mann found particular fascination in the one part of Miami that, back then, even the city's most fervent boosters considered worthy only of the attention of the wrecker's ball.

"South Beach," the southern tip of the barrier island that forms Miami Beach, had been in big trouble long before the Marielitos turned it into a palm-fringed Asphalt Jungle. Once a winter playground for working-class Jews, it had been to Palm Beach in the thirties what Coney Island was to the Hamptons—making up in honky-tonk vivacity what it lacked in chic. Following World War II, however, all that changed. Mass affluence and the disappearance of overt anti-Semitism turned South Beach into a resort without a *raison d'être*. Once one of the liveliest parts of Miami, South Beach was now "God's Waiting Room," an area of somnolent decay where elderly retirees eked out their final years.

As late as 1980, nothing so epitomized South Beach's decline, so far as many people in Miami were concerned, as its Art Deco architecture. Everywhere else along the beach, towering hotels and apartment blocks had long ago replaced the gracious mansions and estates of the twenties and thirties. But here in South Beach, even along the ocean front, there were only old hotels, many of them rising no more than five or six stories. Worse still by prevailing standards, they were ornamented in what, at the time, was considered not merely bad taste, but a complete lack of taste. Yet if you looked closely enough, even the shabbiest of these buildings had what those glittery new Arquitectonica constructions had—a spontaneous delight in color and ornamentation for its own sake, and an irreverent disregard for the good, gray standards of established taste that was utterly appropriate to this new, dynamic and irrepressibly vulgar metropolis.

"I love old buildings," said Abe Resnick, a local developer and member of the Miami Beach Planning Board. "But these Art Deco buildings are forty, fifty years old. They aren't historic. They aren't special. We shouldn't be forced to keep them."

Yet Miami Beach in the end would be forced to keep them because Yerkovich and Mann by then weren't the only out-of-towners fascinated with Miami's visual possibilities—and Laurinda Spear wasn't the only local who perceived in Miami's clashing colors and human tumult new aesthetic and human possibilities. A few years earlier, another woman who was American as American can be—a talkative, opinionated, utterly irresistible old busybody named Barbara Baer Capitman—had set out, along with her two sons, to transform South Beach from a dying slum into a pastel paradise. The Capitmans started by buying several old Social Security hotels and turning one of them, called the Cardozo, into a rendezvous for local artists and writers and, even more important, for hip out-of-town visitors ranging from Louis Malle, the French film director, to columnists for the *Village Voice*. Then, in June 1979, just before Miami was struck by its triple crisis, local preservationists managed to get a square mile of South Miami Beach, containing more than four hundred Deco buildings, officially designated a historic district by the federal government.

The Capitmans, like most people who leave a permanent mark on Miami, were inhabitants of that no-man's-land where the boundaries between reality and fantasy break down. Just as the people at Arquitectonica dreamed of creating a whole new kind of Miami architecture, they dreamed of creating a whole new Miami way of life. It wasn't just that they wanted the Deco district first preserved, then revitalized. They wanted it preserved and revitalized both for the old and poor who were already there and for the young and affluent they hoped would join them. "All the ingredients are here to create one of the most distinctive urban environments in America," Barbara Capitman told me the first time we met, "the architecture, the geographic location, the people. This could be a vibrant community where all kinds of people—elderly retirees, young artists, people from the North, people from Latin America—come together to create an exciting, harmonious community."

What she lacked in capital and expertise Barbara Capitman, who was then in her late sixties, made up in enthusiasm and PR. In Miami, a town where image always takes precedence over fact, public relations usually means a limousine waiting at the airport, a suite at a luxury hotel, a hi-tech video presentation in a darkened executive suite, followed by a banquet at an expensive restaurant. Barbara Capitman, in contrast, drove visitors around in a dented old Dodge. When she spied an architectural detail of interest, she'd drag her visitors into some welfare hotel, step over the drunken Marielitos asleep in the lobby, show them some faded ziggurat. She, too, handed out glossy brochures—then made her visitors pay for them.

Barbara Capitman told me she'd generated $25 million in free publicity for South Beach. In the national media, if not in South Beach, it showed. At the very moment the Marielitos invaded, and the area hit rock bottom, the Deco district became a cultural icon —the symbol of something beautiful, and worth cherishing and preserving—for thousands of people who'd never set eyes on the place.

The ratio was telling: having been ravaged once by anger and despair, Miami had been lashed twice by hurricanes bred of hope. One result, as the boosters lamented, was that no one looked on their city as a tourist destination anymore. But there were other consequences. The Liberty City riots and the arrival of the Marielitos and the Haitians had caused all different sorts of people, for the first time in decades, to take a fresh look at Miami. Prior to these melodramas, Michael Mann later told me, he'd considered Miami "the most undramatic place in the universe." When I asked him what had convinced him that Yerkovich was right, that a TV adventure series set in Miami would work, he replied, "That pink. That incredible Miami pink."

That pink façade of Spear House; those pink façades in the Deco district; the pink sunrises over Biscayne Bay; the pink flamingos at Hialeah. It would be several years yet before it was fulfilled, but a fantasy world had already formed inside his brain.

And in Michael Mann's case, too, fantasy, once transported to Miami, wouldn't be fantasy. It would be reality—a reality that, just like the Liberty City riots and those stunning new skyscrapers, would be both bigger and stranger than even those who dreamed it could foresee.

2

In the Pink

At the precise moment mainstream America had written it off, producers, architects and preservationists weren't the only ones who began to see all sorts of strange possibilities in Miami. Big investors, ranging from the Prudential Insurance Company to the Rockefellers, were buying in. So, at the height of the oil boom, were wealthy Venezuelans and Arabs. But without doubt the two strangest people whose eye Miami caught in those troubled years were a Bulgarian—whose name was Javacheff—and a woman of even more obscure Levantine origins named Choukroun.

Javacheff, or so he claimed, was a sculptor, and said he'd come to Miami to create "a work of art." He hung out on the terrace of the Cardozo, watching an amazing human spectacle parade by each night.

Out in Biscayne Bay, there was an archipelago of swampy mangrove islands. Some people picnicked on these artificial islands, which were really only landfills left over from the dredging of the Intracoastal Waterway. Others found other uses for them. (Syringes and used condoms were among the garbage that littered the islands.) Most people simply ignored them as they hurtled across the causeways linking Miami and Miami Beach. Javacheff proposed nothing less than sheathing eleven of those islands with 6.5 million square feet of undulating pink plastic at a cost of more than $3 million.

He said he'd do all the work for free, and raise the money himself. All he asked was what the boat people asked—that Miami give him a chance. This was, by Miami standards, the most outrageous thing about the proposal. In a city where "art" usually is only another name for "consumer durable," Javacheff's "work of art" would deliberately be made too immense to sell. It would also be utterly ephemeral. Having gone to all that expense and trouble, he intended to dismantle the whole thing after only two weeks.

It was like the Pink House controversy all over again. Miami's cultural establishment was appalled at the utter unconventionality of it all; the environmentalists donned war paint, too. "A loathsome and potentially harmful experiment that clutters the bay, befuddles the manatee and needlessly interrupts the feeding and mating habits of the islands' birds"; "neither art nor outrage, but a frivolous and pointless exercise that says nothing, does nothing and means nothing"—such were only a few of the hostile comments the proposal provoked.

Pronouncements from on high hadn't turned back Marielitos and Haitians. They couldn't stop Bulgarians either, as Javacheff—who is better known, of course, by his first name, Christo—ultimately proved.

By May 1983 the world-famous sculptor's preparations were at last complete. Miami once again was invaded by boat people, as hundreds of volunteers arriving on rafts, barges, powerboats and inflatable dinghies first cleared the eleven islands of garbage, then sank 710 anchors in the bay bottom, and tethered to them immense hexagonal Styrofoam booms. These floating perimeters in place, they then began to surround the islands with more than six miles of a buoyant, luminous frangipani-pink synthetic fiber called polypropylene. The planning had taken years; the preparations had taken months. Now the installation was finally under way—and, as is only to be expected in Miami at such moments, disaster struck, this time in the form of lowering storm clouds, slashing rain and vicious tropical squalls. As hundreds of people battled wind and waves to lash down the fabric, the most fascinating thing about this spectacle was that, out there on those mucky islands, you could find every single kind of person who made Miami, for both better and worse, what it was.

There were elderly retirees and high school students, artists and construction workers, millionaires and people on welfare—all wading around in the mud, working together to wrench into reality what, by anyone's standards, was only a useless fantasy. One island was set aside for Spanish-speakers because a crowd of Cubans from Hialeah had shown up. "They wanted to continue helping, so because they spoke very little English, we set aside one island where only Spanish is spoken," one of the organizers explained. From another island, an appeal was issued: Did anyone speak French? It turned out Christo's twenty-three-year-old son could. He spent days translating instructions for the Haitians working there.

Even when the weather improved, this surreal human endeavor looked so confused, so chaotic, so weird, you could hardly see a pattern in it, let alone a reason for it. Then, suddenly, it all came together. And "it" (there was no word in any language for what had been created) was so amazing, astonishing, extraordinary and unbelievable, it opened your eyes and took your breath away. Where before there had been nothing but water, mud, garbage and mosquitoes, now there was something so immense and delicate, so gargantuan and intimate, so synthetic and natural, so human, so abstract—so utterly, gorgeously, undeniably beautiful—it made even the naysayers beam with pride, pleasure and a newfound sense of Miami's possibilities.

It was called "Surrounded Islands" and, just like the Atlantis, this was something that could only have been created in Miami. Having first denounced it, the local custodians of taste now legitimized this plastic, tropical, excessive, utterly unique creation by comparing it to Monet's paintings of his garden at Giverny.

It was as though Monet's pink water lilies had been fed radioactive isotopes, grown to the size of circus tents, then floated across the Atlantic Ocean and gently, happily taken root in Biscayne Bay. The art world was delighted. (Critics came from New York, California, Japan and Europe to admire the view, and certainly not because it reminded them of some canvas in the Louvre.) The national media were delighted. ("Surrounded Islands" didn't just create a sensation in art circles; it made news on programs like "Night Line.") Even the manatees were delighted. (Far from being befuddled, they, like lots of people, found the sight of those pink islands aphrodisiac.)

Delighted others may have been, but Miami was stunned, thrilled—overcome with emotion, really. Where so recently there had been a paroxysm of hate and terror, now there was an explosion of joy, and for just reason: who could possibly have imagined that, right here in Miami, an object, an event—a work of art—of such immense delicacy, of such unforgettable beauty, could have emerged from nothing except mud, synthetic fabric and a human dream? Other artists worked with canvas and paint. But "the demented Bulgarian," as one local columnist called him, had used a whole city, its whole people, to create an evanescent, gargantuan masterpiece that would be dismantled after two weeks, then live forever in people's minds and memories.

Suddenly Christo was public hero number one. As even Miami's cultural arbiters now recognized, "Surrounded Islands" had confirmed his worldwide fame as one of the most visionary and humane artists of our time.

"For more than ten years I have lived in this community, studied it, loved it," wrote one thrilled Miamian. "But not until now . . . have I seen this community for what it is." "You have made us bloom. You have brightened us. Thank you. Thank you," others said. "You gave us more than a creation quite wonderful in itself. You gave us a new, an essential, perspective on ourselves." People applauded the artist wherever he went; they showered him with pink bouquets.

"What am I going to do with all these flowers?" he asked. Someone asked him how he'd ever come up with the idea of surrounding all those islands with all that floating fabric in the first place.

It was the color pink, Christo explained, it was the color pink that had opened his eyes to Miami's astonishing possibilities. "So colorful, so strong," he said. "It is a temperament here that is unique in the United States. That color cannot possibly be made in Boston or another place in the north." He'd originally planned to surround the islands in pink in 1982. But raising the money, fighting off the court challenges, getting the necessary permits, had delayed the project for nearly a year. Finally the grand event had been scheduled for April 1983, but then there had been more delays. Still more time had been needed for the hundreds of engineers, seamstresses, fabric workers, cargo carriers and others to get everything ready.

So it hadn't finally happened until mid-May 1983. No one much noticed, but the great work had been finished just in time for the third anniversary of the Liberty City riots.

His famous first name gave Christo at least one thing in common with that second foreign eccentric who also revealed to Miami possibilities Miami had never suspected in itself. Her last name, Choukroun, may have been as obscure as Christo's. But her first name was Regine—as in Regine, Regine, the nightclub queen. Some cities are born with glitz, some achieve it, some have glitziness thrust upon them. The latter would be Miami's fate, as Regine set out to turn Miami into a combination Paris and Rio, choosing a locale for her extravaganza that never would have occurred to the conventional mind. For decades, the center of Miami's night life hadn't been in Miami. It was over in Miami Beach, where nightclubs in hotels like the Fontainebleau and the Eden Roc had starred entertainers like Tony Martin and Eddie Fisher. Regine, however, turned her back on the beach. She installed her extravagant new club (only her second in the United States, after New York) in the middle of Coconut Grove—until recently a funky enclave of old wooden bungalows and raw new apartment buildings whose charm derived from its luxuriant foliage and local eccentrics, not its international cachet.

As far back as the twenties, visitors as offbeat as Robert Frost had found "the Grove," as everyone in Miami called it, a refuge from both winter up North and the asphalt-and-cinder-block banality of the rest of the city. (It was on the basis of that slim connection that that freeway traversing Liberty City had been named for Frost; local planners evidently found Wallace Stevens too avant-garde for such an honor.) During the sixties and seventies, the Grove had become Miami's Haight-Ashbury, a mecca for pot-smoking dropouts on roller skates. Without doubt the place had a certain mildewy charm. But would it wash with the Concorde crowd?

If Regine's press releases were to be believed, Coconut Grove was nothing less than a subtropical St. Tropez—"a village quite unlike any other in America. Picassos in tiny art galleries look out at natives in tiny bikinis . . . joggers and Jaguars move along winding streets to the beat of Jamaican reggae and American jazz." Unmentioned were amenities not even the Côte d'Azur could offer —including year-round mosquitoes, a violent crime rate high even by Miami standards and (for sociologically curious jet-setters) its very own ghetto, a district known as the Black Grove, where some of the most vicious incidents during the Liberty City riots had occurred. Also unemphasized was another distinction. According to the Drug Enforcement Agency, Coconut Grove was the favored playground of the cocaine Mafia.

Regine's penthouse disco was only the icing on a $30 million cake. The name of the cake was the Grand Bay Hotel, and no less than the Atlantis and "Surrounded Islands," it proved to be a stunningly successful confection—a fusion of American high tech and exotic fantasy only Miami could have conjured up. Architecturally, the building may not have been up to Arquitectonica standards, but for Coconut Grove it was a revelation. Until then, most new big buildings in the Grove had been dull, boxy and intrusive hotels and apartment houses of the kind that despoiled, and ultimately destroyed, similar enclaves of character in cities from Boston to New Orleans. The Grand Bay, in contrast, actually enhanced its surroundings because, like the Grove itself, it was both bizarre and utterly apt to its climate and locale. A kind of step pyramid, the hotel didn't merely blend in with the surrounding tropical foliage.

It became part of it. Tropical vines, plants and palms were every-where.

Without doubt the building's most admirable feature—stunning in its own way as that big hole in the Atlantis—was its façade. Instead of blank, staring, plate-glass windows, there was a 150-foot blue waterfall running down the front of the building; it was sur-rounded by thirteen stories of cascading bougainvillea. The blue falling water led the eye, indeed all the senses, quite naturally to the nearby blue waters of Biscayne Bay, while the tens of thousands of pastel blossoms paid homage to Miami's Art Deco City Hall, located just on the other side of South Bayshore Drive.

Besides being a tour de force, the Grand Bay was like the Atlantis in another way. In spite of its "foreign" appearance, this was a made-in-Miami fantasy. The building had been designed by local architects. The entire scheme had been dreamed up by local devel-opers. More than that, the hotel's voluptuous fittings—which most visitors assumed were antiques imported from Europe—were all brand-new, and all made in Miami by Miamians themselves. What appeared to be antique wooden paneling had actually been carved a few months earlier by a twenty-seven-year-old Miami Cuban. The hotel's etched-glass doors and panels looked like relics from the Belle Époque, but they were made by a woman living in Broward County. And those glittering crystal chandeliers weren't from Paris —and they weren't crystal either. They were made in Hialeah and the three thousand shimmering pendants in each of them were made of polished acrylic.

Like practically everything of any worth in Miami, the Grand Bay was an ersatz compendium of the fabulous and the fake; and that, above all, was what made it, like Pink House, just right.

Once again, however, people in Miami, having created some-thing worthwhile and unique, pretended they were just successfully copying something someplace else. CIGA, an Italian hotel corpora-tion that owns the Gritti Palace in Venice and the Excelsior in Rome, was engaged to give the Grand Bay the required veneer of imported "sophistication." Far from being celebrated as a trium-phal showcase of Miami's talents, the Grand Bay was marketed as an enclave of "European" chic, complete with a Paris disco on the roof.

On Regine's opening night, it was as if "Lifestyles of the Rich and Famous" had crashed a Marielito transvestite ball. The duke and duchess of Bedford, Prince Jean Poniatowski, Baron Alexis de Rede, the Duke and Duchess de la Rochefoucault, Count and Countess de Rohan Chabot and various other assorted potentates and princelings graced the "honorary committee." Ursula Andress, Guy Laroche, Gina Lollobrigida, Emilio Pucci, Arlene Dahl and the duchess of Seville (whose Bourbon ancestors had once owned Miami, along with the rest of Florida) danced 'til dawn with, among others, Julio Iglesias, Henri Perrier Moët and the stars of *La Cage aux Folles.*

Miami, as always, was thrilled. But Miami is the kind of place where a guy in a burnoose and rented Rolls is treated like royalty —and if your name begins with "de" or "von," you can eat out free for months. What would the verdict of the big league, that is to say, out-of-town social arbiters, be? Such Eurotrash extravaganzas, after all, were no novelty on Park Avenue and Rodeo Drive.

"Exotic, electric and wild," pronounced *Women's Wear Daily.* A sophisticated European alternative to "the glitzy standard issue of most American luxury hotels," added *Vogue,* as it savored the sight of those Hialeah acrylic chandeliers. "CIGA's style has lost nothing in translation." The imprimatur became bi-coastal a little later when Michael Jackson checked in for a night, and stayed for a week. Soon real royalty—people like Prince and Bruce Springsteen—could be seen partying at the Grand Bay. Regine's, of course, is like Kentucky Fried Chicken. It's a franchise, and Ms. Choukroun, like the late Colonel Sanders, doesn't let just anyone buy rights to that fabled name. So with places like Los Angeles, London, Rome and Tokyo still bereft of what Regine herself described as "the style, the quality, the meticulous design, the exciting events and celebrities and, of course, the international status of Regine's," why had Regine chosen to confer her incomparable cachet on Paradise Lost? When a local design critic named Laura Cerwinske posed this question, Regine—just like Christo—saw pink. It turned out she was so crazy about it that she'd decorated not just her Miami club, but all her clubs, in Art Deco. Not only that, she'd accorded Deco an even more coveted distinction: Regine had made Deco her own personal style because, she explained, Deco was just like Regine herself.

"Deco is very classic and simple and structured," she elaborated. "You see these colors and lines. So sophisticated." Regine was shown some photos of the Deco District, and she smiled, as though at a reflection in a mirror: "These hotels, they are very small, yes? But the geometry, beautiful. Now everyone copies what I do. . . ."

Other people found the Deco style beautiful; others found it thought-provoking; still others found it a stylistic link between the yearning in both its time, and ours, for a successful fusion of spontaneity and order. But now, resting from her labors in her Deco disco in her "Art Deco apartment high above Biscayne Bay," Regine looked down at the "pale peach carpeting," then revealed something hitherto unsuspected about all those Miami pastels.

"These colors," she informed Cerwinske, "are good for the skin."

Ralph Sanchez also had what he called "this kid's dream. I have always had this grandiose idea of racing on the streets of Miami." Sanchez didn't mean running rush-hour red lights. He meant Lamborghinis and Maseratis hurtling down Biscayne Boulevard at 160 miles an hour, just like in Monte Carlo and Le Mans.

It all had started back in Cuba, when he was eleven or twelve. The other kids were hooked on *Playboy* centerfolds, but little Rafael, as Ralph Sanchez originally called himself, took pictures of Corvettes to bed. By 1983 the locale had changed beyond recognition, and so had that little boy.

Sanchez was now thirty-four, a U.S. citizen—and one of Miami's movers and shakers. Handsome in the classic Latin manner, Sanchez had a well-developed taste not just for fast cars, but also for dinner jackets with wing-tipped collars. When he drove up to the

Grove Isle Club in his satin lapels and bougainvillea-purple Porsche 911 SC, he looked just like one of those archdukes on Regine's "honorary committee." But here, as usual in Miami, the truth was both more interesting and much more revealing of the human possibility: the guy with all those zippy sports cars had arrived during the first Cuban "invasion," back in the sixties. At the age of thirteen, his parents had sent him to Miami to stay with relatives, but when the relatives moved to Nicaragua, little Ralph was put in an orphanage in Opa-locka. Sanchez was miserable, though not for the usual reasons. "At the orphanage, we weren't allowed to have cars," he later told Liz Balmaseda of the *Miami Herald.* That, however, didn't stop our hero, whose name might as well have been Horatio Alger Sanchez. Somehow he scraped together fifty dollars and bought an old English Ford. He'd been burning rubber ever since. By the early eighties, Sanchez was a millionaire who, like lots of millionaires in Miami, had made his millions out of nothing, that is to say, real estate. But what was the point of having all that money if it couldn't buy happiness? The erstwhile Opa-locka orphan began roaming the world in search of fulfillment.

"I saw the Grand Canyon at dusk," he later explained, "and that was lovely. I saw the Leaning Tower of Pisa at midnight, and it was beautiful. But there was nothing like my first Sebring."

Sebring is a cracker town in a scrubland of central Florida, north of Lake Okeechobee. It has a population of seventy-five hundred, but for twelve brief hours once and only once each year, this flat-chested, stringy-haired truck-stop waitress of a town puts on a glass slipper and turns into Dolly Parton. It becomes the scene of the rip-roaringest hell-on-wheels auto race in the whole United States. "It was the first time I had been exposed to the speed, the noise of the cars, the people, the—what do you call it?—festive ambience," Sanchez said. "I was hooked."

So he did what is only normal in Miami. He "mortgaged everything but my soul" to fulfill his fantasy, in this case the fantasy of starting a $4 million Miami Grand Prix of his own. Then he staked out a 1.9-mile course in downtown Miami, put up the grand prize and—like some high-octane Regine—invited the *Almanach de Gotha* of the racing world to come on down. As usual, even the naysayers were astonished, and for good reason.

The Opa-locka orphan was now Miami's man of the hour. And as he stood there on the reviewing stand surrounded by the fast, the famous and the fashionable, Ralph Sanchez epitomized a truth about Miami as off-center and indestructible as the Leaning Tower of Pisa. This really is a place where dreams, not just nightmares, come true.

The inauguration of the Miami Grand Prix proved something else: it just wouldn't be Miami if, at the most important moments, all hell didn't break loose.

It was more like the America's Cup than an auto race, people remarked, as they tried to escape the slashing rain, the howling winds—the sinking Jaguars and capsizing Aston Martins—the advancing wall of water. Shivering, drenched mobs fled the reviewing stands for hotels, bars, restaurants; some, in their desperation, sought refuge in churches. It was only its first Grand Prix, but already Miami had made sports car history: not a single vehicle had finished the course, a distinction unmatched even by the East African Auto Safari. Tens of thousands of people got soaked, but it was Sanchez who took a bath—to the tune, as he put it, of "over one million hard-earned dollars." Was it worth it?

"It's incredible," he beamed. "I have never seen so many people standing in the rain to watch a race." For months afterward, the question was asked on television, in the newspapers; it was hotly debated in the legislature up in Tallahassee. Would young Sanchez lose his Porsche, his tuxedo—his shirt? To which questions Ralph Sanchez always had the same answer: "Wait until next year!"

A year elapsed. Once again Sanchez set up the bleachers, he laid out the course, sent out the invitations, put up the prize money. Once again he held aloft the white-checkered flag of hope—and now Miami proved something else: if you wait long enough, try hard enough, hope desperately enough, eventually the sun will smile down on you, even in Miami.

Had there ever been such a balmy, beautiful day? Such immense, friendly crowds? Wasn't that Paul Newman up there—slapping

Ralph Sanchez on the back while Miss Universe kissed him on the cheek? Nearly 400 million people had watched the race on TV over a worldwide satellite linkup that, among other outlets, included the whole of Latin America: incalculably more people saw Sanchez fulfill his Monte Carlo fantasy of Miami than ever saw the Liberty City riots on TV.

Suddenly Sanchez was like Christo and the Miami Grand Prix was like "Surrounded Islands." That is to say, Sanchez was a Miami hero, his fantasy a Miami institution.

Sanchez's race was like Christo's islands in another way. Even when it was over, it wasn't over. A newfound sense of all the unexpected, and sometimes quite wonderful, possibilities of Miami lived on, like a lovely 160-mile-an-hour frangipani polypropylene smile.

The terrible events of 1980 and 1981 had revealed how vulnerable the city was to catastrophe, whether the catastrophe was imposed from without or of Miami's own making. But the happy events of 1983 and 1984 proved something else. Miami might be vulgar, it might be violent and, with all those drugs and illegal aliens, it might not even be part of the "real" America anymore. But one thing Miami wasn't was finished. In fact the really astonishing thing was how fast Miami had surmounted its crises.

As early as the end of 1981, for example, Marielitos had made up 69 percent of the Latin prison population in Greater Miami. This —along with the other crime statistics—proved the city was doomed, according to the conventional wisdom. In reality it proved the exact opposite, that Miami was weathering the storm. The American justice system isn't merely unjust some of the time. It's inefficient all of the time—that's one of the more unpleasant prices we pay for the privilege of not living in a police state. But while single crimes, including murders, often go unpunished, a certain rough justice nonetheless applies in Miami, just as it does everywhere else in the United States. The more crimes multiple offenders commit, the greater the likelihood they'll eventually be caught and convicted. That was what was happening with that substantial minority of Marielitos who were indeed criminals. Slowly, cumbersomely, but inevitably, most of the hard-core criminals were being blotted up by the criminal justice system.

What of the more than 100,000 others? When the Marielitos first arrived, nearly all of them were on food stamps. But by 1983 the number dropped to about fifteen thousand, and this, as much as any headline, revealed what was happening. The Marielitos might not be on the way to becoming Ralph Sanchez–style millionaires. But the vast majority were becoming self-sufficient members of the community.

Things were looking up for the Haitians, too, by 1983. Baby Doc was still in power and wouldn't be overthrown until 1986. But a significant victory for the cause of due process and human rights already had been won. As a result of suits brought by local groups, the courts had ruled that not even in Miami could people be rounded up and imprisoned without trial simply because of their nationality and the color of their skin, and that Haitians held without trial out at the Krome detention center must be released. "What started out as an effort to single out the Haitians for special discrimination has turned into at least a modest victory for fair play," Rev. Thomas Wenski of the Pierre Touissant Catholic Haitian Center told me at the time.

The most surprising developments, however, were in Liberty City. "There's hope in the black community now," an old friend named Bea Hines told me. Bea had started out as a cleaning lady, back in the days of legal segregation. Then she'd managed to get herself a job as a typist at the *Herald.* Now she was columnist at the paper and almost a legend among the black community, especially its hard-struggling women.

When we traveled around the city's black neighborhoods together, it was clear Bea was right. Liberty City and Overtown were still shockingly poor. Violence—including police violence—was still rampant. In fact, at the end of 1982, yet another police killing of yet another unarmed black had touched off even more disturbances. But as she put it, "Blacks have discovered they can make a difference." Following the riots, in a development no one had foreseen, black voter registration soared. For the first time, Miami's blacks acquired, and began to exercise, major power at the polls. It was as though the city's blacks themselves had decided that ways other than violence must be found to gain influence over the city's white and Hispanic power brokers.

In November 1983 Liberty City made history again, though this time peacefully, when black voters held—and adroitly tipped—the balance of power to reelect Mayor Ferre over a strong Cuban challenger named Xavier Suarez. "One result of the riots," Ferre told me at the time, "is that blacks are back in the political process, and back to stay." He discovered how right he was just two years later in a rematch with Suarez. Black voters, angered at Ferre's firing of a black city manager, turned against him, and so helped assure Suarez's election as Miami's first Cuban-born mayor.

Everywhere you went people told you the same thing: Miami wasn't just surviving, it was prevailing, so it seemed only prudent to ask the city's elder statesman of PR the fundamental Miami question. Was it real or was it hype?

"Miami has been facing a test of its strength, character and imagination," replied Hank Meyer, who, in the course of forty years of witnessing Miami melodramas, had handled clients ranging from Arthur Godfrey through the Beatles to Regine herself. "And it's passing the test. I never thought I'd live to say it," he added. "But maybe Miami's growing up, and it's wonderful."

Or as Meyer's longtime friend Jackie Gleason might have put it: "How sweet it is!"

It was September 16, 1984, and this warm Sunday night, too, would become a date to remember, and for the same reason. As a result of what happened, the outside world's impression of Miami would be changed forever. There was one difference. This turning point in Miami's history, unlike the Liberty City riots, began promptly at 9:00 P.M. and was over by 11:00.

It goes without saying that the official custodians of Miami virtue were not amused by the premiere of "Miami Vice." Tourism officials fretted the show would create the "impression" Miami was a city of crime, violence and drugs. "The phrase itself—Miami Vice —connotes all kinds of social awfulness," noted the *Herald.* A Coconut Grove woman named Lydia Clark had her BMW stolen after the show went on the air; it was later found burned. She had a ready explanation: "The 'in' thing now on 'Miami Vice' was to burn cars to get rid of the fingerprints." (Actually no such incident ever occurred on the show.) "Somewhere in Kansas, someone will cancel a vacation thinking that's what all of Miami is like," warned a local TV critic.

When those opening credits came on it was like strolling into the lobby of the Grand Bay on a hot afternoon, or driving round a corner and seeing Pink House for the first time.

"Miami Vice" was a revelation because it showed you a Miami you'd never seen before, and for very good reason. Just like the Atlantis, the Grand Prix and "Surrounded Islands," that "Miami Vice" Miami hadn't existed before someone first had the fantasy, then made the fantasy come true.

Like the show itself, those credits were a video collage of the visual excitement that had first drawn Michael Mann's eye to Miami: a pink flamingo, a blue bay, a pastel sunrise, quick cuts to Calle Ocho and the Deco district—then that "sky court" at the Atlantis winking at you as if it knew secrets only Miami could reveal. What fabulous locations! That can't be Miami. If that really is Miami, let me see more: now millions of people were reacting the way Michael Mann first had.

Even more than those clothes, those cars, that music and those stars, what was a revelation to America were those Miami colors: "flamingo pink, lime green, Caribbean blue. 'Miami Vice,' " *Time* noted in its cover story on the show, "has been filmed under what may be the strangest production edict in TV history: 'No earth tones.' "

"Incredible New Miami Has It All," reported the *Washington Times.* "Miami Beach Bouncing Back," added the *Milwaukee Journal.* "New Moon Over Miami," the *Atlanta Constitution* declared. All thanks to a TV show, the most feared city in the nation was now the coolest, hippest, hottest metropolis in the universe.

"At the moment no city in America is hotter than Miami," *Vanity Fair* announced at the end of 1985. "Miami, everyone agrees, is a modern-day Casablanca," it added, echoing both *Time*'s take on the town (a "new-wave Casablanca") and the verdict of the *Washington Post*—"an American Casablanca, a city of dreams and intrigue." "Crime is on the retreat, racial violence is on the wane, the economy is booming," announced *Le Monde,* France's most eminent newspaper, on D-Day 1986. The story ran under a headline describing Miami as—what else?—"Paradise Refound."

"The City You Wouldn't Trade for Any City in the World" ran Miami's latest slogan, and a Miami-mad America seemed to agree. What did it matter that those snazzy "Miami Vice" fashions really came from Milan—that the show's scripts were written in Hollywood, its Florida-exotic characters cast in New York? That that brooding, tropical background music was composed by a Czech immigrant living in a colonial farmhouse in Westchester County?

As Leroy Robinson, seventeen, explained when I encountered him peddling marijuana to stalled motorists on an access ramp of I-95, "When you're hot you're hot, and when you're not you're not," which brings us back to still another Miami constant.

Even in the worst of times, Miami had never lacked in abundance what it clearly possessed in the best of times, a definite resemblance to the Garden of Eden. As always, serpents of all species abounded, people ran around clad in little but fig leaves, and—whether it happened to be on the world's "in" or "out" list—Miami remained what it always had been, an ideal spot to gorge yourself on forbidden fruit.

3

Stayin' Alive

Back in New York, I'd encounter two categories of people. First there were those for whom Miami was an adventure series of a city —the ones who'd ask what Don Johnson, the star of "Miami Vice," was like. Then there was that second category—people like the woman at a Park Slope cocktail party who'd just gotten a residency at a New England writers' colony so she could finish that novel about Miami she'd begun after visiting her mother in Surfside one winter. For her, Miami wasn't a pastel fantasyland; it was the epitome of something darker.

"All those Cubans, all those drugs, all that violence! That's what gave me the inspiration," she confided, "to use Miami as a metaphor of evil." Then she asked me that other, inevitable Miami question: "How did you make it back alive?"

There was only one time I was really certain I'd get killed in Miami; I knew I'd get killed because everything seemed so normal.

It was just past 5:00 P.M. one Friday; I was in a Volkswagen Rabbit that was fighting the southbound rush-hour traffic on Biscayne Boulevard. A friend's secretary was driving, and by then I knew her pretty well because her employer, with that generosity typical of Miami, had put both his office and his office staff at my disposal. It was helpful to have the use of the desk, the computer terminal, the telephone. But this woman's services had been most useful of all. There were days that had twenty-eight hours in them because she'd pulled together all the appointments at the last minute—then suggested someone "it might be interesting" for me to meet, who turned out to be the best interview of the week.

She was in her late thirties and looked like the title of an unproduced film script, in this case "Escape from Far Hills, New Jersey." There was a cold, northern, not–quite–Social Register tension about her and everything she did, though she tried to affect a breezy subtropical informality in both manner and dress. Maybe that undercurrent of anxiety was what made her so eager to please.

This ride downtown was just one example. The workweek was over, and she had offered me a ride back to my hotel, even though it would take her out of her way. "No trouble at all," she said.

We stopped at a light near one of the local TV stations, and I asked her for a cigarette. She shook it out of the Marlboro packet on the dashboard, then handed it to me. I said thanks; she said nothing. I lighted the cigarette.

Then the light turned, and I was slammed back against the seat: she had the accelerator pressed to the floor. We were doing eighty miles an hour down Biscayne Boulevard. We were weaving around trucks and cars. We were running lights. She was pounding the horn with her right fist. Now we were in the left-hand lane accelerating into the face of the oncoming traffic and the car seemed propelled by rage, not gasoline. Little details stick in your mind at such moments, like the Big Daddy liquor store on one corner. It shot by in a blur, but I could see the price tags on the bourbon bottles, along with the rage on her face and the logo of that TV station. Would the wreck be on the TV news tonight?

People in other cars were terrified, too. They'd run full speed into gas stations or turn corners without braking to escape; some jumped curbs to get out of our way. Then we passed a Cuban kid in a Camaro, and he wasn't scared; he was going to teach this *rubia* —Spanish for an uppity, Anglo blonde—a lesson. If she was doing eighty, he was doing ninety. He was just about to overtake us when she swerved straight at him. She would surely have rammed him, if it weren't for those reflexes only kids under twenty have.

When she slammed to a stop in front of my hotel, I hadn't been able to say anything I was so shaken. But after getting out, I'd looked back. She was glaring at me. You could tell from that glare: her rage wasn't directed at the world in general. It was directed at me.

What could I have done to get her so upset? I couldn't figure it out, no matter how hard I examined my conscience. Saturday I went sailing with some friends on Biscayne Bay. We were tacking, and as we came about, the TV station on the Seventy-ninth Street Causeway hove into view; then I remembered something. I'd taken her last cigarette.

Monday morning I bought her a bouquet of roses. The weekend had shown me how unappreciative I'd been; I'd also let Saturday and Sunday convince me I'd overreacted on Friday. After all, I wasn't used to driving in Miami; she lived a lot of her life in that car. She must have known what she was doing, even if she had speeded. After all, I reminded myself, no one was hurt.

Workmen were installing a new computer when I arrived at my friend's office with the flowers. "She let herself in over the weekend and destroyed everything," he explained, "the terminal, the print-er, the hard disk, forty megabytes of data. I guess she liked you, though. She made floppy disks of all your files and left them, carefully labeled, on my desk."

It could've happened anywhere, I told myself. But maybe only in Miami would the reason have been obvious to everyone but me.

"You didn't notice?" he asked, with a look that said, You'll never understand Miami. "She was shooting up in the bathroom all the time. What could I do? After years of loyal service, you can't just let a human life go down the drain. Ten months ago she came in and leveled with me. I authorized a fake Blue Cross claim so she could go to a place up in Georgia. She was fine for a couple of months after she got back; then it started all over again. When you arrived," he continued, "it seemed like a godsend. I thought help-ing you out would restore her self-esteem."

One thing my friend couldn't figure out was what she'd used to smash everything: "You just couldn't do this kind of damage with a hammer or a two-by-four," he said.

"Perhaps it was the tire iron," I suggested. His look changed. In his eyes I was no longer a dunce. But lots and lots of times in Miami I was like some precocious six-year-old who couldn't understand why adults—for no apparent reason—one minute would be tense, distant and irritable, then a little later be expansive, friendly and relaxed.

A six-year-old couldn't understand because a six-year-old couldn't understand sex. It was the same way with Miami and drugs.

Some close friends had a friend who had a boat. One day we all went marlin fishing. The host, a man in his mid-forties, had recently moved to Miami—and not just for the deep-sea fishing. What he liked most, he said, was that Miami was so cosmopolitan. In his spare time, he was taking Spanish lessons. "Back in Pittsburgh," he told me, "there was no chance to speak a foreign language, even if you knew one. When I get a little more fluent, I'm going to take a vacation in South America." He was crazy about Venezuelan girls —those dressy, classy, well-bred Caracas debutantes who, during the oil boom, would fly up to shop once or twice a month. He had one of those Mercedes coupes with a detachable roof, and when you saw him arrive for dinner at our mutual friends' house in Key Biscayne, it was hard to believe he had two kids who'd finished college.

The younger child had been a sophomore at Bryn Mawr when he and his wife, who had some family money behind her, divorced. He'd worked for one of the Fortune 500 companies, so it was easy to get himself named comptroller of its Miami operation. He'd never been able to save much money, but he'd arrived with a sizable nest egg, as well as a good job. After he and his wife had sold the house in Sewickley, paid off the mortgage, provided for the kids and split the remainder, he still had more than $50,000 in cash.

A year after we first met, the money was gone—partly on car and boat payments, mostly on coke. "I started 'experimenting' up in Pennsylvania," he later told me. "But the stuff you got up there was always low grade and enormously expensive. The emotional side of my brain told me I didn't have a drug problem. The financial side convinced me it would really be an economy moving to Miami—I could get better coke here, a lot cheaper."

One night one of those girls from Caracas let him come up to her suite at the Dupont Plaza. She must have come from one of those really sheltered Latin backgrounds. When he made sexual advances, she got frightened; when he offered her some coke, she tried to call the police. Fortunately for him, only the house detective showed up; even more fortunately, the house detective turned out to be a good ole boy who spoke no Spanish. It was only that they'd both had a little too much to drink, he explained to the detective. Besides, he told the guy with a wink, these Latin firecrackers were always so hot-blooded.

Then he coolly excused himself, went into the bathroom and flushed the coke down the toilet. It wasn't his first close call. So when he was fired two weeks later, he didn't know whether it was because the head office had caught wind of that particular incident or another. Within six months the boat and car had been repossessed; he owed Visa and Mastercard more than $10,000. He lost the apartment on Brickell Avenue, too.

That was when our mutual friends had stepped in. For nearly a year, they let him sleep in their guest room and drive around in an old Pinto they had. There was only one condition. They had a twelve-year-old daughter and a seven-year-old son; if any trace of any drug of any kind were found in the house, he'd be out.

"I was an inch from the gutter," he told me. "I had no money. I had no place to go. I had no choice but to stay clean." Sometimes he'd delivered messages for four dollars an hour. "I was the only forty-six-year-old Anglo delivery boy with an M.B.A. in Miami," he said. Mostly he'd earned pocket money doing odd jobs—mowing lawns, laying patios, cleaning swimming pools. Once or twice a month, he'd scrape the dirt from under his fingernails, put on a suit and tie, and go downtown for an interview. Knowledge of his credit rating, if nothing else, seemed to precede him everywhere. "Besides," he said, "who'd want to hire a middle-aged guy who was fired from his last job, and who's had no visible means of support for more than a year?"

One Friday our mutual friend came home from the office early. "He was laughing, he was jumping up and down, he was so happy. It was all fixed. He had a friend who had a job opening up in his accounting department. It wasn't much of a job, but I was as good as hired. Of course I'd have to take the drug test. It was set for ten A.M. Monday.

"He knew, soon as he saw my face. All he said was: 'I just hope it wasn't in this house, I just hope it wasn't in this house.' It wasn't. It was on a yard job that morning. The woman invited me in and said she was lonely. I said I was lonely. She took off her blouse and rolled us a joint."

There was this mixture of anguish and wonder in his voice as he talked about it: "That was the crazy thing. It wasn't coke. It wasn't coke. It was just a goddamn joint and because of that my whole future—my whole chance to have a future—was literally going to be pissed away on Monday morning. That night we were all sitting around trying to talk about something else because the kids were there. Then his wife started crying, and I started crying, and then all three of us were crying. The kids couldn't figure it out."

The next morning he put on shorts and jogging shoes; our friend got behind the wheel of the Pinto, and with our friend pacing him, he ran from one end of Key Biscayne to the other—all the way from the foot of Rickenbacker Causeway to the entrance of Bill Baggs State Park. Then he ran back to Rickenbacker Causeway, and was halfway back again when he sat down on the road, put his head in his hands and said he couldn't do it anymore. They did the same thing Sunday. This time he made two and a half round-trips, a distance of nearly twenty miles. He drank gallons of water.

"They say marijuana, unlike cocaine, is traceable in your system for five days whatever you do," he explained. "But we figured, we've just got to try. At nine sharp Monday," he continued, "I called the man at his office, introduced myself over the phone and told him I'd really overdone it exercising over the weekend. Could I postpone our interview—I was too scared even to mention the drug test—for a day or two? I could tell immediately he was suspicious, so I said I'd be right over.

"The funny thing was, I never had to take the test. The subject of drugs never came up. The guy who owned the firm was more than ten years younger than me, and it turned out he was a health nut. Soon as he saw me limping in, his whole face lit up. He spent the whole interview giving me advice about blisters and stretched muscles. 'I wasn't really sure I was going to hire you,' he told me, 'but I admire it when people your age make an effort to keep in shape. You're on the payroll as of today, but don't come in until Wednesday. You deserve a rest.' "

When I last saw him, it was two years later. He'd found another job that paid a little better. Our friends in Key Biscayne had been transferred to Seattle. He drove a used Pontiac; he lived in a three-hundred-dollar-a-month studio near the Seventy-ninth Street Causeway. He was very lonely.

"I'm almost fifty," he told me. "I take home eight hundred and seventy-five dollars a month. I have two children I haven't seen in five years. I work for people who are all fifteen years younger than me. I meet girls who lose interest as soon as they figure out I'm not into drugs. I watch television a lot, sometimes the religious channels. I envy people who can get solace from Jesus, but I can't. I don't drink anything except beer anymore, because when I drink the hard stuff, it makes me want coke. I haven't got laid in six months."

A few days later, I had a drink with another divorced man about the same age, though there the similarities ended. This man was the classic Miami success.

He owned shopping malls, condominium complexes, an entire island in Biscayne Bay. He was worth millions. He was one of those Miami figures people in New York tell you to call.

His name was Martin Z. Margulies. His island was called Grove Isle; it was populated, indoors and outdoors, with countless objects, with inestimable millions of dollars of contemporary art. It was a collection a Medici might have envied, but this was Miami. Margulies didn't look like a Florentine prince. He looked like a guy with a Toyota franchise. He told me to call him Marty, of course.

I met him four times. One morning he showed me the collection he kept in his penthouse duplex—Pollock, Kline, de Kooning, Rothko, Motherwell, Frankenthaler, Johns, Rivers, Marisol, Indiana, Rosenquist, Lichtenstein, Warhol, Oldenburg, Stella, an austere Morris Louis with blues so blue and reds so red they made a Biscayne Bay sunrise seem both drab and vulgar. Another morning he showed me his outdoor sculpture collection: Calder, Nevelson, more Stellas, Dubuffet, Heizer, Noguchi, Smith, Segal, Di Suvero.

Margulies was like a lot of people in Miami. He made a great trophy if that was why you'd come down there—to bag your glitzy TV hero, your white-collar junkie, your crooked Latin cop, your designer-label art speculator, but one of the reasons I respected him was that he clearly was interested in collecting art, not status. He was also about the only big art collector I've met who was honest about the money. "The role of money is vital if you're a serious collector," Margulies told me, "because it makes you make choices. Anybody can have 'good taste,' in the sense of having a series of opinions on what's good art. What keeps me honest is having to write those checks."

I told him he'd assembled the best private collection of contemporary art I'd ever seen. "There's no such thing as a great de Kooning," he said. "There are just great paintings de Kooning happened to paint. You could assemble a collection of paintings and sculptures by the biggest names in twentieth-century art, and it could still be junk."

I asked Margulies what it was like living in Miami. He had this island; he had money; he had this extraordinary art collection; he was unattached and he was still fairly young. For someone like him, I suggested, Miami really must be paradise found.

When he answered, it might have been the guy with the three-hundred-dollar-a-month studio and the used Pontiac speaking.

"I'm lonely a lot of the time," he said. "You meet a girl you like a lot. You invite her out a few times; she seems to like you. Then she loses interest.

"You see," he said, "I'm not into drugs. I invite a girl up, and I don't offer her cocaine. So, in lots of people's eyes, that makes me pretty square."

In Miami you could refuse to take drugs. You could refuse to associate with people who use them. You could even isolate yourself from drugs, if you were rich enough, on your own island. But whatever you did, drugs would be part of your life. If you were lucky, they wouldn't affect your relations with your family, your loved ones, your friends and co-workers. But there is no way to stop coke or crack or smack from determining whether the girl on the next barstool smiles at you, whether the guy in the car in the next lane rams you. However you make your money, you know at least some of it has to be drug money, because in Miami drug money doesn't just buy Rolexes and Mercedes and condos and automatic pistols. It buys everything from hypodermic syringes to magazines on newsstands. It's on the table when you settle up your bridge scores; it's in the collection plate when you go to church.

By 1985 it had been scientifically established that, statistically speaking, every man, woman and child in the Miami area had not only had drug money, but drugs, on their hands. When Dr. William Lee Hearn, a local pharmacologist, tested bundles of currency randomly chosen from the deposits at seven of the area's most respectable banks, he found "large amounts of cocaine" on all of them.

"At one time or another we will have tainted money in our pocket. If you have over $1,000 in cash," Dr. Hearn told a Dade County judge and jury, "it is a virtual 100 percent probability that there will be a trace of drugs on that money."

It costs $1.4 million a week to produce "Miami Vice." The yearly budget of the Miami Metro vice squad is $1,161,741. Your average undercover cop in south Florida earns in a year about what Don Johnson earns in a week, but in the course of my research I did come to know two different drug enforcement officers who, just like Sonny Crockett, lived on boats. This wasn't because they liked sailing. They lived on boats for the same reason other cops you met lived in seedy trailer parks around the airport, or in dumpy little bungalows out in Sweetwater.

One sunset I visited one of these cops at his marina. He was a man who'd reached that stage in life when he was three or four years past being really young—just five or ten pounds past being really good-looking. His wife, I learned later, had left him a few months earlier for a man who made more money, less dangerously.

He was expecting me and, maybe because he was lonely, he'd made an effort. He'd gone out and bought a six-pack of Dos Equis beer and some Doritos. He'd acquired his taste for Mexican beer, he explained, while intercepting drugs in Texas. Then the Reagan administration had decided to make Miami the showcase of its "war" on drugs and set up a highly publicized task force, headed by Vice-President George Bush, so he'd been transferred here. One problem with his undercover work, he said, was that he spoke Spanish with a Mexican, not a Cuban, accent. Another was that the politicians weren't interested in long-term strategy—programs like antidrug education in U.S. schools and helping Bolivian peasants develop economic alternatives to producing cocaine. "They're hooked on razzle-dazzle," he said, " 'Miami Vice'–type capers. That way they can hold press conferences and get on TV.

"I guess you can't really blame 'Miami Vice,' " he went on. "If you showed what it's really like, the show'd be canceled. You'd have endless shots of guys sitting in cars, sitting on docks, sitting in offices and parking lots and coffee shops, waiting. Then, maybe after a couple hundred hours, something might happen. Maybe you'd catch a guy claiming a suitcase at the airport. Only there wouldn't be clothes in the bottom of the suitcase, there'd be cocaine. Or you'd intercept a fishing boat, only they wouldn't have stone crabs in the hold, they'd have pot. Then you'd show us informing them of their rights, taking them to the station and typing out the report. Then you'd see their lawyers posting bail and them going home. The dramatic climax would come twenty or thirty episodes later, when the judge decided whether they got six months or two years."

A big power craft went by; this man's little sailboat was wrenched up and down in the wake. The passing vessel was more than forty feet long; besides radar, sonar and loran, it carried an auxiliary launch as long as his boat.

"When they pick up the coke tonight," he said, "maybe they'll stow it in the launch. That way, if they pick up the Coast Guard on the radar, they can set up a diversion. Of course," he added, "if we mounted a really serious operation, they could just dump the stuff overboard and go back for more the next night."

He mentioned the name of the man who owned the boat. It was vaguely familiar; he was a real estate developer from up North who divided his time between Miami, Palm Springs and Europe. Once in a while, you'd see his picture in the society pages of those glossy in-house magazines the big hotels and condominiums hand out.

My acquaintance opened another beer and answered my questions before I could ask them.

"He does it because no one ever has enough money," he said. "He and his wife entertain a lot; the kind of people they entertain expect both coke and caviar. The real estate market's shot to hell, as you know. What could be more natural, when the condos aren't moving, than to retail some of the stuff you've been bringing in for your personal use?

"We don't arrest him," he went on, "because his lawyers would tie us up for years. If they were really smart, we might have to settle for, say, a twenty-five-thousand-dollar fine and two years' community service. Meanwhile twenty-five million dollars in coke would get through while we were tied up filing affidavits."

He smiled at me affably. "Besides," he said, "that guy's not Mr. Big. He's like you—just an enterprising free-lancer."

As darkness settled over the marina, the lights on the surrounding boats had come on. It was like looking in windows in some John Cheever short story. People were mixing cocktails, preparing dinner, sitting out in the balmy night air talking and smoking—when the wind blew the right way, you could tell some of them were smoking pot. Across the way a bridge game had started. On another boat they were running a VCR. We couldn't see the screen, but you could tell from that brooding, exotic background music: it was "Miami Vice." Of course there were a few people with dark hair and dark eyes and foreign accents in this tranquil American marina where the jagged edges of Miami merged into the smooth fiberglass normalcy of Broward County. But most of them had that blond, blue-eyed, "real" American Don Johnson look. There wasn't a cocaine cowboy, let alone some *capo* of the Colombian drug *mafioso,* in sight.

I asked him how he coped with the tedium of his work. "It's not that bad," he answered. "It gives you time to think. The really hard thing about this job," he explained as we each opened our third beer, "is that it murders your social life. It's not just when you go to a party; you can't drop in on friends on the spur of the moment. You have to call up in advance and tell them exactly when you're arriving so they can hide the drugs before you get there. After a while," he continued, "you see that look even in the eyes of your closest friends: 'When's this narc going home, so we can enjoy ourselves?'

"It's not the dealers and users who are social misfits anymore," he explained, "it's guys like me."

As he walked me down the dock to the gate, he pointed out the boats he knew smuggled drugs regularly, the ones that did it occasionally and those that, as he put it, were "clean"—not that you wouldn't find drugs on them, but in the sense that they weren't involved in the traffic.

"Figure drugs paid for thirty percent of these boats," he said. "Maybe fifty percent carry some kind of contraband sometime. The remaining twenty percent belong to hardworking, law-abiding guys who like to sail out with a girl, get naked, snort some coke and have some fun.''

As I left, I asked him to join me for dinner that night. I was meeting some people at Cafe Chauveron, Miami's snazziest restaurant: it would be on the expense account. "Nah," he said, "I need the *ZZZ*s. Something interesting might happen at MIA around six-thirty tomorrow morning."

There were, so far as I can remember, about six of us at dinner at Cafe Chauveron that night. I already knew several of them. But the real reason for the dinner was to meet a certain Miami lawyer in his early thirties. He was one of those people whose name you never see in the papers, but whom people keep mentioning. Someone in New York I knew had gone to school with him; several people in Washington I knew knew him, too. Not only was he extremely well connected, they all assured me, he was lots of fun —just the person to show me the "real" Miami.

We ate a great deal of very pretentious, very expensive Miami-French food; we drank a great deal of very pretentious, enormously expensive Miami-French wine. When the bill came, it was nearly seven hundred dollars. The lawyer grabbed the check, and I let him. He was dressed casually—and not "Miami Vice" casual, just plain penny loafers, gray slacks and a blazer you could've bought at Burdine's department store. But with that gold name-bracelet on his right wrist, and the gold Rolex on his left, you could have endowed a small literary magazine. I still didn't know Miami very well so I didn't appreciate the most significant detail until later: the lawyer paid the bill in *cash,* as he invited us all back to his house.

Maybe there were six to start, as I mentioned. By the end there were just us two—and then only me. Did the others, one by one, start disappearing right after dinner? Or did they vanish later? I never did find out.

His house was one of those discreet little half-million-dollar *pieds-*

à-terre you find tucked away behind cypress fences, surreal vegetation and state-of-the-art security systems all over Coconut Grove. There was the Jacuzzi in the garden, the stereo system that cost more than the Rolex. There was the girl who disappeared to slip into something more comfortable and, when she returned, was wearing a bikini and carrying what looked like a tray full of Gitanes cigarettes and a Ming Dynasty blue-and-white vase full of talcum powder.

It only makes me cough uncontrollably, I explained as I declined the marijuana. The lawyer had taken out his wallet again; he was passing around hundred-dollar bills. People were rolling them up, then kneeling beside the coffee table and inhaling so hard the white powder was sucked up the hundred-dollar bill into their nostrils. Why not, I said, though it'll just make me sniffle. It was just before eleven, according to the Second Empire ivory-and-ormolu clock on the mantel of the Art Deco fireplace.

Next time I noticed, the clock said 6:14, and my curiosity was aroused by a couple of things.

First of all I was wondering why it was so cold, even when you huddled on the silk Qum carpet next to the fireplace. After a while I figured that out. Those weren't heat ducts; those were air-conditioning ducts beside the fireplace.

The next anomaly was harder to decipher. Why was someone shining klieg lights through all the windows? It had been so nice when the lights in the garden had been all soft and rosy. I got up from in front of the fireplace; I was looking for the rheostat, when a little voice inside me said, "Sunrise. The sunrise is over. Everything is so bright now because it is now morning."

What I really couldn't figure out, no matter how hard I tried, was that, if the lawyer really was my best friend, why was he leaving me alone in this strange house? He and I had talked all night; we'd told each other the stories of our lives and shared the secrets of our souls. And while I couldn't actually tell you what any of those secrets were, while I couldn't have provided you with such details as what my great new friend's telephone number or address or name was, that didn't matter. What mattered was that he was my Crockett and I was his Tubbs, or maybe the other way around, but whatever the case, we were a team!

Except now these bright lights were making my eyes hurt, and my friend had changed into a tropical-weight pinstripe suit and was holding a machine that sounded like an outboard motor next to his face. And he was leaving! Why?

"Jesus," he exclaimed, as he put down the electric razor and knotted his tie. "It's six-nineteen and I've got to get to MIA in eleven minutes. Fix yourself some breakfast, if you want."

I asked him why he was shouting at me, but the only answer I heard was the scrape of accelerating tires on the white gravel driveway outside. It was too complicated to find the kitchen, so I moistened the tip of my right index finger with my tongue, stuck my finger first into the vase, then up my left nostril. Then I did the same thing with my left index finger and right nostril. Before you knew it, the ormolu clock said nine-thirty and the electric razor had turned into a vacuum cleaner.

Connected to the vacuum cleaner was a Cuban maid in a uniform, and she was vacuuming up the white powder that, in the course of the night, had come to be scattered and spilled all over the room, and I was wandering out across the gravel driveway that went CRUNCH-CRUNCH every time you took a step, no matter how quietly you tried to walk. Outside on the street, all those passing cars were like thirty-three-and-a-third records being played at seventy-eight rpm. I knew one of them was going to run me down. What else could you expect, when everyone in Miami did 180 miles an hour in a thirty-five-mile zone? My impending death in a hit-and-run homicide fascinated me, but not so much as its meteorological circumstances.

How poetic to die in a snowstorm in Miami! I was sweating; sweat was streaming down my face; as I wiped some of it from my face with my hand, the same voice inside me said, "If you are sweating, it is hot, and if it is hot, how can it be snowing?" Then a taxi came along, and the Haitian cabdriver stopped. *"Pourquoi neige-t-il?"* I asked as I got in; then I realized.

My jacket and shirt and trousers were covered—impregnated—with the white powder; every time I moved, a little blizzard of cocaine enveloped me. There was five hundred or a thousand dollars in coke in the folds and creases and pockets and lining of my clothes, but not even in Miami can you pay taxi fares with cocaine. As the driver pulled up to the hotel, I felt through my pockets. It was okay. The meter said $5.75 and in my breast pocket there was, I found, this piece of rolled-up money covered with white powder.

I told the Haitian to keep the change.

The room boy refused a tip when he returned my dry cleaning that evening; he said I could give him my laundry anytime. The red light on the bedside telephone was blinking; the lawyer had called while I was out. I told the hotel operator, if he called again, to say I'd returned to New York. For the rest of the week I watched the drug reports in the local papers closely. It was unlikely, I knew. But it was just possible the narc on the boat had had to get to the airport by six-thirty to arrest the lawyer who'd bought me dinner. And if he was nabbed with the claim checks to a suitcase full of coke, would the police also find the name card I'd given him?

I was also curious about my future mental agility. Would I have to tell myself There-is-the-tooth-brush-You-will-now-pick-up-the-tooth-brush-and-put-tooth-paste-on-the-tooth-brush-And-when-you-put-the-tooth-brush-in-your-mouth-Remember-to-move-it-up-and-down forever? It seemed only prudent to seek expert advice.

"You'll be okay," a colleague who reported white-collar drug addiction said when I consulted him. "But, wow, has that guy got a connection! Sounds like one-hundred-percent purest, finest Colombian. What's his name, Juan Valdez?"

Let us say you're a Colombian businessman. You enter into a perfectly straightforward business agreement with some tourist, to carry ten kilograms of cocaine from Bogotá to Miami. It doesn't matter whether the tourist is American or Colombian. You give him the cocaine and then when he gets to Miami, he says he doesn't have the cocaine. He says the police got the cocaine, and they were about to get him when he saw the plainclothesmen surrounding the baggage carousel, and he walked straight through Customs, saying he had no baggage—nothing to declare, thank you.

It's possible. Sometimes, once in a while, even in Miami, the cops get some cocaine. But if they did get ten whole keys of coke, why hasn't the Drug Enforcement Agency held another press conference announcing the war on drugs is being won? If the cops got the coke, where's the TV *rubia* telling you the cops got the coke, through that microphone she holds between her tits? Above all, where's the story in the *Herald*?

When it comes to these juridical deliberations, that's the only sure grounds for acquittal, the report of the drug seizure in the *Miami Herald*. And what if the *Herald* doesn't send a reporter? Guilty as charged, of ethical impropriety in the transportation of a commercial commodity across international lines.

But in a lax and permissive United States of America, no court of law will convict a mule (drug courier) for welshing on a deal. So justice must be served by other means—the midnight ride out Venetian Causeway; the bullet in the back of the neck; the body floating back up in Biscayne Bay, which is no more newsworthy than some car bomb in Shenandoah Park. It's not an easy job killing people for a living but someone has to do it, and once the work's done, at least it entitles a man to a little relaxation.

One night a friend and his wife took me to dinner at Islas Canarias, one of those storefront restaurants in Little Havana where the decor is Formica and the *arroz con pollo* is great. His name was David Smith, his wife's name Zita Arocha—and like the Arquitectonica couple, they exemplified Miami's talent for fostering interesting cross-cultural marriages. At the time Dave was managing editor of *El Herald,* the city's most respected Spanish-language newspaper; Zita was the court reporter for the *Miami News.* They were typical Miamians in another way: Dave looked very Latin, even though his name was Anglo. Zita was so blond and blue-eyed she could have been from Ohio; she actually was the daughter of impoverished immigrants from Cuba.

The restaurant had been just another hole in the wall until a Cuban family had turned it into one of those thriving little businesses that, even more than the multinational corporations and big skyscrapers, explain Miami's success and appeal as a city—as well as why most Miami Cubans, far from being wild-eyed Latin radicals, are Republicans. Here all the old American pieties about hard work and maintaining the traditional values still clearly retained the capacity not just to arouse people's hopes, but also to make their dreams come true. In this family restaurant, the husband cooked in the kitchen; the sons washed dishes; the wife ran the cash register, and a daughter waited on tables. These people were light-years away from high life in the "Miami Vice" manner, but they had something more valuable than a dozen Maseratis—the certain knowledge that the future would be better to the exact extent they strove to make it so.

After dinner, we drove down Calle Ocho. It was late, but here, unlike in many other parts of Miami, people were still out on the street. Lights were on; shops, gas stations and restaurants were open, and that always made it all the more surprising. I actually met some people who lived in Miami who found Little Havana too frightening—too "foreign"—to visit after dark.

At Southwest Twenty-seventh Avenue we turned right and drove south through the Shenandoah Park district toward Coconut Grove. Here the exotic animation of Calle Ocho disappeared; the normal horizon of the "real" America was restored. You reentered a world of neat little streets and neat little houses with cars parked outside, and it was on one of those neat little streets, right in front of one of those neat little houses, under one of those parked cars, that the car bomb went off.

The fireball must have been thirty feet in diameter. It was burning orange and searing white all at the same time. The heat on our faces was like a blast furnace, even though we were half a block away in an air-conditioned car. But for me the most disorienting thing was that my friends didn't seem to notice the explosion at all. Dave Smith drove on as though nothing had happened.

"What in God's name was that!" I inquired, a question the others evidently found amusing, because they all started laughing.

"Just some drug dealer fire-bombing another drug dealer's car," Smith replied. I asked him if he would send a reporter. Now the others were really laughing. "You send a reporter to cover a scraped fender up in New York?" he asked.

He wasn't scared by the car bomb, but the managing editor of *El Herald* sure was scared a few nights later when we visited the Mutiny Club in Coconut Grove. At the Mutiny, which, according to Drug Enforcement Agency officials, was at that time the favorite watering hole of the more established cocaine cowboys, the patrons arrived in magenta Cadillac convertibles and the parking "valets" wore uniforms out of *The Merry Widow*. The membership cards were gold, and even the baked potatoes came wrapped in gold foil, which matched the gold medallions on the young men at the bar. The waitresses, over black net stockings, wore skirts that ended in the vicinity of the *mons veneris*. At that time there was a soufflé chef at the Mutiny who called himself Pierre but who was really named Mohammed. He was Iranian, and when I asked him one time how an Iranian soufflé chef had managed to get a job in a place where the staff was predominantly Cuban, Mohammed replied, "Compassion for a fellow refugee. I explained Khomeini was just like Castro, a revolution betrayed."

At the Mutiny the tables didn't have chairs. They had leather-covered, swiveling, executive armchairs, and when the guy who ran the discotheque got going, the laser beams bouncing off your baked potato reminded you of that car bomb exploding, but that wasn't why you went to the Mutiny. You went to the Mutiny to look at the killers.

Not, I'm sure, that our fellow revelers saw themselves as criminals. In their eyes they were bulwarks against anarchy—law enforcement officers, if you will, taking a night off at the Mutiny, because these were men who believed deeply in law and order. The only problem was that, in their particular profession, there wouldn't be any law and order if they weren't there to enforce it.

Besides the Smiths and me, our party consisted of Jere Warren, an artist with a Georgia accent broad as the Chattahoochee; also

Minnie Cassatt Hickman of New York, London, Southampton and
Palm Beach, who'd come down from Palm Beach for the evening
because, as she put it, "I may get killed, but I won't die of bore-
dom." Also with us was a vacationing Chinese journalist from
Hong Kong named Donald Cheung.

It had been my idea to invite Cheung to join us; but I'd unac-
countably failed to explain to this foreign visitor certain cultural
idiosyncrasies as fundamental in Miami as the use of chopsticks is
in his homeland. In this case I had failed to warn him that strangers
do not approach professional killers and ask their girlfriends to
dance.

Donald Cheung was at that time a correspondent for the *South
China Morning Post*. But the trip to America was strictly pleasure,
not business. I think he assumed Miami would be all Don Ho hors
d'oeuvres and Trader Vic's cocktails with little umbrellas in them,
just like Waikiki.

The waitress in net stockings hardly had the chance to give us our
menus (leather-bound, written in English pretending to be French).
Mohammed (in his Miami-French accent) hardly had the chance to
ask if *messieurs et mesdames* would like to order their soufflés now so
they would be ready in time for dessert, when the vacationing
correspondent of the *South China Morning Post* quaffed his piña
colada and announced, "I feel like dancing!"

The two ladies at our table looked up expectantly, but quick as
a flash the Chinese had bounded past the first table, then past the
second, and stopped at the third, around which were seated a
couple of enforcers with Incan faces and Yves St. Laurent suits
and accompanied by two bejeweled women in gowns of metallic
silk.

Donald Cheung was tapping the more muscular, the shorter and
more sinister-looking of the two men on the shoulder, and on Dave
Smith's face, as though in hieroglyphics, you could see graven the
terrible dilemma. Should he jump up, run over and tell the Chinese
to stop? Or would sudden movement now only increase the chances
we'd all be killed?

"They have reached for their revolvers," Minnie Hickman observed. "Should we get under the table?" She felt under the blood-red tablecloth. "Plywood," she revealed. "Better to sit up straight and die like men."

The Chinese had committed the social gaffe—occasionally fatal in such circles—of surprising the two men from behind, so they'd swung around in those leather-covered, swiveling, executive arm-chairs as if one, and at the sight of this inscrutable Oriental peering down at them, their right hands had risen instantly, reflexively toward the bulges under the left armpits of their linen suits.

You could see the question in their eyes: Was this the Enforcer from the Golden Triangle? The Chinese was smiling and explain-ing. Their faces were like pre-Columbian stone sculptures, and I was thinking: These guys can't understand English when an Ameri-can speaks it; he doesn't stand a Chinaman's chance.

What followed was remarkable. After about twenty seconds, those stone faces turned to Silly Putty. After forty-five seconds, they were grinning and smiling and then roaring with laughter. The Chinese was laughing, too, and the younger and taller of the two men was saying, *Sí?*

Sí, replied his squatter, more menacing-looking companion. *Sí, sí, sí! Porqué no?* The two girls were also saying *Sí, sí, sí!* Now they were all laughing and saying it, including the Chinese—*Sí, sí, sí!*—and the Chinese and the two girls were bounding down to the dance floor and were cavorting among the laser beams. They were doing a combination rumba-disco routine *à trois*—a Carmen-Miran-da-and-Her-Younger-Sister-Meet-the-Chinese-John-Travolta num-ber—while the two gunmen beamed down on them benignly. This was several years ago; the song, needless to say, was "Stayin' Alive."

"Well, that was invigorating!" the Chinese stated, after returning the two women to their table, shaking hands with their escorts and giving them each one of his business cards. "I think I'll have an-other piña colada."

The rest of the table was speechless; Dave Smith's knuckles were white. Finally, he spoke, gently but firmly, to our foreign friend: "You must never do that again. Never."

A few days later, an official of the Drug Enforcement Agency also invited me to a club. This one was located in the Miami garment district—that warren of dilapidated old warehouses that, like Miami itself, suddenly had become fashionable without warning.

It was indeed a club in the sense that you had to be a member or the guest of a member, but it certainly offered amenities unknown to the Knickerbocker and Yale clubs. Bikini-bottomed go-go girls were dancing on top of the bar. The girls all looked as if they'd passed Pulchritude but failed Seat Belt Drill at stewardess school. No one was wearing a suit and tie there except me.

My host was telling me about some of his exploits down in Colombia. He and another agent were working undercover; two guys had broken into their hotel rooms and tried to kill them. My attention was divided between the go-go girls and his story, so maybe that was why his next comment seemed so out of context.

"They're not faggots," he said. "They may look like faggots to us, but that's not why they do it."

"Become go-go dancers?" I asked.

"No, no," he answered, lowering his voice a little. "Look over there." I didn't see anything except two guys who looked like refugees from an Engelbert Humperdinck look-alike contest. They wore tight-fitting slacks. The top four buttons on their shirts were unbuttoned, the better to permit admiration of their gold chains and hairy, well-exercised chests. Sartorially speaking, they certainly weren't models of that DEA macho look. But the fact that they didn't wear brown suits from Sears did not seem to me to constitute *prima facie* evidence they didn't go for women.

"See, there on the table?" he continued. "They're carrying whatchamacallems—purses, little purses with strings on them." I looked again, and he was right. As millions of completely heterosexual males do all over Europe and Latin America, and even right here in these United States, they were carrying men's purses, those things where you put wallets, credit cards and sunglasses when you're not wearing a jacket.

I nodded in agreement, and the DEA official drove home his point. "Now, normally, you see a guy with a purse and you assume he's a faggot, right?" He answered his own question. "Wrong, dead wrong—at least in Miami!"

I was no closer to getting his point, and I guess it showed on my face.

"The gun," he said. "The heater, the rod, the forty-five magnum —you know that thing that goes bang-bang and shoots bullets?" A little light bulb went on in my brain. "Most of the time it's too hot in Miami to wear a jacket, isn't it?" he asked. I said yes. "So you can't use a shoulder holster all the time, can you?" I answered no; he clearly enjoyed the Socratic method.

"So where do you keep your gun?"

"You buy one of those little men's purses and keep the gun in there," I answered, like some slow learner who's finally getting his multiplication tables right.

"Excellent," he replied. "You get a B-plus on that one and your reward is another beer." I could tell he was like my friend that time the computer was smashed and I said maybe it was the tire iron. He wasn't being sarcastic; I could hear it in his tone of voice, a kind of municipal pride that said, Maybe this out-of-towner is beginning to understand Miami. I asked this narc, whose name was Brent Eaton, how he'd wound up working for the DEA.

"Last thing I expected," he replied. "I was going to be a mortician, but then when I got out of the service one thing led to another. I find this more interesting, though you don't make as much money."

If you wanted to know where the guns were, you followed the guys carrying purses, and if you wanted to know where the drugs were, you followed the guys with beepers. Mostly they hung out at pay phones in shopping centers like Dadeland and the Suniland mall—at pay phones because pay phone calls are hard to trace; in shopping centers because the cocaine Mafia, in a perfect example of American upward mobility, long ago started moving to the suburbs, along with all those honest Latins who've saved up enough for a down payment.

Some of the guys with beepers specialized in Colombian coke; others had connections with Peru, Brazil or Bolivia. Others dealt with intermediaries in the Bahamas or Panama or Costa Rica, and here, at least, Communism and capitalism were a model of hemispheric accord; according to the DEA, even the Cubans and Nicaraguans were in on the act. Once these pipelines flowed into Miami, they surged out again in countless different directions, into every corner of the country. So one guy at one pay phone might be making a Peru-Chicago fit while another linked Bolivia with Boston.

Others might find all this exotic, but in reality these drug dealers were no more exciting or dangerous than Stanford M.B.A.'s, and for the same reason: it was money, not gunfights or glamour, they were after. In fact, in Miami, the shoot-outs are like Yuppie embezzlement scandals on Wall Street. The surprising thing isn't that they happen, but that they happened so seldom.

In the Miami drug trade, you can earn more than on Wall Street. Even penny-ante traders can make $1.5 million annually. Of course there are always a few people who are too greedy, who think they can get away with it and not pay a price. But most people realize the easiest and safest way to make money is to work within the system.

On Wall Street they call them runners—those guys who scurry between banks and brokerage houses carrying hundreds of thousands of dollars in stock certificates and negotiable securities in big manila envelopes. Every time you take a daytime subway ride in Lower Manhattan, chances are there'll be a couple million dollars riding with you. No one considers this exotic or glamorous, least of all the guys with manila envelopes; it's just a fact of life.

It's the same way in Miami, only there the runners are called smurfs and they don't just transport millions, they launder it. How to spot a smurf? It's one thing to look for the purses and follow the beepers, but smurfing is a more subtle Miami occupation because the whole secret of being successful is to have no identifying characteristics at all. Those two men at the Mutiny, for example, would be terrible smurfs because they look just like the kind of people you'd expect to be carrying around a quarter-million bucks in a bowling bag. So who makes the ideal smurf?

"Little old ladies on Miami Beach," a retired smurf named Herb told John Dorschner, a staff writer for *Tropic* magazine, when he asked that question. "You know, they all have three savings accounts, because they got a new toaster with each one. So you get three little old ladies. . . . What do you do? Give them two hundred dollars a week. These people trying to live on Social Security, they'd kill for another two hundred a week." Herb had an even better idea for making big money—though one not without its psychic, as well as physical, risks: "Get ten girlfriends, and figure that the guy running the smurfs keeps three percent of the laundering for himself. I'd be making two hundred and fifty thousand dollars a week."

I can't say the revelation about the men's purses—any more than, say, the incident at the Mutiny—made me scared of Miami, though afterward I did start noticing something. A truly extraordinary number of men did carry purses, and I suppose if I'd ever found myself in a confrontation with a guy with a purse I'd have backed down quick.

But the truth was, even when Miami did look like a scene from "Miami Vice," there was no reason to get worried because it was still very difficult to get yourself shot. To be sure, if you were a cop, if you were heavily into drugs or involved in criminal activities (except for white-collar crime, of course), or if you were a young black male living in a ghetto, Miami was just like the rest of America. The odds skyrocketed that you'd wind up with a bullet in your chest.

But even then, being shot dead was, statistically speaking, far less likely than that you'd get killed in a traffic accident. Even if gunfire broke out all around you (which, of course, was a million-to-one chance), it was still hard to get shot in Miami. What makes the "homicide rate" so high isn't sinister strangers attacking innocent victims, or even innocent victims firing back. It's people shooting friends, people shooting family, people shooting shadows—and four-year-old toddlers and distraught teenagers blowing their brains out with Daddy's gun.

One local station had a regular feature that, quite unintentionally, caught the utter banality of most Miami homicides very well. It was called "Crime Stoppers," and on each episode "Crime Stoppers" would present the Homicide of the Day. The memory of one spot stuck with me for a very long time. It began with some sinister-looking kids—one black, one white and one Latin—cruising down a suburban street in an old car. They spotted an apparently empty house, and so they stopped and slipped inside. They were making off with the portable TV when an old guy came in from the backyard, spotted them, ran into his bedroom, pulled a gun out of the dresser drawer and ran after them. So seeing the old guy waving a gun at him, one of the kids pulled out his own gun and shot him in the face.

Then came the blow-dry voiceover: "This has been a public service message. If you have information concerning the whereabouts of those responsible for this crime, call Miami Metro Police. Tune into tomorrow for another edition of 'Crime Stoppers.' Together we *can* stop crime."

I did call the police. First, I wanted to know, what was the likelihood of your TV set being stolen by an interracial gang? "Zip," my contact replied. "They'd be all black or all Anglo or Latin, not one of each. But you have to have racial balance on TV." The great lesson of today's homicide, according to the announcer, was that the dead man had left his windows open. He warned his viewers, especially his elderly viewers, to keep their houses locked up tight. I asked if this meant you should live life cowering behind locked doors if you wanted to be safe in Miami.

"People should take normal precautions," my contact answered, "especially when they go out. But the real reason that old geyser got plugged is the same reason that jerk kid'll wind up serving twenty-to-life someday. Miami's full of idiots running around with guns they don't know how to use and have no right owning. But you'll never hear them say that on that station for the same reason they run those little soap operas about people getting their guts blown out. They know what's good for ratings."

The big dramatic shoot-outs you saw on "Miami Vice" did reflect a certain unique truth about the relationship between guns and Miami. Where else would saturating a whole society with weapons be considered cause for civic celebration?

The Greater Miami Chamber of Commerce was kind enough to send me a glossy periodical called *Global Gateway,* which provides in each issue, as is only to be expected, an upbeat view of some facet of Miami. I opened it to a special section entitled "The Emerging Industries," and found the latest cause for rejoicing:

> South Florida is becoming a military supermarket. With Ronald Reagan out front, military leaders from around the world are shopping in the Miami area for their combat supplies, listening devices, bullet-proof vests, combat helmets, missile parts, handguns. . . . The new boom has meant expanding profits for veteran military merchants in the area. And it has spawned a new generation of merchants—former boat builders, ex-toolmakers and retirees—who are willing to provide whatever war materials the market demands,

announced an article entitled "War Tech Military Manufacturing: Armaments for Uncle Sam and Our Neighbors to the South."

One of Miami's churches had been converted into a handgun factory, the article related, and there was even more to cheer about. Just like sunshine and palm trees earlier, guns and bullets were attracting a whole new wave of settlers to south Florida. An equally upbeat companion piece, "Plowshares into Guns," profiled one of these enterprising newcomers, a thirty-two-year-old former Philadelphian named Robert Miller whose "idea of fun is a Sunday in the Everglades target-shooting with his machine gun."

"To me, it's self-gratifying to pick the point of aim and put the bullet where it belongs," he explained in the interview. But Miller, the profile added, "has more than a sportsman's interest in machine guns." In fact he and two friends had gotten together to assemble and sell about one hundred machine guns a month—thus doing their bit to help make Miami what *Global Gateway* calls "The Place to Do It All!"

With the whole world at his feet, why should such an enterprising young man have chosen the Sunshine State to seek his fortune? It turned out he'd soured on Philadelphia "after the Pennsylvania Supreme Court made it illegal for individuals to own machine guns in that state," and so started looking around for a new place to live.

"Miller," the article related, "says he chose Florida because it had liberal gun laws, access to the South and Central American markets and nice weather.

"Today," *Global Gateway* added, "both [the legal and illegal] arms markets are flourishing, and the profit-makers don't apologize." But, as always in Miami, the real question about all good things wasn't: Does it make money? The question was: Will it last? A local builder of "commando boats for Third World countries" named John Foster provided a cheery prognosis for those interested in cashing in on the Gun Belt boom.

"Since Biblical times," he reminded the reader, "we've had wars. I see this market for the long term."

In the course of all my visits to Miami, I didn't meet one politician who, privately, wasn't in favor of gun control. And I don't think I met a single one, either, who would say so in public. "You try to tell people they shouldn't have guns down here," one Miami city commissioner told me, "and they won't just run you out of office. They'll run you all the way to the Georgia line. Politics," he reminded me, "is about getting votes."

And TV was about ratings, just like selling machine guns was about making money. So, at the end of "Crime Stoppers," the announcer never said, "If you're really concerned about the safety of you and your loved ones, stop being a chump. Recognize the fact that, if you're one of our typical viewers, you're no more competent to use a gun than to fly a plane. Now you wouldn't put the wife and kids in a Piper Comanche and take off without knowing how to fly, would you? So stop being a jerk. Go into your bedroom and take the gun out of the dresser drawer and put it in the glove compartment of your car. Drive the car out Venetian Causeway, and throw the gun into Biscayne Bay. This has been a public service announcement. . . ."

So most of the time there was no reason to find Miami exciting, let alone to get scared. The drugs and guns were only like the cockroaches, or palmetto bugs, as the PR people prefer you call them—everywhere you went.

Objectively speaking, you knew there was no reason to be scared, because the cockroaches were just like those guys at the Mutiny, those guys with the beepers—practitioners of live-and-let-live. They don't want to hurt you: all they want is to make a lot of money, settle down in a nice nest somewhere and have a couple million kids. And who are you to say that being a cockroach is any less noble, cosmologically speaking, than being you?

But even when you do know all that, when you go into the bathroom at three in the morning and that immense cockroach feeding on your toothbrush flies into your face, it is scary. And when you bound out barefoot into one of those dewy Miami "blessed mornings/ Meet for the eye of the young alligator," and you hear the crunch, you feel the ooze, it's *you* who feels dirty, disgusting, corrupted—like some contemptible insect.

And that awareness was all around you all the time in Miami—along with that glorious sunshine, these interesting people, those curious buildings, that air which, on the good days, caressed you like a fond and complaisant lover.

4

Sonny Crockett and the Suniland Shoot-Out

Critics of "Miami Vice" said a series set in some suburb would have given a more accurate view of their city, and perhaps they were right.

Consider the incident that actually did erupt out in the Miami suburb of Kendall on the balmy Friday morning of April 11, 1986. It no doubt would have been rejected as far too improbable had it been proposed at a TV story conference. At its fade-out on the busy fringes of the Suniland shopping mall, two FBI agents, a professional landscape gardener and a born-again Christian lay dead. Five other law enforcement officers also lay bleeding in the street.

You don't see Kendall too often on "Miami Vice" because it doesn't look the way Miami's supposed to look on TV. A churchgoing, Little League, nine-to-five kind of place, it's the part of town that, local boosters argue, proves Miami is just as American as anywhere else.

The Suniland bloodbath certainly bore out that contention. The two men who initiated what the *Washington Post* called "the bloodiest shoot-out in FBI history" were named William Matix and Michael Platt, and they were about as white, as Anglo-Saxon and as Protestant as you can get.

Matix, thirty-four, and Platt, thirty-two, had been inseparable since they'd met in the early seventies while serving in the Army Rangers in Korea. Both men enjoyed the gardening business; both were interested in boats; both wore beards. Each was a widower with young children, a coincidence that would eventually prove significant. "Cops' Theory on Killers: Each Slew the Other's Wife," one headline would run, after police all over the country began probing the two men's pasts.

Just a month before the shoot-out, *Home Life,* a family magazine published by the Southern Baptist Convention, had singled out Matix as a model of Christian piety. Platt, too, "was very much the American," a friend later recalled. "If he felt our country was being raped or molested, he would rise up and do something about it."

Platt was from Indiana, Matix from Ohio, and following receipt of good conduct medals and honorable discharges, both men headed for the Sun Belt to lead what investigators described as "a typical suburban life." When he wasn't gardening, boating or at church, Matix liked to join Platt for excursions out to a remote rock pit in the Everglades for target practice.

On most weekends you'd find lots of Miamians out at that rock pit, exercising their inalienable right to shoot off guns whenever and wherever they chose. It was in the course of these excursions, nonetheless, that Matix and Platt betrayed their first signs of eccentricity. While the other people at the rock pit shot at rocks, Matix and Platt shot at the people shooting at rocks. Exactly a month before the shoot-out in Kendall, for example, they had forced a young man named José Collazo to lie down in a muddy ditch. Then they'd shot him four times—in both arms, the chest and the head.

In this case practice did not make perfect. Collazo survived to provide police with descriptions of his two assailants, and his statements made it clear they were "real" Americans, not Colombian cocaine cowboys. At first that seemed to simplify the case. Since they were "young white Americans," not exotic, dark-skinned killers, they had to be either desperate criminals or, worse still, subversives. As Sergeant Tony Monheim of the Metro-Dade Police later put it, "We all said these guys are going to be neo-Nazis or escaped murderers. Never in our wildest imagination did we figure they would be family types with no criminal record."

Matix and Platt might have continued their target practice indefinitely, but for another eccentricity. Afterward, they liked to steal their victims' cars, and then, mostly on Friday mornings, use them to knock off banks and armored cars. This produced a curious pattern: the cars stolen in the Everglades tended to show up abandoned in Miami after the banks were robbed. But what could the pattern mean?

An FBI agent named Gordon McNeil hit upon the solution. Since the Cuban, José Collazo, had been the last to be shot at the rock pit, Collazo's car—a black, two-door Chevrolet Monte Carlo —would be the *next* to be used in a robbery. From this axiom McNeil derived a corollary: find the black Monte Carlo, and you'd find both the rock pit killers and the bank robbers.

But how to find the Monte Carlo? Collazo's description haunted McNeil because of what "young white Americans," when described by a Miami Cuban, implied. They weren't Italian or Slavic or Jewish or French Canadian. They were just plain, normal, non-ethnic, "real" Americans.

And what better place, in polyglot Miami, to search for such Americans than in Kendall? And what better place in Kendall than in the vicinity of Suniland mall? And at what better time than on Friday morning, when the bank robbers usually struck? "I guess it was both the luckiest hunch and the unluckiest hunch I've ever had," McNeil said later, when he was interviewed in his hospital bed.

FBI agents Benjamin P. Grogan, fifty-three, and Jerry Dove, thirty, were driving an unmarked lemon-yellow 1985 Buick Century, when they spotted the black Monte Carlo first.

"Attention all units," Grogan radioed at 9:17 A.M. "We're behind a black vehicle, two-door, Florida license NPJ–eight-nine-one. We're headed south on South Dixie, no, north on South Dixie." Between them, that Friday, Matix and Platt carried a .357 Magnum; a .357 Dan Wesson revolver loaded with .38-caliber rounds; also a Smith & Wesson 12-gauge shotgun, capable of firing forty rounds a minute; and a Ruger Mini-14 semiautomatic assault rifle that fires .223-caliber slugs at thirty-two hundred feet a second, all of which can be purchased at gun stores all over south Florida.

Matix and Platt opened fire at a few seconds past 9:20 A.M. Minutes later, Grogan was dead (shot through the heart), and so was Dove (shot four times, twice in the head). Five other FBI agents including McNeil (seriously wounded in the back and chest) had also been shot. The landscape gardener and the born-again Christian had come within an ace of outshooting, outmaneuvering and outkilling a twelve-man FBI attack squad, then escaping scot-free.

Partly this was because passing motorists assumed it was a scene being filmed for "Miami Vice," and so refused to stop even when they heard the gunfire and saw the falling bodies. ("I'm late for my tennis lesson," one woman snapped when police tried to flag her down.) So the cops—unlike Matix and Platt—had to hold their fire while, as one report later put it, "traffic continued to roll down sunny S.W. 82nd Avenue, right through the gunfight."

In part it was simply the result of chance that Matix and Platt almost but didn't quite make it. (When they piled into Grogan's yellow Buick and tried to use it as a getaway car, the ignition wouldn't start.)

But mostly they were stopped thanks to the dogged courage of an authentic Miami hero.

He was a big, ungainly FBI agent with a dark moustache named Edmundo Mireles. Shot by Matix, Mireles had crumpled to the ground dazed and bleeding, a gaping wound in his left forearm, which had been severed in one place and splintered in others. Brian Duffy, when he reconstructed the event for the *Miami Herald,* described what happened next:

> Somehow, Mireles got to his feet. There were almost seven yards between him and Grogan's car. Walking slowly, losing blood and barely conscious, Mireles walked the distance, emptying his Smith & Wesson re-

volver at the two men in the car. He shot Platt in the spine. He hit Matix in the face. Then he shot Matix in the spine. Both men were paralyzed. Moments later, they were dead.

The Suniland shoot-out, it occurred to me when it happened, was like "Miami Vice" in two ways. First of all it confirmed the stereotype. How could you deny Miami really was a "metaphor of evil" when, in real life, the place was as awash in violence as it was on TV? The second similarity was that things weren't what they seemed when you looked beneath the careening cars and bullet-riddled corpses. The Suniland shoot-out didn't prove, to me at least, that all those illegal aliens and all those drugs had turned Miami into a "metaphor of evil." It only showed that if there really is such a thing as evil in this world, you don't have to go to exotic places to find it. You can find it even in a place like Kendall. Sometimes, to be sure, evil does look exotic; but most of the time it is mild-mannered, soft-spoken, well groomed. It could be your next-door neighbor, your college roommate. It could be you.

Of course, even when killers like Platt and Matix do turn out to look just like us, our instincts tell us such persons, underneath, must belong to another species. The rock pit murderers couldn't be people with the same ambitions, the same tastes, the same politics, even the same religious convictions as the rest of us.

This tendency isn't limited to individuals. It carries over into the films we make and the novels we write. That, in fact, was the real reason the Suniland shoot-out would have had such trouble at a TV story conference: it stood all the Miami stereotypes on their heads. Mireles the hero didn't look a hero, and the forces of evil didn't look evil.

Interestingly enough, Matix and Platt seemed to have cast their crimes the same way casting directors do. There was no way after their deaths to be absolutely sure. But of the three victims Matix and Platt definitely shot before the Suniland incident (there probably were others), all had something important in common.

All were young Hispanic males of the type "real" Americans tend to stereotype as drug dealers, bank robbers, or worse. Before Collazo was shot, Emilio Briel, twenty-five, the son of a Miami roofer, was murdered out at the rock pit; a Brink's guard named Ernesto Maranje also suffered multiple wounds when Matix and Platt held up an armored car. The coincidences didn't end there. The cars Matix and Platt stole from Collazo and Briel were both Chevrolet Monte Carlos, only Collazo's was jet black and Briel's was gold.

If this was madness, it had a method. Matix and Platt wore ski masks over their midwestern faces during their holdups. In Miami most people like them don't drive jazzy models like gold and black Monte Carlos. "Real" Americans prefer foreign cars—Volvos, Mercedes and Jaguars. Generally it's young Latins who drive the kinds of cars Matix and Platt stole.

So if Collazo hadn't lived to describe them, and McNeil hadn't made the connection, the police might have spent months staking out Little Havana and Calle Ocho, not South Dixie Highway and the Suniland mall.

If the people Matix and Platt killed resembled those Latin killers you see on TV, the hero of the shoot-out was a typecaster's dream, though not, to be sure, for the hero's role: Special Agent Edmundo Mireles weighed 250 pounds; he looked, quite literally, like Mr. Big.

None of those FBI agents who put their lives on the line that Friday morning in Kendall could've played Sonny Crockett. They were variously too old, too plain, too short, too flabby for that.

But the ones who came closest to looking like TV heroes were the two who got killed. Gerald Dove was a strapping, good-looking young man, and Benjamin Grogan, even though he was fifty-three, was a marathon runner who did fifty push-ups every morning, including the morning he died. Unfortunately events that day proved a law of ballistics that seldom applies on TV. Youth and good looks can't stop bullets; neither can fitness, though sheer bulk sometimes can.

One reason Mireles, that great hulk of an FBI agent, was able to get up again when the others couldn't—to keep walking and firing after he'd lost so much blood—was that he had so much more blood to lose.

Subsequent investigations produced a most interesting revelation. Matix and Platt hadn't killed out of some grand plan or dark vision. They'd killed for the same reasons lots of people elsewhere do.

Following the murder of his wife and another woman up in Ohio, Matix had collected more than $350,000 in life insurance. And once he got the money, he'd moved down to Florida, found a nice house and bought a couple of cars; he'd remarried and joined a local church. Like other newcomers, Matix also told his friends up North about the pleasures of life in the Sunshine State. So Platt, too, had moved to Miami, bringing his wife and children with him; soon the two men were giving new meaning to that old American custom of keeping up with the Joneses.

"Daddy has a lot of money now," Platt's son told friends after Platt's wife, too, suddenly died. "We have new money," his daughter confirmed.

Platt did with his new money what many of us would. He treated the kids to a trip to Disney World. Then, after touring Fantasyland and shaking hands with Mickey Mouse, they drove down to Sanibel Island on the Gulf Coast for a beach vacation. Once back in Miami, Platt, just like Matix, began assembling all the artifacts of the good life, American-style—the new house (in an attractive Kendall subdivision called the Hammocks), the new wife (an attractive blonde in her thirties), a television with a "gigantic screen," a robot for the children that cost more than two thousand dollars. In a city where people change cars the way people elsewhere change shirts, Platt wanted—and got—an automotive stable worthy of a co-star on "Miami Vice." There was the Jaguar for dressy occasions, the white Chevy Blazer for casual moments, the Jeep for camping trips with the children. This wardrobe on wheels was rounded out by two off-the-road vehicles and a motorcycle.

So long as you keep your lawn mowed, the neighbors don't much care how you pay the bills. Cocaine smuggling, real estate deals, public relations, murdering your wife and collecting the insurance —by Miami's, by America's, standards, Matix and Platt had it made. They had the houses, the cars, the devoted children, the love of affectionate, attractive women. (Matix's second marriage had broken up, but he was active on the Christian singles scene.) They had the gardening business, and of course their nest eggs that they had, so to speak, inherited.

So why didn't they just stop and enjoy what they had? Once again, it appears, the narc I visited on the boat was right: they did it because no one ever has enough money. After one robbery the two men approached a woman and offered to buy her forty-foot boat. "They told me cash was no object," she later recalled. "They wanted me to take twenty-five thousand for the boat. They wanted it real bad, not to run drugs, I'm sure."

Following their deaths, the police, the press, their neighbors all tried to find deeper explanations. Yet even after it became clear the villains weren't weirdos, some felt only weird explanations would suffice. They tried to equate Matix and Platt with those crazies who, from time to time, gather out in the Everglades in army surplus fatigues to practice for Armageddon.

But that explanation wouldn't wash either. "Someone living in a one-hundred-thousand-dollar home in the suburbs and driving a Jaguar doesn't sound like a survivalist to me," one federal investigator concluded. Then he said something that's always been true of lots of Americans, and which is certainly true today of lots of people in Miami: "I'd say they were more capitalistic. They would do anything for money."

"Miami Vice" got the colors and rhythms right, but it missed the main point: Miami wasn't just a caldron of conflicting firepower. It was a caldron of human possibility.

Would the Cuban kid selling coke (or flowers) on Calle Ocho wind up dead (or going to Miami-Dade Community College)?

Would that pretty black waitress who only hustled when there really was no other way to pay the rent make it out of the ghetto? What about those old people you'd never see on "Miami Vice," but who still made up nearly 20 percent of the population? Would they find some measure of joyful acceptance of life? Or would they end their lives cowering inside some Miami Beach "pullmanette," heating canned soup on a paraffin ring?

And that Yuppie who'd fallen behind on the mortgage payments? When the real crunch came, would he let the condo go? Or would he call the "investor" who, at that big coke party, said, "There's always a place in my operation for someone like you"?

You could find these dramas in other cities, of course, but what made Miami so compelling was that the jury was still out on the whole shooting match, and so in Miami there was always this sense of infinite possibility. It could become the Paris of the Americas; it could become the Beirut; and that sense of *becoming* wasn't just the secret of Miami's tragedies and its triumphs, the secret that made Miami both scary and fun. It was also, I became convinced, the secret of Miami's double-edged appeal to the rest of the nation. Here the American future, to borrow the title of John Rothchild's book about Florida, really was *Up for Grabs*.

If that was Miami's secret, it certainly was safe with "Miami Vice." Most critics pointed out that the stories on "Miami Vice" never made much sense. But the real problem was that the people seemed made out of laser beams, too.

Initially Sonny Crockett, the character Johnson played, did have a human context, if only a very sketchy one. Tubbs, his black partner, also had a vestigial humanity: he seemed to have some family somewhere up North. Characterization never has been one of the glories of adventure television, yet here again "Miami Vice" broke the mold. While the characters on most shows broaden and deepen as they grow more successful, on "Miami Vice" they shriveled. Crockett lost his estranged wife; even his pet alligator was banished for a while. He was so devoid of human and social moorings, where else could he live but on a boat? Crockett was too "undefined" even for Kendall, and this no doubt explained one curiosity of the show.

Even at the height of the "Miami Vice" craze, not one viewer in a million really wanted to be Sonny Crockett. What the fans really wanted was to be Don Johnson, TV superstar—lead item on "Entertainment Tonight."

As for Tubbs, he embodied an even more seductive fantasy than celebrity, which was escape from race itself. This was because on "Miami Vice" your skin color wasn't part of a social, political, economic or psychological condition. Like Crockett's stubble, it was a Look, a fashion statement. And so you shared this life of high adventure with this cool white guy—you were his best friend and he was your best friend—for a simple reason: you were both absolutely equal, because you were both absolutely cool. Tubbs, as played by Philip Michael Thomas, was the most denatured black character on prime-time TV.

In a city that was constantly evolving, changing, the people on "Miami Vice" didn't evolve, they didn't become. So even when they were careening around at a hundred miles an hour, the characters didn't move. Like a flamingo or a Porsche, these exotic creatures just were, so the viewers, like tropical ornithologists, focused on the clothes, the cars, the colors—the stunning plumage, both physical and human, of the show.

The most interesting of the actors turned out to be Edward James Olmos, who plays Lieutenant Castillo, the show's most compelling character. On screen Olmos is brooding, taciturn, somber—the less he speaks the more he seems to say. Off camera, however, Olmos has a good sense of humor and is extremely articulate.

Many viewers assume Olmos, along with the character he portrays, is Cuban. Actually the ethnic identity of the Castillo character, as Olmos told me, is "undefined," and Olmos himself, far from being Cuban, is a Mexican-American from California. One day, over lunch in the commissary, Olmos talked about being raised a Chicano in L.A., at the precise moment when Hollywood, the sitcoms and Disneyland all seemed to vindicate the total triumph of the dominant Anglo culture over people who weren't "real" Americans. His early experiences had deeply shaped him both as an actor and as a human being. In his most famous stage role, in *Zoot Suit,* a landmark play about Anglo injustice toward Mexican-Americans during World War II, Olmos had played an embittered, vengeful Latin street tough. He'd also starred in an award-winning film about ethnic conflicts in Texas called *The Ballad of Gregorio Cortez.*

Olmos's transformation, thanks to "Miami Vice," from an ethnic character actor into an offbeat American star hadn't diminished his fascination with what he called "the challenge of cross-cultural communication." At prisons, migrant camps and Indian reservations all over the country, he talked about the dangers of interethnic conflicts—as well as about the constructive possibilities of intercommunal cooperation. He also, I found out later, had a degree in sociology, was active in campaigns against drunken driving and had become a major supporter of the Multicultural Career Intern Program, a scholarship fund for refugee and immigrant children. This actor clearly understood the current drama of Miami better than many "experts" did.

"It's not just issues like drugs and crime," he told me. "All the great national dramas are playing themselves out here, including the most important one of all—first the clash, then the fusion, of different cultures, of different peoples, which always has explained both the tragedies and the triumphs of this country."

Then Olmos put his finger on what—more even than drugs, guns and crime—scared people about Miami: "It doesn't matter whether you're Anglo or Jewish or Polish or Cuban," he said. "Every group thinks once they've got it made, the curtain will come down on the drama of America, and they can settle down to the happy ending. Then, suddenly, new people start moving in. An America where the plot once seemed simple and safe now seems complex and dangerous because, just when you think you've got America mastered, it always starts renewing itself."

Later, in another interview, Olmos made his point even better.

Both the cause of America's turmoil and the secret of its dynamism, he said, was that different "cultures are constantly at war with one another, misunderstood. I think that's the theme of America right now." Still he was optimistic about the future of the United States. All these new people, all these unexpected changes, as always in American history, in the end were "going to bring an incredible amount of strength to the country."

When I met Michael Mann, I asked him about the most obvious discrepancy between "Miami Vice" and Miami: not a single major character on the show was identifiably Cuban. Wouldn't it make more sense for the central figures to be Cuban, since most of the real-life police dramas there deeply involved Cubans? Mann never answered that question because something else diverted his attention.

"Black?" he replied, with evident surprise. "I wouldn't say Tubbs is black. Of course Philip Michael Thomas is black, but Tubbs isn't. That's why we named his character *Ricardo* Tubbs, not Richard. We loved the way a dark star and a blond star played off each other—visually, it's very exciting. But on the show Tubbs certainly isn't 'black,' the way, say, Eddie Murphy or Bill Cosby is black. It's possible, sure. Maybe he's a light-skinned black; maybe he's a dark-skinned Hispanic; maybe there's some American Indian in him; maybe he's some combination of all three, plus white American, of course."

I asked about motivation. Did Crockett and Tubbs run around risking their lives for twenty-eight thousand dollars a year so they could wear those clothes? Again, Mann didn't answer my question, perhaps because my questions had a different meaning to him than they did to me. "The important thing," he said, "is to create a situation which lets the viewer see what the viewer wants to see. That's why," Mann concluded, unaware he was using the same words Olmos had, "the character is undefined."

*

The reason Crockett and Tubbs were so alluring was their lack of definition. They didn't have wives or children like the rest of us; they didn't live in houses; they didn't pay bills. True, they shot it out with murderers and drug dealers. Yet they nonetheless had all those things—exotic cars, exotic clothes, exotic women—that, in real life, people in their position usually can get only by smuggling drugs, or worse.

Real Miami cops had to live with the melancholy realization that life is serious, deadly serious. Crockett and Tubbs, on the other hand, personified escape from the "battle between good and evil" that, one way or another, complicates all our lives. On "Miami Vice," you could both battle evil and live it up like Mr. Big. And, whatever kind of American you happened to be, that was only the beginning of the dispensations the show conferred on its heroes and, vicariously, those who watched them on TV.

If you were a "real" American like Don Johnson, you no longer had to shave; even your clothes could be wrinkled. If you were a black American, things were even greater. It was never clear how Tubbs paid for all those clothes; you never saw exactly where Tubbs lived, but it certainly wasn't in Liberty City. The only time he went there was to shoot it out with some criminal, usually white or Latin, who'd betrayed the American way. But wherever the shoot-out occurred, when it was over, he looked as if he'd just stepped out of an ad in *Gentlemen's Quarterly.*

"Miami Vice" risked creating more complicated reactions if you were Hispanic since many of the villains were stereotypical Latins, but in fact "Miami Vice" handled the demographics of Hispanic fantasy best of all. Don Johnson may have been the "coolest guy in the universe." But when you watched "Miami Vice" in East L.A. or East Harlem, Lieutenant Castillo was the coolest guy on the show.

It seems fair to point out there was another reason so many white, black and brown Americans were crazy about "Miami Vice." It wasn't simply that, each Friday night, you entered a fantasy world.

The fantasy entered you. For sixty minutes, life became fast, mellow and dangerous—while all the time it was safe as the remote control on your TV set. Intuition always superseded logic; language itself lost meaning. A glance, a gesture—or the absence of one—told you all you needed to know. "Miami Vice" was hardly a "battle between good and evil." It was the cocaine aesthetic successfully translated to prime-time TV, that is to say, into the mainstream of American popular cultural expression. It was the audiovisual equivalent of the biochemical experience of getting high.

"Miami Vice" wasn't the only thing millions of Americans turned on to the same time each week. People all over the country told me it was their regular Friday-night ritual: first, roll the joints or lay out the lines of coke. Then get high watching Crockett and Tubbs blow the drug dealers out of the water.

In Miami, just like everywhere else, people love rooting for the good guys. Indeed, at the same time the rest of the country was hooked on "Miami Vice," Miami was caught up in its own version of the craze.

Edmundo Mireles was all over the TV channels, his picture in all the newspapers and magazines. Women beamed whenever they saw him; men shook his hand; kids asked for his autograph; he received fan mail by the sack. He was surrounded by admirers, colleagues, friends, well-wishers, journalists, photographers and TV crews. Though celebrity had come to him suddenly, it seemed to fit him as comfortably as his casual slacks, his brown- and blue-striped sports shirts and his loafers. He wasn't flustered, and he didn't play up to the cameras even when dozens of reporters thrust microphones in his face. In fact he said very little, but what he did say he said very well.

"I'd like to take this opportunity to thank everyone who made it possible for me to be here today," he told the cameras. "The public has been tremendous," he added, after thanking many people by name. Then, as the crowd applauded, he entered a waiting car and, in a small motorcade, was driven away.

"The entrance was very small and the exit was very big," a member of the staff remarked that day Edmundo Mireles left South Miami Hospital to begin physical therapy for his shattered left arm. The surgeon was referring to Mireles's wounds, but, it seemed to me, that comment also measured the man.

I watched that tape a number of times on a borrowed Betamax. I also ran tapes of "Miami Vice." Switching back and forth between Edmundo Mireles and Sonny Crockett clarified one thing.

Edmundo Mireles's sports clothes, his modest manner—even that smile—made no difference. He still had the dark moustache, the double chin, the slicked-down black hair, the five o'clock shadow. And this, like so many of the incongruities others found exotic, or even sinister, produced in me a different reaction—one of affection, even admiration, for a city where the real-life hero looked just like a TV villain.

"Miami Vice" was about drugs, shoot-outs, fast cars, fast women and fast money. Miami was about life, liberty and the pursuit of happiness.

"Miami Vice" was about escaping reality; Miami was about the inescapability of reality. "Miami Vice" was the most carefully crafted TV program in history. Miami was plastic, slapped-together, instant.

Miami was romantic. "Miami Vice" was not, as the critics said, a TV classic; it was a triumph of mannerism. Whereas Miami was Aristotelian—always struggling toward, never fulfilling, its *telos*— "Miami Vice" was Platonic. In spite of all those shoot-outs and car chases, this show wasn't about struggle; it was an exercise in defining ideal, unchanging, unhuman, perfect forms.

These asymmetries lead us to the most fascinating aspect of the relationship between "Miami Vice" and Miami—to the heart of the mystery that makes them part of the same city.

Why was "Miami Vice" such a fabulous show? It really was

terrific, at least during the first few seasons, while Michael Mann was directly in charge of production.

The work was dull, tedious, repetitive. The hours were never-ending. "Expect to Work to 5:00 AM," one location call sheet announced. "Everyone should be prepared for rain and sun conditions daily." Being a good actor was almost as grueling as being a good cop. Perhaps what made so many people want to be Don Johnson was that Johnson took such care with his work. He wasn't an "artist," perhaps not even an "actor" in the serious sense of the word. Johnson was a craftsman with a seemingly inexhaustible capacity for honest labor. And that, I have reason to suspect, was why Mann hired him rather than any of a dozen other blond, personable actors with crinkly grins. Producing a TV show, like running an FBI investigation, isn't just about shoot-outs; it's about staying the course. Mireles kept going because his work was catching crooks; Johnson kept going because his work was creating illusion, in fact two illusions—first Crockett the cop, then (much more challenging) Johnson the star.

For all their differences, Miami and "Miami Vice" wound up posing what might be called the Christo question: Why do some people turn mudbanks into garbage dumps? Why do some people turn mudbanks into beautiful great joyous works of art?

"Miami Vice" was good because people knew they were creating something important, so you found none of the cynicism and cut corners that you did on some other network shows. Every aspect of the production bespoke a craving to create something excellent. There were whole episodes when every frame of film seemed perfectly composed. I'll never forget one of them. It was just a shot of one of those big red stop lights dangling over an intersection on South Dixie Highway. But it caught the whole tacky, languorous essence of off-the-freeway traffic in Miami.

The show's secret, however, wasn't the excellence of the details. It was how—just like in the Atlantis—those details first fitted together, then reinforced each other, and so created a whole that was greater than the sum of its parts.

Those clothes Crockett and Tubbs wore are a perfect example of what I mean. It wasn't just that they were visually stunning. They solved a very serious technical problem, in this case: What to do with guns? Think through the problem Michael Mann faced when it came to filming a cop show in Miami. The cops had to carry guns, but how, and where? Not even in Miami—not even when the temperature and humidity both hit ninety—could American TV heroes carry purses. Crockett and Tubbs would have looked equally ridiculous, amid all those palm trees, in all that heat, wearing the kinds of ordinary suits real cops do. What did it matter that no one in Miami dressed that way before "Miami Vice" went on the air? Those snazzy Italian jackets didn't just solve the gun problem. They heightened and reinforced the effect all the other details of the show were making. In fact they did much more than that.

Like the sky court at the Atlantis, they became the embodiment of the entire Miami the show was creating.

"Miami Vice" *was* Miami—and never more so than when it was taking liberties with reality.

To understand why, you have to understand another factor that runs through everything there, what might be called the Ralph Sanchez factor. Michael Mann and the others were refusing to let reality stand in their way, refusing to let even Miami stop them. They had an idea of what Miami should be, and if Miami didn't happen to be this cool, exotic city full of glamour and excitement, so what? You turned the actual Miami into your fantasy.

There was another constant. Like Miami itself, as we'll soon see, the show grew out of a marriage of very different sensibilities. As the *Miami Herald* explained, just before the show first went on the air:

> The original idea to set a police show in Miami belonged
> to Anthony Yerkovich. . . . Yerkovich saw Miami's tropi-
> cal, multiethnic feel and the pervasive drug trade as a
> backdrop for an adult, heavy-on-characterization police

show. His idea was to explore the trying lives of cops who spend most of their time undercover and who occasionally find their masquerade . . . poisoning their lives when they begin to take on the very characteristics of their sleazy prey.

"Michael Mann is the other 'Miami Vice' executive producer," the article noted almost as an afterthought, adding that while Yerkovich was best known for his work on "Hill Street Blues," Mann's most notable television creation was "Starsky and Hutch."

So the show really did wind up portraying a mythic struggle—between Yerkovich's interest in the human reality of Miami and Mann's fascination with its decor. This may not have been "the mythic battle between good and evil." But it did have one thing in common with the classic Westerns of yore.

In the end reality bit the dust. Decor—as usual in Miami—triumphed absolutely, and that was why the show captured the essence of Miami so well. Michael Mann, like all the great inventors of Miami, had thrown away the blueprints once he'd got there.

Take a look at a map of Miami sometime. You'll find the place-names honor achievement in fantasy the way other cities commemorate eminence in politics, the arts, or war. Julia Tuttle Causeway, Flagler Street, Fisher Island, Ponce de Leon Boulevard, to be followed in the fullness of time, no doubt, by Ralph Sanchez Expressway and Crockett Causeway: Miami is like those treasure troves in Mesopotamia—when you start digging, you find all the fads and fashions that have made America what it is in the twentieth century. The whole city is one vast, wonderful tribute to the fact that, in this part of the world, fantasy has the force of history.

A good way to introduce yourself to the meaning of Miami, as well as to its archaeological riches, is to fly down there sometime and check into the Fontainebleau hotel. Everyone knows the Fontainebleau sums up the fashions and follies of the fifties the same way, I predict, we will remember "Miami Vice" as one of the totems of the eighties. It's one of those classic Miami Beach hotels that, as Norman Mailer once put it, are stacked along the Atlantic Ocean

> like sugar cubes and ice-cube trays on edge, like mosques and palaces, shaped like matched white luggage and portable radios, stereos, plastic compacts and plastic rings, Moorish castles heaped like waffle irons, shaped like the baffle plates on white plastic electric heaters, and cylinders like Waring blenders, buildings looking like . . . sweet wedding cakes, cottons of kitsch and piles of dirty cotton and piles of dirty stucco, yes, for ten miles the hotels . . . stood on the beach side of Collins Avenue: the Eden Roc and the Fontainebleau. . . .

My suite at the Fontainebleau still had some wonderful touches, though the winged cupid table lamps and Marie Antoinette vanities were long gone. There was, for instance, the air-conditioned, cedar-lined, walk-in closet—so that even when it was ninety-eight in the shade, m'lady's minks would be cool. There was the "fruit basket," which, besides fruit, contained enough cheese, crackers and candies to feed a Marielito family of four. There was no TV in the bathroom, as there was at the Grand Bay, but the French Provincial color television overlooked a balcony big enough to hold a New York studio apartment. Every morning when I ate breakfast there, a bird would appear, to scavenge for crumbs from my toast. This bird was no Florida cockatoo. Like every other guest at the Fontainebleau, it was an out-of-towner, a good old New York pigeon, in fact. Had someone brought the pigeon down in a suitcase and turned it loose? Or did some mutation of the homing instinct impel this creature to migrate south each winter in search of the very people who, the rest of the year, fed him toast in the Bronx? The pigeon knew, but the pigeon wasn't telling.

The bed was the most fun, but to what use was I supposed to put this stupendous object? The management seemed to provide a discreet suggestion. The bed had three immense pillows, and when the maid turned down the covers, she'd put a chocolate mint on each one of them. So every night when I'd come back alone—or at the very most, with one other person—those three little mints would be leering up at me, and I'd wonder: was I the only one whose nightly exploits didn't include a *ménage à trois*?

In the best Miami circles, there are two opposite and equally acceptable reactions to hotels like the Fontainebleau. A "serious" person has the option of being either appalled or delighted by the vulgarity. It's a great pity that what is not permitted under any circumstances is to take these buildings seriously.

When I said earlier that fantasy has the force of history in Miami, I meant it in the same literal, matter-of-fact way you'd say steel has the force of history in Youngstown, Ohio. To prove that point to someone in Youngstown, you'd take them to the top of some slag heap. You'd show them the darkened silhouettes of the mills, and all the buildings and lives in the city those mills have wrenched into existence.

In Miami the place to stand is in the middle of Collins Avenue, at the point where Collins juts inward from the beach and curves around the Fontainebleau in the direction of the Eden Roc. It's best to do this late at night, for two reasons. You're less likely to get run down, and the darkness makes things clearer. What you'll see is something even more grandiose than the Fontainebleau itself—a gargantuan *trompe l'oeil* mural.

The mural is 120 feet wide and tall as a ten-story building; it covers 13,016 square feet. This Biblical immensity depicts what, back in the fifties, was nothing less than the gateway to a Promised Land. The gateway is a towering Art Deco triumphal arch—and it leads out of the Babylonian Captivity of the Deco district into a land of milk and honey and French Provincial cabanas where the "Gentiles Only" signs have fallen like the walls of Jericho. Specifically this *trompe l'oeil* triumphal arch leads to the Fontainebleau hotel, which, in reality, happens to be located just on the other side of the wall, exactly where this gargantuan illusion promises that you will find it.

It is this illusory Fontainebleau in the mural, however, which is the real Fontainebleau, even though the mural itself was only installed in 1986 and the hotel opened back in 1954. This is because, while the real hotel and the people in it have changed enormously over the decades, this illusory hotel is permanent, unchanging, and so it lets you see the Fontainebleau as those who came there thirty years ago saw it. In the mural the hotel still glistens as brightly as it did the night it opened—glossy as a new mink coat, ultramodern as a new De Soto, a great escapist icon reflecting and defining its age.

When this mural was finished, it was given a formal inauguration the way, in other places, you'd dedicate a real building. The hotel's owner, Stephen Muss, held a reception "for top business, governmental and civic leaders" including " 'Miami Vice' star Don Johnson," as the press release explained. Alex Daoud, the Arab-American mayor of predominately Jewish-American Miami Beach, officiated at this baptism and, as always in Miami, the proud godparents were publicity agents. They christened the mural "the most famous wall in the Southern United States." (What the most famous wall in the northern United States was, they did not explain.) "The mural," as the press release also pointed out, "is guaranteed for ten years against fading and an additional five years against chipping or peeling."

Directly underneath that Fontainebleau mural is some archaeological debris—an old run-down Deco hotel called the Surrey that contains one of the great old authentic Miami Beach bars. There, most nights, you can find some of the great old authentic Miami Beach characters.

That night I checked in at the Fontainebleau, I went over to the Surrey in search of local color. I was out of luck. I only found, on the neighboring barstool, an Amazonian Indian wearing a gold nugget in his left earlobe, a "Miami Vice" T-shirt and about a pint of *eau de cologne.* He was a chef in a kosher restaurant, he explained. He'd started cooking for a living back in Iquitos. He'd only been in Miami a couple of months, but already he'd mastered all the stuff about cloven hooves and different sets of pots and pans. "Ham and eggs is *terefah,"* he said as Jimmy, the Irish bartender, brought him another peppermint schnapps. "Practically everything's *pasul* unless it's got the message from the pope of the Jews on it saying it's okay."

Unfortunately, another aspect of life in Miami had him flummoxed. This was the triangular, interlocking relationship of cars, money and women. To get women you needed money, and to get money you needed a car. But here was the catch: you couldn't get the car until you had the money, and you couldn't get the money until you had the car. So, over there in Miami were all those big-paying jobs, all those big-breasted women. And over here in Miami Beach, here he was, making borscht for four bucks an hour, sleeping alone in a seedy room in the Surrey hotel, all because he didn't have wheels.

No car, no money. No money, no car. In English, in Spanish, in languages—Hebrew? Quechua?—unknown to my ear, he explored the dreadful syllogism and, with Talmudic exquisiteness, its cruel corollary: no sex.

He asked me where I was staying. I said the Fontainebleau, and so the Amazonian was prompted to illumination.

"People who stay there," he observed, "worked for everything they got."

At the Fontainebleau, *Saturday Night Fever* was playing on the French Provincial TV set. Had people once really worn white suits like that? Had people, had I, once really danced those dances? A question formed in my mind: What ever happened to John Travolta? I climbed alone into that immense bed, and as I ate the first mint, then the second, and finally the third, it seemed whole decades were being swallowed up. I'd gone from a thirties bar back to a fifties hotel. Now the seventies, too, were only a look, a style, a decor, preserved on film like a fly in amber.

Suddenly I feared for Miami. What if crinkly linens and pastels went out of fashion? What if, God forbid, "Miami Vice" were canceled? Would planes descending into MIA have to regain altitude, quickly, when they found the runways had disappeared?

The next morning as I ate breakfast on the balcony, I could see I was wrong: everything would be just fine. All along the beach the Moorish castles were still heaped like waffle irons. The sweet wedding cakes of hotels still glistened.

What difference did it make that no one used waffle irons, that not many people bothered to get married anymore? Miami still climbed upward, born aloft by this illusion people had, that they could create perfect forms, toward that great *telos* in the sky.

This year's Don Johnson might be next year's John Travolta, today's Armani jackets tomorrow's minks. But, as the Fontainebleau itself proved, there was always life in reruns. (The Grand Bay Hotel, another artifact in the making, now exquisitely, minutely curated our fantasies of what now defined escape.) But having fallen from fashion, the Fontainebleau had been born again as "Caribbean" convention center.

The thought pleased me as I surveyed this living city, the realization that "Miami Vice" was the real Miami precisely because "Miami Vice" was fake.

Complacencies of the bathrobe, and late coffee and oranges in a sunny chair. First I had to run up to Surfside to meet Isaac Bashevis Singer, Nobel laureate in literature, then down to the very termination of Miami Beach, for lunch with Irwin Sawitz, grand impresario of Joe's Stone Crab.

It was Sunday morning. I hastened in from the balcony. The pigeon made unambiguous undulations as it lurched for the toast.

Part II

City of the Future

5

Golems

"Miami is a place of the future," Mr. Singer told me. "I write about a world that has disappeared in a world that is being born."

In the world of literature, Isaac Bashevis Singer is a titan, but in Miami Beach he is a little bluebird of a man. He wore a powder-blue jacket; he had the prancing blue eyes of an eighty-two-year-old child. He wrote in a dying language about a dead world where evil had triumphed absolutely. He bobbed and hopped his way around the Bal Harbour shopping mall as though it were a candy store.

Even legends, it turned out, fly south for the winter. So while it snowed in New York, Isaac Bashevis Singer sat in his Surfside condo, using a fountain pen and Yiddish to conjure up places and people no Holocaust could destroy. When he had visitors, he took them out for coffee or a bowl of borscht. Every afternoon at five, he and his wife lined up with the other old people at a nearby restaurant for their dinner. He also taught a writing class at the University of Miami.

I asked Mr. Singer what it was like to be a legend. "When you live with a legend, you see he's not a legend," he answered. I also asked him what it was like to be old. "An old man is a young man who is eighty or ninety," he answered. "Nothing changes, only the body changes."

Nobel Prize–winners can go anywhere for the winter. So most of all I wanted to know why he liked Miami so much. "In Paradise you should have drugstores," was his reply. I asked him about his Cuban students at the University of Miami.

"They think in English," he told me. While we were discussing Miami, Mr. Singer offered an explanation as to why the Jews wound up the Chosen People: "They made an effort to be chosen," he said.

Isaac Bashevis Singer also told me about Golems. A Golem, he explained, is a kind of Talmudic R2D2—an artificial being created by the theosophists of the Kabbalah. How is a Golem made?

"You start with mud," he explained. "You shape the mud into what you want it to be. If you get the ritual incantations right, it springs to life."

If you want to get a sense of how Miami is made, you eat at Joe's Stone Crab as I did that Sunday after my meeting with Mr. Singer. On a typical night, Joe's serves some fourteen hundred customers more than half a ton of crab claws dipped in more than three hundred pounds of butter, along with nearly a hundred Key-lime pies.

To do all that takes a fleet of more than fifty fishing boats and, at the restaurant itself, 150 workers and twenty hours a day. It also requires a degree of effort and organization that makes the production of "Miami Vice" seem simple. The work begins around five each morning, when the pastry chef starts baking pies, cakes and biscuits from scratch, and other specialists start weighing, sorting, cleaning and chilling those crab claws that, even those bred on Maine lobster agree, are the most succulent crustaceans this planet produces. Sometimes the work doesn't end until after midnight, when the help finishes scrubbing the floors and scouring the kitchen clean.

For three-quarters of a century, Joe's Stone Crab has survived hurricanes, depressions and changing food fads to become a force of its own in south Florida history. It's conceivable that once upon a time some notable visited Miami without eating there, but only barely. Over the years its customers have ranged from the duke and duchess of Windsor to Jimmy Buffett. Presidents have dined there, so have countless other politicians. Back in 1972 Florida moved the date of its presidential primary up to March. The weather was better then; the earlier date also assured greater national attention. But the real reason, so the story goes, is that candidates and commentators didn't want to come to Florida if they couldn't eat stone crab at Joe's, which is closed from May to October, when the stone crab is out of season.

When I got to Joe's Stone Crab, Irwin Sawitz revealed something as illuminating as what the Amazonian at the Surrey had told me: his restaurant hadn't started serving its famous Key-lime pie until an outsider made it famous for its Key-lime pie. Even more astonishing, no one in Miami had the idea to serve the crabs, either, until a visitor urged them to do it.

Sawitz told the Key-lime pie story first. "This was always a seafood restaurant, never a place for desserts," he said. "But then someone in Chicago wrote an article saying that if anything was even better than the stone crabs at Joe's, it was that tart taste in the pie. He wrote you could only get it from those authentic limes from the Florida Keys they used at Joe's.

"Sure was news to me," Sawitz added. "So we put it on the menu. It's been a big hit ever since."

As Irwin Sawitz recounted the saga of Joe's Stone Crab, I realized why this Miami story seemed so familiar. None of the features that make Joe's Stone Crab what it is existed until people came down to Miami and made them up.

There wasn't even a Miami Beach back in 1913 when Sawitz's grandfather-in-law, Joseph Weiss, established what would become

Miami Beach's most famous restaurant. And the place wasn't even called Joe's, let alone Joe's Stone Crab. It was only a short-order sandwich counter located in Smith's Casino, a public bathhouse in an area called Alton Beach, which was then a swampy sandbar, covered with mangroves and infested with mosquitoes, and could only be reached from the mainland by boat.

By the time the 1919 hurricane struck, Weiss's establishment was still so primitive he didn't bother to batten down the hatches when the big blow came. As Jesse Weiss—Joseph Weiss's son and Sawitz's father-in-law—later explained, "We had nothing, a little furniture. So we opened the windows and the wind blew through. Then the sun came out and dried everything up."

By 1919, however, the restaurant was at last known as Joe's and, having moved a couple of times, it finally came to rest at its present site. By then Miami Beach also had acquired its present name, though the "city" founded four years earlier still had fewer full-time residents than Joe's has employees now. But the restaurant was only one of a dozen unremarkable seafood places, and not a single one of them bothered to serve stone crab, although the species abounded in Biscayne Bay. It wasn't until 1923 that Joe's Stone Crab became one of those essential Miami fixtures—because an outsider, in this case a Harvard ichthyologist, decided to make it so.

Damon Runyon may have been the first writer to get a story out of the stone crab's curious Miami apotheosis: no one in Miami "bothered much with stone crabs as an article of diet," Runyon wrote back in the twenties, until

> the late Jim Allison, of Indianapolis, one of the builders of Miami Beach, who had an aquarium on the shores of Biscayne Bay loaded with aquatic fauna of various kinds, imported a Harvard professor to study and classify the local fish and one day this professor saw some boys with a bunch of stone crabs. He wanted to know what they were going to do with them, and they said they were going to throw them away. The professor said that was

bad judgment as the crabs were good eating, and some-
body tried them and found he was right as rain.

Actually, it was a little more complicated than that. Prior to 1923
people in Miami deliberately refused to eat the crustacean. The
body of the stone crab contains almost no edible flesh and even the
large, lobsterlike claws, when cooked, have an odd, slimy texture,
as well as what many find an odd and unpleasant taste. Scorned
though the crab was by the locals, the visiting Harvard professor
noticed it bore a striking resemblance to the renowned Moro crab,
a famous delicacy of Havana, and he told Jim Allison so. Allison in
turn carried a barrel of the crabs to Joseph Weiss's restaurant and
urged him to add them to his menu. Soon a caldron was bubbling
in Weiss's backyard.

According to most accounts, it was Joseph Weiss himself who had
the idea of chilling the claws after they were boiled. Thanks to this
simple expedient, the stone crab underwent a wondrous metamorphosis. The flesh grew mysteriously firm, but not the slightest bit
chewy. Most important, that memorable taste of the stone crab
emerged. Even today, more than sixty years later, no one has
figured out a better way to eat stone crab than first boiled and
chilled, then dipped in melted butter or a mustardy mayonnaise.
Because frozen stone crab can't equal the taste of the fresh, Joe's,
to this day, is open only seven months a year.

A dish hitherto unknown to the world had been conjured up in
Miami. But it requires more than crab claws to make a legend.
According to Jesse Weiss, it was an energetic promoter named
Steve Hannigan "who started us on the publicity thing." Hannigan
transformed Joe's, just another all-purpose seafood place, into Joe's
Stone Crab, worldwide capital of a seafood empire that nowadays
extends from Europe to Japan.

More than ten years ago, a Miami writer named Jack McClintock
observed that stone crabs were sociologically as well as gastronomi-
cally "very unusual, in that they were first eaten in a restaurant

instead of by the masses." Only in instant Miami did the local speciality appear on a menu before people started serving it in their own homes.

Even the stone crab's name seems to have been made up. (While hard enough, the shell of the "stone" crab is no harder than that of some other marine species.) What is clear is that the creature only became generally known by that name after Hannigan convinced Weiss to call his restaurant Joe's Stone Crab.

That day at lunch, I mentioned to "Say" Sawitz, as everyone calls him, that the saga of Joe's Stone Crab contained all the classic Miami ingredients.

There was, first of all, the leitmotif of escape. (Joseph Weiss had started out as an asthmatic New York waiter. Like countless others, he'd migrated to Miami because he believed the stories that the climate would be good for his health.) There was the essential Miami theme of the outsider manufacturing something out of nothing. There was hype. There was the satisfaction of an elemental human craving. (Stone crabs, it should be pointed out for the benefit of those who haven't tasted them, are as addictive as cocaine.) There was the violation of old taboos. (Not only the Weiss family but most of Joe's customers were Jews. That didn't stop them from devouring the forbidden crustacean in mind-boggling quantities even on High Holy Days.)

There was also another inescapable Miami leitmotif—the price you pay for rapid growth. (The species was on the way to massive depletion, if not extinction, during the early years of the stone crab craze. But, today, in a real triumph of environmental wisdom, the restaurant plays an important role in maintaining the ecological balance. Instead of harvesting the entire crab, Florida fishermen now only break off one of the claws, and then return the rest of the creature, alive and kicking, to the sea. A new claw grows back to full size in two years, permitting a single crab to provide many "harvests" of the delicacy in the course of its life.)

Just as on the set of "Miami Vice," there was also at Joe's the spectacle of multiethnic cooperation as whites, blacks, Hispanics, Jews and Gentiles all labored to serve up those prodigious quantities of food.

That wasn't all. There was also the utterly indispensable motif of air conditioning. (The stone crab, like Miami, would never have amounted to anything without refrigeration.)

"You've left out the most important theme of all," Sawitz interjected. "Survival in the face of disaster."

For some people in Miami, disaster was a hurricane, or the bust that inevitably followed the boom. Or it was race riots or invading Marielitos or drugs or violent crime. For Joe's Stone Crab, however, disaster was summed up in three loathsome words—The American Plan. The great disaster struck in the fifties when, typically, the triumph of a new Miami fantasy subverted the old.

Far up the beach the Fontainebleau, the Eden Roc and the other new hotels were rising. These skyscraper extravaganzas weren't just bigger, they were fundamentally different from the old hotels where people previously had stayed. More than mere lodging places, they were self-contained resorts, with their own nightclubs and restaurants. And under the American plan, three meals a day came with the rooms. That wasn't all. These new hotel restaurants were as lavishly decorated as Joe's was austere, and instead of simply prepared local products, they served heavily sauced and flambéed dishes.

Furthermore, as South Beach deteriorated and the new hotels marched farther and farther north, the restaurant grew more and more remote geographically from where the action was. So why schlepp all the way down to Joe's for crab, when right in your own hotel you could get "continental cuisine" for free? For the time being, the restaurant scraped along by doing what it had always done—serving the freshest seafood to the most people for the lowest price it could. But then another disaster in Miami Beach ushered in a reversal of fortunes.

This time the disaster was the wholesale repudiation of the whole fifties-Fontainebleau ideal of what constituted the perfect vacation. As Miami Beach's traditional patrons—usually affluent, self-made northern Jews—abandoned the big hotels for condos or the Caribbean, the American plan collapsed. Equally important, Miami's transformation from a dowdy hick town into a thriving, cosmopolitan city brought both new kinds of tourists and new kinds of locals to eat at Joe's. These people were much more likely to have their own cars and to come from the Miami side of the bay (and so did not have to pay the cab fare down from the upper reaches of Miami Beach). They were also less concerned with culinary status than previous patrons, and much more interested in authentic ingredients, simply prepared.

As good a time as any to date the turn-around is 1961—year of the Bay of Pigs invasion. That year *Holiday* magazine for the first time named Joe's one of the best restaurants in the nation, an honor repeated every year since. This may not have been an event to compare with Sun Belt shift or the Cuban missile crisis. But like the premiere of "Miami Vice," it marked a cultural turning point— away from the old notion that for a restaurant to be good, it had to offer "cuisine" coated in sauces with foreign names and served up in elegant surroundings. A trend toward appreciation of authentic American regional food had begun. Today that trend reigns supreme from Chez Panisse in Berkeley, California, to Legal Seafood in Boston, as well as every place in between. Like Miami itself, Joe's Stone Crab had seemed so out-of-date for a simple reason. It was way ahead of its time.

Barely ninety years ago there was no Miami. So you didn't just find restaurants older than the city around them. You met and talked with people older than Miami itself—and this in turn created the strangest paradox of this instant city: unless you had a sense of history, you couldn't understand Miami at all.

Most of the time you took Miami's existence as a given. But there were other moments. You could be driving down I-95. Out the window you'd see the pastel neon lights of the bridge that carries the Metrorail, and the downtown skyscrapers twinkling beyond. And suddenly you'd remember driving that road when there'd been no Metrorail and half the skyscrapers hadn't been there either. Or you'd take the wrong turn out of one of those new shopping centers on the Palmetto Expressway, and a hundred yards later, Miami would just stop. There'd be no more asphalt, no more neon, no more air conditioning, no more people—only vines and mud and insects and a strange damp Paleolithic smell.

One morning while I was staying at Turnberry Isle, I awoke to find an immense machine outside my window. Like some gigantic praying mantis, it was diligently scooping up muck, piling muck upon muck. Right there, in front of you, you could see earth without form, and void, and darkness upon the face of the deep being transformed, with biblical inevitability, into dry land, into shopping malls, parking lots, condos—into Miami. I took my bath in a whirling Jacuzzi big as that bed at the Fontainebleau, and as I went out, the Haitian maids, in their white uniforms, were singing a song of the Caribbean, and I realized: five years ago that immense machine, that immense Jacuzzi, those Haitians, this hotel—none of them had been here. The whole damn place was made up! The whole damn place was just made up. The creation of this vast, coruscating metropolis hadn't taken hundreds of years. It all had happened, historically speaking, in the wink of an eye, in the beat of a heart, in a single breath.

Disaster, of course, preceded Miami's creation in the winter of 1895. The coldest cold spell in memory gripped the United States. Temperatures dropped to nineteen degrees in central Florida; as far south as Lake Okeechobee people shivered and crops froze. Many feared for the future of Florida's infant tourist and citrus industries. But where others saw crisis, a local landowner named Julia Tuttle perceived an opportunity worth exploiting. She urged railroad magnate Henry M. Flagler to extend his East Coast Railway south of the frost line, to Miami.

It wasn't the first time Tuttle had made that plea; lots of other landowners were also pestering Flagler to run his railroad through their land. Today there might be no Julia Tuttle Causeway—no Miami—if, as every Miami tot knows, Mrs. Tuttle hadn't sent Mr. Flagler something even more worthless than a barrel of stone crabs.

She sent him a little bouquet of orange blossoms. And so, the legend runs, the tycoon's heart was softened, the railroad did arrive, and Miami was born.

As with Joe's, the real story is somewhat more complex. It was more than a bouquet of orange blossoms. It was a whole miniature botanical garden that was sent to Flagler. And it wasn't Tuttle herself who sent it. At her invitation, Flagler had dispatched his chief land agent, J. E. Ingraham, down the coast to inspect her holdings, to see if the place really was impervious to frost. And following this reconnaissance, it was Ingraham who returned to frosty Palm Beach with the assortment of "choice flowers and foliage" he had collected on Tuttle's land. It was this living proof that Miami was a place where the sun shone during even the chilliest winters farther north that transformed Miami from a private estate into a future metropolis.

They may not have been orange blossoms, and it may not have been Tuttle herself who brought them to Flagler. But the fact remains that Miami is the only major American city conceived by a woman, and a remarkable woman she was. The wife of Frederick Tuttle, an industrialist of wealth and position in faraway Cleveland, Julia Tuttle first set eyes on the Miami wilderness way back in 1875. People compared the Miami of those days to the Wild West. In fact that understated its remoteness. By then the transcontinental railroads had brought the wilds of Wyoming within easy access of civilization. The mouth of the Miami River, in comparison, might have been the dark side of the moon.

The nearest railhead was nearly four hundred miles away, just south of the Georgia border. Whether one traveled overland, riding in a cattle cart along the old Indian trails, or took one of the open sloops that carried the coastal trade, the journey down the east coast of Florida was arduous, long and dangerous.

Even at journey's end, one didn't reach "Miami," because not even the idea of such a city existed until Julia Tuttle made up her mind it should. In 1875 she stepped ashore off a mail boat to find only an Indian trading post, the ruins of a U.S. Army camp once known as Fort Dallas and a couple of plantations scattered along the shores of Biscayne Bay.

Six years earlier two Cleveland men had bought land there. One, William B. Brickell, set up the Indian trading post. His holdings today more or less correspond with the Brickell Avenue area. The other pioneer was Julia Tuttle's father, Ephraim T. Sturtevant. Sturtevant and Brickell had started out as partners but there was a dispute and, hardly for the last time in Miami, two real estate partners became bitter rivals. When Julia Tuttle arrived in 1875 to visit her father, Sturtevant was living in a remote homestead near the present site of the John F. Kennedy Causeway, a thoroughfare today flanked by, among other things, one of the relatively few kosher Chinese restaurants in the world.

These days the drive takes twenty-five minutes, but back then the Sturtevant homestead was nearly a day's journey from Coconut Grove, which at that time was the only real settlement in the area. Elsewhere there was only emptiness, and even at Coconut Grove, "civilization" consisted of only a few white American settlers and a small colony of Bahamian blacks, forebears of the inhabitants of the "Black Grove" of today, who worked their plantations. In this tiny, isolated outpost, the arrival of the mail boat was a major event; the apparition of a respectable white woman created a sensation.

Locals were astonished when Julia Tuttle permitted one of the settlers to take her, unchaperoned, for a sail. Even though she was traveling with her two children and staying with her father, her very audacity in coming to such a place was considered close to scandalous. In a letter a settler named George Parson jotted down a character sketch of Miami's founder that future history would vindicate fully. She was "full of life but not very discreet," he wrote, in fact prone to "rather unbecoming conduct in a married lady. She is unaffected though and possesses a stout heart I think."

Julia Tuttle soon went back to Cleveland and probably did not expect to return. Her 1875 visit might have remained of no consequence—and alligators might still be more numerous than skyscrapers in Miami. But sixteen years later, her husband died, following a long illness that had forced her to take charge of the family business. A little later Julia Tuttle's father died, too.

Alone in the world except for her two children, Tuttle faced a staid but not entirely unenviable fate—that of the widowed society matron, living on the fringes of Cleveland society. But for her, as for the millions who would follow in her footsteps, that wasn't enough. Something sunnier—something wilder—beckoned. So this Ohio matron sold her house and business up North and, as Miami historian Arva Moore Parks puts it, "decided to forge a new life for herself in Miami."

Florida by then already had its share of eccentric, wealthy widows, among them Harriet Beecher Stowe, who had decided to live out their lives on coconut plantations in the back of the beyond. But, it quickly became clear, that wasn't Tuttle's intention. In fact, when she returned to Miami in 1891, she paid hardly any attention to the remote little estate she'd inherited. She had infinitely bigger things in mind.

After considerable searching, she found what she wanted, a six-hundred-acre tract on the north bank of the mouth of the Miami River. Later, people would come to Miami and start orange groves or farms. Then Miami would expand, and they'd find themselves, to their surprise, the owners of cities. Julia Tuttle, however, didn't give a fig about citrus. Right from the beginning, she was looking for the Hollywood and Vine of tomorrow—for that promontory where a tropical Cuyahoga entered a palm-fringed Lake Erie and a new city would arise.

So she abandoned her father's plantation. She bought the triangle of land bounded on the east by Biscayne Bay and on the south and west by the Miami River, the place where all the tallest skyscrapers of the city crowd together today.

But it took more than land to fulfill Julia Tuttle's vision. It took money, lots more money than this affluent Cleveland widow possessed. She had that, too, figured out right from the start. "Someday someone will build a railroad to Miami," she predicted years before it happened, "and I will give to the company that does so one-half of my property at Miami for a townsite."

Year after year Tuttle pestered people—not just Flagler, who, by chance, also had made his fortune in Cleveland, but every other railroad magnate she could find. "It may seem strange to you," she confided to a friend, "but it is a dream of my life to see this wilderness turned into a prosperous country." A strange dream, but not an impossible one because this, after all, was Miami—and Miami, as Julia Tuttle conceived it, was by definition a place where dreams come true.

For years this middle-aged busybody who always wore black, even in the sultry depths of the Florida summer, wrote and argued and badgered. For years the plutocrats said no. Then, in the form of icy winds and frost-blackened citrus, the main chance struck.

The big chill, the orange blossoms, the magnate with an urge to build railroads, the free land to sweeten the deal. Or, in today's idiom: disaster, public relations, the itch not just to escape, but to create new worlds—everything that propels Miami today was there at the creation.

Won over by Julia Tuttle's persistence and vision—above all by the lucrative real estate deal she offered him—Henry Flagler relented. He extended his railroad south to Miami and built the lavish Royal Palm Hotel there, unleashing an influx of fortune-hunters that hasn't stopped since. Hundreds of people, ranging from sharecroppers to real estate speculators, converged on the place, thus establishing the second unique circumstance of Miami's birth.

Other cities have started as forts or foundries, trading centers or ports. Miami is surely the only city of its size to start out as a place to get away from it all. It's also the only major city in the United States, perhaps in the world, that's never produced much of anything in the sense that Kansas produces corn and Pittsburgh produces steel.

Daniel Bell would not popularize the concept of the postindustrial society until 1973. But that's what Miami has been from the beginning—a place where some arrive searching for wealth and happiness, and others are there waiting to sell them land, polish their shoes and pick their pockets. Tuttle and Flagler did not realize it, but they were pioneering, eighty years in advance, America's transformation into a service-sector economy.

In 1896 it was a railroad, a resort hotel and frost-free winters that transformed Miami from a swamp into a real estate bonanza. Today it is the jet airplane, the computer and something far more precious to investors than orange blossoms and sunny skies—a unique combination of U.S. political stability and American technology and a skilled, multilingual Hispanic and American work force—that is transforming Miami into a truly global city.

To understand, think of Miami as a microprocessor chip, for while Miami produces very little, it processes a multitude of things—money, information, cargoes, passengers, hopes, dreams, to say nothing of illegal aliens and cocaine. This may seem like a task that could be performed anywhere, until you consider not just the efficiency of a computer but its vulnerability. It needs skilled technicians who speak its language. The computer also needs a special environment—air-conditioned, dust-free, where the electricity never fails. And it needs linkages to other computers and data banks. Unless all those conditions are met, and met all the time, the computer is nothing more than a whirring, useless piece of junk.

Today the computer language is Spanish. The air-conditioned, dust-free environment is the combination of political stability and economic and personal freedom only the United States can provide. The data banks are the three interconnecting continental economies of North America, the European Common Market and Latin America. And Miami is the microprocessor that connects them all, in millions of different transactions every day. You see it in the busy retail shops downtown, where the Latin American tourists converge with designer blue jeans and video games. You see it in that oldest, most respected and most "American" of Miami institutions, the *Miami Herald,* which is really the daily newspaper of the Caribbean and much of Latin America as well.

"Suppose a retailer in Peru wants eight thousand Swiss watches," said Maria Camila Leiva, executive vice president of the Miami Free

Trade Zone, when I first visited her several years ago. "Or a Texas department store wants some French perfume. In today's global economy," she explained, "the problem is not producing the watches or the perfume. The problem is matching them up with the people who want them."

Mrs. Leiva, a Colombian, led me to a computer terminal and punched out a code. "It turns out," she said after a moment, "that the Swiss watches closest to Peru are in Panama. We'll telex them immediately. As for the perfume they want in Texas, we have it in our inventory here and will fly it to Dallas this afternoon."

Like the Fontainebleau and Joe's, the Free Trade Zone is one of my favorite places in Miami, so I try to visit it whenever I can. It's architecturally surreal yet perfectly functional—like so much else in Miami, an air-conditioned, computerized fusion of foreign capital and American technology that generates enormous wealth. In 1982, after only three years in operation, it had an international work force of 1,260 people and processed $1 billion worth of goods involving 105 countries and 156 companies. Yet the most striking thing about the Free Zone wasn't its size. It was that as late as 1979 there had been nothing but scrubland where it stood. And only a few years before that, not even the notion of such an operation existed in Miami. Only when outside investors—South Americans and people from up North—came up with the idea did it turn into a reality.

On my first visit there, I complimented the Zone's corporate vice president, Robert B. Sproul—not for starting a business, but for building out of cinder blocks and plate glass and silicon chips and air-conditioning ducts a model of Miami itself.

"We didn't realize it at first," Sproul told me, "but it dawned on me when I tried to put together an organizational chart." He handed me a piece of paper. On it were listed, in capital letters, all the elements that combined to make Miami one of the world's fastest growing centers of international trade: INTERNATIONAL COMPANIES, GEOGRAPHICAL LOCATION, PEOPLE,

BANKING, INSURANCE, GOVERNMENT SERVICES, COM-MUNICATION, TRANSPORTATION.

"It was easy to identify the crucial factors, but graphically speaking, there was one problem," Sproul added. "I couldn't figure out where 'MIAMI' should go. Then it struck me. Miami had to go in the middle. Miami was the thing that connected everything else."

The parking lot where I'd left my car was brand-new. All around, housing developments were being laid out, and a giant shopping mall was going up. You could see an immense Jordan Marsh sign, but you still could sense the swamp.

The next time I visited the Zone there were, besides the Jordan Marsh, Italian restaurants and sushi bars and cinemas showing foreign films with subtitles. Within a half-mile radius, you could find boutiques, gun shops, tennis courts, pornographic bookstores and churches.

That wasn't the surprising thing. The surprising thing was that the primeval smell had vanished; it was as though all this had been here forever, as though the wilderness Julia Tuttle saw had never existed.

Many in Miami considered it the most troubling paradox of their city. How could a place with such a genius for creating everything out of nothing also be a city of violence and drugs and hatred and despair?

They were just like Julia Tuttle in that regard. She was out to attract big investors and wealthy settlers. And, sure enough, wealthy northerners did come down on Flagler's railroad and fill his hotel. But retired working-class people from the sweatshops of New York also flocked to Miami. So did poor whites and poor blacks from the rural South, not to mention pickpockets and real estate shysters.

Julia Tuttle had forgotten the truth that constantly renews and despoils America. This is that when you start a stampede toward opportunity, you can't be choosy. If Miami attracts wealthy Venezuelans, how can it not attract poor Haitians? If a hardworking

Cuban businessman can make a small fortune there honestly, what is to prevent a Colombian cocaine don from making a big fortune overnight?

That time Brent Eaton told me about the men's purses, he said something else that stuck in my mind. "Free societies don't have closed borders," he said. And that comment, when you thought about it, explained both Miami's virtues and its vices.

Miami's problems with drugs and illegal aliens were part and parcel of the very internationalization of the city that filled people there with so much pride. Miami's capacity for dizzying growth and change also helped explain the problems of Miami's blacks and old people. The new immigrants, both legal and illegal, enriched Miami—but also filled economic niches at the expense of blacks and other native-born Americans. A similar process had turned Miami into a place where many old folks feel they have no place because the city's stupendous growth hasn't just reshaped the Miami skyline. It has turned many retired persons into urban refugees, as I discovered when I went around Miami talking to old people.

Those who did understand Miami all had two things in common. First of all, they understood Miami was about process, not about getting things right. This was what linked Joe's with the Grand Bay, and Sproul's diagram with "Miami Vice," and Christo with the Haitian boat people. They all understood that whether you ran a restaurant or a free trade zone, Miami was about becoming, not authenticity of detail.

The second thing people who understood Miami had in common was the realization that the real and the fake, the dream and the nightmare, the hope and the despair, were inseparable—that, in Miami, the good always came wrapped up in the bad.

"Whether it's the positive things or the negative things," Maurice Ferre told me the first time we met, while he was still mayor, "this city is going to remain the focus of the most dramatic national and international problems. Miami's unique position is both our biggest opportunity and the source of our most serious problems."

Miami, of course, did not invent any of our great national problems. The problems of the ghetto, of the elderly, of drugs and violence, haunt every American city. It's just been Miami's peculiar fate to have all these things roar through it the way that hurricane roared through Joe's.

Success is the source of all the worst problems. It was true in Tuttle's time; it's still true today.

When I started to write this chapter, I wanted to learn more about Golems. But by then it was August, so Singer wasn't in Miami, of course; he wasn't even in New York. He was over in Switzerland, where he goes every summer. And since neither number in the States was connected to an answering machine, there was no way to get the Switzerland number.

I will ask the questions anyway:

Mr. Singer, you who are more than eighty years old, and write about dead worlds in a world being born, who speak Yiddish and know the secrets of the Kabbalah, once you start a Golem, why can't you stop it?

Mr. Singer, you have won a Nobel Prize, so please tell me: Is the Golem good because it creates, or is the Golem evil because it destroys?

Why do we human beings have this urge to create Golems? And why does God let us? Doesn't He know it's only asking for trouble because the Golem, once we do create it, never turns out to be the Golem we wanted?

Even in Miami, Labor Day comes. Dreams of perpetual glorious summer in Switzerland, dreams of a glorious endless autumn in New York, prove false once again, so people return to Miami and I was able to get Singer on the phone.

"Golems are Golems," he said. "Who are we to say what is good and evil? God can't stop you just because He started you. Why should Golems be different?"

6

Cardboard Waves

"For sixty-five years," said Betty Beckwith, who was then seventy and working for the Dade County Elderly Services, "people have it drummed into them that retirement is their reward for years of work. Then they come to Miami and find it's all a lie. They find retirement is a punishment for being old, and that that punishment consists of being uprooted from your work, friends, family and home and confined to Miami Beach. You know," she concluded, "people get bitter when they're treated like that."

What I hadn't expected to find among so many old people was the anger. "The real problem for old people here isn't the crime or poverty," said Elena Herrschaf, who was active in the Gray Panthers. "It's the sense of worthlessness, the realization that you aren't wanted." She and her husband had settled in Coconut Grove back when it seemed like Greenwich Village South. Now they were planning to move to an old folks' home. "If the blacks don't mug you," her husband told me, "the real estate speculators will."

I guess it was at that moment that Miami taught me another of its lessons—that the elderly were really a lot like the Haitian boat people, the Liberty City street kids, the Colombian drug dealers. They might have been black or penniless or have spoken a foreign language, so utterly alien were their lives from mine.

To visit the old was like getting lost. You had no sense of context; you might have been in a foreign country—a country where you, like everyone else, will live someday. Those old people looked at your youth, and you could see what they were thinking: this makes him the enemy.

In Liberty City the kids stood on the street corners and watched the rest of Miami speed by on I-95. In South Beach the old people sat on park benches and watched the traffic on Collins Avenue pass them by. No one in either place, when you asked them, listed crime or drugs as the main problem. Instead they talked about the trauma of living in a city—a world—that, however full of possibilities for others, had no place for them.

Americans tend to use words like "ghettoization" and "segregation" to describe such alienation, but the sociologists have a better word, because it frees the phenomenon of its racial connotations. They call it marginalization—this tendency to shove whole categories of human beings aside as we create new worlds. As I left one of those old folks' homes in South Beach, it occurred to me that, in the end, we wind up marginalizing ourselves as well.

That night I returned to Coconut Grove, where I was staying in a friend's apartment. It is in Coconut Grove that the Miami ethos of constant newness, perpetual youth, endless affluence, constant success and ceaseless pleasure achieves its purest manifestation. Each day, from that apartment, I looked down on a swimming pool where young and slender human beings ceaselessly bronzed themselves, across a parking lot filled with Mercedes, BMWs and Audis, to a municipal park where at every daylight hour the joggers and cyclists burnished their bodies as though they were expensive possessions.

Coconut Grove has many boutiques and singles bars and elegant restaurants. That evening I decided to have dinner in one of them, and so found myself, once again, in the midst of another revelation. Why, I wondered, did this restaurant in Coconut Grove remind me so much of South Beach and Liberty City? I studied the chic young people at the bar—the careful makeup on the women, the careful hairstyles on the men. They all paid such attention to their dress. They all smiled so much. Perhaps unfairly, I inspected their faces, and so found myself staring into the illusion, much bigger than Miami, as immense as America itself, that if you had enough money and exercised enough and were personable enough and chose the right possessions, you would never know the isolation of the ghetto, the despair of the old folks' home. You would never be lonely, you would never suffer, you would never grow old.

From the beginning it seemed to me Miami illustrated, more clearly than any other city, our American capacity to conjure whole dreamlands out of nothing. Gradually I came to the conclusion that Miami also holds up a mirror to that strange American emptiness that seems always to pursue us no matter how many swamps we turn into cities of tomorrow.

Of the 343 persons, virtually all of them menial laborers, who, at Tuttle's and Flagler's behest, met in July 1896 to incorporate Miami as a city, most were poor, unskilled and landless; more than one-third were black. Streets had to be paved, and sewers dug, before the genteel refugees from winter in New York, Boston and Chicago could occupy Flagler's Royal Palm Hotel.

In one sense these early tourists and laborers were inventing Sun Belt shift and postindustrialization—inaugurating, four years before the end of the nineteenth century, a dizzying metamorphosis that, before the end of the twentieth century, would transform Florida from a half-empty, semitropical near-wilderness into a state whose population would be exceeded only by California and New York.

But these first Miamians were also re-creating a very old America, whose roots went back to Jamestown. From the beginning Miami was organized on the principle of racial segregation, with blacks stringently confined to the least desirable areas—that is, those districts farthest from Miami's alluring waterfront, on the

Everglades side of Flagler's north-south railroad tracks. In fact blacks were entirely barred from all beaches in the Miami area until 1945, when they were granted a strictly segregated stretch of sand reachable only by boat. Until 1947 they would be barred from Miami Beach after dark.

Beneath this racial drama, moreover, lay an older and even darker one. A mound—a man-made hillock rising out of the low, level, swampy ground—obstructed the site Flagler had chosen for his hotel veranda, the place where wealthy, white Americans would gather to enjoy the mid-winter Miami sun. So the sacred burial mound was leveled, its Indian skeletons tossed like refuse into the swamp, the "skulls . . . given to visitors as souvenirs."

The new city would have its tragedies; it would have its triumphs. But here was its founding irony: having established this shining city of the future, Miami's creators furnished it with all the darknesses of the past. So in this city of escape, people would escape nothing.

Today the relics of Flagler's Miami are cast aside to make way for the new skyscrapers, and so are the poor and the old to make way for the new condominiums and shopping malls. The theme of violent dispossession always has defined the dark side both of what Miami is and what it does to others. It is the bedrock not only of Miami's history, but of Florida's as well. Linked to this theme since the days of Ponce de Leon has been the groundless belief in Florida's riches.

Ponce de Leon wasn't looking for a Fountain of Youth at all in 1513, when he set out from Cuba with "eleven cows and six milch goats" to explore the vastness of the North American mainland. Like most *conquistadores,* Ponce lusted for gold, but when he chose Florida, he picked the worst place in the world to hunt for El Dorado because "no metals have ever been discovered in Florida." In that sense he was the original Floridian.

Ponce's adventures, which ultimately cost him his life, foreshadowed future events in another way. Before setting off for Florida, Ponce, who had accompanied Columbus on his second voyage to the Indies, had been governor of Puerto Rico. Political infighting, however, accompanied the Spaniards to the New World, as surely as the sword and the cross. When Diego Columbus, the great captain's son, asserted his family claim to the governorship, Ponce lost power. In an attempt to diffuse intrigue and rivalry in his Caribbean dominions, the king of Spain authorized Ponce de Leon to set out to find, subdue and colonize the mythical island of Bimini.

Ponce found Florida instead, thus becoming the very first of literally millions of political losers in the Caribbean to head north to Florida in the attempt to recoup their losses.

Florida's fate also hinged on superpower confrontation and tropical invasions centuries before the Bay of Pigs and the Cuban missile crisis. France and Spain fought a desultory, undeclared war for control of the peninsula in the mid-sixteenth century, more than a generation before the Pilgrims landed at Plymouth. Florida became a full-fledged pawn in the game of international power politics a century later, when war broke out between England and France over control of the new European empires in the Americas and Asia.

That long struggle for global supremacy between maritime Britain and its allies on one side, and continental France and its allies on the other, was really part of history's first world war. And like the great wars of our own century, it produced results never imagined by those who started it. Before the struggle finally ended with Wellington's victory, and Napoleon's defeat, at Waterloo in 1815, the United States would throw off the yoke of British colonialism. Spain's own New World empire would crack and crumble before the onslaught of the independence struggles of Latin America—and Florida would be moved across the chessboard of international politics like a very small pawn in a very big game. First, in 1763, Spain would be forced to surrender Florida to Britain; then, twenty years later, at the same time it granted independence to its colonies farther north, Britain would be obliged to give Florida back to Spain.

Finally, in 1821, Florida would fall into American hands.

These immense events affected Florida very little. Ponce had discovered a wilderness, and for more than three centuries, virtually into the twentieth century, Florida would remain a remote, undeveloped and underpopulated backwater, populated mostly by mosquitoes, alligators, renegades, runaways, adventurers, smugglers, losers and rats.

Even in those distant days, however, Americans were already throwing over the traces of their lives farther north and heading south toward the promise of escape. Some came to Florida to escape bounty hunters or creditors; others came to escape extinction itself. Even before the American flag flew there, Florida was a place where Americans of all colors and origins were pursued by conflicts they had begun in older and colder places.

To understand the history that almost all Floridians have forgotten, it is necessary to go back to the Revolutionary War era when Spain first briefly lost, and then won back, Florida from England. Our Founding Fathers had declared life, liberty and the pursuit of happiness self-evident truths. But as they desperately sought foreign assistance in their struggle against the might of Britain, they could not afford to let ideological purity stand in their way.

Then as now, the enemy of one's enemy—in this case royalist France—was one's friend, even though the Americans were fighting for republican liberty. France's ally, Spain, was also a friend, even though Spain abused its own American colonies much more than Britain ever did. In the course of our War of Independence, not only did the Spanish Bourbons, devotees of the doctrine of the divine right of kings, provide the American revolutionaries with arms and money in their struggle against the British crown, they diverted British troops by invading Florida.

During the course of the war, the Americans also made several attempts to conquer Florida. These attempts failed because the Floridians of the late eighteenth century—a heterodox, exotic mix of Englishmen, Mediterranean Europeans, and Indians and blacks —had fled to Florida to escape white American domination. They had no desire to throw off British rule, and desired even less to become a part of the infant United States: "As the guns sounded at Lexington and Concord, St. Augustine emphasized its loyalty [to the British] by burning Sam Adams and John Hancock in effigy."

As the struggle for independence grew more and more divisive and bitter, Florida's anti-Americanism was intensified by the arrival of thousands of British Loyalist refugees, fleeing Georgia and the Carolinas rather than fall under American rule. The news from Paris that Britain was not only abandoning the thirteen colonies to the north, but its Florida colonies as well, threw Florida into "despair and chaos."

Rather than endure a reimposition of Spanish rule at home, or face American rule back in what was now the United States, more than thirteen thousand Florida residents fled to the Bahamas, Nova Scotia and British colonies in the Caribbean. As these early American boat people, forerunners by nearly two centuries of the Haitians and Marielitos, took to the sea, one group of Floridians remained behind—the people who rightly may be called the first real Floridians in the modern sense of the word.

Like those who come to Miami today, these people came from many different regions. They had many different customs and spoke many different languages. But gradually their common surroundings and shared struggles had blurred their old distinctions and turned them into one people.

These first Floridians were called the Seminoles.

Today we Americans remember the Seminoles as just another of those Indian tribes that scalped settlers and fought the cavalry in the course of our conquest of the American frontier, but the word "Seminole" is a "tribal" name that no Indian tribe ever had. Even now historians are unable to agree on the derivation. It did not come into general use until the beginning of the nineteenth century. That very fact points to its real significance: the Seminoles weren't a tribe in the sense the Creeks and Timucuas, and all the other Indian tribes that existed prior to the conquests of the Europeans, were. The Seminoles weren't even pure "Indians." Some of their most important leaders were part white; many of their most astute diplomats and military leaders were black.

The Seminole was something new in history. His identity derived neither from the ancient castes and nationalisms of the Old World nor from the prehistoric past of the Americas, but from the chaotic, often violent fusion of them both that really did make America, in human terms, a New World.

The real definition of a Seminole was a person who the white conquerors of the rapidly expanding American frontier believed had no right to life, liberty or the pursuit of happiness at all.

During the War of Independence, the Americans had failed to take Florida. During the War of 1812, American forces, this time led by Andrew Jackson himself, invaded Florida again, even though the United States was not at war with Spain.

In 1818, even though Spain and the United States were not at war, and Spanish sovereignty over Florida was incontestable, Jackson again invaded the territory and marauded through Spanish Florida like an outlaw. His object: to win Florida for the United States whatever the niceties of international and American law happened to be.

In one "incursion," Jackson massacred 270 American blacks who had sought freedom in Florida. "They were American property," was his justification. Jackson also burned Indian villages, hung Indian chiefs and killed countless Indian women and children. Already, so far as Americans were concerned, liberty was synonymous with America. But while Americans proclaimed their own liberties not only self-evident but God-given, "toward another race of humans, that of the Creeks and Seminoles, the prevailing attitude," as Gloria Jahoda writes in her bicentennial history of Florida, "was one of terror and contempt."

Neither the terror nor the contempt was limited to the nonwhite races. In another foray into Florida, Jackson had one Englishman shot and ordered "an old gentleman named Arbuthnot, a British trader," hanged for "conspiring with the Indians." His crime? Arbuthnot, who was seventy years old, was "well known for generous and fair treatment of the Indians," and so, as Jackson saw it, he

—like all others who treated the Seminoles humanely—was an "unprincipled villain." Florida, which until then had been a place where white, red and black men coexisted in harmony, was suddenly in the grip of a veritable reign of terror.

Today Florida still harbors those who proclaim that terrorism in defense of liberty is no vice. Omega 7 trains with submachine guns in the Everglades for a fantasy reconquest of Cuba. Other groups —ranging from Nicaraguan *contras* to the captains and generals of organized crime—find a happy hunting ground in Miami's munitions supermarkets. Even wackier groups, from time to time, gather in the pine barrens and swamps to train for battle against the insidious threats fluoridation and secular humanism pose to American liberty.

Like these Floridians of a later day, Jackson was convinced that even the most outrageous violations of international law were justified by the need to defend freedom. For as he and many other Americans saw it, Florida's Indians and blacks, along with the Spanish, were only the agents of a far-flung and insidious conspiracy that had as its object nothing less than the destruction of both liberty and the United States. It was "the British scalping knife" that explained the opposition of blacks, Seminoles and Spaniards to Jackson's outrages.

As Americans saw it, everything that stood in the way of the fulfillment of their own ambitions, and hence the territorial expansion of human liberty as they defined it, was part of what, as early as 1811, was called the "Red Peril." Or as one U.S. senator put it in 1845—114 years before Castro took Havana—it all came down to "a question between two great systems."

In Jackson's most outrageous violation of Spanish sovereignty, he kidnapped the governor of Florida and stole the Royal Spanish Archives. Publicly, the Monroe administration repudiated Jackson's attacks. Privately it moved quickly to reap the benefits. In 1819, less than a year following Jackson's invasion, the Spanish, in the face of strong American diplomatic pressures, agreed to surrender Florida to the Americans. Two years later, in 1821, Florida finally became a part of the United States.

Centuries later, Marjory Stoneman Douglas—*doyenne* of Florida historians and Miami's most enduring founding daughter—wrote Ponce de Leon's epitaph: "All his . . . high hopes for Florida had come only to this, that he had nothing from it but the most indestructible American myth, the Fountain of Youth, and his own death." Jackson, too, had helped to conjure up an indestructible American myth—in this case the myth that the United States "purchased" Florida from Spain for $5 million.

The historical truth is that, in the treaty of annexation, the United States agreed merely to settle all claims, many of them trumped up, that America's own citizens had brought against Spain, up to a total of $5 million. The Spanish never got a dime for Florida even though, in reality, it was Americans who had destroyed Spanish lives and property, not the other way around.

Today it's hard to imagine America without Miami Beach, Disney World and Cape Kennedy. But for a few thousand Seminole warriors, historical inevitability had no meaning. For forty-six years —from Jackson's first armed attack on Florida in 1812 until the last clash between American and Seminole forces in 1858—Florida was a battleground where American troops met the kind of resistance they would not encounter again until U.S. forces, a century later, began search-and-destroy missions in Vietnam.

The Seminoles fought resourcefully, honorably and with exemplary courage against overwhelming odds. They covered themselves with honor, and lost. The Americans violated every norm of civilized warfare and trampled on every human right. They coated themselves in dishonor and shame—and won.

Just as the story of one American, Andrew Jackson, tells the story of the American conquest of Florida, so the story of one Seminole —Osceola—lays bare the dark stratum of historical injustice that underlies the gleaming new Florida of today, to say nothing of the gleaming illusion of virtue triumphant that underlies so much of what we Americans do, build and are.

Probably the most important thing to understand about Osceola is that he was every bit as "American" as the Americans who hounded him and his people to the brink of extinction. Osceola was born in north Georgia, near the Chattahoochee River, in 1804— just five years before Abraham Lincoln was born in similar obscurity in rural Kentucky. Given the qualities of military leadership, personal honor and zeal for justice he later demonstrated, Osceola might well have become a great statesman in an era that abounded in statesmen like Clay and Daniel Webster.

Osceola, however, possessed one defect that barred him from a position of honor in the United States. Though she was married to a white settler named William Powell, Osceola's mother was a Creek Indian. And, in the early nineteenth century, life, liberty and the pursuit of happiness were considered white American human rights exclusively. Just as American principles of liberty "did not apply to blacks, they applied even less to Indians."

When he was four years old, Osceola's mother, like so many other red- and black-skinned victims of the Americans, sought freedom by fleeing the United States with her young son. It was in Florida that time, circumstance and his own pride would metamorphose Osceola from a "half-breed" Creek into a proud Seminole.

An account of one of Osceola's engagements published as late as 1911 inadvertently reveals the way any attempt by nonwhites to defend themselves and their lands against usurpation by white Americans was automatically viewed:

> In a battle fought [in 1835] at a ford on the Withlachoochee, Osceola was at the head of a negro detachment, and although the Indians and negroes were repulsed by [U.S.] troops . . . they continued, with Osceola as their most crafty and determined leader, to murder and devastate, and occasionally to engage the troops.

Marjory Stoneman Douglas gives us a rather different picture of Osceola:

> Although he was not a hereditary chief, Osceola was the unquestioned leader, surrounded by a band of desperate young warriors with the shrewdest Negroes, such as the interpretor Abraham. Osceola was thirty years old, handsome, well-proportioned, about five feet eight, with small hands and feet, the best dancer, the most reckless ball-player. His eyes were brilliantly expressive in an intelligent, frank, sensitive face. A great dandy, he wore fringed scarlet leggings, a silk turban around his head trailing black and white plumes. . . . He fought savagely, yet he refused to make war on women and children, or permit torture. He was unquestionably the greatest Floridian of his day.

Osceola and the other inhabitants of Florida who had fallen under American rule had every reason to "murder and devastate." Thanks to the U.S.-Spanish treaty of cession, Florida's blacks had been converted, at the stroke of a diplomatic pen, from free men and women into runaway slaves who could be forcibly returned to their owners, or simply sold into slavery for a profit, by whatever white American happened to kidnap them. Florida's Seminoles faced an equally unenviable fate. In 1830 Congress passed the "Removal Act," a piece of legislation reminiscent of the later policies of both apartheid South Africa and Nazi Germany. The law's purpose: nothing less than to uproot every Indian in the territory and forcibly remove them to the barren lands of the West.

In the end, Osceola was defeated by American treachery, not American valor on the battlefield. In 1837 the United States, finding it impossible to defeat the Seminoles militarily, offered them peace negotiations; to prove his honorable intentions, and to assure the Seminole leader safe conduct through the American lines, the U.S. commander, General Thomas S. Jesup, sent Osceola a white flag of truce.

When Osceola and his family reached St. Augustine, they were summarily arrested and sent north for imprisonment without trial in South Carolina. The United States had captured the Seminoles' most gifted statesman, but only by dishonoring its own flag of truce.

U.S. dishonor did not end with Osceola's imprisonment. When Osceola died "of malaria and grief," the American doctor attending him "cut off his head and exhibited it in circus side shows around the country." Florida had produced one of the first, and perhaps even now the grisliest, of the "tourist attractions" for which the place later became famous.

Seminole resistance did not stop following Osceola's imprisonment and death. To the contrary, "the effect on the Seminoles [was] mainly to infuriate them and stimulate their resistance." For the next twenty years, Florida was synonymous in the United States not with sandy beaches and sunshine, but with the spectacle of American troops prodding weeping Indian women and children westward along the Trail of Tears, and hounding thousands of blacks into makeshift concentration camps where men, women and children alike were sold to the highest bidders.

Many Indians and blacks committed suicide rather than face a destiny of dispossession and slavery. Meanwhile U.S. troops pursued a scorched-earth policy that reduced Florida to a state of wilderness such as had not prevailed even under the Spanish. The population of Florida—which is the size of New York State and the southern New England states combined—fell to less than thirty-five thousand, about the same as it had been when Ponce de Leon had arrived more than three hundred years earlier.

The "impressive parallels between the Second Seminole War and Vietnam" were not limited to battlefield operations. The spectacle of U.S. forces exiling Indian women and children from their homelands, and selling black mothers into slavery, excited the same controversy, and soul-searching, that American tactics in Indochina later did. In Congress, John Quincy Adams protested the use of bloodhounds to track down Indians; when Osceola died, Walt Whitman eulogized him.

Such actions may have salved the consciences of some Americans, but they had little effect on the course of the war. Instead, what one historian has called the "moral calamity" of the conquest of Florida seemed only to excite in the conquerors the very savagery they imputed to those they attacked. Arva Moore Parks provides the following description of a U.S. attack on the encampment of the Indian leader Chekaika, which was launched from Fort Dallas, near the site of latter-day Miami, by Colonel William S. Harney in 1840:

> Up the dark waters of the Miami River they paddled, into the south fork where the saw grass grew tall. . . . Finally, [they] sighted Chekaika's island. Ignoring the conventions of civilized warfare, Harney ordered his men to don Indian attire and paint their faces. Whooping and hollering, the U.S. Army "Indians" attacked. Chekaika was shot and killed, along with many of his braves. The squaws and children were taken hostage. At sunset, two braves and the lifeless body of Chekaika were hung from a tall oak and left for the buzzards. The squaws and children were taken to Key Biscayne where boats waited to take them to Tampa and on to the new lands in the West.

The Americans never achieved their objective of making Florida entirely Seminole-free. While thousands of Seminoles were hounded out of Florida, and thousands more of their black allies were sold into slavery, a few hundred people of Indian and mixed blood permanently eluded capture by finding refuge in the vastness of the Everglades. By the time the fighting died down for the last time, white Americans were too preoccupied with their own internal divisions, and the impending Civil War, to pursue Jackson's policy of dispossession and enslavement to its "final solution."

In 1837, as Osceola lay dying in a U.S. military prison, President Andrew Jackson—rich in honors, richer still in the esteem of his countrymen—delivered his Farewell Address. Providence, he assured the nation, had singled out us Americans to be "the guardians of freedom to preserve it for the benefit of the human race."

The Seminoles, however, remember Jackson differently from the way most other Americans do, and place a different construction on what he accomplished. To them, the entwined freeways of south

Florida, the new shopping malls and subdivisions that ceaselessly drive back the Everglades, still embody a betrayal, not a fulfillment, of the American promise of liberty.

As for Jackson, the Seminoles still call him "The Devil."

Even after the Indians had been battered into submission, Florida remained an unformed land, Miami a nameless wilderness.

The great centers of American life—Charleston, Philadelphia, New York and Boston—were very far from Florida. But they were not nearly so remote from Florida as Florida was from itself. The journey from St. Augustine to Pensacola took weeks, and the whole of peninsular Florida was literally trackless: when Key West's delegation to the Florida legislature traveled to the state capital, it went by sea to New York, then by rail south from New York to Atlanta —and from there journeyed by horseback to Tallahassee.

Something of technological importance, indeed of revolutionary cybernetic importance, nonetheless did happen in Florida in those early years. In 1844, in Apalachicola, Dr. John Gorrie invented air conditioning, a device without which Florida, as we now know it, could not exist. Like some other inventions that would reshape the world, Dr. Gorrie's gadget, which grew out of his work with yellow fever victims, was greeted with scorn. "He was considered eccentric and laughed at by his fellow townsmen."

Statehood, in 1845, set off the first of Florida's many population explosions. Yet though the total population had nearly doubled by 1850, it was still only 87,445, including 39,000 black slaves. Florida's population rapidly increased following the defeat of the Seminoles, but it would not top the half-million mark until the beginning of the twentieth century, and would not reach the million mark until the census of 1920. All in all, in the years before the outbreak of the Civil War, Florida's destiny lay in the hands of only ten or twelve thousand adult, white males.

The United States had expended considerably, of both blood and treasure, to secure Florida for these settlers. But by 1860 the

United States, like Britain, Spain and the Seminoles earlier, was just one more threat to "liberty," as Florida's cotton-growing, slave-owning freeholders defined it. In 1860 Florida—which sixty years later would be the only state to reject the Nineteenth Amendment, giving women the right to vote—quickly joined South Carolina and Mississippi to become one of the first three states to secede from the Union.

Although Florida's role in the Civil War was nearly as minor as it had been during previous wars, the conflict nonetheless remains one of the great formative events in Florida history. Defeat and Reconstruction—America's failed social revolution—locked Florida, along with the rest of the Deep South, into a pattern of social, political and economic relationships that would dominate the state's affairs for a century and which, even now, deeply influences events there.

People, particularly of the white, southern persuasion, like to say Florida isn't really part of the South at all. That's nonsense. Florida's southern identity underlies its contemporary social customs, mind-sets and mores as surely as its substratum of porous limestone underlies its condominiums, skyscrapers and retirement colonies.

Back in 1982, when the *Economist* reported that "Miami is not a good city in which to be black," the local Chamber of Commerce reacted with anger and amazement. But the truth is that Florida, including Miami, seldom if ever has been a good place to be black. For nearly a century and a half following Jackson's massacres, the black's place was in the kitchen, the field—or, in the case of undocile "nigras," on the chain gang. Slavery in all but name persisted for generations after the Emancipation Proclamation. The classic 1911 *Encyclopaedia Britannica* entry on Florida related:

> There is no penitentiary; the convicts are hired to the one highest bidder who contracts for their labour, and who undertakes, moreover, to lease all other persons convicted during the term of the lease, and subleases the prisoners. . . . In 1908 the state received $208,148 from the lease of convicts.

Florida did not have a justice system so much as it had a black penal system. "Of the 446 convicts committed in that year, there were 15 negro females, 356 negro males." Only seventy-five white males, and apparently no white females, were leased out for involuntary servitude. "The leased convicts are employed in the turpentine and lumber industries and in the phosphate works," the article elaborated.

Race continued to govern social relationships in Florida long after that. Some of my own earliest memories of a childhood, still no more than thirty years ago, spent partly in Florida, are of "colored" water fountains in grocery stores, segregated rest rooms in filling stations—of little white children chanting, on warm, tranquil Florida evenings, as they roasted marshmallows under an avocado tree, "Eenie, meenie, miny, moe, catch a nigger by his toe. . . ."

In 1954 my brother and I were loaded into the backseat of the Buick, and the family headed north for the summer. This was just before the Supreme Court decision, just before the interstate highway system was started. So we rattled westward on two-lane macadam roads of central Florida, and with each new county line we crossed, my nine-year-old eyes took in a sight my fourth-grade civics class never mentioned: grown-up black men wearing striped pajamas in the middle of the day. And they had on things like handcuffs, only they connected their ankles. They carried pickaxes and their—I didn't have a word for it, he wasn't just a boss—their master rode a horse and had a gun and a whip. I'd never seen colored people like that. They weren't like our yardman and cleaning lady, they were so much darker they might have belonged to a different continent, a different race. But I knew about white people like the man with the whip because one time I met another boy, and he invited me home. He lived in a "project" and his mother wore hair curlers and served me Kool-Aid and a jelly-and-Wonderbread sandwich on a plastic plate with a paper napkin. When I told my parents this, they didn't say anything. But when, the next night, the boy's father came to our house and tried to sell my father a Bible—a great big Bible with a white-and-gold plastic cover—my parents had a discussion, and after it was over, my father told me: You must never play with that boy again.

Another time my parents had a discussion about burning crosses. It sounded very pretty as I listened in the dark, and I wondered if we would have one in our yard someday. Mother said it was inconceivable that in the United States of America this sort of thing should happen and, when you called the police, they didn't come. My father said if it ever happened within a mile of this house, he wouldn't call the police. He'd get the .45 out of the dresser and shoot the white trash scum.

As we traversed rural Florida, I wanted to ask: Where do they go to the bathroom? You could see there were no bathrooms inside the houses we were passing because they had no basements. The houses—and even some white people lived in these houses—just had cinder blocks at each corner, and air and dirt underneath, so you could see: there were no pipes. I figured it out before long, all by myself. The houses with no pipes had little houses out in back, and it was there the people went, though what happened when they got there, I could not speculate.

We saw white and black people plowing fields with mules, but I was only really alarmed once. We had stopped for gas. My brother and I were given nickels to get Cokes from the Coke machine, and we were drinking the Cokes when I saw something very troubling indeed. Across the road some Negro children were playing. The youngest was about my brother's age, four or five, and the oldest was about my age, eight or nine. And they had no pants on! There were girls and boys playing together, and while they had on shirts, they had no bottoms to their playsuits, no shoes either, and they were running around in the dirt: I never saw anything like it again until after I graduated from Harvard, joined the Peace Corps and was sent to Nepal.

*

Miami Beach was not the only municipality in Florida that banned blacks. Black Americans also faced arrest if "found on the streets after dark" in Palm Beach, surely the most "northern" community in all Florida.

For nearly a century, it was as though the South had won the Civil War when it came to Florida politics. State government was dominated by generations of officials, many of them hailing from the small, rural counties of north Florida, for whom "state's rights" and the pork barrel were principles far more important than the U.S. Constitution and efficient administration. As late as 1950, Senator Claude Pepper—a son of Dudleyville, Alabama—was defeated for reelection when George Smathers, his opponent from Miami, tarred him with the brush of racial liberalism, which was tantamount in Florida in those days to being convicted of Communism. What finally "ended the Civil War in Tallahassee," as Gloria Jahoda points out, "was not Appomattox, but the Civil Rights Act of 1964."

Equally important in finally bringing Florida politics into the twentieth century, at least half a century late, was court-ordered reapportionment of the state legislature. Reorganizing government in Tallahassee on the principle that elected officials should represent people, not cotton fields and mules, broke the power of the legislature's Pork Chop Gang and unleashed a political revolution that is still far from running its course.

To the myth that Florida isn't southern is often appended another myth—that the influx of new Floridians produced a fundamental liberalization of attitudes on racial and other matters. The truth is that the settlers from the small towns of the Midwest, the Upper South and the Northeast often brought with them prejudices more subtle in tenor, but little different in practical substance, than had always been known in Florida.

Writing of Miami as it existed in 1916, Marjory Stoneman Douglas observes, "The general attitude toward Negroes, the socially accepted attitude, adopted by most Northerners, was that of the old South." While undergoing many dramatic changes in manner, the substance of racial attitudes, even today, has changed little, except in one regard. As the overt racism of the Old South has faded, the new racism of the great northern cities has flourished.

Liberty City and Overtown—like the rest of Miami—may be little more than a lifetime old. But they demonstrate one of the oldest truths of America: the original sins of our national genesis pursue us wherever we go.

Long after Osceola had been forgotten, the tourist brochures would present Florida as a paradise where southern refinement and gentility merged with Latin elegance and sophistication. Miami's boosters would sell the city as the proud and gracious inheritor of a centuries-old Spanish legacy, but this was only another myth.

In truth Miami's Latinization, which only began in earnest with the arrival of the Cubans, nearly half a century after Miami first acquired its passion for Spanish-style decor, was a case of human demographics mimicking architectural fantasy, not of history repeating itself.

Even the most ancient and imposing of Miami's "Spanish" monuments—the grandiose, Italianate Villa Vizcaya—dates back only to 1916. It was built by James Deering, an International Harvester heir, not by some Spanish grandee. Following World War I, Addison Mizner, "artist-architect, prize fighter and miner . . . introduced the Spanish vogue that resulted in a transformation of architecture along Florida's lower east coast." Among Mizner's "Spanish" innovations—"tiled pools and mosaic murals [that] resembled those of Pompeii."

In the 1920s George Merrick—creator and promoter of Coral Gables—chose a "Mediterranean" theme for his subdivision, and began stripping whole villages in Cuba of their tile roofs in order to give his suburban bungalows the appropriate Iberian veneer. "Spanish" architecture became so popular that, by the end of the 1950s, Miami probably had as many stucco villas with red tile roofs as any Latin city.

But until the Cubans began arriving, en masse, in the early

1960s, Miami was not much more "Spanish" in its human composition than Memphis or Hartford, Connecticut. Nearly three hundred years of Spanish rule in Florida had left no human or physical traces in Miami and, interestingly enough, since 1960, thanks to the Cubans and other Latin Americans, Miami has become much less Latin in appearance than it was before they arrived.

The reason for this increasingly Latin city's increasingly un-Latin appearance is simple enough: the Latin American fantasy of the Florida good life isn't of red tile, tinkling fountains and Spanish moss, but of high-rise condominiums, chlorinated swimming pools and fast American cars. The richest Latins in Miami live in triplex skyscraper penthouses and sprawling "ranch" houses with five-car garages.

Here there are no New England mountains, no Virginia valleys —the very distinction between ocean, bay and swamp on the one hand, and dry land on the other, breaks down. And so in Miami, a place lacking social and aesthetic terra firma as well, the role of architecture always has been to act out in plaster, glass and concrete that most essential Florida impulse—that is to say, the actualization of fantasy.

That impulse hasn't been limited to hotels, restaurants and amusement parks, as the fate of Florida's few surviving historical monuments demonstrates. In colonial times St. Augustine was only a flyblown outpost with sand streets and a few mud-plastered shacks. John J. Audubon, following an 1831 visit, called it "the poorest hole in creation." But that hasn't kept it, in the twentieth century, from undergoing a metamorphosis as fantastic as the metamorphosis of Florida itself—into the "Nation's Oldest City."

Who cares that most of the "oldest house" was built in 1888, or that Ponce de Leon never set foot in Fountain of Youth Park, which is really an old Indian burial ground? That the oldest of St. Augustine's many Fountains of Youth, established in the 1890s, was shut down by local authorities in the 1920s—because it was a health hazard? Or that St. Augustine's cathedral, post office, city gates, old wooden schoolhouse, "oldest store" and "Old Spanish Inn" all are generations, sometimes centuries, younger than similar edifices all over Virginia, New York and New England? It seems only in keeping with Florida's affinity for fable that St. Augustine—which does have the "World's Original Alligator Attraction," founded way back in 1893—should become much more important as a tourist attraction than it ever was as an historical site.

In early 1926, Arva Moore Parks recounts in her history of Miami, real estate speculator Arthur Voetglin not only conjured up an entire Spanish village in Miami Shores, he turned Florida's fantasy history into a floor show in which, needless to say, such themes as Indian massacres played no part:

> Voetglin's glittering Pueblo Feliz (Joyful City) . . . was a walled replica of a Spanish village, complete with small shops and cafes. Its focal point was the grand *Teatro de Alegria* that reportedly could seat more people than Carnegie Hall. Each night a cast of 150 performed *Fountania*—a grand recital of Florida history with enough feathered dancing girls to rival the Ziegfeld Follies. During the breathtaking finale, 48 beautiful girls, each representing a different state, paraded onstage. With the beauties poised, the chorus danced a lively Charleston as the Magic City [Miami] rose majestically from cardboard waves.

Today not one Floridian in a thousand—perhaps not one American in ten thousand—remembers the true story of Florida's conquest. Did we not, after all, pay a fair price for the place when we bought it from Spain?

Yet even now mementos of that long, bloody and dishonorable conflict are no harder to find than the names on a tourist's road map. Fort Pierce, Fort Lauderdale and Fort Myers, like many other Florida cities, started out as bases for attacks on the Seminoles. Only much later did they become, first, the sleepy beach resorts of the early and mid-twentieth century, and then the rising Sun Belt cities of today. Gainesville is named for a Seminole War general, and of course Jacksonville commemorates the conqueror of Florida himself. Up in Palm Beach, Lake Worth—which is not a lake, but a saltwater lagoon—honors Colonel William J. Worth, who "indulged in a punitive campaign [against the Seminoles], burning crops and dwellings, which he sustained straight through 1841."

Dade County, today synonymous with metropolitan Miami, was named for a U.S. Army officer killed by Seminoles in central Florida in 1835. Even though Major Francis Langhorne Dade and his troops incontestably were combatants, and like other American forces had orders to kill Seminole leaders, capture Seminole settlers, seize their lands and property and force them to move West, the Seminole attack on Dade's U.S. Army detachment was not a legitimate act of war, so far as the Americans saw it; it was an unjustified act of barbarism. More than anything else, the "Dade Massacre" convinced white Floridians that only total eradication of the "Red Peril" could secure Florida for "liberty."

Perhaps the most telling example of America's gift for simultaneously conjuring up the future and destroying the past is to be found in the geographical center of the state—where the gates of Disney World rise like gleaming monuments to America's pursuit of happiness in what, only recently, were citrus groves and, before that, Seminole lands.

Only the most careful reader of the tourist road map is likely to notice that the entrance to Disney World is located in Osceola County.

This oblivion seems only a fitting culmination of the historical process that, in less than 150 years, has transformed the heart of Florida from a battlefield where Seminoles desperately resisted extinction into a literal American Fantasyland where cartoon characters are far more real to visitors, adults and children alike than Osceola and General Thomas S. Jesup are ever likely to be.

In the wilds of Adventureland, one encounters another essential theme of Florida. This is not merely the usurpation of nature, but the use of high technology, once nature itself is usurped, to replace it with the illusion of escape: the Swiss Family Robinson's castaway home turns out to be made of two hundred tons of concrete and steel, the surrounding "jungle" garbed in 800,000 plastic leaves. Nearby, Cinderella's castle, a wild amalgam of details from Fontainebleau and Versailles, rendered in synthetic marble, its turrets inspired by "a Bavarian castle built by mad King Ludwig," outstrips the fantasies even of Addison Mizner.

Few visitors miss the Hall of Presidents in Disney World's Liberty Square, where mechanical clones of the presidents, including Andrew Jackson, deliver tape-recorded homilies on liberty, justice and the American way. The Disney empire, the most stupendous Florida tourist attraction of all, sprawls across the county line into Orange County, and it is there at EPCOT—the billion-dollar Experimental Prototype City of Tomorrow—that the fantasy of America's past, epitomized by Disney World's Main Street, U.S.A., merges seamlessly into a future fantasy of an aseptic, climate-controlled, computerized America free of conflict and inequalities of race and income, where microwaves, video waves and laser beams confer happiness on all.

Here, as it so often has been in the American national imagination, it is but a short trip from Fantasyland to Tomorrowland. Indeed both places, though they differ in decor, are parts of the same nation—that mythical blue-eyed America where the poor and the old, like injustice and violence, hardly figure at all.

Even when we Americans destroy the past, we cannot escape it; even an architecture of fantasy winds up reflecting not just our dreams, but our darkest contradictions.

Certainly one reason Miami is such a compelling city is that it lays bare—often shockingly—what Walt Whitman Rostow once called "the double bar-sinister which cut[s] across the fabric of American life." This he defined as the twin legacy of the "African slave trade" and the "decimation of the Indian."

That no doubt helps explain why so many Americans find Miami not just intriguing, but alarming. In an age in which America, hardly for the first time, has opted for "feeling good" about itself,

Miami, even in the shining hour of its celebrity, tells a dark but important truth. Even after we turn off the shoot-outs on "Miami Vice," check the security system and go to sleep, the hulk of the slave ship, and all the rage, guilt and hate it carried with it, still haunts our dreams, just as it haunts our schools, streets and slums.

We have, of course, expunged the Indian so totally from our national life that Osceola might never have existed. But, as Miami and the rest of Florida still constantly reveal, the belief that nature must first be conquered before *we* can be made free still has an appalling ability not only to despoil the world, but to poison our own lives.

Today no Seminole warriors resist the conquest of Florida. The wetlands yield to the developer without resistance. Yet hardly has the saw grass vanished, and another new self-enclosed reservation —for the elderly or for young singles—taken its place, than the brushfires begin.

In their new high-rise apartments, gouged into what, even ten years ago, was wilderness, people lament the arrival of smog. Offshore from the new marinas, coral reefs turn into dying, underwater slums; between Disney World and Cape Kennedy, giant holes in the earth open up, swallowing houses. Along I-95 between Fort Lauderdale and Miami traffic slows; even with the air conditioning on, drivers gasp for breath, as the surrounding landscape—converted from swamp to desert in one generation—burns, and the smoke flows toward the eroding white sand beaches.

Even when the black thugs with truncheons don't attack your car the way the Seminoles once ambushed wagon trains, even after you train your eyes to watch the blue sky, the blue bay—after you train yourself to ignore the sprawling concrete-and-neon ugliness of Miami—the knowledge that Miami not only constantly creates, but ceaselessly destroys, runs through even the balmiest days there like that dark, brooding background music in "Miami Vice."

"Why cannot we live here in peace?" Osceola's successor, Coachoochee, asked the Americans. "I could live in peace with [the white men], but they first steal our cattle and horses, then cheat us and take our lands." Coachoochee ended his appeal with one of the most eloquent statements on liberty in American history: "They may shoot us, drive our women and children night and day; they may chain our hands and feet, but the red man's heart will always be free."

He was wrong.

More than a century and a half after Jackson and his followers set out to create an America in which the Seminole would be deprived of everything, that dream has been fulfilled. Confined to the margins of society, plagued by poverty, lack of education and alcoholism, the Seminoles give human meaning to the abstract concept of human dispossession: in 1970 the Indian Claims Commission awarded them, as compensation for all lands unjustly seized, throughout the entire course of history, in the entire state of Florida, $16 million.

A billion dollars for a theme park, sixteen million for the Seminoles. . . . Certainly the long-forgotten story of Florida's conquest initiated themes that still shape Florida, that still explain Miami to us, today. "The history of white Florida . . . began with violation," and although the real estate magnates and cocaine kings long since have replaced the army generals and railroad tycoons, a history of violation it continues in large part to be.

In the general oblivion to which the darker side of Florida's past has been consigned, we find another very important theme of the present: "When Florida doesn't feel like accepting a truth, it blissfully ignores it."

But of course all that—like so much that is true about Miami—is true of America, too.

154

7

Elsewhere Destinies

No one personified America's rise to unparalleled wealth and power better than Miami's co-founder, Henry Morrison Flagler.

At his whim legislatures enacted laws for the convenience of his love life; on fragile barrier islands, armies of architects and artisans erected palaces a Medici might have envied.

At Henry Flagler's behest, hosts of engineers and laborers drove railroads through malarial swamps; they drew up designs for cities, then imposed those designs on the wilderness, even spanned the ocean by steel. Flagler was the definitive Florida genius. At his touch mere land was alchemized into real estate.

The product of cold, snowy climes, Henry Flagler, like many others, became a Floridian by accident. Born in Upstate New York while President Jackson was still in the White House, Flagler, like many another poor but ambitious young man, went West, at least as far west as Cleveland, Ohio. But there everything typical about his life ended; in Cleveland he fell into a business partnership with another astute entrepreneur named John D. Rockefeller. Flagler, with Rockefeller's help, founded Standard Oil. By the 1870s he was back in New York, living in a mansion just off Fifth Avenue; Henry Flagler was now one of the richest men in the world.

Those were still the days when the American superrich sailed their ocean-going yachts to Europe and the Mediterranean, not Florida and the Caribbean. The age of the private railroad car, nonetheless, was at hand. Although Florida was still one of the most isolated, least developed states in the nation, in twenty years it would become part of a world of conspicuous consumption that began in Newport and New York, and stretched wherever the gilded railway carriages and mahogany yachts of America's *nouveaux riches* could take them.

When Flagler's first wife, Mary, developed a chronic lung ailment, Flagler's New York doctors counseled a winter in the Florida sun. The half-empty peninsula, where land in many counties still sold for a few cents an acre, intrigued the New York entrepreneur as much as its primitive transportation and accommodations appalled him. Hardly for the last time, Florida's rejuvenative powers proved to be a myth, albeit one with an ability to defy all proofs to the contrary: even after Mary Flagler died in 1881, Henry Flagler seems to have believed Florida's sun and waters had recuperative powers. In 1883, as he considered places to spend his second honeymoon, the multimillionaire developed liver trouble.

What better place to find renewed health and happiness than in the Sunshine State? Like many a later wealthy businessman from the North, Flagler went to Florida to get away from it all, and wound up starting a second career even more remarkable than the one he had pursued before he "retired."

For the next thirty years, Flagler—who lived into his eighties, and dominated events until his death in 1913—marched down the east coast of Florida like a conquering general, reshaping Florida in his own image. Where Jackson had led cavalry charges, Flagler pursued a strategy of conquest by railroad. Where Jackson had built forts, Flagler constructed luxury hotels. With gilt-edged bonds and engraved land titles, he secured an empire larger than some European nations. Between 1818 and 1883, the idiom of conquest had changed, but not the substance. Florida was still as malleable as mud —if you were nimble enough to avoid the quicksand.

Steadily, the whole of Florida between Jacksonville and Key West finally acquired its modern identity—that is, the identity

Henry Flagler chose to give it. Charmed by the Moorish excess of architect Franklin Smith's winter home, the Villa Zorayda, Flagler built more "Spanish" monuments in St. Augustine in a decade than the Spaniards had in three hundred years.

Flagler's next conquest was a scrubby, mosquito-infested island in Lake Worth, only five hundred feet wide in places. But where others had seen only a run-down, flood-prone coconut plantation, he saw the outlines of a tropical Newport. Soon Palm Beach was the winter haunt of Whitneys and Vanderbilts and ultimately, as the Gilded Age gave way to the dime store age, of Woolworths and Kennedys.

Flagler found a wilderness; he transformed it into a magic kingdom. The royal palace was Whitehall, his $4 million mansion in Palm Beach. True, republican institutions survived in faraway Tallahassee, but only in form. When Flagler's second wife, Alice, developed the delusion that the czar of Russia was her paramour and attempted to communicate with Nicholas II by Ouija board, the state legislature, at Flagler's bidding, quickly rid him of this embarrassment by making insanity grounds for divorce.

Even the U.S. postal service seemed to confirm Flagler's right to Florida's throne. The postmark "Fla.," it was said, stood for Flagler-land, not Florida.

In 1912 Flagler—like Alexander the Great—finally ran out of new lands to conquer. In a feat of railroad engineering never since duplicated, his Overseas Railway, spanning swamps, coral reefs and open seas nearly seven miles wide at one point, reached Key West. Between 1883 and 1912, Flagler had built a railroad, founded one major city and dozens of towns, and opened up the entire east coast of Florida to massive settlement from the North. More than that, he had dictated the structure of modern Florida. He had laid the foundations—cultural and psychological, as well as economic and political—for a land where men still dare to dream big, usually quirky, and often impossible dreams.

Thousands of speculators would mimic Flagler's land schemes. Hundreds of thousands of northerners would buy lots in Boca Raton and crowd the hotel rooms of Miami Beach.

Florida, indeed the universe, would never be the same again: just fifty-seven years after Flagler's railroad was proclaimed the Eighth Wonder of the World, another Florida newcomer named Neil Armstrong lifted one foot off Florida. His next footfall touched the moon.

Nature had taken Florida and made it a swamp; history had turned that swamp into a backwater. American know-how would make it the place where anything could happen.

Henry Flagler wasn't the only railroad baron to carve out an empire for himself in the Florida wilderness. By the beginning of the 1890s, Henry Plant—whose tastes were even more Disneyesque than Flagler's—had pushed his Savannah, Florida & Western Railroad down to Tampa and built the grandiose Tampa Bay Hotel.

It was as though America's appetite for excess, at the height of the Gilded Age, had taken architectural form. Even today, the minarets and cupolas of Plant's extravaganza dominate Tampa Bay the way Santa Sophia dominates the Golden Horn. It is the kind of eccentric, obsessive work of half-looped genius that might have driven Ludwig the Mad sane with envy.

Plant was not just indulging his aesthetic whims, for this was the age when, commercially as well as aesthetically, nothing succeeded like excess. Build a more grandiose tourist trap, the logic ran, and the world was bound to beat a path to your door.

Did St. Augustine have the "Fountain of Youth"? Plant pronounced one of the oaks on his hotel grounds in Tampa "the very tree under which Hernando de Soto had treated with the Timucua Indians."

Over in Palm Beach, Henry Flagler had "Afromobiles"—mobile settees "propelled by a robust negro," as Henry James described them—to transport his guests around the grounds of the Royal Poinciana Hotel. Not to be outdone, Plant had Oriental rickshaws, pulled by pageboys in "Merry Widow" uniforms, to carry gentlemen in white tie and tails, and ladies in whalebone corsets and steel bustles, the quarter-mile to the grand dining salon of his hotel, where, one evening, "twenty millionaires were observed dining at twenty different tables."

That quarter-mile route was all indoors. Outside, Plant's gardeners had created a botanical fantasyland, lush and bizarre as the jungle of brocade, onyx, stained glass, ebony, marble and gold leaf inside the hotel. Asian orchids hung from native live oaks; flowering vines from the Amazon clutched mulberry trees shipped in all the way from China. At night the hotel's towers, outlined in electric lights, glittered as if celebrating a Moorish Christmas.

The decor was called "Spanish." But, as at Disney World later, the American psyche had run riot, in a wild profusion of the fake and fabulous the Old World never could have conceived. Yet Plant —as astute a merchant of fantasy as Walt Disney—"was scientific enough on his verandahs," as Gloria Jahoda points out. "Each wicker chair had been built to conform to the measurements of the world's fattest man."

It was a prudent measure. This was, after all, the era that would reach its climax with the presidency of William Howard Taft. A skinny millionaire would have seemed as out of place in the gilt-and-velvet Florida of the 1890s as a fat adventure hero would seem amidst the shiny chrome and tropical pastels of "Miami Vice" today.

Not a moment too soon had Henry Plant his stately pleasure dome decreed. His railroad, his hotel and the port for ocean-going vessels he dredged in Tampa Bay were shortly to become stage sets for history.

To a modern reader, the headlines in the Florida papers of the late nineteenth century would seem uncannily familiar. In Cuba's Oriente Province, guerrillas had taken to the hills and begun a revolutionary struggle to overthrow the government in Havana.

This Cuban revolution, however, differed from Castro's in two important ways. First of all, it was not a civil war, but a war of independence. More than sixty years after it had lost Florida to the United States, and its other American colonies to Bolívar and his counterparts, Spain still held on to Cuba, and Puerto Rico as well —and Spanish rule remained both repressive and inept.

The second difference was that this was one revolution the guerrillas lost. The Cubans had first declared their independence in 1868, just after the end of the American Civil War, and for more than ten years the Spanish pursued a scorched-earth policy that made Jackson's treatment of the Seminoles seem chivalrous. Only through "horrible excesses in Havana" had Spain kept the last remnants of its once-immense American empire.

With their families and sympathizers, the insurgents fled north to Florida when their struggle for power in Cuba failed. Like the Marielitos, they landed in Key West and set off an economic and social revolution in Florida. Before the Cubans came, the "Conchs" of Key West, as the natives of the Keys still style themselves, had subsisted on smuggling and "wrecking"—luring ships onto the reefs so that their cargoes could be plundered. The latter skill was as highly developed as the later art of fleecing tourists.

All that would soon change. These Latin newcomers quickly demonstrated an astute sense of the opportunities the American market provided.

What would the Gilded Age have been without a fine cigar? One can no more imagine the era of the cedar-lined humidor and brass spittoon without this article of conspicuous consumption than one can envision Miami high life today without its Jacuzzis, string bikinis and lines of coke. By 1870 these Cubans had made Key West the world's largest manufacturer of cigars; by the mid-1880s, also thanks to the Cubans, Key West's population had doubled to nearly eighteen thousand—enough, even at that late date, to make it the biggest city in Florida.

This prefiguration of later developments would have been incomplete without disaster. In 1886 fire swept through Key West's scrimshaw-ornamented, creosote-cured wooden houses. Half the city was reduced to cinders, including Vicente Martinéz Ybor's giant cigar factory. The Cubans decamped to Tampa, to found Ybor City, and make Tampa the cigar capital of the United States, which it remains to this day.

Florida's late-nineteenth-century Cubans had another trait, besides their industriousness, shared by the Cubans who would arrive in Miami in the 1960s. They believed their sojourn in the United States was only temporary. Once the revolution triumphed, the Cubans assured each other, they would go home again. They had failed to reckon with either the allure or the self-centeredness of America.

The Civil War had transformed the United States, for the first time, into a world-class military power. U.S. intervention, at any point following the outbreak of Cuba's war for independence, would have quickly driven the Spanish out and saved tens of thousands of lives. Instead, the United States, for more than thirty years following the end of the Civil War, ignored Cuba's agony. An age of American generals like Grant and Lee had given way to an American epoch in which the commanders-in-chief of specie and steel—the Plants and Flaglers—dominated national affairs. They had no interest in wasting money and manpower on foreign wars for freedom, especially when there was so much money to be made at home.

Meanwhile, in its campaign to crush the independence forces, Spanish troops rounded up all men and boys in Cuba over the age of fifteen and killed them. Women and children were forced into concentration camps. All houses neither flying white flags, as the Spanish ordered, nor occupied by Spanish forces were burnt to the ground. In order to "contain" the guerrillas, the Spanish impressed thousands of Cubans and forced them to defoliate a thirty-mile strip of land across the island. By the time the Cubans were bludgeoned into submission in 1878, more than a quarter-million people in Cuba had been killed, out of a total population of only about a million and a half.

By the beginning of the 1890s, Cuba lay prostrate, and Flagler and Plant personified the triumph of one of the great forces—the force of America—that has made Miami what it is today. But in Florida in those days it was also possible to make the acquaintance of a quite different kind of historical figure.

His name was José Martí, and he personified that second force that would create modern Miami—the force of revolution in Latin America.

If the habitués of the Tampa Bay Hotel had ventured an excursion into Ybor City in the early 1890s, they might have witnessed a spectacle as revealing of the times, and the forces that were creating them, as Henry Plant's Tiffany-glass skylights and lacquered jinrickshaws. Cuba might still be in Spanish hands, but the exiled Cuban revolutionary had conquered Florida. Martí exhorted immense, cheering crowds:

> Now! Form your ranks! Countries are not created by wishful thinking. . . . Let us rise so that liberty does not run any risk in its hour of triumph through disorder or indolence or impatience in its preparation. Let us rise for the real Republic!

"Anyone is a criminal who promotes an avoidable war," Martí proclaimed, "and so is he who does not promote an inevitable civil war."

Martí would take his message to cities as far away as New York, but in Washington, neither President Cleveland nor his successor, William McKinley, was swayed. The old generation had learned the "lessons" of the Civil War all too well. "We want no wars of conquest," McKinley declared in his inaugural address; "we must avoid the temptation of territorial aggression."

Among a younger generation of Americans, however, the turmoil in Cuba elicited a very different response. It was America's "duty to intervene in Cuba and to take this opportunity of driving the Spaniard from the Western World," a rising young politician named Theodore Roosevelt declared. Change "Spaniard" to

"Communist" and one has a statement another wealthy, youthful and charismatic scion of the eastern establishment—John F. Kennedy—might have made at the Orange Bowl in Miami in 1962.

Martí orated in vain. In 1895 another insurrection did break out in Cuba; once again the United States did nothing. Martí himself was killed a few weeks after the fighting began. As before, the struggle was vicious; as before, the guerrillas fought tenaciously but failed to break Spain's hold on the island.

Nothing had changed in Cuba, but a little to the north, a different kind of revolution had triumphed. In only a few years, thanks to the endeavors of magnates like Flagler and Plant, "Florida, which had ranked last in the South in railroads, wound up leading the nation in mileage per capita." This was just froth on a tidal wave of American economic expansion.

The same year Tuttle and Flagler founded Miami, U.S. industrial production for the first time surpassed that of Great Britain, the nation that had invented the Industrial Revolution and which, hitherto, had dominated the world.

Historians still cite America's victory in the Spanish-American War as the event that made the United States a world power. But Andrew Jackson had shown Spain was a paper tiger eighty years earlier, and America's military power had been evident to the world since Appomattox. It was the economic might men like Henry Flagler had created that would enable the United States, in the coming century, to shake, and sometimes to move, the world.

"Action, Action, Action! Jackson, Jackson, Jackson!" screamed the *New York World* in 1898. Andrew Jackson, of course, was long gone. But the evocation of his rambunctious, conquering spirit, exactly eighty years after America's man on horseback had rampaged across Florida, summed up the new temper of the times.

America was in a Rambo mood. The "lessons" of Gettysburg, like the lessons of the Tet Offensive later, had undergone a fundamental revision: it was time to forget the traumas of the past—time to feel good about America again. And what better way to make

America feel good than to teach wicked old Spain a lesson it would never forget?

As Robert Asprey explains, "The glory of nation building had worn thin. Men were bored, frustrated by the economic depression of 1893; they wanted activity, and a foreign excursion did not seem repugnant." Or, as Gloria Jahoda puts it, "The country longed to forget the lingering lessons of the civil war. Northerners and southerners felt that they could unite in a holy crusade to liberate a comfortably distant people—distant, that is, from the rest of the nation, though not from Florida."

Soon it seemed President William McKinley was the only American uninfected by the war fever of 1898. "The currents of destiny flow through the hearts of the people," McKinley lamented. "Who will check them? Who will divert them? Who will stop them?"

McKinley thought he had an idea. Why not send the U.S. battleship *Maine* to Havana to calm tempers, both in Cuba and at home?

Soon it was impossible to forget the sinking of the *Maine.* But even after Congress had stampeded the McKinley administration into war, the question remained: How, exactly, was the United States to avenge this insult to our national honor and then confer liberty on the Cubans?

Fortuitously, Henry Plant's railroad—like Florida itself—pointed in the general direction of Cuba. His Tampa Bay Hotel waited to billet the U.S. officer corps in the comfort to which it would quickly grow accustomed. And Plant's port in Tampa Bay was ready to harbor the ships that would carry our valiant doughboys off to confer baseball and freedom on their little brown brothers.

It was a test of American valor and virility, the yellow press proclaimed. But it was, no less, a test for Plant's wicker chairs: the commander of the United States expeditionary corps that gathered at Tampa, General William Rufus Shafter, weighed 320 pounds.

Soon Teddy Roosevelt and his Rough Riders were drilling where, hitherto, the only men in uniform had been Plant's rickshaw boys. And, as in Saigon seventy years later, the great and famous were showing up to watch the fun. Stephen Crane, Frederic Remington and Richard Harding Davis, the superstar foreign correspondent of the era, all converged on the Tampa Bay Hotel. One of the most celebrated of these globe-trotting celebrities, even then, was a young British aristocrat named Winston Churchill.

Churchill was as perplexed by the spectacle of guerrilla warfare in Latin America as many later outside observers would be. On the one hand, he reported, the Spanish were cruel and repressive, and there was no doubt that "the insurgents . . . possess the sympathy of the entire population." Yet the insurgents themselves, Churchill wrote, "neither fight bravely nor do they use their weapons effectively." Worse still, from Churchill's viewpoint, the guerrilla forces consisted "to a large extent of coloured men."

This was an age in which the superiority of the white race was considered as self-evident as Newton's law of gravity. The grandsons of British dukes were not the only ones who found a war fought simultaneously for liberty and against white men as disturbing a paradox as, a few years later, they would find Einstein's notion that invisible little atoms contained enough energy to blow up whole cities. When they finally reached Cuba, "American soldiers treated Negro guerrillas with open disdain. On the other hand, Americans got on well with Spanish survivors," even though Spain was the ostensible enemy.

If Martí was right, and it was criminal to promote "an avoidable war," two-thirds of America's newspaper publishers and three-quarters of its elected officials deserved to be hanged. Spain had capitulated to virtually every U.S. demand before the fighting began.

But why let technicalities deny America the thrill of a star-spangled battlefield victory? For ten weeks American sabers flashed, American cannon boomed; almost before the fighting began, the United States had blown Spain's four-hundred-year-old empire out of the water. Never before had the United States fought such an easy war; never again would it win such an easy victory. Prince Bismarck seemed to have the Spanish-American War in mind when he later remarked that Providence seemed to take special care of drunkards, fools and the United States.

*

It had been "a splendid little war," as John Hay wrote Roosevelt, following the Rough Riders' ramble up San Juan Hill. Not only had the Spanish, whenever some American shot off a Gatling gun, fallen down the way Japanese and Nazis, and Vietnamese and Russians, later would in the films of John Wayne and Sylvester Stallone. The United States—all in the name of liberty—had conquered a colonial empire of its own.

On the one hand, the Americans had fought to secure Cuban independence. On the other, most Americans, including President McKinley, were "convinced that Cubans could not govern themselves." As in the future, infighting in Washington and divided public opinion across the country wound up leaving the United States with the worst of both possible worlds. Unwilling either to let Cuba "work out its own political destiny" or to impose direct U.S. rule there, the United States, as Robert Asprey recounts, wound up trying to "reap the fruits of colonialism without accepting the responsibilities of colonialism."

For the time being, this exercise in "colonialism on the cheap" suited the Americans, if not the Cubans, well enough. The U.S. Army occupied Cuba, on and off, until 1909, and even when formal U.S. military rule ended, Cuba remained an American colony in all but name. By the time World War II began, U.S. citizens owned 85 percent of Cuba's sugar mills and controlled most of the rest of the Cuban economy.

For the United States, probably the most satisfying aspect of this arrangement was that it allowed Americans both to eat of the fruit of foreign domination and keep their illusions of liberty, too. What was wrong with Americans owning Cuba's factories and plantations? Or with the United States deciding who ruled Cuba and dictating what policies the Cuban government pursued? Hadn't we Americans given the Cubans their freedom and independence in the first place?

For the Cubans the arrangement was less advantageous. For

more than half a century, with the habitual acquiescence, and often with the full support, of the United States, a series of inept, repressive and brutal regimes abused the Cuban people. Even more demeaning to Cuban pride, generation after generation of Cubans grew up to discover that their flag, their government—their nationhood itself—was only the cheap façade for a military, economic and political system whose chief function was to enrich a handful of foreign investors and a small elite in Havana whose powers and privileges flowed, directly or indirectly, from their services to the *Yanquis.*

The worst consequence of the U.S. "liberation," however, was that it denied the Cubans the right to liberate themselves. As professors Thomas D. Boswell and James R. Curtis of the University of Miami point out:

> The Spanish army surrendered to the American forces, not the Cubans. Rebel Cubans were not allowed to participate in the surrender ceremonies. Because neither rebel representatives nor their flag were present when the agreement was signed, the United States gained the undying enmity of the Cuban people. Cubans rightly claim that they fought a lot longer and lost far more lives seeking their independence than did the Americans. They feel that the Americans intervened at the last minute, once it was clear that the rebels would win. They resent their rebellion being called the Spanish-American War, instead of the Spanish-Cuban War.

Revolution denied was revolution deferred.

Sixty years later the United States government would come to the conclusion that Castro and his followers were bent, as President Kennedy put it in his inaugural address, on making a "peaceful revolution of hope . . . the prey of hostile powers." The truth was that Fidel Castro, whatever he owed to Marx and the Soviet Union, was—as much as Kennedy himself—the inheritor of the whirlwind the United States had sowed in 1898.

Martí had been right. Countries are not created by wishful thinking. Not even after the United States had edged to the very brink of nuclear war would Cuba achieve the "real Republic" of which José Martí had dreamed.

The establishment of United States control in Cuba was only the beginning of an era of American conquest that would see this country dominate the Caribbean and Central America as totally as any European colonial power ever had.

Just as Jackson's violation of Spanish Florida had made him a national hero, so Theodore Roosevelt's adventures in Cuba helped propel him into the White House. Under Roosevelt and his immediate successors, U.S. troops would intervene in "a half-dozen Caribbean nations during the next twelve years, and within two decades dominate at least fourteen of the twenty Latin American countries through either financial controls or military power—and, in some instances, through both." The high point of this "most ignoble chapter in United States–Latin American relations," as the distinguished American historian Walter LaFeber calls it, was Roosevelt's seizure of Panama from Colombia, and the Panama Canal Zone from Panama.

There was really no way the United States could justify such abuse of its neighbors, but that didn't keep Roosevelt from trying. "Well," he asked his secretary of state, Elihu Root, on one such occasion, "have I answered the charges? Have I defended myself?"

"You certainly have, Mr. President," Root replied. "You . . . were accused of seduction and you have conclusively proved that you were guilty of rape."

Florida did very well out of the Spanish-American War.

Wartime government spending pumped millions of dollars into the local economy; thousands of American soldiers enjoyed a taste of the Florida sunshine. When the war ended, many of them, along with the Cubans, would never go home again.

For the first time in history, Florida had found itself at the center, not on the far fringe, of great events—and in Tampa this produced the same results that, more than sixty years later, another war in Cuba would produce in Miami: "Long eclipsed by Tallahassee, Tampa now began to become a cosmopolitan city that made the state capital look like the country town it was." On a smaller scale, Tampa acted out the current drama of Miami three generations in advance. The steady Americanization of Tampa's Cuban population offers clues to the future of Miami's much newer Cuban community.

The most important benefit to flow to Florida as a result of the war, however, wasn't social, political or even economic.

It was medical. A mere 385 Americans had died fighting in Cuba. Two thousand more had died of malaria, yellow fever and typhus. The U.S. military occupation of Cuba, Puerto Rico and Panama made the conquest of tropical disease a vital strategic American necessity. The subsequent discovery that both yellow fever and malaria were transmitted by mosquito would prove as important in terms of Florida's future development as the invention of air conditioning. With these advances in public health, large-scale settlement in Florida, on a year-round basis, would soon become feasible.

The Spanish-American War had another important side effect in Florida. Henry Flagler, with his habitual clairvoyance, recognized the conflict for what it was—a magnificent business opportunity.

Hardly had the *Maine* been sunk when Flagler's lobbyists began petitioning Washington to send troops to protect Miami from the Spanish peril. No matter that the settlement was of no strategic importance, and that the Spanish would have been unable to attack it, even if it were. If Flagler could lure a U.S. Army detachment to Miami, Henry Plant over in Tampa would not be the only one to make a bundle.

Miami had almost been wiped off the map even before the war

got started. On Christmas Day 1896—less than five months after its incorporation as a city—fire broke out in a grocery store; the settlement's ramshackle wooden business district quickly burned to the ground.

Others might have taken this as a portent that Miami, contrary to its promoters' claims, was bound for perdition, not triumph. But Tuttle and Flagler characteristically chose to regard the fire as an opportunity to launch Miami's first urban-renewal project. On the ruins of the old wooden buildings, new structures of brick and stucco were erected. Miami's infant construction industry, which to this day follows a frenetic cycle of boom and bust, was given the first of its many new leases on life.

"Miami Arises from Its Ashes," the *Miami Metropolis* exclaimed. The "Spirit of Miami" had been born.

Fire was followed by invasion—by American, not Spanish, forces. In a classic case of U.S. military overkill, the War Department dispatched no less than seven thousand lonely, bored, hungry and hard-drinking troops to defend Miami's twelve hundred people against the Spanish peril. What did it matter that, so far as the prosecution of the war was concerned, these troops might as well have been sent to Alaska?

Not only was the defense of Miami a strategic necessity, Flagler assured the generals, the troops, once they got there, would find Miami "the most pleasant place south of Bar Harbor to spend the summer."

Even for Miami, this was a stunningly outrageous bit of hype. Even today—with air conditioning, swimming pools and indoor ice-skating rinks—summer in Miami can be as trying as winter in Buffalo. Back then, it was like vacationing in a vermin pit.

"If I owned Miami and Hell," one soldier wrote home, "I'd rent out Miami and live in Hell." Though they'd never fire a shot in anger against the Spanish, the troops did find good use for their military training in the course of their Saturday-night rampages through Colored Town. In the worst of these assaults, the entire black population had to flee their homes and seek safety in Coconut Grove. The soldiers killed at least one man, injured others, and some blacks only barely escaped lynching. But no white soldier was ever arrested—let alone tried or convicted—for such assaults.

Rape was also a popular antidote to tedium, in addition to pillage. Soon it was unsafe even for white "women to walk the streets —or even to stay at home." Only Spain's speedy capitulation prevented what locals called the "Battle of Miami" from engulfing the place in full-scale war.

Fire and invasion were followed by pestilence.

The soldiers departed—leaving behind mumps, measles and typhus, to say nothing of syphilis and gonorrhea, as souvenirs. Then came the yellow fever epidemic. For three months in 1899, Miami was sealed off from the outside world, with armed guards on patrol to stop those who tried to break the quarantine.

Hardly had the yellow flags come down, and the last bodies been buried, when yet another fire struck.

These cumulative disasters had the same effect on Miami that later catastrophes would. As the new century—the American Century—began, and Miamians surveyed their city's first four years of conflagration, confrontation and upheaval, "few residents felt anything but optimistic about the city's future." Hadn't Miami and its people survived just about every calamity man and nature could dish out?

What more proof could anyone want that Miami was "the coming Metropolis of South Florida"?

8

Oolite

Julia Tuttle never saw the American Century. In late 1898 she died
suddenly, in the midst of her fiftieth year. In an instant town with
an instant history she was already a legend. Hundreds of people
gathered at the new cemetery to inter the "Mother of Miami."

She had survived the founding of her city by less than three years,
but enough time had passed for her death, like her life, to teach
another of Miami's essential lessons: when your dreams do come
true, watch out.

The establishment of Miami had not made Julia Tuttle rich; it had
impoverished her, even though Flagler himself had done quite well
out of the deal.

Tuttle's debts, like Flagler's wealth, flowed inescapably from that
most primal of all Miami relationships, the relationship between
land and money. Flagler could draw on his immense Standard Oil
fortune to develop his Miami holdings. But to develop her own real
estate, Julia Tuttle, like many a later Miami landowner, had to go
to the banks. Even going into debt, however, couldn't solve her
essential problem, a problem that dogs Miami to this day.

This was that people in this frontier city never wait for the customers to show up. Instead they first build their railroads, their
hotels, their shopping malls, their skyscraper condominiums. Then

they set out, with all the ballyhoo they can muster, to create a demand for what they have supplied. The result, even now, is that Miami most of the time has a glut of office buildings and housing, built in anticipation of the next wave of buyers from Latin America or up North.

This isn't a totally irrational approach in a self-invented city where, sooner or later, growth has always surpassed even the wildest predictions. But, financially speaking, it raises a question as important now as it was back in 1896. What to do until the people with down payments show up?

Speculators with lots of cash and outside sources of capital, like Flagler, could afford to wait until demand caught up with supply—and, once it did, plow their profits back into a new cycle of build, bust and boom. But people like Tuttle, whose whole wealth was tied up in land, couldn't afford that luxury; the banks demanded their payments every month. The ensuing scramble for cash only made matters worse, because the only way to get cash was to sell more land, driving prices down even more.

This tendency always to put the real estate cart before the financial horse accounts for many of Miami's present idiosyncrasies—its often hysterical reliance on public relations, its consequent tendency to confuse image with reality. It's no accident, for example, that today Julia Tuttle's former lands are covered with skyscraper banks and that Miami is a big financial center. This always has been a place with more schemes than cash—a great lender's town, an even better place for foreclosures.

This also helps explain why, behind the compulsive boosterism and glossy brochures, the real Miami drama is so often a riches-to-rags story. In Julia Tuttle's day as now, the place had no natural resources; it didn't produce much of anything. Its only essential reason for existing was that a lady from Cleveland had decided it should, and then set out to convince others.

In a city lacking both capital and natural wealth (and this is absolutely crucial for understanding not just Miami's origins, but its present condition), the only real way to get money was the same way you got kerosene or computers—to import it. And in Miami this need to attract outside capital always has raised an even more important question.

What were Julia Tuttle and all her successors to exchange for all this imported wealth, whether the outside money was Flagler's fortune in oil or the fortunes in drugs and flight capital that help propel Miami's growth today? Then as now, muggy, insect-infested swampland was a poor medium of exchange for gold, oil, dollars, steel girders and all the other things you need to build a city. So right from the beginning Miami was fated to traffic in orange blossoms.

This commerce in fantasy, in turn, has always had an implication of the greatest practical importance: before some people can get rich in Miami, many others must go broke. Dreamers tend to make inept financiers. So Tuttle, the dreamer, got her city, and Flagler, the financier, got even richer. Flagler was not a heartless man, but he hadn't built Standard Oil by paying off his competitors' bank loans. "I do not want you to suffer but I cannot accept the responsibility for your suffering," he informed Julia Tuttle when she appealed for help shortly before her death. "For months past, I have advised against your becoming so deeply involved in debt."

So Julia Tuttle wound up with a final distinction. She was only the first of countless thousands to arrive in Miami rich and leave, for Heaven or Havana, with the creditors in hot pursuit.

Actually Julia Tuttle was a lot luckier than many a future Miami visionary would be. She'd lost her money, but she'd hung on to most of her land. Eventually her children would make some profits selling it off, though not even they would wind up rich.

Today Miami, unlike New York, Pittsburgh or L.A., still lacks its Rockefellers, Mellons and Chandlers. Things still move too fast there, the foundations are still too porous for the dynastic principle to thrive. Instead Miami goes on doing what it's always done, trading dreams and taking money.

During a 1986 visit to Miami Beach, I was intrigued when Stephen Muss, a real estate magnate with a reputed personal fortune of $200 million, asked me to meet him at the Fontainebleau, rather than at the deluxe Alexander Hotel, as he had on my previous visit.

The Fontainebleau, of which Muss is the latest owner, is of course the most famous hotel in Miami. But the Alexander is also known to millions because the flamingo-pink skyscraper on Collins Avenue is one of the regular backdrops of "Miami Vice." More than that, all the stars of the program—Don Johnson, Philip Michael Thomas, Edward Olmos and its producer, Michael Mann—are familiar faces there. The hotel is headquarters for the show's production.

At the Alexander the corridors leading to the Jacuzzi are lined with Persian carpets. Tapestries and paintings in rococo gilt frames hang everywhere. When I'd seen him last, the year before, Muss had sent a yacht to ferry me across Biscayne Bay in order to show me the Alexander and explain why he had conjured it up. The family fortune had originated in New York, but it was here that Stephen Muss had decided to create a living monument to the memory of his father, Alexander Muss. "I set out to make this one of the great hotels of the world," he said, "because my father's name is on it."

After that original lunch, Stephen Muss had shown me to a waiting limousine, apologizing that it was only a Cadillac. The customized Rolls, he explained, was in the shop. Then this car the size of a yacht spirited me off for a helicopter tour of his domains.

All that was back in 1985. A year later the Alexander's parking valets still snapped to attention whenever a pastel Porsche drove up, but both the Muss Cadillac and the Muss Rolls-Royce were gone. He told me most of the story when I met him at the Fontainebleau; real estate sources filled in the rest.

Year after year he'd pumped millions into the Alexander, and in Miami terms, the place was a dream come true. The rich, the famous and the beautiful all flocked there. On slow days it might have been a layout from *People* magazine; on fast nights it was like an episode out of "Lifestyles of the Rich and Famous." There was only one problem with this Miami monument to Alexander Muss, who'd started out on the streets of Brooklyn. When the party was over, Stephen Muss was always left to pick up the tab. "There was no way to make that place pay," another Miami developer told me.

So after Muss had poured at least $26 million—some people said more than $50 million—into the Alexander, the dream had led where it so often leads in Miami. The banks now owned Alexander Muss's memorial. Stephen Muss now held his lunch-hour levees in the less elite, but more fiscally viable, precincts of the Fontaine-bleau.

Ninety years later the Julia Tuttle lesson was also being taught on the other side of Biscayne Bay. During his twelve years as mayor, Maurice Ferre—a man no less wealthy, complex and funda-mentally eccentric than Stephen Muss—virtually invented a new Miami. When he was first elected in 1973, Miami was still, in spite of the arrival of the Cubans, not much more than another Jackson-ville. By the time Ferre left office in 1985, Miami was billing itself as the world's newest great city and, thanks largely to Ferre's vision of what Miami could become, this was no public-relations ploy. That cosmopolitan Miami you see in the background in "Miami Vice" was from the beginning Ferre's conception and, to an impor-tant extent, its realization was his work.

Down to his well-manicured fingertips, Ferre personified Miami's transformation into a suave, exciting and prospering inter-national metropolis, and this was no mere matter of cultivating an image. Ferre took a largely ceremonial office and turned it into a position of real leadership, but not without paying a certain price.

The Byzantine intrigues involved in keeping his five-hundred-dollar-a-month job had not left the mayor with much time for other matters. While he was in office—while he was building his dream Miami—his family's fortune, estimated as high as $300 million, disappeared in a melodrama of bankruptcies, corporate mergers and court cases that made headlines for years. The man who, more than any other, had conjured up this latest new Miami had wound up like Julia Tuttle.

After he left office, I called on Maurice Ferre. Stephen Muss had shown me his penthouse residence, which, among other amenities, possessed a rooftop swimming grotto; when you swam east, you saw the Atlantic Ocean and when you swam west the skyscrapers of downtown Miami came into view. Ferre's walled estate in Coconut Grove epitomized another Miami dream come true. Here Hispanic artwork and antiques, some of it dating back to the *conquistador* era, filled book-lined drawing rooms with cathedral ceilings. Outside there was a manicured jungle—lush as the Amazon, well-ordered as a botanical garden.

Muss had showered me with helicopter rides, boat rides, limousine rides. Ferre, no less lavishly, served up odd ideas, recondite connections, lateral concepts to explain this city where, beneath the Cartesian street plans, nothing was solid, nothing straight lines.

"Oolite!" Miami's former mayor exclaimed at one point, as we sat in the garden and a uniformed maid brought us refreshments. "You can't understand Miami unless you understand oolite." This, my 1911 edition of the *Encyclopaedia Britannica* later informed me, was a "rock structure characterized by the presence of minute spherical grains resembling the roe of a fish; if the grains become larger," the entry elaborated, "the structure is said to be pisolitic," from the Greek word for pea.

Though most of us know oolite as calcium carbonate or porous limestone, Ferre compared the city he had governed for twelve years to a metropolis built on a bed of soggy rice. "Underneath there's nothing solid," he went on. "You take out the water and everything sinks." He jabbed the ground, to show how, in Miami, things connected. "You pour some pink dye in the ground here," he said, "and it doesn't stay here. You dig a hole over there the next day, and you find the soil's turned pink. It's seeped over there."

It must have been the color pink that caused the former mayor to make his next connection. "You see the progression, of course, starting with Art Deco in the twenties, and then going through the pink flamingos at Hialeah and Christo's wrapped islands to 'Miami Vice' today." I took a sip of my pink Campari, with the green lime in it, and Ferre said, "The pastel essence of Miami never changes;

it just migrates from form to form." I took another sip, and realized that when you boiled it and chilled it, even the stone crab turned pink.

We moved from the garden, and its moist languorous breezes, into an air-conditioned study. Ferre said, "Everything in Miami depends on the movement of air," and I asked him if he had paid too high a price to be mayor.

"I had a dream of Miami, that it should be the first hemispheric city," he said, "and I helped make that dream come true. You can always make money," Ferre added, referring to his family's losses the way you or I might discuss an overcoat the dry cleaners had misplaced. One idea he was considering now that he was out of office, Ferre added, was the establishment of a professional baseball team. "You don't have a major city," he explained, "until it plays in the major leagues."

"You plant an orange tree down here," Ferre once told me while he was still mayor, "and you get pineapples. You plant mangoes and you harvest banana splits." That was what had allowed him, for twelve years, to dominate the imagination, not just the politics, of Miami. In this oolite city, the mayor had an oolite mind.

A few days later, with Marjory Stoneman Douglas, the Florida historian, I discussed one of those curiosities that, like the oolite, the porous air and the pastels, runs through everything in Miami. This is that the creators, as opposed to the inheritors, of this get-rich-quick city have always cared so little about money.

We were having dinner at the Grand Bay Hotel; the crowd around us looked as if it had been borrowed from a soiree at Regine's, which in fact was upstairs. Mrs. Douglas at that time was ninety-five, deaf, nearly blind and in possession of the subtlest intellect I encountered in Miami. She took a sip of Chivas Regal and said, "The secret of Miami's success is that even more than it excites avarice, it excites the imagination." Then she told me a story about Ferre before he became mayor.

"Long before it all happened," she said, "Maurice would tell me about this idea he had for Miami, that it should become a great international city. He was always reading books—historians, poets, economists, philosophers. One time he telephoned, and said there was a social anthropologist I must help him meet; he had just read his book and said it had the future of Miami written on every page. I told Maurice there were only two problems: this man lived in England and he was deaf.

"A few months later," Mrs. Douglas went on, "I was in London, doing some research at the British Museum, when suddenly I heard a loud voice which I recognized. It was Maurice Ferre questioning the deaf anthropologist, and of course he had to shout at the top of his lungs to be heard. Maurice was a very rich young man back then, and he took us all to lunch at Annabelle's."

Marjory Stoneman Douglas had first arrived in Coconut Grove in 1916, when it was not much more than a few plantations by the water. But history happened so fast in Miami that, in considerably less than her own lifetime, a literal coconut plantation had become a forest of stately mansions, couturier boutiques, theaters, discotheques, yacht marinas, restaurants and luxury hotels.

As for Marjory Stoneman Douglas, she had started out as a society columnist in the wilderness—for the infant *Miami Herald,* which her father, Frank B. Stoneman, had founded—and had wound up battling to save that wilderness from total extinction. Her most famous book, *The Everglades: River of Grass,* was to Florida conservationism what Rachel Carson's *Silent Spring* was to environmentalism. She'd also written seven other books and, among other things, campaigned for female suffrage and served as a Red Cross nurse on the western front during World War I. One of her earliest memories, she told me, was of visiting Havana while it was still a Spanish colony. "It was very exciting," she recalled, "because of all the revolutionary agitation. There were demonstrations in the streets and, of course, a short while later the *Maine* blew up, and President McKinley took us into war."

To meet with Mrs. Douglas in Miami was like being able to telephone Dolley Madison in Washington and then have dinner with her at the Watergate. She had become the most enduring of Miami's many living legends, and in this celebrity hotel where even the pats of butter seemed to have designer labels, the presence of a legend did not go unnoticed.

A Cuban waiter came up to congratulate her on having been one of the founders of the city. She pointed out he was one of Miami's founders, too. The couple at the next table—he in a ruffled tuxedo; she in a black strapless—looked like an ad from *Vogue.* But it turned out they'd just returned from camping in the Everglades.

"Mrs. Douglas," the woman said, "my children will be thrilled when they hear we've met. I always tell them about what you've done to preserve our natural heritage."

"Well, thank you, my dear," she replied. "Did the alligators try to steal your sandwiches? They always try to steal my sandwiches."

I noticed something odd about the woman at the next table, but thought it better to inform Mrs. Douglas of it only after the couple had left. This woman had become so animated upon discovering that this elderly lady was the savior of the Everglades, that in the course of their conversation her left nipple had popped out of her dress.

"The poor child," Mrs. Douglas replied. "I hope she wasn't chilled, with all this air conditioning. So much in Miami," she elaborated, "depends on the movement of air."

Back in New York, when people asked if Miami was really stranger than it looked on TV, I'd tell them Miami was stranger than television *could* show, because a TV camera couldn't get inside people's brains.

They had to understand that down there, even underneath the neatest blow-dry all-American hairdos, you found minds as rampantly eclectic, as porous, as full of strange connections as calcium carbonate. These minds not only demonstrated a tendency to excess when it came to fantasies; they were characterized also by wanton disregard for authenticity of detail.

Not even the songs of Jimmy Buffett were safe from this rampant eclecticism. Take "Margaritaville," his best-known song, and practically the national anthem for a whole stratum of white English-speaking people under forty in south Florida who liked marijuana, pickup trucks, sailboats and jukebox music (as opposed to cocaine, sports cars, powerboats and disco music). Wherever these folks gathered and drank, you heard that song. And as "Margaritaville" played in those bars, on those jukeboxes, Julia Tuttle's old dream came alive again: maybe in Florida you could still have it all—manatees and money, a tropical paradise without Cubans or Haitians, marijuana and all these really interesting ideas. Maybe, down here, the sixties could put on a palm-tree sports shirt and go on forever, without delayed stress syndrome.

None of these people actually drank Margaritas. The sour rigor of lime, the hard bite on your tongue when you raised the icy, salt-rimmed glass to your lips—these were tastes as alien to these Americans who had chosen to live in this soft, waterlogged land as the Mexican rhythms of "Margaritaville" were to Miami's Cubans. Miami, along with the rest of south Florida, wasn't tequila; it was like rum, refined from sugar, and if the waitress in the net stockings liked you, when she served you Miami she put in an extra maraschino cherry.

Once when I was visiting Jimmy Buffett on his boat in Key West, I met a friend of his who, quite literally, pursued Florida's oldest profession. Middle-aged and white-haired, though athletic, he might have been a vacationing corporate executive until he explained he was a fortune-hunter.

This guy was after gold doubloons, pieces of eight, sunken treasure. The sun was setting and he gestured outward from the bridge of Jimmy Buffett's boat to the immensity of darkening water that surrounds the Keys, Miami and everything else in Florida. "It's out there," he said, "there's no doubt it's out there. The only problem is finding it."

That really was one of the things that made people in Florida different. People down there really thought the only problem was finding it. They never quite grasped that the real problems only began when Flagler did bring the railroad to town.

Buffett summed it all up in one of his songs—this belief that the problem only had to do with getting there, because whatever you wanted, it was

> . . . *waiting in front of me,*
> *And I know that I just can't go wrong,*
> *With these changes in latitudes, changes in attitudes.*

As for the man who knew the gold doubloons were out there, he just didn't know quite where, I decided he was a true native son of Piña Coladaville and didn't even bother to keep his card. I forgot all about him until six months later when it was in all the newspapers, in all the newsmagazines, on all the networks.

It would take years to bring up all the sunken treasure he'd found, years more to appraise it. The state of Florida, which both encourages and regulates such enterprise among its citizens, would take its cut. So would his backers and the IRS. But according to the reports, the value of the gold, silver and jewels he'd found out there, sleeping in that sunken galleon just out of sight of the condos and motels and gas stations, was, roughly speaking, one quarter of a billion dollars.

Sometimes I think of this white, middle-aged American searching the surface of the dark, unconscious water, obsessed with finding that one, exactly one, essential spot where, if only you can find it, the pursuit of happiness will end. Then, in my mind, another boat passes over the same stretch of water, though this boat does not contain diving equipment and metal detectors.

It contains a cargo of Haitians, and the funny thing is that the Haitians looking for Miami are just like the American looking for the sunken treasure. If you tell the fortune-hunter, Stop now: go back to Miami and drive a taxicab, and your life not only will be happier, it will be richer than if you find the sunken galleon, he will not stop. He will keep on searching. And if you tell the Haitians, Stop now: do not go to Miami, there is more wealth right here, just beneath this leaky hold where you huddle, than all of you will ever find in all your lives driving taxis, they will not stop. They will keep on going to Miami.

In his Florida novel, *Continental Drift,* Russell Banks portrays a scene similar to this moment I have just described. I read Banks's novel twice, once up North, once in Miami. It was a wonderful book to read in the cold, but with the changes in latitude, it lost something. What it lost was the realization that Miami's not about death, it's about hope. It was easy to forget that up North, but when you read the novel in Miami, you saw that Banks, while getting the consequences, missed the truth. In this book about pursuit, he didn't mention the really exotic thing about Miami—that so many people actually get what they're after.

In his novel the Haitians never make it to Miami. The Coast Guard intercepts the boat, which is piloted by Robert Dubois, the central character of the novel—a former oil-burner repairman from New Hampshire, now a smuggler of illegal aliens, whom the good life has eluded. When the cops show up, the Haitians are pushed overboard at gunpoint the way drug dealers flush cocaine down the toilet. Ultimately Dubois himself, following a voodoo trial in Little Haiti, finds deliverance, in the form of death, at the hands of some black thugs.

The name of the sunken galleon was the *Atocha,* and its discovery turned Mel Fisher into another Ralph Sanchez, into another Christo, that is to say into a hero. Producers and publishers competed for rights to his life story. People congratulated him wherever he went. Dozens of journalists did stories on him.

All the articles and broadcasts emphasized the struggle, the dedication, the sacrifices that went into the search. One of these sacrifices had been Mel Fisher's son.

The young man had drowned, while on a salvage operation in

one of the many wrong places his father picked before he found the right one. Fisher had found the treasure at the cost of his own son's life.

In the passage from *Continental Drift* that follows, Dubois is thinking about one of the young Haitians on the boat. That is to say he is thinking about the dream he himself once had:

> Bob looks down at the boy's black profile, and he thinks, You'll get to America, all right, kid, and maybe, just like me, you'll get what you want. Whatever that is. But you'll have to give something away for it, if you haven't already. And when you get what you want, it'll turn out to be not what you wanted after all, because it'll always be worth less than what you gave away for it. In the land of the free, nothing's free.

As I said, I like the logic and consistency of all this. Now that I am no longer in Miami, Banks's rigorous symmetry appeals to me even more. But the truth is, Florida isn't rigorous, and Miami certainly isn't symmetrical, which is why both serious literature and TV shows so often lose sight of an important main point: in Florida, people don't hunt for sunken treasure because the human condition is tragic. They hunt for sunken treasure because there really is sunken treasure. It's the same with the Haitians. They don't keep coming because they drown. They keep coming because, for every one who does drown, a thousand get through.

9

Circumspice

Tuttle and Flagler had founded a city, and a spunky little street-brawler of a city it turned out to be. But a host of other places, by 1910, also had their big railroad stations, their little business districts, their grandiose hotels, their even more grandiose dreams of a place in the sun.

It was another odd but well-matched pair of real estate eccentrics, Carl Fisher and John Collins, who would turn Miami into one of those trick-or-treat places that grabs the world's imagination and doesn't let go.

Together they transformed a slender, low-lying offshore strip of shifting sand, roach-infested palmetto groves and slimy mangrove swamp into one of the most bizarre, most illuminating wonderlands this nation has ever seen. There all that was shiny and gay and carefree in the American spirit would be realized, all that was selfish and destructive and vicious in the American psyche, too.

Never before had Americans conjured up such a place. If we are wise, perhaps they never will again. It was called Ocean Beach or Alton Beach at first. But quickly it acquired the name that, even now, for all its tarnished luster, still has the capacity both to enthrall and appall: Miami Beach.

*

Like Henry Flagler, Carl Graham Fisher had made a lot of money up North. Like Flagler, he also decided, now that he had made his money, to head south for some sun and fun. And once he got there, Fisher, too, discovered that what he enjoyed most was making even more money in Florida real estate. Flagler, presciently enough, had made his money in oil. Fisher was one of the very first Americans to get rich on the automobile. Back in Indiana, he had made more than $5 million by inventing and manufacturing the first headlight that actually let a driver see where he was going at night. Fisher was a fabricator of grand schemes even before he arrived in Miami. He started the Indianapolis Speedway; he also was one of the original promoters of America's first coast-to-coast motorable road, the Lincoln Highway.

Fisher's visionary projects were always models of capitalist self-interest. A nation intoxicated by fast cars and the romance of the open road would need billions of headlights. And if only a fraction of all those Americans, in all those cars, could be lured into driving down to Florida, then real estate prices in Miami would soar like rockets. Flagler had opened Florida to the plutocrats in private railway cars; Fisher would open it up to the Main Street masses in Tin Lizzies.

Like Julia Tuttle, John Collins had a dream, and lots of land. But without Fisher's money, vision and drive, Ocean Beach might still be what the environmentalists say it should have remained—an untouched barrier island, acting as an ecological buffer between the Atlantic Ocean and the maelstrom of human development on the mainland.

Carl Fisher transformed Collins's sandbar into a city, setting the stage for many future confrontations between those who wished to preserve Miami as nature had created it and those for whom a quick profit always took precedence over the quality of life.

Environmental conflict came with the territory in Miami. The coastal ridge on which the new city had been laid out was on average only about four miles wide. Hemmed in by the mangrove swamps of Biscayne Bay and the saw-grass swamps of the Everglades, Miami could grow big only by draining the wetlands to the west and by filling in the bay to the east.

As early as 1904, this environmental battle had begun to determine the course of Florida's political wars. Promising to transform south Florida into a new, high and dry "Empire of the Everglades," a former steamboat captain named Napoleon Bonaparte Broward campaigned for governor on a massive program of dredging and drainage. Even though Frank Stoneman denounced the scheme in the *Herald* as "superficial and dangerous," Broward was swept into office.

These days it's still customary for high-minded Miamians to take to the opinion pages of the *Herald* and lament the political power the criminal element has acquired. Napoleon Bonaparte Broward, like many a current Miami notable, had made his fortune as an arms smuggler. The high editorial tone of the *Herald* also goes back to the beginning: Miami in particular and frontier Florida in general have always had good newspapers. Perhaps it's because in a society in which government, political and social institutions were so new, so fragile and so corruptible, only the press could defend the public interest with any independence and consistency.

Good as his word, Governor Broward soon did as much violence to the geographical contours of south Florida as his Corsican namesake, exactly a century earlier, had done to the political contours of Europe. By 1905, Government Cut, a man-made ship canal, had sliced through Ocean Beach, opening Biscayne Bay to the Atlantic Ocean and making it possible, for the first time, for Miami to function as a deep-water port. Miami's days as a major ocean port were still far in the future, but with the opening of Government Cut small freighters from the Bahamas and the Caribbean, often carrying contraband, began to tie up at the mouth of the Miami River. They were the forerunners of today's merchantmen of marijuana, munitions, cocaine and illegal aliens.

By 1909 dredging of the Miami Canal had begun. When this

massive water-diversion scheme was finished, countless billions of gallons of Everglades freshwater, and millions more tons of Everglades sediment, surged into Biscayne Bay, in a double act of ecological despoilment and real estate creation.

At a stroke thousands of acres in the Everglades were drained dry and so opened up to the speculators; simultaneously the once crystal-blue waters of Biscayne Bay, now mucky brown, began to be filled in with artificial islands. As gangs of black laborers uprooted the mangroves on Collins's sandbar and Fisher's dredges scooped up millions of tons of muck from the bottom of Biscayne Bay to create the "unspoiled tropical paradise" his real estate brochures promised, the stench of dead, decaying marine life made Miami stink worse than any northern mill town. By 1916 the dredges had drained the lands that, by then, already were beginning to be called "Greater Miami." But conservationists had also acquired the first of the lands that later grew into Everglades National Park.

Government Cut and the other early dredging projects prefigured the government spending that would have such an impact on Florida's growth in the future.

First state, then later federal, tax dollars financed the canals and levees that transformed south Florida from a primitive swamp into a real estate bonanza. The Intracoastal Waterway, built by the U.S. Army Corps of Engineers, provided the yachts of the wealthy a free ride south to the Florida sun just as, later, the Interstate Highway System would help make mass motorcar tourism a vital sector of the Florida economy. By the 1960s the space shots at Cape Canaveral would inject billions into the Florida economy.

Without doubt Florida's most lavish government benefactor has been the Social Security system. Every year it pumps tens of billions of dollars southward into Florida shopping malls, real estate and service sector industries, ranging from hospitals to hotels. Even the Horatio Alger story of Miami's Cubans, financially speaking, is a myth: These refugees received lavish U.S. government grants to help them build new lives under capitalism. "In fact, the federal

Cuban assistance effort was the largest in the history of the country."

Today transfer payments—whether the money transferred is flight capital from Latin America, drug money or the savings people from up North spend on condominiums, vacations, medical care and retirement homes—remain the mainstay of the south Florida economy, thus continuing another theme that goes back to Miami's very origins. It always has been a place where people spend—and frequently squander—the wealth they have accumulated elsewhere.

Broward's election demonstrated just how far Miami had come in less than ten years. Before 1896 hardly anyone had heard of the place. By 1904 the debate over Miami's development was dominating state affairs. Broward also personified how times had changed in another way. Dade County had been named for an Indian fighter. But when the area to the north of Miami, around Fort Lauderdale, was organized into an independent county, it was named for Governor Broward himself. The heroes of the real estate wars were beginning to supplant the heroes of the Seminole wars on the political map of Florida.

It still took a week to drive to Miami from the big cities in the North, but, as in the past, travel within Florida remained even more arduous. In 1923, when an expedition of ten cars, twenty-three drivers and two Indian guides left the Gulf Coast for Miami, it took them three weeks to traverse the peninsula, "during which they were reported lost several times" in the Everglades. Not until 1928, when the Tamiami Trail was completed, did direct overland travel between the Atlantic and Gulf coasts of Florida become feasible.

The new highway reduced travel time from Miami to Tampa to less than a day; it also achieved something the U.S. Army never had. Attracted by the prospect of making money off the tourists, the Seminoles at last began to abandon their enclaves deep in the swamp and, under contract to tourist promoters, build "Indian villages" along the highway. Thanks to the irrepressible transformation of land into real estate, even the Seminole wars became the source of a tourist attraction.

By then Miami, in spite of its comparative isolation, already had been a motor car metropolis for a long time. In 1915 Carl Fisher had led a fifteen-car safari, called the Dixie Highway Pathfinders, all the way from Chicago to Miami. As usual, the local papers hailed the latest development as "the beginning of a new era." As usual, they were righter than they knew. Though the age of mass automobile migration to Florida would not reach full flood until after World War II, the car would do even more than the air conditioner to make Miami what it is today.

Not even Miami's most imaginative boosters could have predicted the city's future as the aviation nexus of North America, Latin America and Europe. But the town went wild when one of the Wright brothers' biplanes was shipped down on Flagler's railroad and performed stunts in the sky overhead. By 1915 local publicists had convinced Glenn Curtiss, who, along with the Wright brothers, was one of America's premier aviators, to establish a flying school there. Amelia Earhart began her ill-fated flight to immortality in Miami, and both Eastern and Pan American airlines were founded there. From the very beginning there was passion, not just love, in Miami's affair with the airplane.

Palm Beach, St. Augustine and Tampa all attracted their share of the rich and celebrated during the winter season. But Miami had another trait that set it apart from its rivals—a knack for luring both the famous and the infamous on a year-round basis.

Robert Frost, for example, in the course of his Miami sojourns, composed many of his poems about New England snowstorms amidst the tropical verdure of Coconut Grove, back when it was the Greenwich Village of Miami and he and Marjory Stoneman Douglas were neighbors. Zane Grey wrote many of his thrillers about brave gunmen taming the Wild West in a city where the pioneers were mostly fast-talking real estate sharks. By 1913 Andrew Carnegie had chosen to settle there, James Deering had begun building Villa Vizcaya, and over in Miami Beach, Harvey Firestone—another of the automobile era's first millionaires—had erected a "vine-covered, many-chimneyed Georgian Colonial mansion" on what later became the site of the Fontainebleau hotel.

Without doubt the city's most celebrated early resident was William Jennings Bryan, the three-time populist candidate for president. Like many another midwesterner, Bryan had his first taste of Florida during the Spanish-American War, while serving as a colonel in the Third Nebraska Volunteers. It seems both poetic and historical justice that the boy orator of the windswept northern prairies should have wound up spending his old age in muggy, buggy Miami, like so many others from his neck of the woods.

Apparently he, too, was lured there by the myth of Florida's healthfulness. Mrs. Bryan was sickly, but the Florida sunshine was of no more help to her than it had been to the first Mrs. Flagler, and during the Scopes Monkey Trial it was suggested that the Miami sun had addled Bryan's brain. "If I had my health," she later confided to Marjory Stoneman Douglas, "Papa would never have gone in for this evolution business."

In the winter of 1921, William Jennings Bryan was followed to Miami by another midwestern politician, Warren Gamaliel Harding. By 1921 Prohibition was in force, but that didn't keep the president-elect of the United States from enjoying Carl Fisher's stock of contraband whiskey. Although Julia Tuttle had wanted her city not only to be as prosperous, but as proper, as her hometown of Cleveland, Miami already had become a place where Americans went to escape the social, moral—and legal—constraints of life up North. Fisher had prepared well for the "noble experiment." "Cases of Scotch were buried around his Miami Beach home, and his yachts were fitted with secret compartments to bring in refills from the Bahamas when necessary."

When Harding wasn't drinking or playing poker, during his visit, he went golfing. Carl Fisher, never slack when it came to generating free publicity, provided the president-elect with a caddy—an elephant named Carl II. Soon the president-elect, the elephant and

Miami Beach were in the photogravure sections of newspapers all over the country.

Winter guests like Harding came for the illicit booze and illicit gambling; for famous year-round settlers like Bryan and Glenn Curtiss sunshine was also a secondary consideration.

When Glenn Curtiss wasn't giving lessons at his flying school, he was hustling real estate. And when William Jennings Bryan wasn't teaching Sunday school, he was hustling real estate, too. George Merrick, having laid out Country Club Prado, had hired the famed orator to sell the masses on Coral Gables the same way he'd sold them on free silver twenty-five years earlier.

Now the former secretary of state "gave special promotional lectures at Venetian Pool" while such "well-known orchestra leaders as Jan Gerber and Paul Whiteman played 'When the Moon Shines on Coral Gables' at the Coral Gables Country Club." Bryan's salary was $100,000 a year, twice what he would have made as president of the United States.

George Merrick spent his money not only lavishly but well—and not just on publicity. To this day Coral Gables remains a model of what Miami might have been, and a living rebuke to the greed, tastelessness and irresponsibility of those who, by and large, have made Miami what it is. Where others viewed the land as a battleground—first to be assaulted, then bludgeoned into unconditional surrender—Merrick treated his surroundings with something akin to reverence.

Perhaps he showed such respect for real estate because he was one of the very few entrepreneurs of the boom years with any real human ties to the wilderness he was transforming. Merrick's family had arrived in Miami in 1898, just two years after the town was founded. Though Merrick's holdings ultimately encompassed three thousand acres, the nucleus of Coral Gables was the 160-acre farm that his father, originally a New England Congregationalist minister, had purchased for only eleven hundred dollars.

The family grew vegetables for sale in the new city; as a boy George Merrick hawked produce from the back of a mule-drawn cart. Later he studied law at Columbia University, but his real passion was always poetry. As his development of Coral Gables proved, Merrick was a kind of poet, destined—as Rex Beach later put it, with a floweriness Merrick would have cherished—to "write in wood and steel and stone, and paint his pictures upon a canvas of spacious fields, cool groves and smiling waterways."

In a metropolis built by eccentrics, Merrick's vision was the most daring. He operated on the assumption that you could build the future in south Florida by enhancing, not destroying, the natural amenities that attracted people there in the first place. He wound up teaching a lesson Miami still hasn't fully learned: if you want to make big bucks, cash in on that elemental human yearning for quality. In 1924 alone, Merrick sold more than $12.5 million of real estate.

Merrick's life ambition, quirky even by Florida standards, was summed up by his sales slogan—he wanted to create "The City Beautiful." This was one of the few instances when hype accurately mirrored the nobler impulses of the soul. Then as now, Coral Gables was a little too well planned—a little too smug in its self-conscious graciousness—to have the spontaneity necessary for true beauty. But in a metropolis of defoliated swamps, treeless boulevards, tacky storefronts, neon-lit motels and plastic drive-ins, Merrick's enclave to this day remains a marvel of respect both for its natural setting and for the people who live and work there.

To help him plan his dreamland, Merrick convoked a brain trust of artists, landscape architects, planners, historians and designers. Though he never once in his life ventured outside the United States, Merrick was as fastidious when it came to the authenticity of the Mediterranean, French, Dutch and Chinese details he incorporated into his buildings as he was with his plumbing. This obsession with quality cost Merrick millions—he spent $10 million alone on the Biltmore Hotel, which was modeled on the cathedral of Seville.

Where other builders uprooted vegetation, Merrick planted

trees compulsively. Like other developers, Merrick dug drainage ditches, but then he went on to landscape the banks, convert the ditches into canals and float Venetian gondolas on them. So instead of the open sewers crisscrossing other parts of Miami, Coral Gables wound up with "Forty Miles of Inland Waterways."

Today, as in the twenties, it seems ugliness is never destroyed in Miami, only created, as if in obedience to some natural law of aesthetic entropy. Grandiose skyscrapers inevitably create their slag heaps. In order to create marketable land here, the speculators create gaping holes in the earth there. More than sixty years ago, however, Merrick proved that profit and despoilment need not necessarily be bedfellows.

Like many other builders in Miami, Merrick had dug a quarry—and, as usual, the result was a great ugly hole in the ground. Rather than leave things at that, Merrick filled this empty, gaping hole with sparkling blue water. Then—in a triumph of landscape engineering that still delights the senses—he surrounded his erstwhile hole in the ground with moss- and vine-encrusted boulders. He planted the adjoining grounds with stately palms and, instead of a typical Miami bathhouse, built a tile-roofed and arbored palazzo worthy of a doge.

There was nothing effete or elitist in Merrick's approach, in spite of his insistence on quality. In a city full of "exclusive" country clubs and sports clubs, Merrick's Venetian Pool was—and still is—open to the public for a nominal fee. Like every true Miamian, of course, Merrick was also a passionate believer in the legitimacy of publicity. Soon the former quarry was being ballyhooed as "The World's Most Beautiful Swimming Pool."

Excellence wasn't the only secret of Merrick's success. From the beginning he actively excluded mediocre designs and cheap construction by obliging all who bought land in Coral Gables to submit their building plans to an independent architectural review board. Detractors not only proclaimed Merrick's approach financially suicidal; they accused him of subverting the American Way. Didn't every red-blooded U.S. citizen have the right to build whatever he wanted on his own property, no matter how much it degraded its surroundings?

It was a clash of sensibilities as revealing of Miami's current conflicts as the early battles between the preservationists and the diggers and drainers. George Merrick—the closest thing Miami had back then to a native son—turned out to have a better vision of how both to preserve the past and build the future than the supposed sophisticates from up North.

Today most of the "dream communities" built by Merrick's competitors have either been bulldozed or degenerated into slums. Coral Gables is the only Miami boomtown of the twenties that today is even more attractive, and more profitable, than when it was built.

Glenn Curtiss was destined to leave a much darker—and much more typical—mark on Miami. Curtiss's first real estate scheme was the "city" of Hialeah, which consisted essentially of a dog track, later converted into the famous racehorse track. In time Hialeah would boast both the world's largest bougainvillea trellis and the universe's most immense electrically operated bet-totalizing board, "said to contain nearly 100,000 miles of wiring." There also was a thirty-two-acre artificial lake in which two hundred pink flamingos were trained to arrange themselves so that, "seen from the stands," they resembled "a bed of pink water lilies."

Nature was already imitating artifice in Miami. Curtiss's flamingos had been imported from Cuba and, for a time, they seemed to regard their Miami sojourn as only temporary. Periodically they would take to the skies and return to their native land. Over the generations, however, this homing instinct faded, and today—I was told when I visited Hialeah—the birds consider themselves every bit as American as you or I. Hialeah's human population is now almost entirely Cuban. It was one of the first municipalities in the Miami area to elect a Cuban-born mayor.

For Glenn Curtiss Hialeah was only the beginning.

Without any doubt whatsoever, the wackiest Miami real estate scheme of all time was his "city" of Opa-locka, a Hollywood stage set of a town built in the epoch of Rudolph Valentino.

The Tampa Bay Hotel had proven any millionaire could lounge beneath a minaret in the Florida sun. At Opa-locka, coming home to the casbah became Everyman's right. Curtiss had originally planned a Sherwood Forest motif for his suburban development. But after happening upon a lavishly illustrated edition of *The One Thousand and One Tales from the Arabian Nights,* he decided to create the "Baghdad of Dade County" instead.

Soon bulldozers were crisscrossing muddy pastureland where free-range cattle previously had grazed; red slashes in the earth were being given names like Sherazad Street and Ali Baba Avenue. Real estate was sold at Curtiss's mosquelike sales center—today the Opa-locka City Hall. Supposedly modeled on the emperor Kosrou-shah's Persian palace in the tale "The Talking Bird," it was a Moorish extravaganza of domes, minarets and arches, painted blue, green, amethyst and rose-toned ivory. All this, the salesmen assured customers, was only the overture to a symphonic suburb worthy of Rimsky-Korsakov. Each section of Opa-locka, the prospectus promised, would be modeled on a different story from *The Arabian Nights.*

Curtiss, who had moved to Miami in 1916, was made in the mold of the classic Florida real estate *conquistador.* A compulsive tinkerer like Fisher and a multimillionaire like Flagler, Curtiss had invented both the world's fastest motorcycle and the first flying boat to cross the Atlantic. Sales of his airplanes—notably the "Jennie," used by U.S. forces during World War I—had amassed him a personal fortune in excess of $35 million.

Like Fisher and Merrick, Curtiss was also an authentic publicity wizard. The racetrack drew buyers to Hialeah as surely as the seashore beckoned investors to Miami Beach. Not content with that, Curtiss also built America's first jai alai fronton, and imported athletes from Cuba and Spain to play there. It was in Opa-locka, however, that the aviator-turned-real-estate-impresario revealed a knack for PR that put Fisher's golf-club-carrying elephants to shame.

In January 1927, when the first train pulled into Opa-locka's Arabesque railroad station, local "sheikhs" on horseback waylaid the passengers, including the governor of Florida. Hardly had the startled dignitaries collected themselves, when they heard "screams from a nearby harem and it was seen that one of the Grand Wazier's favorite wives was escaping and the Opa-locka Arabs took off in hot pursuit." What amazed the visitors most, however, was that that day's edition of the *Opa-Locka Times,* which carried banner headlines describing the "attack on the train," had been printed hours before they arrived. Curtiss had thoughtfully alerted the editor in advance of the news he planned to make.

Curtiss was better at selling sunshine than building houses with roofs that could keep out the rain. Build a big-enough tourist attraction, get enough people to buy land around it and then—his theory ran—the streets, schools and sewers would take care of themselves.

Hialeah quickly degenerated from a chic resort for the sporting set into a jumble of tacky bungalows and trailer parks. Curtiss also lacked Merrick's eye for detail and passion for excellence. Opa-locka was a Levantine fantasy executed in concrete, water paint and flaking plaster so cheap it made Kosroushah's palace look "old even when the building was new."

Curtiss's disdain for authenticity extended to names. Opa-locka's real Indian name was "Opatishawockalocka," but the middle syllables were excised lest potential buyers find it too difficult to pronounce. For the same reason, Scheherazade became Sherazad on the street maps. Even Curtiss's land office—aesthetically as well as structurally—was a fraud. Though the scene supposedly inspiring the building was Persian, Curtiss's architect, Bernhard E. Muller, had opted for an Arab design.

What did it matter? Back then not one buyer in a thousand could distinguish Greek from Gothic, let alone an Arabic from a Persian design. As always in Florida, you didn't sell land; you didn't sell buildings. You sold dreams—in this case the dream that, for the price of a lot in Opa-locka, anyone could become the Valentino of the Everglades.

Curtiss and Muller—who previously had designed Christian Science churches for a living—each claimed sole credit for their grand vision. Curtiss asserted it was he who had the genius to first pick up a copy of *The Arabian Nights*. But as far back as February 1927 Muller attributed the inspiration to his own bedtime reading. The architect told a reporter:

> Having passed from one scene of oriental mystery and splendor to another, I went on and on until I had completed the story. Finally sleep overtook me and I lived the stories over again in my dreams. My mind [was] so filled with the beauty of what I had read that the idea had flooded my consciousness to create a city of oriental splendor, a veritable Arabian Night's dream, and upon meeting Mr. Curtiss, I conveyed this to him.

The Casbah craze died with Valentino, and what Muller called "the phantom city of my mind" became a true phantom of a city. Ticky-tack villas filled the vacant lots where Moghul harems had been supposed to rise. Palmettos—and palmetto bugs—thrived where the blueprints called for formal gardens and playing fountains. Five of the Opa-locka City Hall's six domes collapsed. When I visited Opa-locka in 1986, half the great structure was closed as a risk to life and limb; the tile frescoes of the abandoned railroad station were marred by graffiti and barbed wire. What little remained of Curtiss's "city of oriental splendor" resembled nothing so much as a long-abandoned and vandalized amusement park.

Glenn Curtiss's initial obsession, aviation, had a greater long-term impact on Opa-locka than his dreams of Araby. He also built an airfield there, and when World War II broke out, Opa-locka enjoyed a short-lived camp-town boom. When the Navy decommissioned the airfield in 1947, the CIA took it over. Dirty tricks and hush-hush operations, including preparations for the Bay of Pigs invasion, replaced the high living of the war years.

Gradually Opa-locka became the refuse bin for everything else Miami wanted to brush under the carpet. Warehouses, depots and dumps unwelcome closer to Biscayne Bay filled the town. The cheap cinder-block housing the military had thrown up during the war was converted into ghettos for the welfare rolls of Dade County. By the early sixties, "slum clearance" in downtown Miami was ravaging Overtown. All in the name of social progress, the thriving "Colored Town" that dated back to Flagler's time was devastated by federal "urban renewal" projects long before the 1980 civil disorders delivered the *coup de grâce.* Thousands of the homeless blacks were forced into Liberty City, but many moved north to Opa-locka, where they encountered traditions older than Miami itself.

Blacks were barred from Opa-locka's parks, prevented from voting, and when they took the civil service examination for employment with the city government were invariably told they had failed. In fact blacks were welcome at the Arabesque City Hall for only one purpose. "As a general rule," Freeman Collins, one of Opa-locka's first black residents later recalled, "blacks were to pay their bills at City Hall and leave as soon as their business transactions were complete. If they attempted to linger for any length of time, they were run off."

The breakdown of legal segregation in the sixties produced the same result in Opa-locka that it did in working-class neighborhoods up North—white flight. By the end of the decade, Curtiss's erstwhile paradise was a black slum patrolled by white cops, an Arabian Nights version of Harlem and Watts.

In a prefiguration of the Liberty City explosion nine years later, racial conflict broke out there in 1971 when black crowds, enraged by "the use of excessive force," attacked white policemen arresting a black motorist "at the corner of Ali Baba and Northwest 22nd Avenue." In May 1980, as the Liberty City riots leaped municipal boundaries, arsonists vented their fury on the run-down remnants of Glenn Curtiss's fantasyland, and "Opa-locka . . . glowed as if it had come under a large-scale incendiary attack."

Curtiss's Levantine reverie was at last fulfilled, though not the way either he or Muller had intended: with the genie of racial violence let out of the bottle, Opa-locka had become a Florida Beirut.

At the time I visited Opa-locka, I happened to be staying in Coral Gables, so the journey between the two "cities" turned out to be doubly revealing. In less than forty minutes, I could make a round-trip between the dream that had created Miami, and which ceaselessly re-creates it, and the nightmare that so many people, in pursuit of the dream, have wound up inflicting both on Miami and on themselves.

Most Americans, of course, like to believe they live in a Coral Gables of a nation, but Opa-locka, like most "ghettos" white Americans never visit, was a lot more like their own neighborhoods than they ever suppose. This was a place where there never was enough money for decent schools or health care, but where it seemed at least one family on every block could afford a satellite dish. Here as almost everywhere else—even after the construction of Miami's billion-dollar Metrorail system—there was no reliable way to get around by public transportation. Everyone, whether they could afford it or not, had to have a car. So here, just like in Coconut Grove and Key Biscayne, people complained about the monthly payments even though in Opa-locka, as in the rich neighborhoods, there always seemed to be enough spare cash for a bag of marijuana or a line of coke.

Opa-locka resembled the rest of Miami in an even more important way. Here, as in the most fashionable waterfront locations, all the larcenies, felonies and scams you see on "Miami Vice" weren't distant menaces. They were next-door neighbors.

In the white Miami, there were superficial differences, of course. Along Biscayne Bay the exclusive residential compounds had names like the Palm Bay Club, Quayside and the Jockey Club. Life looked more like an advertising supplement to the *Miami Herald* than the crime pages of the *Miami News*. But the underlying commerce was all the same. The developers of these establishments didn't sell houses and apartments. They sold what Curtiss sold at Opa-locka—the illusion that a thirty-year mortgage can buy you escape.

In fact what $250,000 mostly buys you in those places is what $25,000 gets you in Opa-locka—life in a ghetto. The walls are high and, in the better-designed establishments, the barbed wire and broken glass are disguised with luxuriant foliage. The security guards are courteous, efficient—and well trained in the use of the loaded firearms they carry.

But just outside, every evening, the prostitutes and drug dealers begin their nightly patrols along Biscayne Boulevard. The neon vacancy signs on the thirty-dollar motels wink on with a leer. Along the little side streets leading down to the bay, white people living in those old bungalows slapped together during the boom—like black people in Opa-locka—sit down to dinner wondering if this will be the night the madman with the loaded revolver breaks in.

Opa-locka, I discovered, was like the rest of Miami municipally, too. The officials I encountered in the remains of Kosroushah's palace, like the officials I met elsewhere, had no solutions to problems like drugs, violence, poverty and pollution.

But they had come up with a slogan: "Rebuilding the Dream." The mayor, John B. Riley, was away—in Saudi Arabia, seeking petro-dollar investment in Opa-locka's "Arab" heritage—but the director of city planning, Lincoln D. Chandler, outlined the fundamentals of the grand design.

In a town with a tiny and fragile tax base, where most people's incomes hovered just above or below the poverty line, the city council had decided it was time for action. So it had appropriated $900,000 to refurbish Curtiss's fantasy palace.

Once City Hall was restored to its former splendor, city officials reasoned, it would become a great attraction for affluent people of all races. Already, an Arabian Nights Festival was planned, and as a result of the publicity all this would generate, I was told, people would start moving into Opa-locka and fixing up the old houses with minarets over the garages. Opa-locka once again would become what people in City Hall assured me it once really had been —a city of true Oriental splendor.

Outside City Hall there were boarded-up stores and burned-out buildings; unemployed youths were hustling drugs. Curtiss had been dead for more than fifty years. But his fantasy lived on, there in the ruins of his fantasy palace: just build the right tourist attraction and your dream of the city beautiful was bound to come true.

Actually, there were one or two signs of revival. A Cuban family had opened a restaurant. On another block one of the few surviving Arabian Nights villas had a new coat of paint on it. The owner was out in the front yard, working on his pickup truck.

He turned out to be a Marielito, not some gentrifying Yuppie. He still couldn't speak much English, but in Spanish he said the minaret on his roof hadn't dissuaded him. Where else in Miami, he asked, could you buy your own home for twenty-five thousand dollars? Within four years of getting off the boat, he explained, he'd saved up enough for a down payment. He had a little subcontracting business, of which the used pickup truck was the principal investment.

He gestured to the houses of his black neighbors—most of them weren't Arabesque bungalows at all, but small-scale versions of the "ranch" houses you see in richer, white neighborhoods. "I don't bother them, and they don't bother me," he said.

For this man, Miami was not some dream out of the Arabian Nights. It was a mundane practical place where, if you worked hard enough, you could actually own a home of your own—even if, for some inexplicable *Yanqui* reason, it turned out to have a minaret on the roof. As for the people around him, they could be zebra-striped, so long as they did not disrupt his daily routines.

Miami was neither a dream nor a nightmare for this man, it occurred to me, for a simple but very important reason: he wasn't an American. And it was that accident of birth that had freed him of both the fantasies and the phobias that are the heritage of "real" Americans, whatever their income or skin color happens to be.

On the way back to the freeway, I took a wrong turn and found myself in one of those black neighborhoods that only white people regard as "ghettos." It was working-class by white standards, middle-class by black standards. There were Chevrolets and Fords in the carports. Behind the picture windows you could see big-screen TV sets and those plastic-covered living room suites people buy on the installment plan at discount houses. There were pink plaster flamingos in some of the front yards, but no swimming pools out back. The kids rode around on old-fashioned American-style bicycles, not those ten-speed, European-style racing bikes you see in neighborhoods where the parents drive Volvos.

It was hard finding your way out of this little enclave whose existence seemed decipherable not so much in terms of race, as in the persistence of some color-blind American ideal where everything—street plans, TV screens, houses, garages, swimming pools and lives—remained rectilinear, no matter how many minarets the salesmen sold you.

It was difficult to find a way out because this corner of Opa-locka turned out to be surrounded on three sides by a big drainage ditch. So whichever way you drove at first, you wound up back at the ditch. Had this been Coral Gables, George Merrick would have turned the ditch into a Venetian canal, complete with a Bridge of Sighs. A current Miami developer, in a more upscale neighborhood, would have lined it with jogging paths.

But this was Opa-locka, so the ditch remained a ditch—its banks covered with litter, the water between the banks sluggish and brown. The people here didn't have the money for improvements, and in truth, I suppose, they were like the people who buy condos on Biscayne Boulevard: their interest in paradise ended at the property line.

Back in Coral Gables, it wasn't just the flesh tones of the people. The shape of things was different—curving and oak-tinted, rather than rectilinear and plastic. Merrick built so well that his buildings are about the only ones in Miami that have actually improved with the passage of the years. The small hotel where I was staying was an example of that. Sixty years ago it had been done up in the "Spanish" style that then was all the rage, and called the Hotel Seville. Now, in an age of Perrier and Cuisinart, it had been converted into a "French" restaurant and hotel, called the Place St. Michel.

One evening the young owner of the hotel—his name was Stuart Bornstein—offered me a brandy and told me his story.

Just as the officials at Opa-locka, although they were black, were Glenn Curtiss's real reincarnations, so Bornstein was the true heir of George Merrick, son of the Congregationalist minister. He had Merrick's dream of creating a self-contained world where everything would be beautiful—also Merrick's fastidiousness with details. This building had been a dowdy relic of the boom until Bornstein had transformed it into one of the city's most stylish gathering places. He showed me his latest scheme, for a luxuriant roof garden. Rock stars and oil sheikhs might stay at the Grand Bay when they came to Miami, he conceded. But when Joan Didion came to Miami, he told me proudly, she stayed here.

Besides the innocent Miami delight he took in this song of himself and the world he had created, there was, in everything he said, a definite southern inflection. I assumed he was a native Floridian. So I asked him if the influx of so many foreigners bothered him. "Damn," he replied, "when you grow up the only Jewish kid on your block in Richmond, Virginia, and then you come down here, Miami is paradise."

By the time I got back from Opa-locka that night, the bar and dining room of the hotel were full of bright, earnest young people, dressed for success and knowledgeably discussing the wine lists. These days we call them Yuppies; in Merrick's time their critics would have called them boosters, maybe even Babbitts. What defined them, even more than their affluence, was their self-certainty. In this wide-open town, they not only had standards, they set them. They had nothing to do with drugs—except for a little "recreational" cocaine on the weekends. Violence wasn't their problem—their handguns were registered. They weren't profiteers like the traffickers in munitions, flight capital and human beings. They were journalists, bankers and lawyers.

And so to set themselves apart they congregated here, in this establishment where every detail said "I'm not vulgar, I'm not plastic, I'm not like the rest of Miami"—and, in truth, they were right. A whole stratum of America, both white and black, would have found the Place St. Michel very strange. They would have wondered why there were ceiling fans instead of air conditioners, and old-fashioned furniture instead of the consoles and couches you see advertised on TV. They would have noticed, with disfavor, the absence of a parking lot and the lack of a swimming pool.

What perhaps most of all they would have disliked about the place was that, unlike the Hyatts and Holiday Inns, it was not new. Indeed, in a city where "newer" and "better" were synonyms, this place flaunted its antiquity—even though, by anything except Miami standards, it was not old at all.

That was both the problem with this place and the secret of success. Like George Merrick's Venetian Pool, Stuart Bornstein's hotel did not look the way most people in Miami expected things to look.

Whenever I went swimming there, Venetian Pool was never crowded. People in Miami spent thousands to join sports clubs, tens of thousands more to install rectangles full of chlorinated water in their backyards. But at Venetian Pool the swimmers mostly were visiting foreigners. It was as though, for real Miamians, Merrick's compulsion to beautify was only a distraction from the real business at hand.

To get from one place to another in Miami, after all, you didn't need curving tree-lined streets, you needed nine-lane freeways. And if you wanted exercise, the place to get that was in a real swimming pool—with the lanes marked, for swimming laps, just the way the traffic lanes were marked on I-95. Occasionally some-one who lived in Miami would point out Venetian Pool as a kind of archaeological monument—as though they were Roman and it was the Baths of Caracalla. But I never met anyone who actually went swimming there.

Even in Miami, of course, there is what sociologists call a direct correlation between status and the shape and age of the objects used to establish status. As I consumed my expensive little French dinner, I wondered if my fellow patrons here at the Place St. Michel in Coral Gables realized they were just like the blacks of Opa-locka. True, the details varied. If your fantasy, in this instant raw city, was that you weren't an uprooted newcomer like everyone else, but a person of cosmopolitan refinement, you sought out Merrick's sixty-year-old enclave of aristocratic antiquity the way people in Paris converge on the Île St.-Louis. And if your fantasy was that you, in spite of your skin color, were just as American as anyone else, you bought a lot by that drainage ditch in Opa-locka; you built a house with a rectilinear picture window in the living room, a rectilinear air conditioner in the bedroom and a rectilinear refrigerator in the kitchen. But running through everything in both places was the belief that, in Miami, you didn't have to be what you were.

Upstairs, the Cuban maid had turned down the bed and placed a chocolate truffle on the pillow. The soap in the bathroom was Gilchrist & Soames English Rosemary Herb Soap. The new plumbing fixtures were Empire-style and gold-plated.

In a similar hotel in Paris, the soap would have been Common Market Camay, the faucets brass, and so this world Mr. Merrick had created, and one corner of which Mr. Bornstein had embellished, turned out to be part of the real Miami after all.

Even here in Coral Gables, in spite of both their best efforts, things could not help being *de trop.* Here—as much as in Opa-locka —the unquenchable excess of Miami, as always, crept into things, no matter how "authentic" and "tasteful" people tried to be. The bedside radio was tuned to the classical music station, and as I turned it on I remembered that, after all, the Place St. Michel wasn't really a French hotel, any more than Opa-locka was a tale from the Arabian Nights.

It was the Miami fantasy of a French hotel. Was that, I wondered, why—like so many other things here—this place was so appealing?

Precisely because people here were always trying to fulfill some idea of places they'd never seen, of people they'd never been, you were always encountering strange new worlds you'd never find anywhere else, even if you traveled all the way to France or Arabia.

The voice on the radio announced a Mozart concerto, and it seemed even the announcer proved a rule as old as Osceola: whatever you were before you got to Florida, and whatever you intended to be once you got there, you wound up becoming something neither you nor anyone else could predict.

By then, I knew this voice on the classical music station very well. She announced Mendelssohn quartets while I fought the traffic on I-95; she introduced Rossini overtures while I shaved in the morning; she played Brahms as I fell asleep at night.

This woman—or to put it more correctly, this woman's voice—was like the English soap in my "French" bathroom and the Arab minarets on the "Persian" City Hall in Opa-locka. Just as you needed gold faucets if you wanted to create a chic little Parisian hotel in the heart of Coral Gables, so if you wanted to broadcast classical music in Miami, you needed someone with an aristocratic English accent to announce it.

It struck me the first time I heard this woman's voice. That cultured "English" accent wasn't English at all. Instead, as I listened to her announce Schubert and Chopin in this chaotic, sweaty metropolis, I could hear echoes of some other sprawling, disorderly tropical cities I'd known.

The radio station confirmed it, when I called. She was a real Indian, from India, not some Seminole, of course.

One reason people like Merrick and Curtiss left such different and enduring marks on Miami was that Coral Gables and Opa-locka, like Hialeah and Miami Beach, weren't mere real estate developments. They were "cities"—at least in the eyes of Florida state law. Flagler and Tuttle had pioneered the practice of incorporating parcels of near-vacant real estate as full-fledged municipalities. During the boom of the 1920s, as the great real estate bubble inflated, Dade County was Balkanized into dozens of "cities." In many cases they weren't much more than a real estate sales office slapped down in a swamp.

What did it matter that, when it was incorporated in 1915, the city of Miami Beach had a grand total of thirty-three voters? Or that as late as 1960, the "cities" of Medley, Pennsuco, Indian Creek and Hialeah Gardens had a combined total population of exactly 461? Until 1949, under Florida law, if any group of twenty-five persons "met and agreed to form a municipality, they could select a corporate name, choose their officials, and possess those powers granted by the general laws of Florida to municipal corporations."

In consequence, the general avarice, and occasional beneficence, of each individual real estate magnate acquired first the power of law, then the force of history. If you liked trees, like Merrick, you could enact ordinances making everyone plant trees. But if, like most developers, your favorite greenery was hundred-dollar bills, you could strip-zone your suburbs, the way up in central Florida they strip-mine phosphate. Whatever the case, generations after you'd made your money and gone, the "laws" you and your hand-picked city government had laid down continued to shape the "city" you'd established.

In this PR-oriented society, one of the most important powers these municipal corporations possessed was the power "to select a corporate name." The reason was that in the race to attract gullible buyers, the trick was to conjure up a rendezvous of tropical magic, where dulcet ocean waters lapped against palm-fringed beaches, and elegant sophisticates played in an American Garden of Eden where hurricanes and frosts were unknown, and the mosquito never stung.

But how to do that, when all most people really had to sell was "land by the gallon"? Fortunately enough for such developers, Florida had no truth-in-packaging law when it came to "cities." By the 1920s the myth and magic the promoters were selling was summed up by one word. Scores of wide places in the road were racing to cash in on Miami's chic and cachet.

So just as Ocean Beach had become Miami Beach, soon other

Dade County hamlets were renaming themselves West Miami, North Miami, Miami Shores and Miami Springs. Who cared that the chief attractions of little Larkins—named for the local grocery store owner—consisted of a tomato packing plant and an abandoned limestone quarry? The very day after the unfortunate Mr. Larkins died, the locals hastened to rename their metropolis South Miami—so they, too, could cash in on the "Miami" real estate craze.

Today the map of south Florida is still a Baedeker of illusion. Places like Miramar, Margate and Royal Palm Beach are miles from the ocean. Belle Glade, on the swampy shores of Lake Okeechobee, has the lowest incomes in south Florida and the highest incidence of AIDS in the United States. Sweetwater is one of those brackish exurbs where the tap water tastes of chlorine.

There is, needless to say, no coral in Coral Gables.

These snake-oil place-names parted many a fool from his money back then. Even today they befuddle the visiting motorist. Surely North Miami Beach must be that town just north of Miami Beach? No, that's Bal Harbour, spelled with a *u* to imply—falsely, of course—an atmosphere of British-style upper-crust gentility. North Miami Beach is way over on the mainland and was originally called Fulford; it has no beaches at all. But that didn't keep Fulford's founding fathers from appreciating that mail-order real estate sold faster when the chumps up North imagined they could become Harvey Firestone's next-door neighbors for ten dollars down.

The proliferation of such "cities" from the beginning frustrated efforts to develop coherent policies and a rational administration to govern "Greater" Miami's growth into a major city.

They conferred virtual sovereignty on the city's shoddiest impulses, and they fostered a system of American apartheid—along class as well as color lines—which, in spite of attempts to establish effective metropolitan government, flourishes to this day.

Florida's mom-and-pop municipal incorporation laws nonetheless did produce one result of future utility. Today the tidy street plans of downtown Miami tell us as much about Julia Tuttle as the undulating avenues of Coral Gables tell us about George Merrick. The dehumanization of Miami Beach judges Carl Fisher's legacy as dispassionately as the tract housing of Kendall in due course will pass judgment on the purveyors of today's "dream houses." Of course the tenements of Liberty City and South Beach bear witness to the perennial American impulse to treat whole categories of people as expendable commodities. But the armed guards at the gates of Indian Creek Village—a town from which all uninvited outsiders, whatever their race, are banned—also deliver a verdict on the continuing segregation of our society, even though the guard may be black and those he turns away are white.

As for Glenn Curtiss, Opa-locka's motto might be that double-edged sword of a Latin epitaph, which always reveals so much because it cuts so deep: *Si monumentum requiris, circumspice.*

If you seek a monument, look around you.

Even in Curtiss's day, Miami was a mirror. You gazed into it looking for escape, paradise, for the New World.

And Miami winked back.

Then, with a grin or grimace, it reflected you, your times, your follies—your inadvertent nobilities—in that same exact measure a Miami Beach matron's facelift reveals her age.

10

The City of Tomorrow

In the Jazz Age America went Miami-mad.

Lovers spooned on darkened verandas while Victrolas played "Moon Over Miami." They kissed in darkened nickelodeons while Ramon Novarro found romance against a Miami backdrop. And, in an unstoppable torrent, they surged south to act out the Miami romance for themselves.

Sun was in. Sand and heat were chic. What only recently people of cultivation and taste had considered a dreadful, insect-infested swamp, unappealing and unfashionable as the Dakota prairies, now seemed an exciting, alluring place not just to visit in the winter, but to live year-round.

In 1900, Florida's entire population had been less than 530,000. Between 1920 and 1930, it would soar by nearly another 530,000. Between 1920 and 1925, a million and a half tourists, more than the state's entire population, surged into Florida every year. So many stayed that, during that same period, Florida's population increased four times faster than that of any other state. At the peak of the boom, in 1925, more than two and a half million outsiders inundated Florida, and most of them headed straight for Miami.

Did the out-of-towners want Moorish skyscrapers? In one year alone, a local firm designed three replicas of Seville's Giralda

Tower—the Miami-Biltmore Hotel, the *Miami News* tower, and the Roney Plaza in Miami Beach—and every one of them was built.

As the money pelted down, even the naysayers got rich. By 1925 the *Herald* led the entire nation in newspaper advertising and was carrying a larger volume of advertising "than any paper anywhere had ever before carried." Its rival, the *News,* celebrated the city's twenty-ninth anniversary by publishing a commemorative "issue of 504 pages, the largest in newspaper history."

Individual promoters were spending millions on advertising—George Merrick alone was spending $3 million a year to publicize Coral Gables—and never had it paid more to advertise. By 1925 hysterical buyers were offering $6 million for downtown office buildings that had cost $350,000 six years earlier—and the owners were holding out for more. Undeveloped pine barrens eight miles out of town were selling for $25,000 an acre, and downtown building sites were going for $20,000 for a foot of frontage. In 1925 more than $100 million was spent on construction in Miami alone. So great was the demand for building materials that freight cars carrying steel beams were backed up into the Carolinas, and ships carrying cement had to wait weeks before their cargoes could be unloaded.

Miami had surpassed the wildest dreams of Tuttle and Flagler in less than thirty years; in less than fifteen it had outstripped the most extravagant expectations of Collins and Fisher. What explained America's Miami-madness?

Between 1896 and 1926, the definition of the American Dream underwent a profound revision.

This was the change that took America from corsets to short skirts, from waltzes to Charlestons, from Henry James to F. Scott Fitzgerald, from tea dances to speakeasies—from telegrams and railway Pullmans and nights at the opera to telephones, airplanes and movie matinees.

Between 1912 and 1922, America's bedroom mores and business ethics, its national temperament and its psychic fashions, all changed more than they had since the American Revolution—more than they have in all the decades since. Every national statistic, from sales of common stocks to sales of condoms, reflected this change. But in terms of what this all meant for Miami, it is easiest to sum up what had happened simply by imagining two pretty girls strolling along two different beaches more than twelve hundred miles, but less than five years, apart.

The first young woman of fashion is walking on Bailey's Beach in Newport, Rhode Island. It is, let us say, a sunny afternoon in late August 1916. She carries a parasol to protect her ivory complexion from the contagion of the sun. Though the sun is hot and the cool water inviting, she will not go swimming: she wears, besides a bonnet over her long hair, a blouse, lace-up shoes, silk stockings and a full-length petticoat and skirt. By today's standards, this debutante is plump. But by the standards of her own time, she is as delectable as an overripe peach. Let us give her the thrill of an unexpected flirtation. A handsome young man in a seersucker suit approaches her and tips his straw boater. Even this is a seductive impertinence: they have not been formally introduced.

But let us further imagine that, daringly flouting convention, she gives him leave to call on her nonetheless. A few afternoons later, under the watchful eye of an elderly chaperon, the two take tea together. Perhaps, as the scones are being passed, the maiden aunt or widowed cousin notes an absence of marmalade and leaves the room for a moment.

In a burst of romantic impulsiveness that leaves them both breathless, he grasps her hand and kisses her full on the mouth.

The second girl might be the first girl's younger sister; it might be the same girl, though you'd have to look closely to tell. It is four and a half years later—the spring of 1921—and this young woman of fashion is strolling on Miami Beach. She is the same height, but fifteen pounds slimmer than the Newport girl. Her hair is bobbed short. Her skin is suntanned; her one-piece bathing suit reveals most what it conceals.

This time her young admirer is sitting on a beach blanket. He wears only a bathing suit (though men's bathing suits still have tops). He smiles; she smiles. He offers her an iced martini from his thermos. She accepts.

That evening they dance to jazz music in a speakeasy; that night they make love in the backseat of his car.

Back in the 1890s, Americans hadn't cared much about Florida until first Flagler and Plant, then Teddy Roosevelt and the yellow press, had sold them on the idea that Florida was the ideal stepping-stone to perpetual youth—as well as to conferring white Anglo-Saxon freedom on the dusky Latin heathens.

By the twenties America's imagination of itself had undergone another of those historical sea changes that punctuate our entire national experience. For neither the first nor last time, in the years following World War I, Americans were tired of making the world safe for democracy. The energy that had turned New York and Philadelphia and Chicago and St. Louis into world-class cities had run its course. Miami was now the place to scratch, to relieve America's restless itch to conjure up New Worlds out of nothing.

People wanted to make money; they wanted to have fun. Most of all Miami catered to the mania for the new.

Like some other national beliefs, this conviction that Miami was the necessary metropolis of tomorrow existed independent of the facts, if not in downright defiance of reality. In this case the reality was that Miami, for more than three hundred years, had remained a stagnant backwater for some very valid reasons.

Climate was first and foremost why so many people had avoided Miami for so long. Though even now it's still tantamount to treason to say so, Miami's climate can be, and frequently is, dreadful. It is a curiosity that, in a state so fond of superlatives, the chambers of commerce never make the point that Florida indisputably is the insect capital of the United States. In less naturally blessed states, the nature lover must mount an expedition to field, forest or sea-shore to contemplate such marvels of nature firsthand. But only move to Florida, and this inconvenience becomes a thing of the past.

There even the invalid—incapable of stirring from the Barcalounger in front of the TV set—is not denied the privilege of communion with the wonders of nature. Sand flies, deerflies, dog flies, yellow flies and red bugs all show a happy disdain for screening, glass and the other artificial barriers normally isolating man from his natural environment. The friendly termite shows a particular affinity for the human race and colonizes many a Florida home.

In such a paradise, scampering lizards, slithering snakes, gaily colored giant spiders procreate with abandon, though evidently in vain: blessedly free from any threat of extinction, by either these or human predators, is that most abundant of all Florida's natural marvels, the mosquito. Prior to the great PR campaigns of the twenties, in fact, Miami and mosquito meant the same thing.

"I passed some nights and days without being able to sleep for an hour," wrote Brother Francisco Villareal in 1568 of his sojourn in the Indian settlement of Tequesta, future site of Julia Tuttle's townsite and Henry Flagler's hotel. The friar's complaint about "the three or more months of mosquitoes we have endured" was the first known historical reference to Miami.

"Of all the places in the world for mosquitoes, Key Biscayne is entitled to the preference, saying nothing of sand flies. Their everlasting hum never ceases," observed Dr. Benjamin Strobel, a visitor of the late 1820s. "Excursion trains brought in a large number of people . . . who, on arrival, were attacked by the mosquitoes," reported Isidor Duncan, one of the first three Jews to settle in Flagler's new Miami. "These poor victims begged the railway officials to take them back to civilization."

"We are also tormented by a vicious breed of giant horse flies," he added. To discourage the mosquitoes (to eliminate them was impossible), early settlers kept "punk piles burning—little saucers of mosquito powder which sent up smoke and odor repulsive to the mosquitoes . . . underneath the dining table, the bed, and just outside the front and back doors." "We put newspapers under our clothes," Dorothy Dean Davidson, whose family had arrived in Miami in 1904, later told Arva Moore Parks.

In 1962 Lou and Nick Nicolaides moved to Miami—and inadvertently became, respectively, the nine-hundred-thousand-nine-hundred-ninety-ninth and one millionth inhabitants of Dade County. The Chamber of Commerce, never slack to publicize such momentous occasions, showered the lucky couple with five thousand dollars in prizes; the Department of Motor Vehicles gave them a special license plate—"Mr. and Mrs. 1,000,000." Three months later Mr. and Mrs. Million got into their car, drove to Arizona and never came back.

"Mosquitoes eat you alive in Miami," Lou Nicolaides said.

Long after Miami became a big city—even after Florida's rise to Sun Belt preeminence had begun—mosquitoes weren't the only species to contest man's sovereignty over land and home. One of my own earliest memories is of my mother shooting a sixteen-foot alligator between the eyes when it invaded her riverside Florida retreat. Another time she had to hack off the head of a five-foot black rat snake with a hoe when this serpent decided to play with my infant brother in his sandbox.

In those innocent days, people still believed in better living through chemicals, and the sight of low-flying airplanes bombarding us with DDT was a frequent, and welcome, sight. One winter my brother found himself covered with tropical ringworms. They formed large red circles and burrowed beneath his skin. He had to be flown north to a clinic in Boston, where each and every one of these creatures was burned away with dry ice.

One sweaty evening in 1953, while phalanxes of flying insects assaulted the screening of our living room and Bing Crosby sang "White Christmas" on the radio, I read in my geography book that the industrial and cultural supremacy of the white nations derived from their bracing temperate climate. The brown and black nations, this textbook approved for primary instruction by the Florida Department of Education elucidated, were doomed to lethargy, poverty, dictatorship and effeminacy because tropical heat and humidity stifled initiative and rotted the brain.

That Dixiecrat hokum contained a kernel of truth. Sultry, swampy places like Miami were odd sites indeed to build big cities, by past historical standards. Even today Miami's intemperate climate helps explain its tempestuous personality, for in Miami the social, economic and political rhythms of life often are more redolent of the Orinoco than they are of the Hudson.

If Chicago has only two seasons, winter and August, Miami also has only two—summer and January, though in this case January often begins in December and sometimes doesn't end until March.

In January in Miami, I've shivered under three blankets while chill winds rattled the palm trees outside my window at the Grove Isle Club like matchsticks. Sailing off south Florida in February, I've found long johns, two pairs of heavy woolen socks and a ski sweater under a hooded, down jacket weren't enough to avoid being chilled to the bone. Every winter off Miami Beach the Gulf Stream kicks up like a cold caldron and freezing whitecaps whip across Biscayne Bay; anyone foolish enough to dive into an unheated swimming pool risks pneumonia.

More than fifty years later, Marjory Stoneman Douglas still shivered when she remembered her first winter in Miami. The winter of 1916, she wrote in 1967, was

> surprisingly chill and rainy, with pools of white water standing in the white rock streets. Bay water was seething pewter color in an edged northeast wind. The sun, covered with milky-white clouds, left the landscape without brightness or color, the leaves without glitter, the city dull and shabby. The people, huddled in all the warm clothing they had, sweaters over cotton dresses, inadequate coats, were not warmed. The thin board houses had no heat. In empty corner lots of colored town, men without work huddled over fires.

The truth is that all Miamians remember their first winter there as "surprisingly chill and rainy." Subsequent winters don't become any warmer. It's only that even when the PR fails to convince outsiders, it successfully indoctrinates the locals. After all, if Miami really isn't paradise, what was the point of leaving Indianapolis or Cleveland?

Miami's peculiar climate—unpredictably chilly precisely when Americans farther north want reliable heat, and hot as Hades when temperatures in the rest of the country are more or less tolerable —explains why, prior to the twenties, the notion that Miami was a natural paradise never gained much ground.

People had even more reason to avoid south Florida. As a consequence of its climate, the place was positively dangerous to health. Modern public health measures, of course, would do away with active menaces like yellow fever, typhus, malaria and, later, polio, which thrived in south Florida's countless ponds and canals. But how to convince the prospective real estate buyer that living in Florida was not merely safe, but positively beneficial?

Way back in 1821, a St. Augustine publicist invented the first, and still most durable, of all Florida's PR campaigns. He proposed that Florida make itself "the retreat of the opulent, the gay, and the fashionable," by inducing northern doctors to recommend winter in Florida as a panacea to their patients.

The subsequent transformation of dozens of Florida springs and ponds into "fountains of youth" would eventually prove more valuable for its long-lasting subliminal message than for the tourist dollars such attractions produced at the time. The historical small print might reveal that most of Ponce de Leon's expedition had been wiped out by infection and fever. But in millions of Americans' minds, perpetual youth and Florida henceforth were synonymous.

By the turn of the century, a whole army of writers was churning out paeans to Florida's healthfulness, and not all who sang Florida's praises were hacks. William Cullen Bryant and Harriet Beecher

Stowe were among those who wrote guidebooks to Florida or positive accounts of their travels there. But not all eminent literary visitors could be persuaded to sing Florida's praises—not for love, not even for money. In 1905, eager to finance his return from England to visit his native country after an absence of twenty years, Henry James agreed to write a book about his American travels.

In *The American Scene,* James's visit to Florida resulted in some of the most impenetrable prose The Master ever wrote. But James also had keen insights. He saw two Floridas even back then—the swampy, feudal backwater bypassed even by the Civil War, and the synthetic, high-tech fantasyland that would come to full fruition only eighty years later.

The inept servility of the black retainers James encountered appalled him, but not so much as the white obsession with maintaining racial supremacy. Could it possibly be "that it was for *this* they had fought and fallen" in the Civil War, James wondered, as a black porter dropped his valise in the mud, and he observed white patrons lording it over a bumbling black waiter.

Safe inside Flagler's luxurious hotel compound at Palm Beach, Henry James sensed the same alienation from life one finds today inside the guarded condominium compounds of Miami and Fort Lauderdale. James found the vacuous bonhomie of the adult guests at the resort "decent, gregarious, and moneyed, but overwhelmingly monotonous and on the whole pretty ugly." But he was troubled even more by the materialistic vacuity of the children he encountered inside this luxurious, artificial and utterly up-to-the-minute pleasure dome.

"As for the younger persons, of whom there were many, as for the young girls in especial," James wrote, "they were as perfectly in their element as goldfish in a crystal jar: a form of exhibition suggesting but one question or mystery. Was it they who had invented it, or had it inscrutably invented *them?*" It is a question one might as well ask in any Coconut Grove discotheque today.

Underlying both the racial obsessions of the Old South and the social obsessions of the *nouveaux riches* from the North, James sensed uncertainty and fragility. The locals might tout the Royal

Poinciana Hotel as the American Versailles. They might treat the "poor little scraps of Florida's antiquity so meagre and vague," in St. Augustine, as though they were the Roman forum. But James's most powerful "impression, in the great empty peninsula, [was] of weakness." Beneath all the boosterism, he found "a void furnished at the most with velvet air."

Florida, he wrote a friend, was

> a fearful fraud—a ton of dreary jungle and swamp and misery of flat forest monotony to an ounce or two of little coast perching-place—a few feet wide between the jungle and the sea. Nine-tenths of this meagre margin are the areas of the hotels—the remaining tenth is the beauties of nature and the little walk of the bamboozled tourist.

All this half a century before the high-rise condominiums of Miami Beach blotted out the sun!

Between 1915 and 1925—in a mere ten years—dredging and hype had transformed Miami Beach from "a 1,600-acre, jungle-matted sand bar three miles out in the Atlantic" into a 2,800-acre "world of moneyed industrialists, boulevardiers, and stars of stage and screen, its atmosphere gay, carefree and expensive."

Will Rogers once said, "Had there been no Carl Fisher, Florida would be known today as the Turpentine State." In *Florida: A Guide to the Southernmost State,* the anonymous writers of the WPA provided a classic description of the city Carl Fisher had created—"a world of speculative make-believe," as J. K. Galbraith later put it, where you could "get rich quickly with a minimum of physical effort" because this was "a world inhabited not by people who have to be persuaded to believe but by people who want an excuse to believe" that they were the pioneers of "a new and remarkably indolent era." The WPA's evocation of Fisher's fantasyland still reads like an opening passage from *Tender Is the Night:*

Northward along the Atlantic, where palatial hotels, apartments, and homes face Loomis Park and the beach, are terraces and swimming pools, bright with sun parasols and cabanas. Back from the beach and Collins Avenue that parallels it is Indian Creek, a placid, sea-walled lagoon winding southwest to the bay. . . . Well-kept golf courses border the waterway, boulevards follow its irregular palm-fringed shores, gleaming yachts and houseboats moor in the sheltered coves, and broad stretches provide a course for speedboat races. On both sides are private piers and landing docks, some trellised with allamanda and bougainvillea, waterway entrances to winter estates of celebrities.

On Lincoln Road, the Fifth Avenue of Miami Beach, the double sidewalks were painted pink, and lined with "theatres and exclusive shops, many of them branches of New York, Paris and London establishments." Strolling down Lincoln Road, one could imagine encountering the last tycoon, or Nicole and Dick Diver—even though many of the people, already beset by too little money and too much booze, were only rhinestone versions of Zelda and Scott.

Blacks, of course, were banned entirely from living or playing in Miami Beach. Jews were confined to the southern tip of the island "with its preponderance of open-front bars, sandwich stands, bingo establishments, kosher restaurants and delicatessen stores." As for Hispanics, they remained nearly as rare as Seminoles, in spite of Miami's infatuation with "Spanish" decor.

Lincoln Road was more than a shopping district. It was a boundary line. South of it were "the greyhound track, the pier, and its burlesque theatre"—along with the kinds of people who belonged in such places. North of it was a blond, blue-eyed, forever youthful and affluent America where "residential sections and beaches are highly restricted," the WPA writers noted.

It wasn't that less "American" Americans had no place in this bright new world. In fact it couldn't have existed without them. Black laborers had dug Fisher's paradise out of the muck and built most of the rest of Miami. And, right from the beginning, Jews had played an essential role in making the schemes of Tuttle and Flagler and Collins and Fisher and all the others a profitable reality. It was just that, here in the Florida sunshine, America at last became as simplified. There was no need to close your eyes to poverty and violence and injustice. The real estate developers did it for you. Here was a vision of a new kind of America where the sun always shone, property values always increased, where the right kind of people always lived on the right side of the tracks.

And what was so wrong with that? Hadn't fantasy, almost over-night, turned Miami into a metropolis of 150,000? Hadn't fantasy, by the end of 1925, put over $1 billion in Miami banks?

Previously Americans had pursued happiness in covered wagons, across prairies, toward homesteads where the corn and wheat waved in the wind—or so, at least, the national mythology in-formed us. Henceforth they would pursue, into the suburbs and Sun Belt, a new kind of happiness that came with the swimming pool, the two-car garage, the air-conditioned "ranch" house with the barbecue out back. Over the next half-century, this redefinition of what constituted happiness would change Florida and the other Sun Belt states unimaginably. America itself would be redefined.

By Christmas 1925 even a blind man could see it, if he just stood at the corner of Flagler Street and First Avenue downtown. The shops were packed with well-dressed, free-spending tourists. The streets were jammed with cars with out-of-state license plates. Everywhere tall, ornate buildings were rising. People had already started comparing the skyline of Miami to the skyline of Manhattan. A mere thirty years had elapsed since 1896, thirty years that had proven, everyone agreed, that Miami was "the most Richly Blessed Community of the most Bountifully Endowed State of the most Highly Enterprising People of the Universe."

By joint proclamation, the mayors of Miami, Miami Beach, Coral Gables and Hialeah decreed a "Season of Fiesta" throughout Dade County to celebrate the advent of 1926. All over what the mayors called "our Broad Boulevards, our Beautiful Plazas and Ballroom

Floors, our Patios, Clubs and Hostelries," there was, as the official edict ordained, "Love, Good Fellowship, Merrymaking and Wholesome Sport."

As 1925 gave way to 1926, Miami was toasted as "The Wonder City," "The Fair White Goddess of Cities," "The Magic City"— even "The City Invincible,"

In the words of the great orator William Jennings Bryan, Miami was "the only place in the world where you can tell a lie at breakfast and it will be true by evening," although, in another panegyric, one local poet did acknowledge in passing Miami's dependence on "Friendly Sun, Gracious Rain and Soothing Tropic Wind."

In the predawn hours of September 18, 1926, the hurricane struck.

The previous evening winds were almost calm—eight miles an hour, the weather bureau reported. The local papers had carried big headlines about the approaching storm, but not even old-timers took the warnings seriously. A hurricane of this predicted magnitude hadn't hit south Florida since 1906 and had never hit Miami since the time it had become a real city.

As the full fury of vengeful nature bore down on them, however, there was another reason 150,000 complacent human beings did nothing. Their city's whole quick rise to magnificence, no one doubted, proved Miami really did exist beyond nature, outside history—that, like America itself, it was a special case.

By 1:50 A.M. that night the winds had accelerated to 57 miles an hour.

By 5:00 A.M. they had accelerated to 115 miles an hour.

A few minutes later, the weather bureau's meteorological instruments were blown away.

By 6:30 A.M., however, the winds were "variable at 10 miles per hour." By 6:45, all was calm again. It was the dawn of a whole new era in Miami.

People surged out onto the streets, causeways and beaches and found that things didn't really look so bad. A lot of trees, houses and boats had been blown around, but the city was still standing. Almost no one had been hurt.

Half an hour later, the eye of the hurricane passed.

The winds, reversing direction, crashed into the city at 138 miles an hour. The Atlantic Ocean burst over Miami Beach; the water level of Biscayne Bay rose twelve feet, twice the height of Miami's mean elevation. "Paradise," as David Nolan later put it, "had turned into a windy, watery, seaweed-drenched hell on earth."

Lured out of their homes and hotels by the false calm, hundreds of people had climbed into their cars and driven out on Venetian Causeway to view the damage at Miami Beach. As the eye of the hurricane passed and the storm began to rage again, "more than 100 people were trapped and drowned on the causeway by rising water."

In Miami Beach the ocean shattered hotels. It swept away apartment buildings; it splintered giant piers into driftwood. As the atmospheric pressure plummeted, some buildings exploded.

Hialeah was ten miles from the Atlantic Ocean, but distance offered no protection. As the hurricane drove inland, Lake Okeechobee burst its levees; fresh Everglades water poured down the Miami Canal, reclaiming the land. The hurricane of 1926 "just about wiped Hialeah off the map," George Keen, whose insurance agency lost nearly half a million dollars in claims, remembered nearly sixty years later. "Real estate stopped immediately. You couldn't give property away."

Arthur Voetglin's Pueblo Feliz was totally destroyed, along with dozens of other boomtowns. "Biscayne Boulevard looked like a yacht basin," so many boats had been swept ashore. Downtown, streets were full of mud and fish; hundreds of houses and cars had been swept into the bay. Hungry, homeless people wandered the streets. So many were destitute that department stores were converted into shelters. Typhus broke out.

As in the future, local boosters made the crisis worse by pretending nothing had happened. The mayor of Miami, who'd been away when the storm struck, returned and pronounced the city's recovery "absolutely amazing." The tourism magnates, faced with catastrophe, came up with a slogan: "Miami by the Sea Is Ready." "The same Florida is still there with its magnificent resources, its wonderful climate, and its geographical position," one official assured the *Wall Street Journal*. Nonetheless even he discerned one dark cloud in paradise—the effect of the hurricane on PR. He offered the opinion that the Red Cross relief effort would "do more damage permanently to Florida than would be offset by the funds received." Relief workers complained that the Chamber of Commerce hype "practically destroyed" their efforts to help the victims, at a time when nearly twenty thousand people lacked food and shelter.

When the damage was toted up, it was revealed that 242 people had been killed and many more injured. "Between Ft. Lauderdale and Miami, 4,725 homes were destroyed and another 9,100 damaged." Total losses—in terms of both damaged property and lost business opportunities—ran into the hundreds of millions of 1926 dollars.

These losses were inconsequential in comparison to the main casualty the hurricane inflicted. The belief that Miami was the city of the future had been blown away.

In 1925, bank clearings in Miami had soared to more than $1 billion. By the end of 1927, they had dropped to $260 million. Waterlogged lots in the Everglades had sold sight unseen, in the winter of 1925, for tens of thousands of dollars. By the winter of 1927, mansions in George Merrick's Coral Gables—so well built they had survived the hurricane without damage—couldn't be sold for any price.

Before the hurricane Americans had converged on Florida in a frenzy. Now they stayed away in droves: it was as though the hurricane had revealed something about the American Dream Americans did not want to know.

Now Miami truly was the city of tomorrow—plunging into the Great Depression three years before the rest of the country. Whole neighborhoods, full of frenzied buyers in the twenties, would remain tacky ghost towns until the sixties, when the Cubans would begin to settle, and revive, them. Into the forties, fifties, even the sixties, Miami would remain peppered with the skeletons of construction projects begun just before the hurricane hit and abandoned just after it struck. The city's skyline would remain stagnant, virtually unchanging, until the big building boom of the 1970s. The construction of the University of Miami, abandoned following the hurricane, would not be resumed for nearly two decades and would not be completed until after World War II, when the GI Bill starting pumping federal money in Miami's direction.

Carl Fisher had arrived in Florida with $5 million, made $50 million out of Miami Beach before the hurricane—and would die, drunk, and with less than $50,000 to his name, in 1939. As for Glenn Curtiss, the hurricane not only bankrupted Hialeah, it killed Opa-locka before it was born. Curtiss, too, died in debt—his high-flying career, in the end, the classic case of the Miami riches-to-rags syndrome.

High winds couldn't destroy Coral Gables. George Merrick had built too well for that. But even steel beams and concrete foundations couldn't resist the ensuing storm of panic.

After the hurricane Merrick also lost everything. He was reduced to running a fishing camp in the Keys, according to one account, though in 1986, when I met Marjory Stoneman Douglas, she had a different story to tell. "Everyone felt so sorry for George," she recalled, "they got together and arranged for him to become postmaster."

"No malevolent Providence bent upon the teaching of humility," Frederick Lewis Allen observed five years later, "could have struck with a more precise aim."

Providence wasn't finished.

Seven killer frosts were followed by an infestation of fruit flies. A second hurricane hit in September 1928, killing 1,810 persons and injuring 1,849, according to estimates given by the American Red Cross.

In 1935 one of the most violent storms in American history

struck the Florida Keys, just south of Miami, where thousands of Bonus Army veterans had been sent south to work on the highways by the New Deal.

The laborers—paid a dollar a day, and living in makeshift huts and tents—were in the direct path of the two-hundred-mile-an-hour winds. A train headed south, down Flagler's Overseas Railway, to save them. At Islamorada, in the upper Keys,

> a tidal wave overwhelmed the train, leaving only the locomotive on the rails. Wind and waves crushed the frail wooden shacks of the veterans. Many tied themselves to boats at anchor in an effort to survive. Miles of railroad embankment were washed away. Entire towns were obliterated; more than 500 bodies were recovered immediately after the storm subsided, and for months unidentified corpses were found in the mangrove swamps. The number of victims was estimated at 800.

"We did it," Henry Flagler had proclaimed in 1912, when his Overseas Railway reached Key West. "Now I can die in peace." People said that with this last great triumph—of steam and steel over water and wind—Flagler had achieved immortality, but his Overseas Railway had endured only twenty-three years before it was blown away like a Seminole tepee.

Following the 1935 hurricane, what roadbeds survived were sold for three cents on the dollar.

In the nether depths of the Depression—at the precise moment when "real" Americans had decided the place was finished—characters you'd never encounter in *This Side of Paradise* began to revive Miami.

The real estate bubble had burst. But Cuba—with its rum and casinos—remained, blessedly enough, just ninety miles off our shores. And the Bahamas, where Scotch was as plentiful as marijuana later would be, was even closer.

Crackers like Claude Pepper opened up law offices. Blacks, settling in Overtown and Liberty City, opened gas stations. Perhaps because it still had the allure of forbidden fruit, Jews flocked to Miami Beach. They didn't have to worry about anti-Semitism this time. The hurricane, the income tax and the Depression, for the moment at least, had produced a triumph of Christian charity. Episcopalians, Presbyterians and Baptists didn't give a damn any more if buyers' names ended in "stein." You could walk into the real estate office wearing a yarmulke and still buy a showplace on Indian Creek, so long as you carried a suitcase full of money.

For forty years Americans with WASPy names like Flagler, Deering, Fisher and Merrick had covered Miami with "Spanish" skyscrapers, "Italian" villas, "Moorish" country clubs and "Mediterranean" bus depots. Now people who'd been born in the ghettos of Lodz, Minsk and Odessa created an authentically American, an authentically Miamian, architectural style for the first time.

Like Florida, Tropical Deco was a bravura exercise in surfaces. Structurally, the Deco hotels, apartment houses, cinemas and ballrooms that began to cover Miami Beach in the thirties were the same mass-produced, urban industrial buildings these newcomers had left behind in Chicago and the Bronx. Corridors were narrow, ceilings low, rooms cramped, windows small—even when they faced the ocean. But what geegaws and doohickeys the Miami imagination conjured up to transform these banal structures! Pink, flamingo-shaped mailboxes; sunburst screen doors; bathroom windows shaped like portholes; kitchen cabinets etched with picture postcard compositions of the inescapable Florida palm tree. Everywhere friezes, façades, even front doors, were ornamented with "Greek keys, scrolls, floral design and ziggurats." And all were rendered in an eclectic, exuberant "palette . . . stretched to include the greens of our forests, the reds and sands of our deserts, the pastels of tropic sunsets," as Barbara Baer Capitman later put it.

Actually this was an utterly urban architecture, designed for city people who continued to live city lives even when they moved to Paradise, and every detail showed it. Neon lighting no longer was the monopoly of Times Square; now, in Miami Beach, it entered the preserve of domestic architecture. At night the apartment houses and hotels of the Miami Beach Deco district flickered like an amusement park, which was only appropriate. The Florida architecture of men like Flagler, Plant and Deering had been inspired by *Debrett's Peerage* and the Grand Tour. They were archdukes of the railroad, sovereign princes of real estate, and so they built themselves palaces where a Bourbon, or at least a Grimaldi, would have felt at home.

These newcomers, however, had labored in the sweatshops of the Lower East Side, not in the boardrooms of Wall Street. And so they came to Florida with different plans—for a frost-free Coney Island where the Social Security Administration paid everyone the minimum wage.

Tropical Deco revealed that not even the absence of affluence could stifle the Florida aesthetic of excess. No one could afford onyx and ebony anymore. So out of lengths of wrought iron, aluminum tubing and cheap water paint, out of glass blocks, pipe-railings and plastics, local architects now "evolved a style that was vital, inviting, and perfectly suited to the time and place of its being." Miami, as Laura Cerwinske puts it in her book on *Tropical Deco*, at last had an architecture as "flamboyant and self-promoting," a decor as "exaggerated and profuse," as Miami itself.

When Al Capone moved to town, the *Herald*—playing its habitual role of the parson preaching in the bordello—lamented the decline in social standards. The *News* dismissed the city's most eminent new investor as "the notorious beer and brothel baron of Chicago." In courtroom hearings Carl Fisher testified—while *Il Capo* himself glared at him "with all the ferocity of an infuriated beast"—that the gangster's presence hurt real estate sales. Here was Carl Fisher, the fallen hero of the twenties, hurling the twenties' most damning moral indictment—"bad for business"—at Al Capone, the man who would make more money out of the Depression than Fisher ever made out of the boom.

It was a brave but pathetic gesture: the Chicago Mafia was as welcome in Miami in the thirties, in spite of the ritual lamentations of "respectable" Miamians, as the cocaine Mafia would be in the eighties, and for the same reason.

Al Capone was great for business.

In the thirties, as in the eighties, no Miami bank was ever recorded as having turned down suspicious deposits, scrupulous though it might have been to report them to the competent authorities. No Realtor—or car dealer or yacht broker or jeweler or haberdasher—raised moral objections to a 100 percent down payment, paid for goods sight unseen.

Miami has always been capable of a pharisaical niceness when it comes to distinguishing between the fruit and the tree that bore it. "Priests, ministers and civic leaders" might preach hellfire and brimstone in the pulpits and editorial columns, but that didn't stop them from accepting Capone's contributions to local charities. Then as now, American hundred-dollar bills only came in one color. They didn't turn red when their owners had blood on their hands, any more than they turned white when they filled the wallets of the pure in spirit.

Mr. Alphonse Capone—formerly a Chicago "second hand furniture dealer"; now a Miami Beach "antiques dealer"—proclaimed Miami "the Garden of America." He turned himself into the new William Jennings Bryan, using his national reputation to attract like-minded settlers. "I believe many of my friends will also join me," Capone ventured to predict, after settling into his white stucco, green-tile-roofed mansion on Palm Island. Even after he shifted his residence to Alcatraz, an island with an even more stunning view, the racketeer was as good as his word.

Miami was Murder Capital, U.S.A., even before Capone arrived, and this distinction at least had the virtue of proving Miami's future boosters right in one way. Whenever you visit Miami, people always tell you that the homicide rate is going down, and historically speaking, they are absolutely right. In 1926 one out of every 908 residents of Dade County was murdered. In 1986 a mere one out of every 2,600 was. Should this wholesome trend continue, Miami will have one of the lowest murder rates in the nation by the year 2106.

The Mob would dominate Miami Beach for decades; truth to tell, it still can give the *arrivistes* from Colombia and Bolivia a run for their money. Beginning in the late twenties, gentlemen in white ties, black pinstripe suits and cement shoes would join the stone crabs and marlins in enriching the marine life off Miami Beach. Landmark restaurants like The Forge would serve countless platters of linguine to characters with bulges under their left armpits. At the Roney Plaza, and later the Fontainebleau and the Eden Roc, and still later at the Bal Harbour Sheraton, enough hoods would savor the delights of enough molls to keep late-night cable TV going into the twenty-third century.

In the 1980s, when Al Pacino chose to set a remake of *Scarface* there, Miamians were rightly outraged by the results. That simpleminded, foul-mouthed film didn't begin to do justice to the subtlety and finesse with which the Mafia, both American and Latin American, had ingratiated itself into every warp and weave of Miami's great gaudy tapestry.

In 1896 and 1926, Miami had been the city of tomorrow; so it was again by 1936, as Arva Moore Parks relates:

> By the mid-'30s, while the rest of the nation was still suffering in the slough of the Depression, Miami was showing signs of recovery. "If one were to judge Florida by the appearance of Miami," reported a writer for the *Nation,* "one would have to say the Depression is over."

By 1939 even the unemployed members of the Federal Writers' Project found in Miami a city that did not so much hearken back to the boom of the twenties as it foreshadowed the mass affluence of the fifties. They reported:

231

In less than a quarter century, miles of rainbow-hued dwellings, bizarre estates, ornate hotels, and office buildings have grown from mangrove swamp, jungle, coral rock, and sand dunes. Islands dredged from the bay are glorified by exotic plantings, and houses of many types and styles. Great wealth, lavishly spent on these synthetic isles and shores, has gone into the building of a winter playground designed to attract those, pleasure-bent, who follow the sun. To the first-time visitor its shining spires, its tropical foliage, the incredible blue of its water, the cloud formations that tower in the background—all sharply etched under an intense, white sunlight—appear as a motion-picture set.

Even during the Depression thirties, Miami was a city of hyperkinetic contrasts:

Open-front shops sell boxes of fruit, fruit juices, neckties and innumerable souvenirs. Drugstores and department stores present the latest in show-window artistry: bewildering displays of sports equipment, beach togs and accouterments.

Pitchmen spiel endlessly to sell their wares. Astrologers read one's future—and pick winning horses—in the stars, and astronomers with portable telescopes show the wonders of the heavens, sometimes including the Southern Cross, for a dime. Theatre doormen, resplendent as admirals on dress parade, advertise orally the current screen attraction; policemen in sky-blue uniforms with white belts and pith helmets direct traffic. Adult newsboys hawk their papers and racing forms like sideshow barkers, and stroll between cars held up by lights, a vociferous performance that continues far into the night. Pedestrians wear what they please. Sun glasses, eye shades, and lotions advertised to promote a quick tan are among the best sellers, for with the majority of newcomers a sepia complexion is a midwinter achievement.

"Gambling is both legal and illegal," the WPA writers reported —singing the national anthem of a city that would always flourish most in that twilight world where, at the boundary between the legal and illegal, no passports are inspected. "Planes and leisurely sight-seeing blimps are almost constantly overhead. The playboy and plowboy, the dowager in pearls and the sylph in shorts, the banker on vacation and drifter on prowl keep the turnstiles clicking."

Forty years later I'd marvel at the cocaine Lear jets lined up at MIA; I'd find my mind warped, at seven in the morning, by elevators that announced the latest Dow Jones averages as they took you down to breakfast.

Miami never would be, never could be, a St. Pete or Orlando. In the 1930s, for most Americans, it became the place where rum runners shot it out with G-men. (Miami's most notorious smuggler, Big Bill McCoy, was eventually captured, but not before his high-quality booze won him immortality. He was the original supplier of the "real McCoy.") It was the place where crazed gunmen roamed the streets—shooting at President Roosevelt, killing the mayor of Chicago. Miami was no longer Ramon Novarro. It was Edward G. Robinson, making a broken-down songstress sing for a drink, while the hurricane raged outside, in *Key Largo*.

And this notoriety, far from being the problem people have always pretended, was, and remains, part of the secret, possibly *the* secret, of Miami's success. Writing more than fifty years before the premiere of "Miami Vice," Frederick Lewis Allen put his finger on the reason why not even hurricanes and real estate panics could stop Miami.

"A paradoxical, widespread, but only half-acknowledged revolt against the very urbanization and industrialization, the very concentration upon work" that made American affluence possible, underlay the virtually irrational appeal not just of Miami real estate, but

233

of Miami itself. Compliance with the Chamber of Commerce virtues

> might bring the American business man money, but to spend it he longed to escape from them—into the free sunshine of . . . some never-never land which combined American sport and comfort with Latin glamour—a Venice equipped with bathtubs and electric iceboxes, a Seville provided with three eighteen-hole golf courses.

So long as salesmen in Cincinnati skip alimony payments and waitresses in New Hampshire hitchhike south, there will always be a Miami because this still will be a nation with an urge to switch off Ozzie and Harriet—and turn on to Crockett and Tubbs.

By the late thirties, it was as customary as it is now for the old-timers to lament that the city had gone to the dogs. It hadn't. It was only that Miami once again had demonstrated its essential genius, which is not merely to change and grow with the times, but to exploit them.

Charming, resourceful, brazenly unsentimental as a Biscayne Boulevard hooker, Miami always gave the customer what he wanted, even if it seldom gave him an even break. Were tile roofs and stucco roofs now out of fashion? Miami applied its Deco decor as thoughtlessly, as innocently, as some Lauderdale adventuress chooses a new shade of lipstick before heading to the singles bar.

The hurricane of 1926 hadn't destroyed Miami Beach. But the very process Fisher had unleashed on that sandbar guaranteed that his dream of a *Juden-frei* paradise would never come true. For if Carl Fisher could fulfill his fantasies there, so could Al Capone. And if Al Capone could, anyone could. By 1939 Fisher's paradise hadn't been lost. The dream had just been taken over by other kinds of people: Fisher's WASP Republican playground was on the way to becoming one of the first majority-Jewish cities in the United States.

Even after the last "Gentiles Only" signs came down, the Miami

sun continued to work its wonders. Jews, like Cubans later, underwent metamorphoses every bit as zany as Presbyterians ever had:
bleached-blond beehive hairdos and suntanned face-lifts on the
daughters of Orthodox cantors; graduates of yeshivas wearing gold
chains and sports shirts that showed their nipples; synagogues that
doubled as booking centers for nightclub acts.

Starting in the forties and lasting into the sixties, but reaching a
frenzy of tropical excess in the fifties that might have made Henry
Plant gasp with envy, the Catskill Aesthetic, like Art Deco before
it, achieved, in Miami Beach, an architectural apotheosis impossible
in more austere climes.

The Fontainebleau, the Eden Roc, the St. Moritz, the Bel Aire,
the Shorecrest, the Sahara, the Catalina, the Garden of Allah: year
after year they marched north along the beach—gas-guzzling De
Sotos and Edsels of hotels, fated, like every work of man in Florida,
to act out the life cycle of glitz, tawdriness and abandonment—
followed, of course, when prices dropped low enough, by reincar-
nation: new sellers, new buyers, new dreamers starting the cycle all
over again.

The most racist conceit of the old guard had been that these
newcomers weren't "real" Americans. Who could be more American than Roy Cohn and Barbara Walters, growing up together in
Miami Beach?

By 1940, 40 percent of Miami's males had been born in Georgia.
It seemed Miami's fate to become just another Deep South city with
some midwestern affectations, one of those many locations in the
Sunshine State where your white cop and your colored cleaning
lady lived in Florida funky bungalows, where gray-haired grocers
from Indiana and blue-rinse salesladies from Michigan flirted on
park benches—and, on big nights out, sampled the culinary delights
of Morrison's cafeteria.

But, even back then, there were some traces of internationalism.
Every time another government fell in Cuba, more Cubans, as
always, headed north. Almost all of them went to New York or

Tampa. But the planes landed in Miami, and so, inevitably, a few of them got off. By November 1955 there were enough Cubans in Miami to hold a meeting. They rented the old Flagler movie palace.

A twenty-nine-year-old Cuban exile strode out on the stage where, earlier, Ramon Novarro had strutted. "Liberty is not begged, but is won with the blade of a machete," he announced, quoting one of the slogans of Martí's time. Then he asked the audience for money.

"Real" Americans paid no attention. Nor did Miami's tiny Latin community. For decades fiery young men had toured the United States, promising national liberation in return for dollar donations. Only years later did the name, and the young man who bore it, Fidel Castro, seem worth remembering.

There were other omens in those years. "Miami Seen as Possible Dope Capital," one headline suggested as early as 1947. Officials dismissed the possibility.

Some sixty-five years after Miami had been founded—let us take the election, in 1960, of John F. Kennedy as president of the United States as the moment—Miami seemed to have reached retirement age as a subject of any compelling interest. It wasn't that what had happened in Miami was unimportant. To the contrary, what was so important about Miami was also what, by then, made it of no particular interest.

Here, as everywhere else in America, the Alexander Hamiltons in time had lost out to the Thomas Jeffersons, and in the end the Andrew Jacksons won the Democratic primary. Here the great leveling law was proved again: millionaires didn't really become archdukes, even when they built archducal palaces. In a great, albeit negative vindication of American democracy, they went broke. Meanwhile, the funniest foreign people became as American, sometimes a lot more "American," than people whose families had been here three hundred years.

Of all Miami's founders, Julia Tuttle remains the most important and the most enigmatic. What, in heaven's name, in 1891, could have possessed this widowed Cleveland society matron to pack up all her belongings and, on the thirteenth of November that year, float them on a barge across Biscayne Bay, into the mouth of the Miami River?

In all the photographs of Julia Tuttle I've seen, she's dressed like a dowager, in a long black dress, with her dark hair drawn back. There is more softness and more humor in that face, but every time I look at those photographs, I can't help thinking of Gertrude Stein.

Stein once explained why she ran away to Paris, when she described her hometown of Oakland, California. "When you get there, there's no there there," she said.

With Tuttle it was the opposite. Rejecting all that another American city of the second rung could offer, she did not flee to some cultivated, first-class metropolis. She plunged into the wilderness. Yet from the moment Julia Tuttle stepped ashore in Miami, there was a there there. From the beginning Tuttle had a particular, a coherent, vision, and that is what distinguishes her from Flagler, Merrick, Collins, Fisher, Curtiss and all the other founders and developers. For her, Miami was never a grand railroad scheme, never a "Florida-Mediterranean" extravaganza or a "Baghdad of Dade County." She was determined that Miami should be a great new *city*.

After she'd made her deal with Flagler, she sweetened it by giving him even more land. But the new parcels were interspersed, like black spaces on a white checkerboard, with her own holdings. If Henry Flagler wanted to make a profit out of Julia Tuttle's generosity, he'd have to dig the sewers and pave the streets that would service her real estate holdings, too. Flagler didn't hesitate. He did what she wanted him to do—and so, instead of turning into another Palm Beach, Miami turned into the city Julia Tuttle had wanted to build.

I can't answer the question, but I can ask it: Does all that Miami would become have anything to do with the fact that Julia Tuttle was a woman? Women are supposed to be the romantics of the species, but the history of Miami, like most serious anthropological studies, suggests the opposite—that men are the romantics, fighting wars, making grand political pronunciamentos, building garages modeled on the Taj Mahal. Meanwhile women domesticate grains and clean up after the hurricanes. Certainly Miami, for all its pretensions to *macho,* is as feminine in its survival instincts as its founder.

By 1960, historically speaking, Tuttle seemed as much a failure as Carl Fisher or George Merrick. The daughter of a second-rate city, she'd become the mother of a third-rate city.

Actually—like all the others who'd created Miami—she'd been the right person in the right place. Only her timing had been off, by a mere sixty-five years or so.

It would take a guerrilla war, Sun Belt shift and a nuclear confrontation for the world to be ready for Miami. Even so, Julia Tuttle would not have been surprised. "Someday," she'd announced in 1896, "Miami will become the great center of South American trade."

11

The Mouse, the Moon and the Toilet Seat

Miami had never really recovered from the hurricane of 1926, and by the early sixties, to judge from the Havana datelines, it once again was in danger of being shattered by shock waves from the south.

But the city had always risen and fallen on a double tide. Miami would thrive on the tempests stirred up by the Bay of Pigs invasion and the Cuban missile crisis. But revolutionary changes farther north would confront it with perils far graver than the Cuban revolution.

What made Miami's problems all the more surprising was that, following World War II, the predictions of the boom years had all come true. The palm tree and the automobile had proven to possess truly astonishing powers of mutual attraction. By the millions, Americans were jumping into their cars and heading for new lives in the sun.

But Los Angeles, not Miami, was America's new city of the future, California the new national dreamland. Between 1950 and 1960, the increase in Los Angeles' population amounted to more than three times Miami's total population. California attracted more than five million new settlers, more people than the entire state of Florida contained.

"Hollywood" was everywhere. Thanks to network TV, the California life-style was now a permanent guest in everyone's living room. Out west the surf was up; Ventura Highway beckoned—and all America was "California Dreamin'."

In comparison, Biscayne Bay was a boring puddle, the Spanish-revival skyscrapers that so impressed Miami visitors before World War II kitschy and old-fashioned. America was tired of the kind of neat, narrow city streets Flagler's planners had laid out—and of the Deco and Mediterranean bungalows that lined them. It yearned to race tail-finned convertibles down Santa Monica freeway. It dreamed of diving into kidney-shaped swimming pools and partying with movie stars in Beverly Hills.

What Miami had lost in 1926—what it would not really regain until "Miami Vice"—was the capacity to excite America, nor was that the only problem. At the beginning of the 1959 tourist season, it rained for sixty days straight. As houses sank, streets flooded and sewers overflowed, a series of lurid real estate scandals erupted. That—combined with the usual Florida tendency to overbuild, oversell and overcharge—was sufficient to sound "the funeral dirge for the postwar boom." Once Miami had seemed to incarnate America's future; now, so far as the rest of the country was concerned, it was a dowdy refuge of retirees and other people of the past. The recent arrival of the Cubans, following Castro's victory over Batista at the beginning of 1959, only reinforced the belief that Miami was a place "real" Americans had left far behind.

Florida was about to be conquered again. As early as 1958 the advance guard, including both spies and secret agents, had begun its infiltration. The new *conquistador* himself had slipped into Florida and, disguised as a vacationing businessman, conducted reconnaissance of the terrain.

In 1967 the surprise attack, years in the planning, was launched. As in the past, the ostensible government of Florida opted for the traditional policy of instant and total capitulation: the legislature in Tallahassee quickly rendered unto Florida's newest Caesar nothing less than virtual sovereignty over a veritable empire—a 27,400-acre tract of land, twice the size of Manhattan, dominating the epicenter of the state. On the official documents, this new Florida kingdom was called the Reedy Creek Improvement District. Every household in America soon knew it by another name: Walt Disney World. Not since Carl Fisher had turned Ocean Beach into Miami Beach had a real estate scheme more radically redefined Florida and its relationship to the rest of the nation.

At a stroke Florida was transformed from a place with connotations variously shabby or sinister into a wholesome family vacationland. But, as with the old Fountains of Youth, Disney World's most important impact was subliminal. By creating Disney World, Disney conferred California's compelling allure on Florida; he made it the other great locus of the middle-American imagination in the Television Age.

Not since the United States "purchased" Florida from Spain had there been a more lucrative Florida real estate deal. By keeping both his plans and his own identity a secret, Disney had paid all of $6 million for his magic kingdom—which today has a market value, conservatively estimated, of at least $6 billion.

The Disney conquest was the most important economic, social, cultural and psychological event in the history of Florida since the Flagler conquest. Anyone could build an amusement park—though it must be emphasized that Disney's gargantuan playground bore about the same relation to a traditional Florida "tourist attraction" as Plant's Tampa Bay Hotel had to one of those old St. Augustine boardinghouses. True, you could say Fantasyland and Adventureland were descendants of the old alligator farms—but that was like saying a Cape Canaveral moon shot was just another firecracker. More than a hundred times bigger than the original Disneyland in California, Disney World gave a whole new meaning to the old Florida obsession with excess.

Disney's accomplishment went far beyond fulfilling the edifice complex Florida excites in all its conquerors. No less than Flagler, he wound up dictating a whole new structure of development—and imposing a whole new architecture of profit—on Florida.

Previously the cutting edge of change had sliced down the coasts, leaving the hinterland largely untouched. As early as the twenties, virtually the entire Atlantic coast between Jacksonville and Miami was lined with towns, hotels, developments and resorts. But into the sixties, real wilderness began only ten or fifteen miles inland from Palm Beach and Miami. Proximity to established towns and railroads and, most important of all, waterfront location and (at least relative) winter warmth had dictated the value of Florida real estate. The inland areas of central Florida, prone to frost and far from the ocean, might as well have been in Iowa, so far as entrepreneurs like Flagler and Fisher were concerned.

It was Disney's genius to grasp that the old factors no longer mattered in the new age of interstate freeways and year-round family tourism. Perhaps his most revolutionary insight was that Florida's greatest supposed asset—its climate—was also its greatest liability, and that Florida would not enjoy permanent year-round growth until its prosperity was based on something more than winter sunshine. Though people in Florida had always refused to admit it, Disney was right.

One good freeze was always enough to ruin Florida's tourist industry, not just its citrus and tomato crops. And even if temperatures never dropped below eighty between December and March, that still left the other eight months of the year. It was a simple law of mathematics. A Florida enterprise which could attract customers year-round would be immensely more lucrative than one which had to pack its profits into the winter months.

But how to overturn the seasonal dictates of life in Florida and create a year-round empire? Disney's experience in seasonless southern California gave him an insight into human nature that eastern developers—whose whole calculus was based on the antithesis of winter and summer—had failed to grasp: people don't care all that much whether it's hot or cold when they visit an amusement park.

It didn't even matter all that much if it rained, so long as there was plenty to do indoors—as there always would be in Disney's climate-controlled paradise.

Disney's choice of location also bespoke strategic genius. Before Disney World was built, there was what amounted to a geopolitical power vacuum in the middle of Florida. Jacksonville, Tallahassee and Pensacola hugged the northern fringes of the state; Palm Beach, Miami and Key West were wedged into the southern extremity of the peninsula. With the partial exception of the Tampa Bay area, the main commercial, political and tourist centers could not have been located farther from Florida's geographical center.

More experienced Florida entrepreneurs were astonished when Disney said he actually *preferred* to locate his kingdom inland—and not just because of lower real estate prices or because his transistorized, plastic paradise was safer from salt air corrosion and hurricanes in the interior. By locating his magic kingdom in what previously was "nowhere," Disney assured that Disney World was on the way to everywhere else. Disney defied every known Florida law of moneymaking: he located his kingdom in a landlocked tract in the interior of the peninsula, not only far from both the Atlantic and Gulf coasts, but well north of the usual winter frost lines as well.

When people pointed out that tourists didn't drive all the way from Indiana to look at dry land, Disney replied, "We'll create our own water." Coming from anyone else, this might have amounted to folly, not just arrogance; for Disney it was just a statement of fact. Not merely would Disney World offer its tens of millions of visitors plastic jungles, synthetic deserts and an artificial Grand Canyon. In due course a "six-million-gallon man-made ocean which duplicates the environment of a Caribbean coral reef" would be constructed, too. "Only the dropping of an atom bomb could have wrought greater, more immediate changes in Central Florida," it was later observed.

Disney had not merely made all the old laws of Florida obsolete; he had redefined the entire state.

Just three years after Disney chose Florida as the site of his magic kingdom, the government of the United States of America selected

Florida as the site for the actualization of a no less audacious fantasy. At the end of May 1961, only a month after the disastrous Bay of Pigs invasion, President John F. Kennedy summoned a special joint session of Congress.

"I believe this nation should commit itself to achieving the goal, before the decade is out, of landing a man on the moon and returning him safely to earth," the president announced. He added, "No single space project in this period will be more impressive to mankind, or more important for the long-range exploration of space; and none will be so difficult or expensive to accomplish."

Congress, the nation and the world once again thrilled to the young president's vision and audacity. But so far as Florida was concerned, the operative word was "expensive." As David Nolan points out, just one structure at Cape Canaveral, the Vehicle Assembly Building, would "cost more than Henry Flagler's entire investment in Florida." Over the next twenty-five years, the space program would pump more money into Florida than twenty-five Spanish-American Wars.

With the space shots from Cape Kennedy, Florida excited the world's imagination. But Disney World excited Florida's imagination more than the space program did.

One reason was that, in Florida, science fiction always had been the handmaiden of reality. As early as 1865, in a fantasy entitled *De la terre à la lune,* Jules Verne had promised that man would take off from Florida when he visited the moon.

What thrilled Floridians about Disney World was that it proved Florida could give California a run for its money, too.

Space shots may exalt the spirit and advance the cause of science, but they are poor ways to get rich quick. Fisher and Flagler had once provided the models. Now, as every used-car dealer and fast-food franchiser rushed to turn his business into a year-round theme park, it was Mickey Mouse.

Florida at last was really growing. Between 1950 and 1970, it went from being the twentieth to the ninth most populous state in the Union, outstripping such well-established population centers as Massachusetts and New Jersey. That was only the beginning. By 1987 it had surpassed Ohio, Michigan, Illinois and Pennsylvania to become the fourth most populous state. By 1990 the Census Bureau predicted, Florida would overtake even Texas, to become the most populous state in the Union after California and New York.

More than that, this population boom was manifesting itself in the strangest places. The previously bypassed counties of central Florida were growing four times faster than the state as a whole—twenty times the national average. What made this spectacle all the more intriguing was that Florida, not just Disney, was breaking all the rules. The rivals Florida was overtaking had become rich and populous for reasons an economist or historian could explain. They had oil or coal and iron ore—the bases of industries. They had history and culture, accumulated wealth and educational institutions—and so became centers of research, finance, commerce and technology.

Even today Florida doesn't have a single nationally dominant industry—not even a service-sector industry like health care or a high-tech industry like computers. It has no natural resources in the conventional sense of the word: even its electricity has to be generated farther north and then transmitted south, making the state vulnerable to blackouts. Florida has no Silicon Valley, no eminent universities, almost no corporate headquarters of the Fortune 500.

Underlying Florida's stupendous new popularity was a constant old as Florida itself. More than anything else, Florida still excited dreams of escape—though the definition of escape, like the definition of the American Dream, had by then undergone a startling and illuminating revision. Even more than winter warmth and sunshine, Florida now promised year-round escape from all the nagging dilemmas that, beginning in the sixties, afflicted the nation. The squeaky-new stucco and cinder-block subdivisions that sprawled south from Gainesville through Orlando and Lakeland to Sarasota and Fort Myers might be architecturally banal. Cultural amenities might be rare as mountain ranges in this horizonless new world of polyester and plastic.

But here, in contrast to Miami or the northern cities, blacks, foreigners and the poor were out of place. Street crime was almost unheard of in these new communities where no one walked. So were mass demonstrations, "subversive" ideas and "alternative" life-styles. This new, prepackaged Florida was as remote from the crazy, exciting, truly adventurous heterodoxy of Miami as it was from all the conflicts and complexities of life up North. The model homes were all basically the same, whether you chose Fort Pierce or Cape Coral for your new Florida home. The menus at Denny's and Roy Rogers never changed, whatever shopping mall you chose for a big night out.

Were you young and single, or married and over fifty? Living on Social Security—or on the profits from that corporation you owned up North? Was home a "ranch" house in Sun City Center, a showplace in Sarasota or a trailer park in Ocala? Wherever you lived, whatever your age or income, the new Florida offered an amenity older, colder, more complicated places could not: everyone around you thought and acted—because they were—just like you.

In an age of total change, Florida—the fastest-changing state in the nation—offered the fulfillment of what, for millions of Americans, had become the ultimate fantasy: life in a world from which uncertainty as well as choice had been banished.

Main Street lived on, immortalized in plastic, in Disney World. Disney's greatest insight, and it amounted to true genius, was that America had reached a stage in its development where it wanted no dangers, no challenges, no unpredictabilities in Adventureland.

So Disney World, as Florida always had, gave America what it wanted: simulated trips to the moon in air-conditioned theaters; landlocked coral reefs where no sharks or barracudas lurked; plastic jungles where orderly groups of explorers passively followed well-marked trails leading to spotless rest rooms; synthetic Jeffersons and Lincolns who, with lifelike gestures and in stereophonic sound, reaffirmed that the secret of America's greatness remained its rugged individualism and willingness to take risks.

At Disney World the guides, ticket-sellers and waitresses were cast like starlets in a TV series. If you had that youthful, healthy, slim, smiling "American" look Darlene and Bobby and all the other Mouseketeers personified, the job was yours. But what if you were old or fat or black or brown—or unshaven, or had a foreign accent, or a big wart on the tip of your nose? The days of "separate but equal" rest rooms and "Gentiles Only" signs were gone. But in the Disney Era, as much as in the Gilded Age, narcissism was the constant.

Like Palm Beach and Miami Beach, Disney World was the prototype of a new way of life. So just as the space shots at Cape Kennedy became mass tourist attractions—the countdowns and blast-offs orchestrated as carefully as any Disney spectacular on TV—even Florida's few industries became variants of Disney World, too. By the early seventies, for example, the Anheuser-Busch brewery in Tampa was drawing more visitors than any Florida beach resort.

It wasn't the beer that made Busch Gardens famous. It was the monorail tours through a plastic Africa—called "The Dark Continent," to the chagrin of local blacks—that made the brewery second only to Disney World as a Florida attraction. Here, without having to sweat or swat insects, one could explore "sanitized versions of Morocco, the Congo and Timbuctu"—and when the rigors of jungle exploration became too arduous, repair to a Foreign Legion outpost offering "an air-conditioned Oktoberfest" year-round.

In more comprehensible times, every coal seam up North had spawned its company town, every steel mill its city. Now Florida was overtaking Pennsylvania and Ohio in Electoral College votes because operating theme parks was more profitable than, say, manufacturing automobiles or television sets. Once, on a road map of Florida, I tried to count all the "attractions" within a three-hour drive of Disney World. I gave up after compiling a list that included, in addition to Busch Gardens and Cape Kennedy:

> Spongerama, U.S.A. of Yesterday, Lion Country Safari, Cypress Kneeland, the Circus Hall of Fame, Circus World, Florida's Big Tree, Gatorland, Alligator Town U.S.A., Alligatorland Safari, African Safari, Masterpiece Gardens, McKee Jungle Gardens, Ravine Gardens, Ve-

netian Gardens, Cypress Gardens, the Rodeo Bowl, the Tangerine Bowl, Blue Springs, Rock Springs, Homosassa Springs, Rainbow Springs, Weeki Wachee Spring, Weekiwa Springs, Ichetucknee Springs, Ponce de Leon Springs, the Museum of Old Dolls and Toys, the Bone Valley Phosphate Museum, the Museum of Sunken Treasure, the Museum of Dishes, Bellm's Cars of Yesterday, Baker's Tropical Aquarium, Don Garlitz' Museum of Drag Racing, the Silver Springs Reptile Institute, the National Police Museum, the Early American Museum, Six Gun Territory, Parrot Village, Marineland of Florida, Citrus Tower, Singing Tower, Happiness Tower, Placid Tower, and the Stars Hall of Fame Wax Museum.

Also on my list were Sea World (located fifty-three miles from the nearest sea); Adventure Island (to be found just inland from The Dark Continent); the Wet and Wild Surf Lagoon (situated in landlocked Orlando); and the Black Hills Passion Play, which is performed in the flatlands of Polk County. Florida, whose highest elevation is a 345-foot hillock on the Alabama border, is also blessed with the Mountain Lake Sanctuary, located on the "summit" of a 290-foot mound. At the Walk of Fame in Winter Park, you can touch a rock Helen Keller touched, and at The Tragedy in U.S. History Museum in St. Augustine you can see Jayne Mansfield's death car.

Though their residents didn't think of it that way, the immense new housing developments sprawling out from Disney World in every direction were theme parks, too. Walls, fences and gates with armed guards kept out those lacking the price of admission. Whole little cities with catchy names were organized around boating, or tennis, or games of golf. It now became possible to live in self-contained—self-centered—new worlds where, within a margin of ten years and $10,000, everyone was the same age, and had the same amount of money, as you.

In this new Florida it might be true, as the critics claimed, that life lost its edges—that the human horizon became featureless as Florida itself. But the bulldozers not only leveled the land; by filling in the swamps, they extended it, and the same was true with the human condition. By flattening the cliffs and ravines of life, life itself could be extended—or so, at least, people liked to believe.

"I'm glad she moved down there," an acquaintance once told me, after visiting his mother in a Florida "retirement community." "It wasn't the cold up North that got her," he said, "it was seeing all the changes around her. They made her realize she was going to die. Now she's the youngest person on her block and loves it, and I bet she makes it to eighty."

Disney, with his unerring sense of what America wanted, had selected for his Florida paradise the one part of Florida where the crashing waves, the shifting sands, the high tides and lashing hurricanes of life could not intrude.

And so just as the racy glamour of Fisher's Miami Beach had once beckoned Americans by the hundreds of thousands, so the synthetic turrets of Disney World now summoned Americans of all ages, by the millions, to a Florida where life, in its every aspect, was like watching TV.

Florida was booming again—but for Miami there was a big difference between this boom and the one in the twenties. The city of tomorrow was being left behind. Even within "Greater" Miami, the laws of Disney now prevailed.

Back in 1950, for example, Fort Lauderdale and Broward County had a population of less than eighty-four thousand. This region was Hicksville, so far as the sophisticates of Biscayne Boulevard and Collins Avenue were concerned.

Suddenly, Fort Lauderdale—not Miami—was "Where the Boys Are." The boys were there because they, like Connie Francis, Annette Funicello and all the other starlets of the Mickey Mouse Club generation, had discovered a new world even more alluring than Disney's—that Adventureland which opens its gates with the advent of puberty.

As tens of thousands of teenagers converged on Fort Lauderdale each April and May, Broward's old WASPy winter colony might have been expected to howl in protest—except that, by the time the kids headed south for the rites of spring, most of the old folks had gone back North. Fort Lauderdale had managed to transform itself into two completely different resorts—a winter haven for the elderly and a spring rendezvous for the young.

This was an epochal development, and not just for the beer and suntan-lotion industries. Fort Lauderdale had learned the Disney lesson; it was one of the first Florida cities to turn itself into a year-round resort.

It couldn't do that by changing the weather, of course. But it could exploit the fact that the weather, in a new age of total mobility and mass affluence, now meant different things to different people. For wealthy, older northerners, Fort Lauderdale still offered what it always had, escape from winter. Aggressively peddling it as a spring vacationland for college students extended the town's seasonal profitability to June. Fort Lauderdale soon was going Miami one better even than that—selling itself as the ideal *summer* resort for families from the Deep South.

It certainly was no hotter in Fort Lauderdale in July and August than it was in Atlanta, Birmingham and the other big inland southern cities. And however hot it did get, Fort Lauderdale, unlike them, had blue water and ocean beaches. Although people in Miami didn't notice it, the demographics of mass tourism had changed. For the first time, teenagers had the money, independence and mobility that once had been the rewards of adulthood. Just as important, a burgeoning New South middle class now could afford to head for Fort Lauderdale and similar resorts.

Besides beer blasts and beaches, Broward County had other amenities Miami could not offer: into "the middle 1960s, Fort Lauderdale tended to exclude Jews," as *The Almanac of American Politics* points out. Not until the early eighties would blacks and Cubans begin to arrive in significant numbers from nearby Miami. This, in short, was a place where both the Ohio fraternity brother and the family of four from suburban Chattanooga could feel right at home.

In the twenties Miami had cashed in on the boom; now Fort Lauderdale was cashing in on a mass affluence that, for the first time in American history, transcended both age and the legacy of the Civil War. Between 1950 and 1960, the population of Broward County tripled to 334,000; by 1970 it had doubled again to 620,000. By 1980 Broward County, deluged both by settlers from outside Florida and by migrants from Miami itself, had a population of more than a million—an increase of 1,213 percent in just thirty years.

"Miami" wasn't just Miami anymore, no more than New York or Los Angeles could be defined by their municipal boundaries in this new age of freeways and shopping malls. It had become a sprawling conurbation in which the center city no longer necessarily dominated its surroundings, either economically or politically.

One important result was that here in America's newest big city, as in older cities all over the United States, some characteristics that once had seemed specifically urban—wealth, rapid growth, economic opportunity, upward mobility—now seemed to have left the city center behind.

Another supposedly urban trait had moved to the suburbs. Just as the big city sophisticates once had looked down on the poverty and provincialism of the sticks, so now the suburbanites of Broward, no less than those of Nassau and Westchester, felt superior to the problems of the inner cities. If Miami was increasingly "black, brown and broke," that was no more Fort Lauderdale's concern than the travails of Cleveland were the concern of Shaker Heights.

Even inside Dade County, Miami's glory years seemed ended. The very name "Miami" had lost its old allure. Now people no longer said they lived in Miami. They lived in Bal Harbour or Indian Creek or Coral Gables or Key Biscayne or "on Biscayne

Bay," whatever the postmark said. It was as though Miami was some far-off, foreign place where other kinds of people—rednecks, blacks, Cubans—lived.

Miami Beach, of course, was stuck with the name it once had clutched to itself like a designer label. So it opted for a different way of dealing with Miami's fall from grace. To hear people in Miami Beach tell it, their bustling resort, not the tacky town over on the mainland, was the real Miami. So far as they were concerned, Miami ended, and the Everglades began, on the opposite side of Biscayne Bay.

Certainly there seemed no stopping Miami Beach's time-tested formula of equal parts garishness, celebrity and hype. Back in the early fifties, Miami Beach had lured Arthur Godfrey and his radio show to its shores by naming an extension of Julia Tuttle Causeway after him. Then, in the Age of Television, Jackie Gleason Boulevard would join Harding Avenue and all the other thoroughfares named for the heroes of Miami Beach's brief history. It was a telling migration: even "The Honeymooners" was abandoning the old neighborhood and heading south.

On the chilly evening of December 18, 1954, Miami Beach's triumph over Miami seemed complete. On that historic night, half the world—the richer, faster, flashier half—had gathered at the site of Harvey Firestone's old Miami Beach mansion to inaugurate the latest, and still one of the most illuminating, of Florida's architectural extravaganzas.

The Georgian colonial mansion where Thomas Edison, Henry Ford and President Harding had once dined had not been gargantuan enough, bizarre enough—and not nearly vulgar enough —to survive with Florida's fittest. In its place a veritable dreamland of kitsch and consumerism had arisen. "I wanted to design the world's most pretentious hotel," the real estate developer Ben Novack later explained. With the help of a designer of department store windows named Morris Lapidus, he had succeeded beyond belief.

This joint apotheosis of the megalomania of Miami Beach and the follies of the fifties, it goes without saying, was the Fontainebleau.

*

That opening night Eastern Airlines' propeller planes (the commercial jets would not start flying for another four years) flew in formation over the hotel and tipped their wings in tribute. Liberace played the piano, and Miami, as always, rejoiced in the sunny certainty that excess was the midwife of art.

The local press agents exulted in the quantitative aspects of the achievement: it had taken twelve hundred workmen two and a half million hours—and more than one hundred miles of plumbing, 140 miles of electrical wiring, twenty-five acres of carpeting, eighty-five thousand square feet of glass, two thousand mirrors and more steel reinforcement than the Empire State Building contained—to give birth to the gaudiest hotel Miami had ever seen.

The Fontainebleau's "intimate" supper club sat eight hundred. Its main dining room could feed three thousand people at a time. Every year the Fontainebleau's fourteen hundred employees would serve its guests 1,560,000 eggs for breakfast. In the course of the 6,500,000 meals taken in the hotel each year, customers also would consume 78,000 chickens, 109,200 pounds of seafood, 486,000 pounds of steaks and chops—and, even though the clientele was predominantly Jewish, eat 41,600 pounds of bacon. While partaking of this nourishment, they would use 1,825,000 napkins and 547,500 tablecloths. Every year the Fontainebleau's guests would sleep on 1,095,000 sheets, wash themselves with 539,280 bars of soap and dry themselves with 3,285,000 towels.

They also would send out 7,300,000 pounds of laundry and make 3,650,000 telephone calls from their 1,224 rooms.

In its heyday the Fontainebleau's guests would include Joe Di-Maggio, Rocky Marciano, Joan Crawford, Walter Winchell, Tony Martin, Jerry Lewis and every U.S. president from Dwight Eisenhower on. James Bond thrillers would be filmed against the Fontainebleau backdrop. Real-life assassinations would be plotted, by the CIA and others, in its suites; men would be shot dead beneath the half-ton crystal chandelier in its lobby.

Frank Sinatra would start a scrambled-egg fight in the Fontainebleau's coffee shop; in the shopping arcade beneath the main lobby, a former lightweight boxing champion of the world named Beau Jack would polish shoes. Ed Sullivan and Jack Paar would broadcast from there; Karl Wallenda would walk a tightrope. John F. Kennedy would hold a presidential ball, and in celebration of Richard Nixon's 1968 presidential nomination, an elephant would be dyed pink and given the run of the Fontainebleau's courtyard.

Surveying its undulating towers, Groucho Marx conferred on the Fontainebleau the accolade once bestowed on Flagler's Overseas Railroad. He called it the Eighth Wonder of the World. But the "Fountain Blue"—as everyone pronounced it, in unconscious tribute to its Technicolor fountains, and the predominant hair color of the mink-stoled matrons who congregated beside them—was more than that.

Not since Plant opened the Tampa Bay Hotel had a Florida structure more perfectly realized, in its design and ornamentation, the absurdities and obsessions of its age.

Years later Ben Novack was asked how the grand conception of the Fontainebleau had come to him.

The spare, rectilinear designs of Gropius, Mies van der Rohe and the other arbiters of Bauhaus modernism, he explained, appalled him. He did, however, like the rococo palaces of Europe. In fact Novack found a certain fourteenth-century French château so much to his liking he had decided to confer upon it a signal honor: he would give his own hotel the same name.

There was a problem with the original Fontainebleau over in France, however. True, Novack found the name "kind of catchy." But the palace itself—which Francis I had started and Napoleon had embellished, at the cost of twelve million gold francs, for the empress Josephine—was not up to Novack's standards.

"It's not fantastic enough!" he exclaimed.

Then nature called—and divine inspiration intervened.

"The idea came to me in a bathroom," he later told Mike Capuzzo of the *Miami Herald*. "When I thought of the Fontainebleau I was in the john and I was sitting on it. My wife was witness to it."

The next day, Morris Lapidus later confirmed, Novack "called me and said, 'Morris, I've been sitting on a toilet and thinking and it suddenly came to me, how about a curved building?' "

Tuttle and Flagler; Collins and Fisher; Novack and Lapidus— once again the visions of two eccentrics combined and the romance of real estate took conjugal form. This particular union, however, was unlike the earlier two. Far from being tranquil, it was fated to be just as stormy—and, if anything, even funnier and longer-running—than the Jackie Gleason show.

In this particular version, Novack was the irrepressible schemer, Lapidus his long-suffering friend, but with a crucial difference. Not even when Lapidus was in his eighties and Novack in his seventies would the two partners cease their bickering. The feud, deepening into legendary bitterness, would last for decades—and, as much as any scheme Kramden and Norton ever hatched, bring ruin on them both.

Success, as is often the case in human affairs, was the catalyst behind this catastrophe.

Had Novack and Lapidus slapped together just one more gaudy, gargantuan Miami Beach hotel, their relationship might have remained so tranquil that years later they'd still have been eating cheesecake together at Wolfie's. But the truth was they'd created a loopy, zany, crazy wonderful masterpiece—a *succès fou* that would go on amazing architects and turning tourists' heads long after the partisans of minimalism had perished of ennui.

Who deserved the glory for this pioneering essay in postmodernism—the Bronx-born Novack and his toilet seat? Or Brooklyn-born Lapidus, who, after decades of dressing windows for Saks and Macy's, had created, in the form of the Fontainebleau, the most stupendous window display of all times? Even as the finishing touches were being applied, Novack, irked at his partner's claims to authorship of their masterpiece, refused to pay Lapidus; Lapidus, vexed by this slight, tried to kill Novack.

"I was running after him with a three-by-six screaming at the top of my lungs—everything stopped on the job—and saying this man must die," Lapidus later reminisced. "He ran away and I ran after him and it took about three of the partners to restrain me. I blacked out . . . or I would have flattened him."

Thirty years later both angry old men would have been long dead, if words could kill.

"He couldn't design a toilet," proclaimed Lapidus, when asked about the importance of Novack's supposed inspiration.

Rejoindered Novack: "He's full of crap."

Their partnership had radicalized notions of what constituted legitimate architecture. Their rivalry would revolutionize the whole of Miami Beach as year after year, in skyscraper after skyscraper hotel and apartment house, each tried to prove he, not the other, was the real genius behind the Fontainebleau.

Hostilities commenced only a year after the Fontainebleau opened. Just north of the hotel was a vacant lot. And for it, Lapidus designed what was to be his grand riposte to Novack's pretensions.

Certainly the Eden Roc, as Lapidus called his new invention, did mark a significant conceptual advance over the Fontainebleau: in terms of inspiration, it seemed to derive more from a bidet than a commode.

Lapidus had thrown down the gauntlet; Novack snatched it up. Of course Novack couldn't prevent the Eden Roc from stealing the Fontainebleau's thunder, but he could, quite literally, overshadow Lapidus's creation with a new construction of his own.

Even as Lapidus began building the Eden Roc, a new wing of the Fontainebleau began to rise just next door. Novack's North Tower, seventeen stories high, doubled the Fontainebleau's capacity. By itself it would have been one of the biggest hotels in Miami Beach. Yet in spite of its immensity, the new building's south-facing, blue-and-white façade, full of spacious balconies and picture windows, fitted in well with the rest of the Fontainebleau.

Only when viewed from the north—that is to say, from Lapidus's

Eden Roc—did the deeper, and darker, purpose of Novack's design became clear.

For the back side of the new wing—the side facing the Eden Roc —had no windows, no balconies, no ornamentation of any kind; it was utterly featureless.

Novack had created a stupendous, ugly, immense, two-hundred-foot-high monstrosity—and wherever one went in the Eden Roc, there was no escape. This gray, grandiose overhanging cliff of concrete dwarfed the human perspective and dominated the view.

This was an aesthetic crime, of course, but in Miami Beach mere ugliness had never been an indictable offense. What made Novack's creation the *causus belli* of the bitterest architectural controversy in Miami Beach history was its *position*. With absolute precision, Novack had situated his North Tower so as to inflict on Lapidus's Eden Roc a permanent eclipse of the sun. The hotel, its gardens, its bars, restaurants, cabanas and lavish new swimming pool all were permanently bathed in darkness. Guests at the Eden Roc had as much chance of getting a suntan as on the dark side of the moon.

Now the Novack-Lapidus skirmish erupted into full-scale war. The press agents sharpened their bayonets, the lawyers loaded their artillery. In Washington black-robed wise men pondered the conundrum. Was equal access to sunshine protected by the U.S. Constitution?

For once the Warren Court opted for a strict constructionist approach. Property rights triumphed, in the form of a ruling upholding Ben Novack's right to commit whatever architectural crimes he pleased on his own land.

People still tend to cast furtive glances in the direction of the Fontainebleau as they amble through the shadowy grounds of the Eden Roc; even on the sunniest days, Novack's monstrosity, oppressive as a tombstone, excites subliminal dread among innocent holidaymakers.

*

Novack had won the battle; Lapidus won the war.

Just as the Fontainebleau begat the Eden Roc, the Eden Roc would beget the Americana, and the Americana beget the Saxony, the Doral, the Deauville, the Carillon and dozens more.

This was the period in American history when, just after Labor Day each year, Detroit created more suspense and excitement than most presidential elections by unveiling its new-model cars. Each winter Miami Beach did Detroit one better as the latest, newest, most extravagant "Hotel of the Year" was opened with the ballyhoo befitting a new Corvette or Lincoln Continental.

Whoever was responsible for the Fontainebleau's success, these new buildings—whether Lapidus, Novack or their many imitators designed them—proved one thing: architectural eccentricity, if not architectural genius, certainly can be mass-produced, but only at the gravest aesthetic and environmental peril.

As these endless spin-offs and rip-offs of the Fontainebleau arose, a concrete curtain descended on Miami Beach, dividing Biscayne Bay from the Atlantic Ocean, turning Collins Avenue into a windswept canyon, severing human beings from contact with all the balmy elements of nature that drew them there.

Soon it seemed all Miami Beach north of the Deco district had been taken over by gigantic mutants of the pink, blue and green fixtures plumbing contractors install.

Even into the sixties, Miami Beach still continued to stake out its claim on the world's imagination. When the Beatles arrived, thousands cheered—and hundreds wept in ecstasy. To solemnize the occasion, they were presented with plastic inflatable dolphins. The next night, from Miami Beach, on live national television, the Beatles sang to America for the first time.

Four years later Miami Beach was host to an event even more indicative of the times—the 1968 Republican National Convention. Never had the promise of Florida, the promise of escape, taken more revealing political form. While the Democrats, up in Chicago, grappled with the reality of mass demonstrations and police truncheons, with the reality of assassination at home and free fire zones abroad, the Republicans savored Miami Beach's greatest amenity—the illusion that America could go on like this forever.

Lapidus, Novack and their imitators had done to sand and sunshine what Disney had done to the majesty of America, and there was no better measure of the times than that the public loved it.

With the erection of each new tower, the shadows blocking the sun might grow longer, the beach erode a few more feet. What did that matter—so long as the hotel beauty parlor had sunlamps, and one could lounge, in Gimbel's rhinestones and Macy's makeup, beside a chlorinated pool? This, after all, wasn't just the consumer age; it was the age of built-in obsolescence. Just as the Deco district, after serving its purpose, had been abandoned to the frail, the poor and the old, so now it didn't matter if, after two or three seasons, walls cracked, paint peeled and the plastic Aphrodites and Apollos acquired a mildew patina.

There would always be another beach to despoil—another "Hotel of the Year" to beggar its neighbor.

Wasn't that the infinite promise of America?

"Are Cities Un-American?" William H. Whyte, Jr., asked in an essay of that title published in 1958—the same year Disney picked Osceola County as the site of his new kingdom. Whyte came to praise cities, not bury them. But even he had to concede that for most Americans by then the "popular image of the city" was not just an unattractive but a sinister one—"a place of decay, crime, of fouled streets, and of people who are poor or foreign or odd."

Macrocosmically, the Sun Belt became America's suburb. Were you tired of the challenges of life in that great northern megapolis, sprawling south from Boston to Washington, and west to Chicago? Just drive out onto the federally financed interstates and point your car west toward California, or south toward Florida. Better yet, put your boat in the federally financed Intracoastal

Waterway. Before you knew it, you sailed your fiberglass *May-flower* into a sunny, low-tax fantasyland where government dams and drainage canals first created the frontier your down payment conquered, then watered the lawn you planted on it, and—even when free enterprise faltered—federal transfer payments buoyed up the local economy.

By the time Americans chose Richard Nixon for their president, Florida, as its new settlers liked to believe, was indeed the real America: here, to an extent never known in the northern ghettos, the pursuit of happiness had become a federal entitlement.

The phrase "urban crisis" wouldn't be heard for another ten years, and then it would conjure up visions of arson, crime and abandonment in old Frost Belt cities, not in new Sun Belt cities like Miami. But by the early sixties, Miami already was a city in crisis, and this wasn't some symptomatic crisis. It was systemic, because it went beyond problems like crime or economic stagnation to the question of Miami's whole reason for existing.

So far as the people over in Miami Beach, and up in Fort Lauderdale and Orlando were concerned, the answer to Whyte's question was obvious. Miami, like the northern cities they'd fled, had become as obsolete as the Edsel, and it must be admitted that this view had a certain logic.

No one needed rail depots anymore. All over the country, not just in postindustrial Florida, fewer and fewer people were working in factories and mills. Why shouldn't the downtown movie palaces and big department stores board up their windows, now that the suburban shopping malls offered first-run films and shiny new branches of Gimbel's and Macy's? The new interstates bypassed the cities, and now so did the airplane. You didn't need to fly to Miami anymore to get to your favorite "attraction." Disney World, like Fort Lauderdale, had its own international airport; it also had more hotel rooms than Miami.

In this new posturban America, cities seemed to have only one real remaining utility.

They were ideal places to dump all those who weren't "real" Americans. So in Miami, as in other cities, blacks were packed into cheap public housing—safely isolated, by distance and lack of public transportation, from the new opportunities multiplying in the suburbs. Cities also were good places to put the poor and unemployed, whatever their race. In fact they were about the only places left for such people, along with the indigent old and even the insane.

After all, in the new suburban Sun Belt America, there was no place, quite literally, for those who couldn't afford the mortgage payments or who could not drive a car. So just as cities up North became dumping grounds, Miami, too, became the refuse bin for everything, and everyone, the new Florida did not want.

The rich might spend their "golden years" in antiseptic retirement colonies. But it was in Miami that the poorest old folks clustered in run-down boardinghouses and dusty trailer parks. Up in Lauderdale, when you went fishing, you revved up your speedboat and headed out into the Gulf Stream in search of marlin. People fished in Miami, too, but they were only those downtrodden folks, white and black alike, you saw dangling lines off bridges into the Miami River and Biscayne Bay.

Most of all, Miami was the perfect place for all those Cubans coming to Florida and all the "problems" they brought with them. To judge from the newspaper accounts of the "freedom flights," the whole Miami area had been overrun. But thanks to the new segregation, that wasn't the case at all.

The truth was that you could go to work, go to school, go swimming, go shopping, go for years, without hearing a word of Spanish or personally encountering the brown-skinned foreigners you saw on TV. You had to leave your condo or subdivision and mount a special expedition into downtown Miami to gain any sense that you now lived in an increasingly cosmopolitan "Greater Miami."

It was all Julia Tuttle's fault, of course.

*

"ARE ALL BIG CITIES DOOMED?" Thus, in April 1976, would one of the national newsmagazines, using capital letters nearly an inch high, and of funereal black, sum up one of those great national questions that seem so pressing at the moment—so meaningless only a few years later. By then the Age of the Suburb was already giving way to the Age of the Young Urban Professional; the Yuppie, not the suburbanite, would become the new national trend-setter.

Miami's great problem, by the time the Cubans arrived, was the exact opposite of what its detractors supposed. Miami's problem—and it amounted to a real crisis—was that, once again, Miami was ahead of the times. It, not Orlando or Fort Lauderdale or Miami Beach, already was the city of the future, and for the very reason that, for the moment, made cities everywhere seem obsolete.

In this new Florida of separate homogenies, only Miami was left to harbor what Wallace Stevens, in his poem "O Florida, Venereal Soil," called

> The dreadful sundry of this world,
> The Cuban, Polodowsky,
> The Mexican women,
> The negro undertaker
> Killing the time between corpses
> Fishing for crayfish . . .

Miami's dreadful diversity would breed tumult unthinkable in less diverse places.

But out of catastrophe, as always, would come opportunity—and, in Miami's case, triumphs unimaginable in less sundry worlds.

Part III

The Americanization of Miami

12

The Shark in the Water

Thirty-five thousand people, according to the Secret Service estimate, packed the lower stalls of the Orange Bowl.

Some carried banners ("Cuba Without Coexistence," one of them read); some wept. Many more laughed and cheered. The crowd anticipated a turning point in history—one of those decisive moments when one human being decrees the fate of generations.

A helicopter appeared overhead. A pulse of electricity surged through the stadium; suddenly it seemed everyone was waving handkerchiefs. From the helicopter the stadium looked like a sea awave with flags of hope and welcome.

The president and Mrs. Kennedy were not in the helicopter. Before leaving the family mansion at Palm Beach that morning, they had decided, after flying to Miami, to go to the Orange Bowl by car. At that moment they were approaching the stadium in an immense convertible like the one, less than a year later, they would ride in Dallas, only this convertible was pure white.

The helicopter carried a sightseeing tourist. But faced with a greeting worthy of a president, the pilot did what anyone might have in the face of such a spontaneous demonstration. He waved back, as though this outpouring of love, admiration and hope had been meant for him. And, so, into this moment of deep solemnity was introduced one of the essential Florida leitmotifs—of lightness, confused identity, of high-flying absurdity.

If one looked up, one could see a second sign that, even here, even now, history did not necessarily obey when an American president spoke. While the lower levels of the Orange Bowl were packed, the balconies were mostly empty. Even with 35,000 people there, the stadium, which seats 72,880, was more than half-empty.

One reason for the empty seats was that not even hatred of Castro and love of their homeland—not even the commingled humiliation of defeat and subsequent rapture at the ransom of the survivors of the disastrous Bay of Pigs invasion—could unite Miami's Cubans. They had been divided at home; they would remain divided in exile, no matter how hard the CIA tried to unite them into an effective force against Castro. Today was no exception. Large numbers of Miami Cubans, angered at the place of honor given supporters of Cuba's former dictator, Fulgencio Batista, boycotted the ceremony.

There was an even more significant reason why the Orange Bowl was not full that day. Less than three months earlier, the normal routines of America had come to a stop; for four days Americans had awakened wondering whether this would be their last day on earth. No event before or since the Cuban missile crisis so graphically illustrated the threat of nuclear annihilation. For Miami's "real" Americans in December 1962, the liberty of Cuba, no matter how desirable abstractly, was something for which they had no intention of risking, or even disrupting, their lives.

So except for a few Anglo politicians—already, in broken Spanish, courting the Cuban vote—Miami's English-speaking residents, both white and black, had stayed away from the Orange Bowl. One native-born American explained why. "We're glad these boys are home—sure," he told a local reporter. "But we don't want to get involved in another war."

Inside the stadium people were shouting *"Guerra! Guerra!"* The security men were tense; a stick of dynamite had been found earlier that morning. In the melee two photographers were roughed up.

"Watch the crowd," Miami's public safety director, Donald Pomerleau, told his men. "Never watch the old man."

He was probably the only one to associate the person of John F. Kennedy with age, let alone with any prospect of mortality. The president, as one news account put it, looked "bronzed and seemingly aburst with energy and health" that day.

Exactly twelve minutes after the helicopter buzzed the stadium, the white convertible limousine pulled into the Orange Bowl. It was a little after ten-thirty on a sunny, seventy-nine-degree Miami morning in late December.

The veterans of the Bay of Pigs invasion, many of them wearing khaki uniforms, swarmed around the limousine, and the Kennedys reached out to them. The president, using an interpreter, told the soldiers, freed from Castro's prisons less than a week earlier, that they were heroes great as Martí. Some of the ransomed prisoners were still in their teens; yet the forty-five-year-old president looked younger than many of them did, so gaunt and lined were their faces after their twenty-month ordeal as prisoners in Cuba. Clearly moved, the president reached out from his limousine and touched the faces of some of the young men.

Speaking softly in Spanish, Mrs. Kennedy called the veterans of the defeated CIA force "the bravest men in the world." She said it was "my wish and my hope" that someday her own son would "be a man at least half as brave as the members of Brigade 2506."

Just four years earlier, almost to the day, Batista had fled Havana, Castro's guerrilla war of national liberation had triumphed, and America's sixty-one-year dominion of Cuba had come to a sudden end.

Forfeiture of hegemony had been followed by humiliation. First, in April 1961, the CIA's Bay of Pigs invasion failed. Eighty men were killed in the fighting, 37 drowned before they could reach the beaches, and no less than 1,180 members of the 1,400-man assault force had quickly surrendered as Castro's forces drove them back into the sea. The nuclear confrontation had come next. For a few days in October 1962, humanity had teetered on the brink of self-destruction. Then, in its aftermath,

Americans had been subjected to still another lesson in the powerlessness of power. Only through the most demeaning of processes—paying a ransom of $62 million in medicine and food—had the United States been able to secure the prisoners' release. Now the president of the United States had come to Miami to reassert America's mastery of events.

In a news photo taken that day, the president, his back to the camera, stretches out his right arm toward the crowd, as he prepares to tell the world what the United States would do next "to assure the survival and success of liberty," as he had put it in his inaugural address. Before him a mass of humanity waits silent, motionless, on his word. Behind him Mrs. Kennedy, taking advantage of that brief instant, adjusts her hair. One of the ransomed Cuban prisoners, wearing a khaki uniform, stands behind the president, near an American flag, clenching his hands behind his back in nervous expectation.

"Cuba," the president proclaimed, "shall one day be free again, and when it is, this Brigade will deserve to march at the head of the free column."

Earlier, the young Cubans had given the American president the flag they had carried on their doomed adventure. Now—even before his words could be translated, even before the president finished speaking—the stadium erupted.

Kennedy made his pledge, "exuding abundant vitality and self-confidence," the *Herald* reported.

"I can assure you," he promised Miami's Cubans, "that this flag will be returned to this Brigade in a free Havana."

A little more than twenty-two years later, one of the prisoners whom Kennedy touched that day drove me over to the Orange Bowl. Balmy December had just given way to January in Miami; it was chilly and raining. The stadium was empty; the Dolphins had just lost the Super Bowl. Humberto Cortina, whom everyone in Miami called by his American nickname, Terry, still walked with a limp from the wounds he had received at the Bay of Pigs. He was approaching fifty, the time in life when a man starts finding it easier to look back than ahead.

That day in 1962 at the stadium—enraptured by the president's promise—Cortina and all the others had vowed they would never disband Brigade 2506. "We do not have the right to demobilize," the brigade's commander, José Perez San Roman, had said. "We have a debt of honor and we must return to Cuba to fight."

Now, as we stood in the rain, I asked Terry Cortina if he still sometimes thought about returning to Cuba. "You mean if Castro's overthrown someday?" he answered. "Sure I'd go back. I'd like to see Havana again, visit the old family house, maybe do some business there. But I'd never renounce my American citizenship or anything." He gestured to the overcast city all around us—so different in substance from the sunny image it purveys. "I think I'd find it difficult living in Havana now. Life here is so much more interesting."

Like many Miami Cubans of his age and situation, Cortina had the small business, the big American car. He had the kids of college age who, depending on their SATs, studied computer science or business administration up in Gainesville—or premed or American literature at some elite university up North. He also had the divorce which, in a community that prided itself on maintaining traditional Cuban values, was now as commonplace as the Betamax and frozen TV dinners.

Back in 1962 Humberto Cortina had thought of himself as another José Martí—one of those heroes who, rifle in one hand, manifesto in the other, writes a new and glorious page in the history of Latin America's long struggle for liberty. But Terry Cortina had wound up with another historical distinction instead. He had become the first veteran of the Bay of Pigs to be elected to the Florida state legislature.

That is, he'd been a legislator in Tallahassee until another veteran of the Bay of Pigs—they'd shared one of Castro's cells together— had defeated him in the Republican primary in Little Havana.

As we left the Orange Bowl and drove through the rain to his house, Cortina pondered this second great defeat in his life. That a president of the United States had betrayed one of his great hopes seemed to bother him less by now than that a fellow member of Brigade 2506 had turned against him. "I don't know," he said. "You get wounded with a guy. You share a prison cell with him. Hell, we roomed together at college after that. . . . You try to tell yourself, 'That's politics.' But, sure, it hurts. Time passes and it's like you aren't the same person anymore."

The veterans had kept their pledge even after it became clear the Americans would never "help wrest Cuba" back. Nearly a quarter-century later, Brigade 2506 still was intact. Only now it was a kind of chamber of commerce, one of those fraternities where vigorous, affluent men just past their prime gather to remember the times when they were filled with the ardency and certainty of youth—and also to keep in touch, to keep the network functioning. Once they had thought of themselves as Cuban revolutionaries. Now they were politicians, real estate developers, lawyers, corporate executives—the kind of people who believe it's their civic responsibility to provide leadership and direction.

Some months earlier such men had decided it was time for stock-taking. So hotel suites and conference rooms were reserved, a kind of seminar organized. By the scores they'd flown—or driven across the Tamiami Trail, in their big, fast cars with the digital dashboards —to a luxury resort hotel on Marco Island, on the west coast of Florida. For a couple of days, as one of the organizers, Guarione Diaz, later told me, "we just talked—about us, about Miami, about our kids. We were trying to get a fix on who we were and what we might become next.

"Of course we talked in English," Diaz said when I asked him. "I mean there was no fixed agenda, nothing that said which language we were going to speak. Everyone just naturally started talking in English. You know how they say we have to communicate these days in English because of the kids, because they're forgetting the old ways?

"That's not why. None of us can conduct a serious discussion entirely in Spanish anymore. I mean our grammar wouldn't be correct all the time, and we'd keep reaching for English phrases to express exactly what we mean. Even at home, when something is very important, we explain it in English. So," concluded Diaz, who heads a Miami group called the Cuban National Planning Council, "we all sat around on Marco Island talking about what it meant to be a Cuban in Miami, in English."

"This is my home now," Terry Cortina said as we entered the house he'd bought following his divorce from his Cuban wife and remarriage to a young American woman. It had the Touch-Tone phones, the microwave oven, the hanging plants, the answering machine, the big hi-fi, the walk-in closets. Only the American car in the driveway hinted that a Cuban lived here.

Inside, Cortina showed me his scrapbooks. The memory of Kennedy was still vivid, but by now the newspaper clippings of that day in the Orange Bowl flaked when you touched them. They might have dated back to another Cuban war.

How could Kennedy have promised so much? How could he have given nothing at all? Surely he knew by then that no one—not he, certainly not the divided, disorganized remnants of the CIA's ragtag force—could overthrow Castro?

For years after that rapturous moment of certainty in the stadium, Miami's Cubans—first in tense expectation mingled with growing doubt, then in sorrow and anger, finally in contempt and bitterness—would ask themselves those questions.

In the end they would decide, on the whole, that John F. Kennedy had deliberately betrayed them. That decision would permeate their whole experience of America, producing all sorts of unanticipated results. (Those Cubans who so rapturously cheered the Democratic president that day would become, in time, fervent Republicans.)

But even as Cortina described the sense of betrayal the brigade members felt, a sense of how the world inevitably works crept into what he said: "What's the point of bitterness? We couldn't know, so what's the point of blaming Kennedy for not knowing what life has in store for you?"

As I listened to him, it occurred to me that we often take the present too literally. Certainly that was the Cubans' problem with Kennedy. They took the promise of this bronzed, charismatic incarnation of America literally. They did not realize that actual words and events, as much as our own emotions, can mask reality. They forgot that the passage of time not only obscures but reveals—that, as present becomes past, politics becomes history, and fact becomes myth, even myths eventually come to tell us truths. In 1892, for example, if you looked at José Martí literally, you saw only an exiled Cuban orator. It took time and Martí's own death to reveal his true identity—the immortal voice, full of hope and despair, of Cuba's unrequited love of freedom.

Today few survivors of the Bay of Pigs would deny that they were destined to retrace Martí's footsteps more completely than they imagined. Like Martí, they were fated to rise for freedom. Like Cubans in every generation, they would fail. Martí was not just Martí. As time and their own transformation into myth would show the survivors of the Bay of Pigs, Martí was them.

Today all Americans remember Kennedy vividly, sometimes more vividly than actual friends and relations they knew twenty-five years ago. But very few think of any of the literal issues—Cuba, Vietnam, civil rights, "the missile gap," the Alliance for Progress, the president's religion—that once seemed to determine Kennedy's significance.

They remember Kennedy for what he really was, the most convincing personification of America's vaunting faith in itself as a chosen nation this century has produced. Of all our other presidents, only Jackson and Teddy Roosevelt had it in equal measure, that gift not merely for promising, but for *being* all that America dreams itself to be.

What did it matter that 1962 was not 1898 or 1818? Kennedy knew that nearby Cuba, faraway Vietnam, the whole world, would be free for the same reason that, in 1898, other Americans had known Cuba and the Philippines would be free and, earlier still, had known the whole vast wilderness beyond our original borders was destined for liberty.

It was what we Americans wanted—and what America wanted was not only inevitable, not only good. Even when the immediate way could not be seen, it was the destiny of the world. "In the long history of the world, only a few generations have been granted the role of defending freedom in its hour of maximum danger. I do not shrink from this responsibility; I welcome it," Kennedy had proclaimed at his inauguration.

So, at the Orange Bowl, the president not only had told the vanquished men he had ransomed from Castro's prisons that they were "the point of the spear, the arrow's head" of freedom. He urged them, now that they were safe in Miami, to "take every opportunity to educate your children, yourselves, in the many skills and disciplines which will be necessary when Cuba is once more free."

No doubt Kennedy knew, even as he spoke, that as a result of the missile crisis, there was no foreseeable way that Brigade 2506 could fight again in Cuba, let alone that U.S. forces could liberate the island. But he also knew, as he made his promise, that time was on his side. He knew he had youth and vigor; he knew he had determination. He would outlast and prevail over Castro and all the others who dared presume that when an American president promised something, the way would not be found.

Like all the great heroes of American nationalism, Kennedy never imagined that reality could permanently bar his way.

Soon after leaving the Orange Bowl, the president was back in Palm Beach. Peter Lawford met the helicopter when it touched down, and just half an hour later, the president, Lee Radziwill, and Lawford and two of his sons were out on the Atlantic Ocean, on the presidential yacht *Honey Fitz,* named for Kennedy's Irish grandfather, Mayor John F. Fitzgerald of Boston.

The day had begun balmy in Miami. Now it was hot. The president of the United States stripped down to his swimming trunks and plunged into the Atlantic Ocean. At the Orange Bowl, he had personified one shining face of America. Now—vigorous, tanned and youthful—the president embodied another of America's great romantic visions of itself, the vision of perpetual youth in an American paradise, of an America not only omnipotent, but in full and permanent mastery of the joy of living.

Yet in these dulcet, warm waters there were signs, as much as in the power of the atom and in the force of foreign revolution, that even we Americans live in a world governed by circumstances we cannot ordain.

Sharks had been sighted in the water off Palm Beach. So the president, as a wire service report put it, "hustled back aboard his yacht." The president and his party returned to the Kennedy family mansion. It was one of those "Spanish" compounds designed by Addison Mizner, back when Flagler's men had stripped away the mangrove on that improbable island, and America's richest and most powerful people had begun fulfilling their vision of what an ideal world should be.

That rendezvous in the Orange Bowl really had been a turning point in history. This wasn't because of what the president had promised; it was because Kennedy's pledge meant nothing.

The United States would never overthrow Castro; but never would it reconcile itself to him either. And so, in the absence of either apocalypse or reconciliation, Cuba and America would cease being neighbors. They would become hallucinations to each other —a fantasy America justifying all the phobias, all the excesses and doctrinal rigidities of the Cuban revolution; a fantasy Cuba justifying all the phobias, all the excesses of an American nationalism that, even as it proclaimed the world's freedom, could not free itself from the specter of darkly sensed conspiracies, toppling dominoes.

Between Kennedy's America and Castro's Cuba there nonetheless was an interstice. It would be in Miami that the veterans of Brigade 2506 and hundreds of thousands of other Cubans would use those "many skills and disciplines" the president had urged them to acquire. Propelled, as America's settlers always have been, by impossible dreams, these Cubans would grow rich, they would grow old—they would grow American—in Miami.

The helicopter in the sky, the shark in the water: there was a third sign of the future that day.

You can see it in many of the photos. Behind the president and to his right, as I mentioned, there was an American flag. But there was another flag on the platform—also behind the president, but to his left, near the metal folding chair where Mrs. Kennedy sat.

This second flag hung there motionless, as if finding it, even in these circumstances, needless to emphasize its point.

"E Pluribus Unum," read the motto on the president's own flag.

13

Years of Destiny

Only two weeks after his speech at the Orange Bowl, President
Kennedy challenged America's critics to "compare the disillusion-
ment of communist Cuba with the promise of the Alliance for
Progress." Disillusionment certainly flourished in the aftermath of
Castro's revolution, but America's own efforts to liberate Latin
America from poverty and repression also yielded bitter fruit.
Within a few years, Kennedy's Alliance for Progress, launched with
the same ringing rhetoric Kennedy had launched his own presi-
dency, had collapsed.

Conditions in Latin America had not improved under the Alliance. Between 1960 and 1968, unemployment in the region rose
from eighteen to twenty-three million. The gap between Latin
America's wealthy elite and its impoverished masses widened, as
the region's population exploded.

Human freedom was the most dramatic casualty of those years.
By the end of the decade, Cuba was not the only country where,
as President Kennedy put it, "a small band of ruthless conspirators"
had ensured that "the promise of a revolution of hope is betrayed."
Everywhere in Latin America—with the sole exceptions of
Venezuela, Colombia, Costa Rica and Mexico—dictators either
held sway or were about to seize power, often with full U.S. sup-

port. Far from fostering democracy, "the Alliance for Progress," as a European historian later observed, "seem[ed] to have encouraged Latin American coups against constitutionally elected governments."

Latin America's future was also being mortgaged. Between 1960 and 1968, its external debt, most of it owed to U.S.-controlled lending agencies, doubled to nearly $20 billion. This sum was trivial in comparison with the more than $360 billion Latin America would owe by the end of 1985, when annual interest payments alone exceeded $37 billion, and some Latin countries would be paying nearly half of all their export earnings to foreign bankers. Nonetheless the handwriting was already on the wall. "The developed nations are not aiding Latin America. It is the other way around," the Chilean foreign minister, Gabriel Valdes, managed to protest before his government, too, was overthrown.

The Latins blamed their misery on generations of U.S. avarice and arrogance—and, though no American president would acknowledge it, they were right. U.S. officials, when they were not blaming Castro and Communist subversion, blamed Latin America's own corrupt and exploitative social, political and economic institutions and, though Latin pride stood in the way of acknowledging it, the American critics in this instance were also right.

Not all was disaster in those years. Even before Japanese cars, OPEC oil and American computers flooded the world, economics and technology were unleashing changes more revolutionary than those politics and ideology produced. The growth of an interdependent global economy plunged many Third World countries into debt; but the rising tide of intercontinental trade, in everything from television sets to marijuana, also created new possibilities. First Venezuela, then Ecuador and Mexico, experienced oil booms; Brazil, Mexico and a few other countries developed important industrial sectors. In a change fateful for Miami, mass hemispheric tourism became a reality for the first time, as the new commercial jets brought the Caribbean far closer to the cold, northern cities of the United States than Miami itself had been during the Miami mania of the twenties.

Positive developments were the exceptions, but even in the poorest Latin American countries, per capita incomes would rise, if only marginally, fueling a new revolution far more potent than Castro's —the revolution of rising expectations.

Nonetheless the two decades following Castro's triumph in Cuba would be notable for an entirely different reason. The amazing thing in retrospect is that both the "threats" which so obsessed U.S. officials in those years, as well as the promise of progress and freedom which the United States itself held out to Latin America, produced so very few changes. Far from being swept by revolution, Communist or capitalist, most of Latin America remained what it had been in Teddy Roosevelt's time—a hemisphere of crushed hopes and looted resources, "so far from God," as the famous saying has it, "and so close to the United States."

God is equidistant wherever one stands on this earth. But as the second half of that aphorism makes clear, by the time the Cubans began arriving in Miami, the peoples of the Caribbean and Central America, along with their nearer South American neighbors, found themselves in a situation fundamentally different from that of people suffering poverty and repression in places like Asia and Africa.

We in the United States have always seen Florida as a finger of destiny, pointing to a special role for us in the lands to the south. But only turn the map around, and one comprehends a different reality: Florida is a bridge, leading north to freedom, opportunity and profit, and Miami is the turnstile through which, in times of both feast and famine, people, money and commodities flow.

For our Caribbean neighbors, the United States was only a few hours away by plane or a few days away by boat.

The colder it got up North, the bankers, merchants and real estate magnates had always known, the better it was for Miami. Now another, even older law of human thermodynamics reasserted itself.

The hotter, politically speaking, it got in the countries to the south, the better it was for Miami. Fear of Communism, not fear of frost, was now Miami's great civic booster, though ideology really had little to do with this tide of foreign capital and human skills flooding into the United States. It didn't matter whether the killers were left-wing terrorists or right-wing death squads, whether the reigning *caudillo* quoted Marx or modeled himself on Mussolini. Miami's most important natural asset—year-round freedom from fear—only grew in value.

Over the next twenty years, Miami would prosper when Latin America prospered. It would also prosper when Latin America faltered, attracting money and people north to the safe haven of Miami's bank vaults and walled condominiums.

Today all that seems obvious. One looks at a map and sees what Julia Tuttle saw in 1896, that it was inevitable Miami should become to the Caribbean what Venice once was to the Mediterranean. But Miami's unique geographical position had existed since time immemorial. The actual circumstances of Miami's transformation into the premier inter-American metropolis, however, prove something else, that nothing is inevitable. Only "thanks to an accident of history—the Cuban Revolution" did Miami acquire the human skills and hemispheric connections necessary to exploit its natural advantages, and emerge as the capital of "the Western hemisphere south of the Rio Grande and the Gulf of Mexico."

Political expediency, in both Washington and Havana, would provide the foundations on which the new Miami was built.

"Power is the hallmark" of the Cuban revolution, Kennedy declared in 1961, "power and discipline and deceit." Americans back then saw Castro as a murderous ogre, bent on enslaving his nation, subverting his neighbors and killing all who dared oppose him. For Cuba's new Marxist rulers, the United States was the classic incarnation of imperialist capitalism—villainous in the short run, but doomed in the long run to strangle in the tightening noose of its own contradictions.

Events soon exposed the folly of both those notions.

The United States, contrary to Marxist doctrine and in spite of its own phobias, was not about to be swamped by the worldwide tide of revolution and subversion both Che Guevara and the domino theory predicted. In fact the United States was on the way to a new era of global influence and technological innovation that by 1987 would make it even more powerful abroad, and prosperous at home, than it was in 1962.

As for Castro, he turned out to be a practical politician; a survivor, not an ideologue—at least when it came to dealing with the two greatest threats to his power, the United States and his own internal opposition. Following the Bay of Pigs invasion, another Latin American dictator might have massacred his defeated opponents. Instead Castro, as he always would end up doing, had dickered with the United States. When the price in dollars was right, he had let his captives go.

Of course there was nothing new in that. Since 1513 Florida had been the escape valve for the Caribbean's political tensions. But it was Castro's achievement, in cooperation with the U.S. government, to systematize this ancient tradition. Beginning in December 1965, with Castro's full approval, two flights a day took off empty from Miami and flew to Cuba. Before the flights ended seven and a half years later, they returned to Miami with more than a quarter-million Cubans.

Americans called them "Freedom Flights" and heralded them as proof that Communism had failed in Cuba. But what did the rhetoric matter to Castro? Kennedy's stirring pledge at the Orange Bowl had coincided with the end, not the renewal, of U.S.-supported attempts by Cuban exiles to overthrow Castro militarily. Now the Americans, at their own expense, were solving another of Castro's problems for him.

Between 1962 and 1980, with U.S. help, Castro would eliminate domestic discontent by exporting it. Eventually about a million and a quarter people would leave Cuba, which, when Castro gained power, had a population of less than six million. Hundreds of thousands of Cubans settled in Europe and Latin America, but ultimately about three-quarters of all those leaving, some 900,000 Cubans, would make their way to the United States by various routes. Today the Cuban population of the United States, which was less than 125,000 in 1960, numbers more than a million, or about 10 percent of the present population of Cuba itself. Cuban-born Americans and their children are now the third largest Hispanic community in the country, after those of Mexican and Puerto Rican origin. It has been one of the largest single waves of peaceful immigration in recent history, comparable to the mass abandonment in 1846 of Ireland following the potato famine.

As befits such an epic, the Cuban exodus was from the beginning encrusted in legend, romance and myth.

Americans fervently believed it then; even today most Americans assume the Cubans they welcomed to their shores were anti-Communist "freedom fighters." Castro's quarter-century and more in power, however, is founded on an incontrovertible reality no number of anti-Communist rallies in Miami can refute: had only a fraction of those Cubans who came to the United States given Castro any effective resistance, his regime would have collapsed decades ago.

In truth, many of these people initially, and sometimes for many years, had supported Castro; many others had been willing collaborators of the Batista dictatorship and violently opposed all efforts to democratize Cuban life. The majority had been politically inactive in their homeland. Apart from the survivors of the Bay of Pigs, only a few hundred of them ever had or ever would fire a shot in anger against the regime they were deserting.

The belief that the Cubans reaching the United States were desperate, endangered "refugees"—like the Indochinese boat people or European Jews fleeing the Holocaust—also belongs to the realm of legend.

In the whole twenty years between 1960 and 1980, only about sixteen thousand Cubans actually "fled" Cuba, in the sense of eluding Castro's military patrols and escaping the island, at the risk of their own lives, in small boats or by "other extremely dangerous means." For the overwhelming majority of all those leaving Cuba, the "escape to freedom" was a matter of running quite a different kind of gauntlet. They would have to patiently work their way through the cumbersome, capricious, but on the whole surprisingly orderly and efficient process of officially approved migration that the United States and Cuba had established.

Like that rendezvous with destiny in the Orange Bowl, the Bay of Pigs had turned out to be a real turning point, though for reasons entirely different from those its participants supposed. Precisely because the invasion had failed, the negotiations leading to the ransom of the members of Brigade 2506 had established a new and definitive pattern in U.S.-Cuban relations.

The clamorous public hostility between the two governments would make headlines decade after decade. But it was this private willingness in both Washington and Havana to quietly negotiate specific solutions to specific problems that made history by turning the Cuban exodus from an isolated incident into a long-term demographic process of great importance for both Cuba and the United States.

This peaceful, orderly mass migration poses a question most people never think it necessary even to ask: Why did so many Cubans come to the United States?

Then as now, it went without saying: They were fleeing Communism.

Msgr. Bryan Walsh is in a unique position to know. He played an historic role in the Cuban exodus, and is now executive director of Catholic Community Services in Miami, and chairman of the Dade County Community Relations Board as well. According to him, "Fidel or no Fidel," Miami today would have an immense Cuban population.

The academics agree. According to professors Thomas D. Boswell and James R. Curtis of the University of Miami, "It would be incorrect to assume that all Cubans have come to America strictly to escape . . . Castro." They describe "the lure of economic opportunity" and "the quest for family reunification" as "powerful migrational 'pull' forces" which caused many Cubans to leave.

Walsh goes on to cite other nonideological forces—"tourism, cheaper airfares, television, the movies, even efforts at economic development." All these, according to him and other immigration experts, would have drawn hundreds of thousands of Cubans to the United States no matter what regime was in power.

Even today, in Miami's Cuban community, some consider it treasonous to suggest that anti-Communism was not the essential reason so many Cubans came. But those who doubt the importance of factors having nothing to do with Communism should ask themselves another question: What would have happened had other Caribbean peoples been offered the same opportunity the Cubans were given to emigrate to the United States?

Over the next twenty-five years, immigrants from non-Communist Caribbean nations like Haiti, Jamaica and the Dominican Republic would get quite a different reception. They would be categorized as "illegal aliens," not welcomed as "freedom fighters." But the labels would make little difference because the human as well as the economic boundaries between the United States and the rest of the world were breaking down. By the mid-1980s, in fact, the combination of Latin America's continuing misfortune and the enormous appeal of life in the United States—what specialists call the "push and pull" factors in immigration—had produced a most revealing result. Approximately 10 percent of the population of *all* the island nations in the Caribbean was living in the United States. "Puerto Rico, Cuba, the Dominican Republic and Haiti—whether the regime is a democracy or a Communist dictatorship, whether it is of the left or the right, the result," as Msgr. Walsh observes, "seems to be the same. The surplus population migrates."

The Cold War melodramas of the early sixties had produced a dramatic result: for the first and only time in history, the United States had thrown its doors wide open to virtually unrestricted migration from a Latin American country—and the Cubans moved quickly to seize that opportunity, just as they would seize so many of the other opportunities life in this nation offers.

But the myth that if it weren't for Communism Miami would not be what it is today, oddly enough, sells short the American Dream. Then as now it didn't take a Marxist dictatorship to teach Latin Americans that immigration to the United States is the most practicable route to the fulfillment of their longings for a better life.

As the Cubans prospered in their new homes, another legend flourished that, as they gained access to all that the American consumer society could offer, even Cubans of the humblest origins came to half-believe.

This was the notion that those leaving Cuba were not chiefly poor and unskilled, like those coming to the United States from other Latin American countries, but predominantly members of a refined, gracious and accomplished prerevolutionary Havana elite.

Once again the truth could not have been more different, as Boswell and Curtis point out. Cubans "emigrated to the United States from virtually all regions of the island, stretching from the province of Pinar del Rio in the west to Oriente province in the east; they came from the rural areas, the cities, and the suburbs." Far from being limited to the rich and educated, the Cuban exodus encompassed "the full spectrum of socioeconomic classes and ethnic groups that existed in Cuba prior to the Castro revolution."

Those who had been wealthy and well placed under the Batista dictatorship, of course, had both the greatest opportunity and the greatest reason for fleeing Havana when Castro took power and, at least initially, the demographics of the Cuban exodus reflected that fact. Most came from Havana and other urban areas, and tended to be older, better educated and more religious than the Cuban population as a whole.

Yet even among the so-called golden exiles, those who came to the United States immediately after Batista fell, the wealthy and skilled were vastly outnumbered by quite ordinary Cubans. Laborers, clerks and sales personnel, farmers, fishermen and domestic servants accounted for about 60 percent of this supposed "elite." Doctors, serious as their loss was for Cuba, constituted less than 1 percent of those Cubans initially coming to the United States. The same was true, within one order of magnitude, of engineers, scientists, professors, even of electricians and plumbers.

Among the first wave of migrants, less than a third were entrepreneurs, managers and members of the professions. With the beginning of the 1965 airlift, the proportion dropped to about 15 percent, as the incoming flights "brought to the U.S. tens of thousands of Cubans from small towns and medium size cities throughout the island." Even today only a small minority of Cubans in Miami are highly paid professionals and wealthy entrepreneurs. By 1983, for example, only 29.5 percent of all Latin households were headed by white-collar workers, and that included technical, clerical and sales personnel, not just doctors, lawyers and businessmen. About 21 percent were retired, students or unemployed.

But by far the biggest group, 50 percent, were blue-collar "craftsmen, operatives, service workers, laborers and farmers." These proportions have varied hardly at all over the last decade and more. And there is no indication they will change dramatically in the foreseeable future.

Contrary to myth, the Cubans always have been, and are likely to remain, a preponderantly working-class community even though, in postindustrial Miami, the work is much more likely to be in the service sector than in traditional industries. Indeed that —not their supposed professional skills and elite origins—is one of the great secrets of the Cuban community's stability and cohesion: the Cuban success story has not been a matter of a few individuals becoming immensely wealthy and leaving the others behind, but of almost all Cubans steadily building a modest affluence for themselves and their families in which their friends and neighbors share.

Why did the rich and well educated constitute such a small proportion of Cubans coming to the United States? Just as Castro's success in retaining power can only be fully explained by the lack of effective resistance on the part of the supposed "anti-Communists" who came to Miami, the fact that the vast majority of all Cubans settling in the United States came from quite humble backgrounds also reflects a reality that, even now, many Cubans in the United States are unwilling to accept.

Had all, or even most, of those leaving actually been either wealthy or skilled, the Cuban revolution no doubt never would have occurred—because Batista's Cuba, instead of being a corrupt tropical slum, would have been, proportionate to its population, one of the happiest and most highly developed nations on earth.

Like all America's immigrants, the Cubans came here for a mixture of reasons: freedom, there is no doubt about it, is a powerful magnet; but equally irresistible—to downtrodden people all over the world—is the glittering allure of America's wealth.

Understanding the disadvantages the Cubans brought with them to America is also important for another reason. It makes their future accomplishments in the United States all the more admirable.

The belief that the Cubans built new lives for themselves entirely through their own efforts gives full credit to their own industry and determination. It also has become an essential theme in the mythology of the Cubans' success.

But it ignores an important fact: between 1962 and 1976, the federal government spent a total of $2.1 billion on direct assistance to Cuban refugees.

City, county and Florida state agencies, along with private religious and philanthropic organizations, notably those affiliated with the Catholic Church, spent hundreds of millions of dollars more. Indirect government expenditures—for services ranging from education for the young, through medical care and welfare, to Social Security for the elderly—probably bring the total to at least $4 billion. But even if only direct federal expenditures are counted, the $2.1 billion in aid for the Cubans was greater than the entire budget for the Alliance for Progress—designed to finance what

President Kennedy called "a true revolution of progress and free-dom" throughout the whole of Latin America.

Later, and nowhere more so than among Miami's Cubans, the domestic faiths of the New Frontier and the Great Society would fall into disrepute, as Americans decided the United States could not solve its human and social problems by throwing government money at them. Back in 1966, however, that unrepentantly capital-ist publication, *Fortune,* took a look at this particular federal "give away" program and came to quite a different conclusion.

Fortune marveled at the smooth efficiency with which U.S. offi-cials welcomed the arriving Cubans, escorted them to a comfort-able, four-hundred-bed processing center called "Freedom House" and then, after a few days' rest, whisked most of them off to be resettled, at government expense, in other parts of the country.

Thanks to a wide array of government subsidies, the magazine reported, not only Cuban doctors and engineers, but even "small farmers, fishermen, industrial workers" were on the way to becom-ing productive, self-sufficient Americans. In Miami alone, the num-ber of Cubans on welfare had declined, since the exodus had begun, from "nearly 70,000 to about 12,000, with most of these being elderly, juvenile, sick, or otherwise unemployable."

That figure was doubly revealing. First of all it proved the Cubans were making great strides toward self-sufficiency. But it revealed something else of equal importance. In addition to all the other forms of direct government aid they had received, more than a third of all Cubans initially coming to Miami had gone on welfare; and even after their economic success story was well under way, many of them would continue to require government handouts in order to survive. Today, nearly a generation after they first started arriving in the United States in large numbers, and in spite of all the economic progress they have made, Cubans are still nearly twice as likely to be on welfare as their American-born neighbors.

Fortune singled out for special praise the resettlement program's director, "John Thomas, fifty-nine, a hardheaded bureaucrat of mixed Negro-Indian and Swedish descent, who has twenty years of refugee resettlement experience, most of it with displaced persons in Europe after World War II." In a Washington interview, Thomas credited the operation's success to the speed with which the newcomers were inducted into their new lives. "Only two weeks in a refugee camp is enough to destroy a person," he emphasized.

It was a truth that U.S. officials would unfortunately forget fourteen years later, as both the Marielitos and the Haitian boat people were shunted into makeshift camp sites, barbed-wire compounds and walled prisons where they would be detained for months and, in some cases, for years.

Not all was perfect in Miami, *Fortune* conceded. "Loud, anguished cries came from the Negro community and some labor unions because the Cubans were going to work for half the prevailing wages." A new social problem was being solved in Miami but only, in part, by making America's oldest social problem worse. The Cuban "economic miracle," later studies confirmed, to a significant extent "took place at the expense of the Black community in Dade County. Not only in the service sector, but in the entrepreneurial area as well," Cubans displaced American-born blacks.

Even as the resettlement program solved problems for Miami's Cubans,

> urban renewal—President Lyndon B. Johnson's "Great Society" panacea—created a new set of problems. In Overtown, many blacks were forced to move to other crowded ghettos while new housing was built. Expressways cut Overtown in half and caused many homes to be plowed under. Liberty City—once considered a model black community—received most of the overflow. Serious overcrowding, substandard housing and lack of hope turned Liberty City into a time bomb.

The time bomb would not go off until 1980. But when it did, Miami would be shaken to its foundations; the tremors would be felt throughout the whole United States.

In the meantime the Bay of Pigs fiasco had produced one of its strangest, and certainly one of its most overlooked, results—a practical triumph of American philanthropy. To this day the Kennedy administration's most successful "foreign aid" program—for Miami—reveals what the official class in Washington actually can achieve when its programs are, as the Potomac jargon has it, successfully "targeted."

Following the ransom of the Bay of Pigs survivors, both the president and his brother, Robert F. Kennedy, kept in close contact with the Cubans coming to the United States. Many were invited to the attorney-general's home in Virginia. Practical suggestions Cubans sent to the White House were speedily implemented, often after the president himself had read them.

The Kennedys had political as well as personal reasons for helping the Cubans. Even after Khrushchev withdrew his missiles, Cuba remained the greatest single foreign policy humiliation of the Kennedy presidency. More than that, the Cuban crisis contained the seeds of domestic political disaster if not handled adeptly.

An uncontrolled flood tide of impoverished, embittered Cuban exiles—jobless, homeless and eager to launch free-lance attacks on their former homeland from south Florida—not only would have unleashed havoc on Miami and created a new threat of war in the Florida Straits. As the Carter administration's inept handling of the Marielitos later showed, it would also have risked generating immense public hostility to the administration in Washington—not merely in Florida, but throughout the nation.

One of Kennedy's first actions following his speech at the Orange Bowl, therefore, was to establish a special refugee-relief program within the Department of Health, Education, and Welfare—and to fund it, interestingly enough, with special allocations taken out of the foreign aid appropriation. By the time Lyndon Johnson became president, the program was well managed, well entrenched and successful. Most important, the relief spending for the Cubans was beyond criticism either in Congress or the White House.

After all, what other federal program so dramatically vindicated the great official American contention of the era—that the American Way fulfilled human hope to the same immense extent Communism crushed it?

Between 1962 and 1980, the influx of Cubans into Miami occurred so gradually, and was managed so smoothly, that the area, on average, had to accommodate less than twenty-seven thousand new Cubans each year. It may have been the most adroitly handled immigration crisis in the history of the United States.

When the Cubans first started arriving, metropolitan Miami's total population was less than one million. By 1970 Miami's Latin population, then almost entirely Cuban, had risen from 100,000 to nearly 300,000. By 1980 it had topped 580,000; by 1983 it exceeded 780,000. By the end of this decade, it will reach at least a million, of which about 85 percent will still be Cuban, in spite of increasing immigration from other Latin American countries.

Even more important, the increase in the Latin *proportion* of Miami's total population was just as gradual. In 1962 Latins accounted for a little over 10 percent of Dade County's total population; by 1970 they accounted for just under a quarter, and by the beginning of 1980 for just over a third of the total. Today Latins, even though they now comprise about 45 percent of Dade County's population, are still a minority there.

Even those figures, however, exaggerate the disruptive impact of Latin migration, because over the last twenty years Greater Miami itself has not been static. One of the most dynamically expanding metropolitan areas in the United States, it has jumped jurisdictional boundaries to encompass Broward County to the north and much of Monroe County to the south. Today the three-county Miami metropolitan area includes nearly three and a quarter million people, of which less than 900,000, or about 28 percent, are classified as "Latin," even though hundreds of thousands of them are totally assimilated into American life.

The result, in these days when "real" Americans are increasingly apprehensive about the "illegal aliens" in their midst, should be deeply reassuring to those who sometimes have apocalyptic fears about the future of the American way of life. Even exotic Miami is still very much a part of the "real" America. And as Cubans and other Latin settlers adopt American ways, "real" Americans no doubt will continue to predominate there, even when people of Hispanic descent come to outnumber those with Anglo-Saxon, Jewish and other surnames. Already in Miami it is possible to hear the "refugees" of ten or fifteen years ago complain that the more recent arrivals from other Latin countries, even from Cuba itself, are "too foreign" for their taste.

To an extent perhaps not even its organizers anticipated, the Cuban relief program succeeded in fulfilling two essential policy objectives in Washington. First, it really did help the Cubans. Today it is difficult to find a Cuban banker, lawyer, civic leader or real estate magnate whose success story did not start out with the receipt of U.S. government support of some kind. Equally important, it helped the politicians in Washington—by diffusing this flood of migration away from Miami and the rest of Florida, and more evenly distributing it throughout the rest of the country.

Today America's vision of the Cubans is inseparable from its vision of Miami. People who think favorably of Cuban-Americans imagine a community of shopkeepers, of hardworking families running little *bodegas* in Little Havana. For others, the Cubans conjure up a darker but more exciting image, of a people thriving on Miami contraband, both material and moral. Certainly few Americans think of the Cubans without simultaneously thinking of palm trees and *paella,* of street fiestas, car chases, drug deals and all the other gaudy civic plumage that now defines Miami in the American mind.

But all that is as much a myth as the similar stereotypes of the Boston Irish—or the notion that all Italian-Americans are somehow connected with the Mafia.

Perhaps the most widely accepted and most unfounded myth about the Cuban refugees, in fact, is that almost all of them settled in Miami. The truth, and it is of enormous importance, is that the majority of them initially settled *outside* Florida. About a third of the Cubans settled in the New York metropolitan area, where many of them found blue-collar industrial jobs and helped stabilize decaying neighborhoods in the troubled New Jersey factory towns on the other side of the Hudson.

Nearly 10 percent settled in California, where the Cuban designer Adolfo Sardina would find a fashion fan in Nancy Reagan, and her husband an adept political fund-raiser in Tirso Del Junco, a medical officer during the Bay of Pigs invasion, later chairman of the California Republican party. Cubans also formed sizable communities in Illinois, Louisiana, Texas and Georgia, where another Cuban, Roberto C. Goizueta, would become chairman of the board and president of the Coca-Cola Corporation.

In time Cubans also would find themselves owners of Chicago TV stations, baseball stars in Minneapolis, professors at Pittsburgh, Georgetown and Harvard, and in the case of Alberto Salazar, a world-famous marathon runner living in Eugene, Oregon.

None of these Cubans, however, more deeply affected America's perception of itself and the world in the years following the Cuban missile crisis than Antonio Prohias, who had been a cartoonist in Havana before coming to New York in May 1960. Two months later he walked into the offices of *Mad* magazine and sold them the first of his endlessly funny "Spy vs. Spy" comic strips. The cloak-and-dagger absurdities of the Cold War had brought both Cuba and America to the brink of thermonuclear annihilation. Now, thanks to a Cuban émigré to the United States, the same absurdities found immortalization in cartoon characters as compulsively addicted to dirty tricks as any top-secret schemer in Washington.

Not that politics had forfeited its capacity for manufacturing situations more bizarre than those even the blackest humor could invent: eleven years after the CIA broke into Cuba, veterans of the Bay of Pigs broke into the Democratic National Committee headquarters at Watergate.

The ensuing constitutional crisis, in addition to much else, revealed that even when the United States "lost" a country like Cuba, it gained something as well. For both better and worse, Cubans would have an immeasurably greater impact on the United States, as a result of the U.S. failure to control events there, than they ever had back when U.S.-supported dictators made the island a safe and secure bastion of the "free world."

Another powerful legend is that the Cubans were somehow "different" from other immigrant groups.

From the beginning the Cubans prided themselves on being less assimilable than previous immigrants, and much more determined to retain their separate national, cultural and political identity. Their critics, surveying the Cuban "takeover" of Miami, agreed.

Yet everywhere they went, the Cubans showed a remarkable ability to adjust themselves not merely to the dominant national rhythms, but to the regional nuances and local idiosyncrasies of American life. Black and mixed-race Cubans, for example, showed a marked preference for settling in New York and New Jersey—as opposed to Miami, which hardly had a reputation for being the ideal place for blacks to make their fortune. Miami—always a post-industrial town in every sense of the word—attracted waiters, chefs, florists, salesmen, maids, to say nothing of prostitutes, drug dealers and service-sector professionals like bankers, lawyers, accountants and nurses.

This knack of the Cubans for fitting into whatever niches they found was so remarkable that even as most Americans became aware of the exotic transformation the Cubans had wrought in Miami, very few of them realized there were well-established Cuban communities in their own cities and hometowns. In New Jersey the Cubans worked on assembly lines; in southern California they worked in garment factories; in Chicago they did all the hard, dirty jobs Carl Sandburg romanticized, not excluding the butchering of hogs.

And in Miami? One of the least-founded myths about the Cubans is that, without them, Miami today would be a *normal* kind of place.

True enough, these Cuban "freedom fighters," once transported to Miami, would not just become electricians, real estate salesmen, bookkeepers, philanthropists, nurses, newspaper reporters and computer programmers. In this city where the boundaries between North and South, Latin and Anglo, good and evil, water and dry land always were fluid, the Cubans would develop enough schemes and scams—inside the law, outside the law, most of all in that no-man's-land in between—to turn "Miami Vice" into a nightly show.

But what was so "Cuban" about that? Flagler had started out in oil and wound up in ocean-going railways; Fisher had started out in headlights and wound up with elephants that doubled as golf caddies. Even the hardheaded Mr. Alphonse Capone, once he transferred his syndicates south from Chicago, was not immune to the existential zaniness Miami unleashes in all sorts of people.

Miami had not lost its essential genius; even as the Cubans changed Miami almost beyond recognition, Miami would change the Cubans almost beyond recognition, too.

One reason Miami today is such an important international center of trade, communications and finance is that so many Cubans did *not* settle there.

As the Castro diaspora unfolded, Cuban communities sprang up in Europe, especially in Madrid, but also in other Spanish cities, and in Paris and London. Others headed to Venezuela, Mexico and Puerto Rico, as well as Canada. Soon there was hardly a Spanish-speaking country anywhere that did not have its nucleus, large or small, of Cuban émigrés. Meanwhile the great commercial centers of the United States developed important Cuban communities, too.

Thanks to another accident of history, Miami's Cuban community did not find itself an isolated enclave in a foreign land—a "ghetto" cut off from the outside world. To the contrary, the Cuban exodus had created a complex and efficient intercontinental network of personal, professional and financial relations, with Miami and Miami's Cubans at its center.

Today it is customary to give the Cubans major credit for "building" a new Miami. But skyscrapers, freeways, shopping malls and airports don't make a "city." They are only the physical manifestations of the invisible economic and human processes that bring a community into existence and make it prosper. In the twenties the Spanish-revival skyscrapers of Miami were only incidentally copies of belltowers and palaces on the other side of the Atlantic Ocean. Monumental manifestations of America's twin compulsions both to build and to escape were what they really were. The same is true today. The sleek glass towers downtown aren't monuments to the cold, northern rationalism of Walter Gropius and Mies van der Rohe. They are by-products of the tropical proliferation of human, technological and economic linkages that underlie Miami's success as a city.

Miami today is a place where so many things converge so profitably because, beginning with the arrival of the Cubans, it developed an almost vegetal capacity to reach out and absorb every manufactured and natural product of this earth—not excluding drugs, guns and every other imaginable contraband, including money and people—and photosynthesize them first into energy and then into wealth.

Geography from the beginning had singled out Miami for this special role as nexus. Then, beginning in the 1960s, technology—the jet airplane, communications satellites, the computer—virtually eliminated the barriers of distance and time that previously had impeded Miami's emergence as a great international nerve center, linking the continental markets of North America, Latin America and Europe. But strategic location and advanced technology, in and of themselves, would not have sufficed.

Miami needed the right people, rightly placed, not just in Miami, but around the world, to animate its intercontinental possibilities. By dispersing the Cubans, instead of concentrating them in Miami, the U.S. refugee program unintentionally helped make Miami a center of human relationships as financially valuable as any confluence of trade or air routes.

This achievement, it should be emphasized, was not exclusively a triumph of philanthropy and "freedom." Had they been given the choice, much larger numbers of Cubans would have stayed in

Miami instead of settling in other parts of the country. But even when they reached "Freedom House," the Cubans found that U.S. officials, as much as those in Havana, were determined to shape their lives for reasons of their own. Only those with family ties or other strong reasons for settling there were allowed to stay in Miami. Others—sometimes almost at random—were sent off to places ranging from Alabama to the Pacific Northwest, and in these decisions, "freedom of choice" played no part. Those refusing to settle outside south Florida were "denied further federal government assistance" and left to fend for themselves as best they could.

Another U.S. government policy—the American trade embargo against Cuba—inadvertently assured Miami's future importance by making exploitation of the Cubans' international network a necessity, not just a possibility. By banning all commercial relations between the two countries, the United States cut these exiles off from their traditional sources of income. As a result no Cubans in Miami would survive, let alone grow rich, by importing sugar or cigars from Cuba, or by exporting U.S. manufactures to Havana, as earlier Cuban settlers in Florida had. Instead the Cubans were obliged to become actors in a much vaster, and more lucrative, drama of capitalism that, with Miami as its nexus, would embrace not just the Caribbean, but the whole of North and South America, parts of Europe, and in the end include both the far Pacific and Asia.

Like the overseas Chinese in Southeast Asia and the European Jews of the diaspora, these Cuban exiles would grow wealthy and influential in scores of countries because economically, as well as politically, they could not go home again.

Several other "accidents" were also vital in assuring the Cubans' —and Miami's—later success.

One of the most important was that, from the beginning, the U.S. refugee program, in spite of its frankly political motivation, was not organized around the ideological principle of anti-Communism. Instead John Thomas and its other directors ran the operation, wisely enough, on the humanitarian basis of family reunification.

That is to say, eligibility for admission to the United States did not depend on whether the migrant had actively opposed, or even passively supported, Castro. It depended on whether the migrant had close relatives already inside the United States.

The Cuban revolution had divided almost all Cuban families, even the most powerful. One of Castro's own sisters, Juanita Castro Ruz, would end up running a small *farmacia* on Southwest Twenty-seventh Avenue in Miami. But the exodus did not destroy humanity's most important economic unit. The Cuban family was strengthened, as the first to leave Cuba were joined by their spouses, children and parents, and together they struggled to build new lives for themselves.

Today wealthy middle-aged Cubans—as they relax beside their suburban swimming pools or aboard their boats in Biscayne Bay—like to reminisce about the bad old days when they first reached Miami. The years spent waiting tables or sacking groceries have become to the Cuban success story what the log cabin and the one-room schoolhouse were to an earlier version of the American Dream.

It is quite true that, in the early days of the Cuban colonization of Miami, surgeons washed dishes and engineers swept floors. But even when such menial labor was actually a step up, as it was for some Cubans, these newcomers were motivated by something much more powerful than mere ambition for money and success. They knew they were fighting for the future of their children, to assure a comfortable old age for their parents—and to sustain what not even dispossession and defeat could take from them, their dignity.

Long before they began to predominate there, the Cubans—in spite of the loss of their homeland and all the other disruptions overtaking their lives—often felt much more "at home" there than native-born Americans did, and for good reason.

Unlike young ghetto blacks, unlike the elderly in their retirement ghettos—unlike the single or childless American-born professionals who, in whatever shiny new Sun Belt setting they pursue happiness, so often find themselves alone, and without a sense of purpose—the Cubans arrived in Miami with an asset even more valuable than U.S. citizenship. Because of the sense of purpose and belonging their shared struggle gave them, the Cubans were liberated from the feeling of alienation that scars the lives, and limits the possibilities, of so many people in the United States.

Family ties also help explain Miami's future economic dynamism. In a functioning family unit, no man, woman or child is an island. Over the next twenty years, the Cuban "economic miracle" would not be limited to the achievements of the men who transformed themselves from waiters into bank presidents, and from janitors into real estate developers. It would also be the accomplishment of the women who worked as waitresses and secretaries, of the children who delivered newspapers, mowed lawns, hawked flowers at traffic intersections and, when they reached their teens, drove taxicabs and delivery vans. And behind them all would be the grandmothers who made beds, washed dishes and cooked dinner while the others earned American dollars.

All this had been true in Havana, of course. But, oddly enough, in Miami the economic advantages of traditional Cuban family life were actually multiplied. In the United States, education for the children was not only free, but compulsory, and when a grandparent turned sixty-five, the family's economic strength was actually increased, because now the monthly Social Security check arrived in the mail. Most important of all, relocation to the United States not only preserved the strengths of the traditional Cuban family, it liberated it, economically speaking, from its traditional inefficiencies.

In Miami, unlike Havana, the idea of a wife working was no longer heretical: now the *macho* thing to do was to adjust resourcefully to the challenge of survival in America. Back home, the spectacle of an engineer becoming a waiter—or of a waiter becoming an engineer—would have been profoundly offensive to some Cubans. Now everything was permissible because everything was necessary.

In that sense the two decades between the overthrow of Batista in December 1958 and the arrival of the Marielitos in May 1980 were not a period of privation, but a charmed era for Miami's Cubans. Freed from the constraints of life in their homeland, they were also immune, for the time being, from all the subversions of the American way of life. Behind them lay all the threats to personal dignity, hope and ambition that poverty and life under dictatorship entail. Ahead of them lay all the threats to their traditional values —drugs, violent crime, divorce, rampant individualism, the generation gap and the breakup of the family itself—that affluence and life in a free society contain.

They regarded it as an ordeal at the time. But today Miami's Cubans already are beginning to look back on those first decades in the United States not only as a heroic, but as a golden, age, and quite rightly so.

Never again would life be so hard—or so challenging, rewarding and simple.

The unique circumstances of the Cuban exodus do more than explain the Cuban community's economic success; they also help explain the difficulties some other immigrant groups have faced in the United States. Today our prevailing image of the "illegal alien" is of a young, poor and uneducated male entering the United States in search of employment, usually illicit, in the nether regions of our society.

That stereotype is far from correct: women are also pouring into the United States from the poorer countries, and the "brain drain" of doctors, scientists and other skilled professionals from Third World nations to the United States both helps us and hurts the countries they are leaving. But it does reveal one important truth: by turning migrants into criminals, by refusing them protection of the law and access to U.S. social services—above all, by denying them the possibility of sharing their new lives with their families and loved ones—we don't stop migration. The stupendous "push" north created by poverty in Latin America is far too great for any

U.S. domestic policy to do that. But we often do guarantee that the migrants we get are doomed to be liabilities, not assets to American society.

Myths do tell great truths, and the greatest truth the Cuban epic tells is that the magnetic power of the American Dream cannot be switched on and off by officials in Washington. Today the Haitians, the Salvadorans, the Jamaicans, the Guatemalans, the Colombians, the Mexicans and all the others are coming here for all the same reasons our own ancestors, as well as the Cubans, did. After nearly half a millennium of superpower confrontation in the Caribbean—after two hundred years of Americans proclaiming alliances for progress—life for all too many of our closest neighbors is still brutal, nasty and short. And the United States, for all its failures and follies, remains one of the last best hopes of mankind, both because of itself, and in spite of itself.

Whether we welcome them as "freedom fighters" or treat them as criminals, the success of future immigrants without any doubt will depend principally on their own industry and ambition.

But their future, and our future, also will depend on a kind of grace—on whether we bestow on them, accidentally or not, the same kind of welcome, the same degree of legitimacy, the Cubans received when they brought their hopes to our shores.

The U.S. government was not the only benefactor of Cuban refugees.

Castro's decision to permit wholesale migration ensured that virtual whole communities reestablished themselves in the United States.

One crucial result was that, even when the flow of immigration became much more indiscriminate, few Cubans would be alone upon arrival. In Miami almost every district of Cuba established its own *municipio*—a veritable municipal government-in-exile, complete with its own "mayor," elected by former residents of the same neighborhood. So whether he arrived from downtown Havana, a provincial capital like Camagüey or a remote village in Oriente

Province, the exile, even if he knew no one personally, found himself among relatives of relatives and friends of friends. American officials provided the money; family ties and the *municipios* provided crucial stepping-stones to a job, a home, and to something even more important—that sense of community without which a person, even in his own homeland, is a stranger.

By forbidding military-age males to leave Cuba, and encouraging "unproductive" Cubans—young women, unattached mothers and old people—to go to the United States, Castro inadvertently helped strengthen the social fabric of the Cuban exile community: to this day Cubans remain unique among recent Latin American immigrants to the United States in that women outnumber men, and that young, uprooted males—always the most violent and volatile sector in any population—do not predominate.

As a result, the Cubans wound up perpetuating, not destroying, another theme from Miami's past. In that raw, volatile town, where every decade brought its new upheaval, women and old people always had played a unique constructive role—introducing into what otherwise might have been total chaos a modicum of common sense and social stability.

Now, in the midst of Miami's greatest human upheaval ever, the calm, clear vision of Julia Tuttle once again would play its role, even as the rambunctious spirit of Carl Fisher and Al Capone found countless Hispanic incarnations, too.

It had taken both Tuttle and Flagler, both Fisher and Collins, to create the previous Miamis. This time, too, a bizarre and unforeseeably fecund conjugality provided the foundations for the new city the Cubans would create.

Passions there still run too high for it to happen. But perhaps in another generation or two, Miamians—Americans—of Cuban descent will agree that their accomplishments, impressive as they have been, are not theirs alone.

They will recognize that defeat always contains the seeds of victories, and victory the seeds of defeats both stranger and more fertile than we human beings can predict—and so decide to erect a monument to the two figures who, more than any others, were responsible for creating, for both them and Miami, such an interesting future.

I shall not propose a specific design for the monument. That should be left to some Miami architect of the future, and no doubt that design will be as idiosyncratic and illuminating as any in Miami history. But it's not too early to suggest the wording of the tribute to be chiseled in marble—or perhaps etched with laser beams in some synthetic wonder substance of the twenty-first century: "Homage to Kennedy and Castro: Co-Founders, in Spite of Themselves, of Modern Miami and Its New Place in the World."

14

Fantasy's Child

Two entirely new cities were born thanks to the Cuban exodus. Even as Miami became a city richer and more powerful, more full of both the light and darkness of human potential than Havana had ever been, Havana itself—metropolis of the heart—also underwent a wondrous transformation.

As the skyscrapers of Miami climbed higher, the courtyards of Havana grew more gracious. As the Cubans raced along I-95 to their next appointments, the evening strolls along the Prado became longer, slower, sweeter.

In the new Miami, the Cubans sat down at Formica dinette sets to eat instant rice and microwave chicken. While game shows blared out from the television, they discussed car payments in fading Spanish and broken English. In the new Havana of these exile's imaginations, life was made up of cool siestas, followed by candlelit soirees.

After 1962 the Cubans of the diaspora would live simultaneously in two countries—a real America, a mythic Cuba. And much more than the facts of diplomacy and politics, the psychic relations between these two countries, unfolding in the minds and emotions of Miami's Cubans, would account for both the triumphs and the follies of their lives.

*

In the minds of Miami's Cubans, at least at the beginning, both the real Miami and the imaginary Havana were populated by the same people. In Miami each Cuban was now a heroic freedom fighter, even if he had not actually fought at the Bay of Pigs. In Miami each Cuban would become rich again, even if he had only been a poor *guajiro,* a landless peasant, back home.

Miami, the Cubans told themselves, was only temporary, imaginary. Havana was real, enduring; only wait, work, save your money and, in another year or two, the inevitable would surely happen. The Americans, at last, would understand their responsibilities as a great power and act like men. The *guajiros,* at last, would disenthrall themselves from Communist propaganda; they would understand where their true interests lay and rise up against Castro.

It would all begin when a few brave men, once again, landed on some moonless beach. The dictator, once again, would flee the false Havana. And this time, naïveté and betrayal would not prevail! Havana would be revealed for what it was, what it always had been —the city of the true Aleph.

There was nothing unprecedented in this, of course. Martí's "real Republic" had never existed either. But that had not stopped Martí's mythical land of liberty from being a much more powerful force in the lives of the Cuban exiles of his generation than Spain's bedraggled Caribbean colony had ever been. Martí's Cuba never died because, like all myths, it would live so long as it retained the power to make people believe. But after 1962, Martí's Cuba would have to coexist with three other fantasy Cubas.

One of these was the Cuba of the U.S. military and ideological imagination—that bottomless font of Communist subversion that, if U.S. officials were to be believed, had a far-flung ability to dictate events that much surpassed that of the larger, richer and more powerful United States. Then there was Castro's own socialist utopia—that shabby, isolated workers' paradise of run-down factories, dwindling sugar crops and love motels that, as the years passed, would become as dependent on the Soviet Union, and indebted to it, as Cuba had earlier been on the United States and Spain.

To explore the mythology of the Cuban exodus is also to explore a third fantasy Cuba—the Cuba that flourished in the imagination of the exiles after 1962. The exact opposite of the Cuba of history and headlines, this was a charmed, prosperous and happy land. But for a series of historical follies and tragedies—the naïveté of Americans like Kennedy; the treachery of Cubans like Castro—it would be rich and free as America, but with an essential difference. *Their* Cuba—the Cubans of Miami never doubted, even as they created an ungainly, sprawling and vital new Miami out of neon, plastic, asphalt and concrete blocks—would be more humane, more cultured; it would be more gracious and civilized than the United States, in its relentless materialism and irresponsible individualism, could ever be.

What judgment is one to make of this particular Cuba? To disprove its existence is easy enough. But that cannot deprive it of its immense power. In fact, after 1962, it turned out to be the most powerful Cuba of them all.

True, the Cubas in Washington and Havana could muster armies, but the great revelation following the missile crisis was how impotent the fantasies of the state turned out to be. Like Kennedy's missiles and Khrushchev's missiles, all they could do was destroy worlds.

The Cuba in Miami was very different. As the future would show, it had a great constructive power. This Cuba, precisely because it was illusory, could propel human beings into great constructive endeavors and sustain them at the task.

They had a lot in common, Kennedy and Castro, besides personal charisma, a way with words—and the fact that, in terms of the great tasks they proclaimed for themselves and their nations, they were failures.

Perhaps the most important thing they had in common was that both were captives of the ideological fantasies of their time, and so each insisted on generalizing his personal leadership, and the nation he led, into a universal paradigm for the rest of the world. For Kennedy and Castro, power in their own countries, even supreme power, was not enough. They had to believe that, because they led them, their nations were destined for a greatness totally transcending any possible glory of the past.

For more than four hundred years, Havana had been the incontestable fulcrum of the Caribbean, the great port and emporium where all the natural riches of the Indies, all the manufactures of North America, all the luxuries of Europe had converged. But that wasn't enough for Castro, any more than the American preeminence of the Eisenhower era was enough for Kennedy.

So Castro set out to give Havana an entirely new importance—to make it the new beacon of revolutionary change throughout Latin America and the rest of the world. As a result revolutionary changes in Cuba's place in the world did occur. For the first time in history, commercial and cultural, not just military and political, control of the Caribbean would shift north of the Straits of Florida to the North American mainland, as Miami became the new Havana. Havana, like Shanghai and Petrograd before it, became a city of the past. Castro, the Western Hemisphere's most renowned anti-imperialist, would become one of the principal creators of a vast new inter-American empire, this one with Miami as its capital.

The future held similar rebukes in store for John F. Kennedy. Greatest of them all was that the "long twilight struggle" to which Kennedy summoned America would prove to be of such little consequence.

"The message of Cuba, of Laos, of the rising din of Communist voices in Asia and Latin America," Kennedy proclaimed as the Bay of Pigs invaders were driven back into the sea,

> —these messages are all the same. The complacent, the
> self-indulgent, the soft societies are about to be swept
> away with the debris of history. Only the strong, only the

industrious, only the determined, only the courageous,
only the visionary . . . can possibly survive.

He could not have been more wrong. Even when Cuba was lost
irretrievably, no hurricane of revolution swept the world. Even
very close to Havana, the self-indulgent were not swept away. If
anything, the sybaritic life of Key West, just ninety miles from
Cuba, became more frenetic, more rococo. Following the Communist victory, José Martí's headquarters in Key West became a gay
guesthouse—and when the Cuban invaders finally did arrive, in
1980, the Marielitos' objective was not to sweep away all the complacencies, all the self-indulgences of America, only to join in the
fun.

Over the next twenty years, much more than Cuba would be
"lost." But even when some dominoes did fall here and there, it
was of no greater general significance than the "loss" of Florida had
been, back in the days when Florida had been traded around like
a four of clubs. Kennedy's "relentless struggle in every corner of
the globe" turned out to be of such little importance for two reasons: the president both grossly overestimated and grossly under-
estimated the power of the United States.

The negative lesson of the Kennedy era was also the lesson of
Teddy Roosevelt, of Andrew Jackson: even when we Americans
conquered foreign peoples, we could not confer liberty on them,
because freedom is something that cannot be imposed from without.

But America has always taught another lesson, that liberty and
opportunity are forces more powerful, and infinitely more productive, than bullets and bombs. After 1962 it would be Miami—not
Green Berets and White House speechwriters—that would teach
this lesson anew, to the whole of Latin America.

Castro's Cuba would also wind up teaching, if not learning, some
equally old lessons. The most important of them was that ideology
and politics, in the end, count for so very little when it comes to
mastering the fundamental human problems of this world. Ideologically, of course, Castro's decision to allow so many Cubans to

abandon their country made perfect sense. The unproductive old people, the dependent wives and children of the men who had fled —revolutionary Cuba was better off without them. What did it matter even that with the departure of doctors, engineers and other professionals, Cuba was losing so many of its most highly trained citizens? Marxist dogma itself proved the flight of the bourgeoisie was a blessing in disguise.

So right from the beginning, Castro's Cuba found itself a "classless society" in the most disastrous sense, and over the next twenty years, it would go on paying an enormous price for its ideological uniformity as hundreds of thousands of the country's most productive and highly motivated citizens opted for exile.

In his quest to revolutionize Cuban society, Castro had forgotten that standing guard in uniform, or shuffling papers in government ministries—whether men do it or women do it—doesn't create wealth; it only consumes it.

Kennedy and Castro nonetheless shared a notable achievement: thanks to them, Miami's Cubans were given the whole key to their future success. This was nothing less than a unique sense of historical mission—a powerful belief in a shared, and very special, destiny.

By first approving the disastrous Bay of Pigs invasion, then by ransoming its survivors, Kennedy had laid the foundations for this sense of mission. He gave these exiles what was, to them at least, an epic past of courage and valor on the battlefield. More than that, he bequeathed to them a sense of unfinished business.

No American politician, the Cubans vowed to themselves, could take away from them what they now saw as their appointed historical task. Whoever held power in Washington, however much he "betrayed" them, *they* would keep alive in Miami the "real Republic" of Cuban culture, tradition, achievement and liberty. More than that, they would be as good as Kennedy's word—seizing "every opportunity to educate" themselves and their children, as the president had put it, "in the many skills and disciplines which will be necessary when Cuba is once more free."

Castro's contribution was even greater. For over the following twenty-five years, the determination to prove that Castro, not they, was on the losing side of history would drive Miami's Cubans on to success. This determination would be the force that shaped, defined—and gave meaning and purpose—to every aspect of their lives.

The political and military dimension of the Cubans' "anti-Communism" has attracted enormous attention, and for justifiable reason. It would be the great negative theme running through the generally positive contribution Cubans made to the United States. After 1962, mindless, pointless, often violent and criminal actions, not excluding the most vicious acts of terrorism, all would be condoned by the supposed sanctity of the Cubans' anti-Communist crusade for "freedom."

Following their ransom, the vast majority of the Bay of Pigs veterans led normal, honest, law-abiding lives. But a minority of them forever after worked on the assumption that any action was patriotic so long as, in some twisted way, it could be linked to *la causa*—the sacred duty of continuing the struggle against Castro and all other "Communists," even when they were American citizens.

Even today U.S. officials habitually blame Cuban "subversion" for the problems of Latin America. But one consequence of the Bay of Pigs was that subversion, thereafter, wasn't limited to Communist Cubans. In Guatemala, Nicaragua and many other nations—certainly not excluding the United States—Cuban "freedom fighters" would also subvert democracy. The Watergate break-in was only the logical culmination of this corrupt fanaticism that, far from controlling, some U.S. officials, notably in the CIA and the White House, cynically exploited.

After 1962 there was no real possibility, however much they refused to accept the fact, for Miami's Cubans to defeat Castro militarily. And so the worst among them opted for a fantasy crusade that, while harming Castro not at all, besmirched the honor of Cubans everywhere. No Cubans in Havana were endangered by these antics, but Cubans in Miami were not so fortunate. Periodically the city would be swept by terrorism as local "freedom fighters" turned on local "Communists." In a typically cowardly murder in 1974, an "anti-Communist" sniper shot one exile leader, José Elias de la Torriente, through the window of his Coral Gables home. In February 1975 Luciano Nieves, who had advocated peaceful dialogue with Cuba, was shot dead in a hospital parking lot.

Over a twelve-month period, "anti-Castro" terrorists bombed more than twenty "targets" in Miami, including Spanish-language radio stations. In April 1976 one of the most shameful incidents of all occurred, when the car of Cuban radio commentator Emilio Milian was bombed, and his legs shattered. "Anti-Castro terrorists," investigators concluded, "wanted to silence Milian for his editorials condemning bombings in Miami."

Such crimes were not the only price Miami and its Cubans would pay for habitually tolerating, and frequently encouraging, this kind of "anti-Communism." Like "state's rights" racism and McCarthyism, it would cheapen, corrupt and poison the entire political process for long periods of time. The need for successful Miami politicians—Anglo and Latin, Democratic and Republican—to prove their "anti-Communism" to Cuban voters would lead many candidates to run for office against Castro, rather than on any positive platform. As a result Miami, supposedly a sophisticated, pragmatic and tolerant city, at times would witness some of the most primitive and hate-filled political campaigns in the nation. It would also elect some of the most embarrassingly inept local and state officials the U.S. political process has recently produced.

The Cuban community's sometimes fanatical "conservatism," which usually works to the advantage of Republicans, may not be historically justified. After all, it was Eisenhower, not Kennedy, who really "lost" Cuba, and Nixon and Reagan did no more to win it back than Johnson and Carter. But that has not stopped it from becoming a crucial factor not just in Miami, but in the politics of Florida as well.

*

310

The need to court the Cuban vote may well be of national significance in 1988, when Florida's burgeoning population, and immense bloc of electoral votes, could possibly decide who is the next president of the United States. One candidate who already has assiduously courted Miami's Cuban voters is Vice-President George Bush, whose son Jeb is head of the local Republican party.

The Cubans' growing influence on the political course of Florida, and Florida's growing influence on the political course of the whole United States, is of great international significance as well. This is because the Cubans, like some other American ethnic groups, have acquired a virtual veto over change in United States foreign policy in the area that concerns them most, in this case relations with Cuba.

Though Jimmy Carter, with disastrous consequences, came close, no American president has ever been really willing to pay the domestic political price of normalizing relations with Cuba the way Richard Nixon did with China. This is so even though Castro, on many occasions, has made known his interest in cutting a deal. In the future the Cubans' growing political clout will only increase the dangers of such an effort for any future president, whether Republican or Democrat, "liberal" or "conservative."

Many Cubans have long realized that mindless anti-Communism serves no one's interests, least of all their own. "A community of seven hundred thousand people cannot have for its sole political agenda that Castro is a son of a bitch," a prominent banker and community activist named Bernardo Benes told me when I visited him at his house in Miami Beach. But Benes himself is living proof of just how risky it can be to deviate from that agenda. Back in the late seventies, he cooperated with the CIA in opening informal channels of communication between the United States and Cuba. Though his good offices were fully in keeping with U.S. policy at that time, Benes was denounced as a "traitor" for his meetings with Castro. His bank was picketed, his daughters were insulted in Miami department stores, and he was ostracized from the Cuban community's leadership. There were also the usual death threats, and anti-Semitism was not absent, either, from this campaign of abuse against Benes, who describes himself "as very Cuban, very Jewish and very American."

Years later Benes was still unrepentant. "I feel sorry for people who want to do something," he said, "but let three little radio stations and a bunch of little newspapers terrorize them. . . . Those 'anti-Communists,' " he added, "are only helping the Soviet Union."

Whomever they help, there is no doubt whom such tactics hurt. Miami Cubans have paid the highest price for our long estrangement from Cuba. Yet the Cubans themselves remain one of the biggest stumbling blocks to the kind of normalization that not only might let many Cubans go home again, but also peacefully pave the way for some fundamental political changes inside Cuba itself.

This is unfortunate for the United States because this country, in terms of its national security interests, potentially has much to gain from reducing Cuba's dependence on the Soviet Union. It is all the sadder for another reason. The exiled Cubans could play a great constructive, perhaps even an historically decisive, role in Cuba—using "the many disciplines and skills" that President Kennedy, so long ago, urged them to acquire, to help Cuba build a better future, in much the same way overseas Chinese are now helping post-Maoist China to chart a more pragmatic course.

Mindless "anti-Communism" is no longer the political force in Miami it once was. The Cuban community nonetheless is still far from ready to embark on a new "success story"—one that would not feed on, but at last heal, the wounds of the past. Fundamental changes in U.S.-Cuban relations will be extremely difficult until they are.

As a result the Cubans' successful political integration, like their successful economic integration into American life, also winds up proving one of the oldest lessons of America: in a democracy people may not always get what is wisest or best.

But they usually wind up getting what they want.

After 1962 no more than a few hundred Cubans would be directly involved in "anti-Castro" acts of violence, in spite of all the publicity such incidents received. For the overwhelming majority of all Cubans in the United States, the "anti-Communist" struggle would take quite a different, and much more constructive, form.

The exiles would fulfill their "determination to prove that Castro was wrong," as Msgr. Walsh puts it, through "a commitment to hard work and to risk-taking" that would make their Miami, not Castro's Havana, the city where Latin America's dreams of material progress came true.

In that endeavor at least, the Cubans won a victory surpassing anyone's expectations. Between 1963 and 1980, the average annual income of a refugee family in Dade County increased by more than 1,000 percent—from $2,229 to $22,356. By 1986 per capita incomes for Cubans in the Miami area exceeded $6,000, considerably more than seven times the average in Cuba.

The approximately 750,000 Cubans in the Miami area today have a combined annual income of about $4.5 billion—or more than half of what the entire Cuban population of about ten million people earns. This is a truly remarkable achievement. In less than one generation, they had established for themselves a standard of living never known in Havana at any time in history, under any regime. But that was only the beginning of it. In twenty years the newest of this country's Hispanic communities had outstripped Mexican-Americans, Puerto Ricans and all other major groups to become the wealthiest of all Americans of "Spanish" origin.

More than that, the Cubans had achieved a degree of affluence rivaling that of "real" Americans as well. By 1983 the average Cuban-American household in Miami had a higher income than the Florida state average. Even more impressive, young, upwardly mobile Cuban families—those headed by men and women between twenty-five and thirty-four—had higher incomes than white, native-born Americans in comparable circumstances. Perhaps never before in American history has such "a large non-English-speaking immigrant group . . . exhibited more rapid upward socioeconomic mobility."

In 1983 two Miami radio stations—WSUA, also called Radio Suave, and WQBA, which calls itself *La Cubanisima*—commissioned the Strategy Research Corporation to conduct and then publish, in English, its ninth major market research and public opinion study of the Miami Latin community.

Their findings documented just how great were the strides Cubans made in Miami between 1962 and 1980. As early as 1975, nearly 70 percent of all Latins in Dade County owned their own homes; 94 percent of all Latin households had telephones; 88 percent owned cars. By 1978 nearly two-thirds of all Latins in the Miami area—that is to say, virtually all employed adults—used credit cards. By the end of the 1970s, Cuban families in Miami were spending considerably more on groceries a week than similar families in Havana earned altogether, and they weren't merely cooking plantains and black beans.

Miami's Cubans, the survey showed, had developed an appetite for American food and were dining out in American-style fast-food restaurants an average of 105 times a year. Kentucky-style fried chicken and pizza, the survey revealed, were particular favorites. American network television, it turned out, was also very popular —more popular than Spanish-language programming, though the Latins did prefer Spanish-language radio shows.

It is now conventional to regard the Cuban success story as a triumph of capitalism, and for understandable reasons; in the purely factual sense, that is exactly what it was. But to see it simply in those terms misses the essential point of what happened, and *why.*

So far as the Cubans were concerned, their success was *not* a mere matter of some hardworking, self-interested people exploiting a major, and very profitable, economic opportunity. To the contrary, Miami's Cubans saw themselves as embattled heroes in an epochal struggle in which good, in the end, must triumph over evil. So, once again in Florida, illusion conquered: Miami did in fact become the glittering vindication of America's capacity both to excite hope and to create plenty, precisely because the Cubans in Miami refused to let the reality of defeat and poverty stand in their way.

The immense advantages the Cubans' sense of community and shared purpose gave them were documented in the course of a six-year study of the Cuban immigrant experience, conducted by Alejandro Portes, Juan M. Clark and Manuel M. Lopez.

From 1973 to 1979, the three sociologists followed the experiences of 590 Cuban newcomers. They wanted to discover which were the worst problems they encountered in adjusting to life in a new country, and what dissatisfactions and personal problems adjusting to a foreign culture produced.

They made an extraordinary discovery.

There were no dissatisfactions—and virtually no problems, except for learning English—in adjusting to life in Miami at all. Nearly 94 percent of those questioned said they were satisfied or very satisfied—and only 9/10 of 1 percent said they were dissatisfied—with life in the United States.

When asked to name their biggest problem in adjusting to life in America, by far the most prevalent answer, 44.8 percent, was "None." More than 27 percent said they had language problems, but only 11 percent mentioned economic difficulties. Only 3 percent complained that life in Miami had created family and other personal problems.

More than that, the overwhelming majority seemed to view Miami not merely as a land of opportunity, but also as a paradise. Their answers documented an extraordinarily positive—indeed a downright unrealistic—faith in the possibilities life in Miami offered, in the Cubans' own potential for accomplishment and, even more remarkably, in the goodwill of their American neighbors.

Ninety-seven percent said they were satisfied with the economic opportunities Miami offered. Even more surprising, manifest as Miami's social and racial problems are, were their answers to three other questions. Seventy percent of these Cubans declared there was no racial discrimination, in terms of economic opportunity, in Miami and the rest of the United States. Nearly two-thirds said there was "no discrimination" of any kind against Cubans. By an even larger majority they described their relations with their American neighbors not merely as friendly, but "close." These people were also clearly filled not just with esteem for Miami and their American neighbors, but with a most healthy self-confidence as well. In spite of their newness in America, their language problems and their generally lower levels of education and income, only

1.5 percent considered themselves in any way "inferior" to native-born Americans.

This perception of Miami as a city of racial equality, intercommunal harmony and economic opportunity, of course, could not have conflicted more with the prevailing stereotype of Miami as a city of riots, crime, drugs, social disintegration and death of the American way. What explains this veritable euphoria about a city that, at the time the survey was conducted, already had one of the highest crime rates in the United States?

One of the more intriguing discoveries of this and other studies is that what Cubans *believe* about themselves and their new country is far more important than what the objective facts of the situation happen to be.

In the study the two radio stations commissioned, for instance, Miami Cubans simply refused to stereotype themselves according to the good-vs.-bad, Cuban-vs.-American and Hispanic-vs.-Anglo categories outsiders sometimes try to impose on life in Miami.

Nearly 97 percent did say they were "proud to be Latin" and believed their "culture, tradition and ways should be preserved." More than 96 percent also believed it was vital for their children to be proficient in Spanish. But more than 98 percent said it was vital for them to be fluent in English, and 93.4 percent said it was also important to vote in American elections.

Even though the Cubans sometimes are accused of being clannish, considerably fewer than half said it was important to them that their children marry Latins, as opposed to native-born Americans. Only a quarter said they preferred to live in Latin neighborhoods. Surprisingly, nearly a third preferred not to—but the largest group didn't care about the ethnicity of their neighbors one way or the other, so long as the housing itself was adequate and the streets were safe.

Those questioned also refused to make either/or choices when it came to the pursuit of happiness. By decisive majorities, the Cubans declared they liked to socialize with *both* Latin friends and

American friends, to listen and dance to *both* Latin and American music. More than 80 percent of the Cubans described themselves as Americanized to a greater or lesser extent. But this didn't seem to bother them, in spite of their pride in their culture. The same immense majority said they were "still Latin" or that they had kept their Latin culture, in spite of their adoption of American ways.

One of the most interesting revelations of the study Clark and the others conducted was that those asked consistently overestimated their fluency in English—and, by implication, the degree of their success in integrating themselves into American life. After six years in the United States, for example, 79 percent of the migrants described themselves as either fluent or knowledgeable in English. Yet when the sociologists administered a quite simple, nine-question, multiple-choice test in English, they discovered this wasn't the case at all.

Only 8.7 percent managed to answer eight or nine of the questions correctly—an accomplishment that the investigators took, rather generously, as a sign of "fluency" in English. Fifteen percent managed to answer six or seven of the questions, and so showed "moderate knowledge" of English. But more than three-quarters were unable to answer more than five questions, and nearly half could decipher only one of the questions, or none. Such highly optimistic "self-evaluations can obviously not be confused with actual" success in learning English, the sociologists concluded.

That certainly is the case in terms of something quantifiable like language skills. But the exact opposite is true when it comes to understanding the *quality* of the Cuban success. Precisely because their "self-evaluations" of themselves, of Miami and of their future prospects were so high—unrealistically high, by any factual standard—the Cubans embarked on their adventure in America not only with a sense of communal purpose, but with a personal optimism and self-assurance that made all the contradictions in who they were, and what they were trying to achieve, irrelevant.

Was their purpose to grow rich in Miami? Or to liberate Havana? To become Americans? Or to prove that they, not Castro and his Communists, were *Cubanisima*?

The Cuban answer to those questions was the same as their answer to questions about Latin music and American music, the importance of knowing Spanish and the importance of knowing English: All Of The Above. Just as it had with earlier migrants, Miami had convinced these newcomers you could have it all.

Following the Bay of Pigs, U.S. official "misinformation" would do Castro no more harm than the dirty tricks did. But as the ensuing decades proved, no number of revolutionary pronunciamentos in Havana could diminish the allure of the life the Cubans in Miami had created for themselves, let alone drown out the appeal of the commercial radio stations in Miami.

Kennedy had feared, and Castro had hoped, that revolutionary Havana would unleash enormous changes in the hemisphere. But thanks to Miami's Cubans, the opposite happened. Miami would exert a ceaseless destabilizing, subversive force on Cuba. The "loss" of Cuba had produced its most paradoxical triumph for the United States.

There was a moment in the late seventies, just as there had been in the mid-twenties, when Miami's triumph seemed complete. It was early March 1977, and just as "real" Americans had back at the end of 1925, Miami's Cubans poured into the streets to celebrate their belief that at last, here in Miami, their every dream had come true.

That first Calle Ocho festival was hardly more than a family picnic. These days the annual festival has a budget of more than $2 million, and the preparations for it go on 364 days a year. Then, for an entire day, more than a million people of all ethnic backgrounds turn Little Havana into a stupendous celebration of all that Miami, since the Cubans arrived, has become. At the 1986 Calle Ocho festival, hundreds of performers from all over the hemisphere performed on fifty outdoor stages. More than five hundred street vendors sold everything from Argentine *parrillada* to Colombian *empanadas*, along with hot dogs, hamburgers and every conceivable kind of Cuban food. One restaurant prepared what, almost certainly, was the biggest platter of *paella* in history. It contained 4,000 mussels and clams, 440 pounds of rice, 150 gallons of chicken stock and fish broth, and more than half a ton of chicken, lobster, crawfish and squid, along with gallons of sherry and olive oil. "You mix everything in an eight-foot pot with two wooden oars," the chef explained.

At the height of the festivities, it took nearly an hour to walk a single block. Thousands of young girls swooned as the Latin world's biggest teen heartthrob group, Menudo, performed. There were professional boxing and street dancing and puppet shows— magicians and musicians from Trinidad, Peru, Honduras and dozens of other countries. One popular attraction, the *Herald* reported, was the opportunity to be photographed with "a life-size likeness of President Reagan."

Back in 1977 the budget for the first Calle Ocho festival was only $34,000, and a comparatively tiny crowd of 100,000 showed up. Yet it was already clear. These erstwhile "refugees" were already dynamic assets to the city, to America. The Cuban "problem" had turned out to be a solution to problems that had dogged Miami since the hurricane of '26.

Fifty years earlier, Miami had called itself "The City Invincible." Now, in 1977, it was invincible again, or so people imagined. But, even in the hour of its triumph, Miami remained Miami. No one then could foresee the consequences, but the Cuban "success story" was destabilizing Castro's Cuba all too well. Soon the Marielitos, along with the Haitians, would be on their way, and why not? If the revelers at the Calle Ocho festival could find the city of their dreams in Miami, why not everyone else with a plane ticket, or a boat, and a dream?

One reason Miami recovered from the hurricane of 1980 so much more quickly than it had from the hurricane of 1926 was that, from the beginning, the Cuban exile community—a community born of failure—demanded a total commitment to success. As the years passed, this fierce insistence on accomplishment evolved into a social force of stupendous power, capable of shaping people's lives, and influencing their behavior, even more powerfully than class, education and all the other sociological factors.

In 1980, as the Marielitos poured into the city, Miami's Cubans faced the greatest challenge yet to the powers of their beliefs to shape reality. The response of one Cuban leader, Carlos Arboleya, summed up the response of the entire community. Rather than making excuses for his newly arrived compatriots, or pretending that the Marielitos' shortcomings were no concern of his, Arboleya took to the editorial columns of the *Herald* to lay down the law to these latest rowdy newcomers to Miami, just as some Anglo notable might have done back in the days of Al Capone.

His ultimatum—to both the Marielitos and Miami's Cuban community:

> To the new influx of refugees, we must clearly say, "You must live up to the examples of those who came here before you and who became the pride and joy of our great city, and you must assimilate this obligation as you are received in this country."

Exactly twenty years earlier, Arboleya had arrived in Miami with only forty dollars in his pocket; his first job had been in a shoe factory. By 1980 Arboleya had become the first naturalized Cuban-American to become president of a national bank and had successfully transformed himself from a poverty-stricken refugee into one of the most powerful financiers in south Florida. But the Cubans weren't the only ones in Miami who had undergone a metamorphosis. Simultaneously, the *Miami Herald,* the oldest and most influential of Miami's Anglo institutions, had transposed itself into the authentic mouthpiece for the highest aspirations of the new Miami, too.

In another Miami triumph, the Cuban community would be as

good as Arboleya's word. Within three years, thanks to their efforts, the vast majority of the Marielitos had been so successfully assimilated that they, too, were contributing, as Arboleya had put it, "to the economic health and vibrancy of this community."

The facts inform us that entrepreneurs and professionals formed only a small minority of the Cuban diaspora, that those who had actually fought Castro were only an infinitesimal proportion of the whole. But Miami's transformation into a major international metropolis reveals something else—that what people are is sometimes less important than what they imagine themselves to be.

Even today some Cubans still cling to the belief that their sojourn there is only temporary, that one day the false Miami surrounding them will disappear.

But right from the first moment they stepped off the "freedom flights," these Cubans turned out to be real Floridians because like Ponce and Osceola, like Plant and Merrick and Fisher and all the others, their lives were propelled by the power of a great irrational dream. And, as Theodore White once noted, "For all dreamers, Miami held indulgence."

In spite of all its upheavals, Miami's life was still a history of dissonant repetitions, of off-angle symmetries.

Now it finally would become the real city of the future, the dreams of its American founders at last really would come true— because the Cubans, too, were propelled by the idea of a city that never existed and, in their lifetimes, never would.

There was nothing new in all this except for the power of it, the importance of it, and the scale. Potential and fantasy had always circled each other in south Florida, like alien yet complementary strands of DNA. Now, at last, thanks to a kind of psychoeconomic fusion, the strands were joined, the double helix fused: Miami began its self-mutation.

15

The Americanization of Rosario

The Cubans had become Americans; the Haitians were becoming Americans. Sometimes it seemed only the Americans were left to provide the foreign touch. At the very moment Miami seemed so exotic to America, Miami was becoming more American than ever before.

At the end of 1985, a headline in the *New York Times* epitomized this latest paradox: "Cuban Refugee Elected Mayor in Miami Vote," it announced.

The new mayor was named Xavier Suarez, and his election marked some less-noticed "firsts" for Miami, in addition to his Cuban birth. At thirty-six, he was the city's youngest mayor. He was also the first with a Harvard degree. In fact Suarez had two of them —a master's in public policy from the Kennedy School and a Harvard Law School diploma.

The most interesting thing about the new mayor of Miami was that he wasn't from Miami at all. His hometown was Washington, D.C., a place where, even now, there's not much chance to speak anything except English. This in turn gave him still another distinction.

Miami's first Cuban-born mayor had beaten two rivals who could easily have outscored him in a Spanish exam. First Suarez had defeated Maurice Ferre, who, in addition to being bilingual in Spanish and English, also spoke Creole, the language of the Haitian community. Then, in the runoff, Suarez decisively outpolled a banker, civic leader and Bay of Pigs veteran named Raul Masvidal whose first language, after twenty-five years in the United States, remained Spanish.

Normally mayoral contests in Florida don't attract national attention, yet the new mayor's picture was in the *Washington Post* as well as the *New York Times;* he was also to be seen in *Time* and on all the network newscasts. His election made the kind of headlines you might expect had there been, say, a *coup d'état.* That was the implication—that, with Suarez's victory, the Cuban "takeover" of Miami was complete. Following Suarez's victory, the *Times* described Miami as "the capital of the Cuban exile." "Mayor of 'North Cuba' " was the way *Time* announced the news.

None of the headlines read "Yuppie Lawyer Elected Miami Mayor" or "Harvard Urbanologist Elected Miami Mayor." Nor did any newspaper carry what would have been the most accurate headline: "Melting Pot Works!" This made Miami's latest notoriety all the more delightful. As usual, it was defying all the stereotypes.

"My Spanish wasn't that good when I moved down here," Suarez told me ten months before his election victory. "It's okay now."

We were drinking Scotch in his living room, which was filled with the oriental curios he and his wife, Rita, love to collect. Suarez, fresh from a shower after playing basketball in the driveway, was wearing blue jeans and barefoot. Their house, modest but comfortable, was located on a quiet side street in Little Havana. But with children riding bikes on the sidewalk outside, and the kitchen filled with all the suburban appliances, it might have been Queens or Dorchester—any of those big-city neighborhoods with a small-town air about them where millions of Americans live.

Suarez was no "refugee" and never had been one. His family had emigrated to the United States in 1961, when he was only eleven. "We knew from the beginning we'd never go back," he told me.

Within two years the Suarez family had moved to the Maryland suburbs. By the time he was a teenager, his Spanish "had practically disappeared." When they first settled in Washington, his father, a nuclear physicist, had taught engineering at Catholic University. Later he joined the Bechtel Corporation, a consulting firm whose alumni include Secretary of State George Shultz, among many other influential Washington insiders. So from childhood Xavier Suarez was immersed not in Cuban exile politics, but in the subculture of American government, as well as in the English language.

Suarez's middle-class, mainstream northern upbringing broke the mold for Miami's mayors in another way. Most earlier mayors had been white southerners; Maurice Ferre was an aristocratic Puerto Rican. Suarez personified the continuing impact of northern migration on Miami, though in a new way.

By the late seventies, tens of thousands of affluent Cubans—having made their fortunes up in New York and other cities—were heading down to Miami to buy land, look for investment opportunities and start new careers.

The Marielitos got all the attention, but after 1980 these Cuban-Americans from the North actually came to outnumber both Marielitos and Haitians—which is certainly one reason the city rebounded from these "invasions" so easily. The skills and capital the newcomers had accumulated elsewhere in America played a vital role in Miami's growth into a major city. In the form of people like Xavier Suarez, they would also bring fundamental political changes to Miami. The Cuban Refugee Program had produced another of its unforeseen benefits.

During the years Suarez was growing up in Washington, Miami youths his age might start out washing dishes or pumping gas, and be lucky to speak heavily accented English by the time they finished high school. "Success" consisted of getting rich and, someday, when Castro was overthrown, going home to Cuba. Suarez grew up in a world where, even in English, the words had different meanings. For him, success was attending a prestigious Ivy League university, then walking, as an American, through all the doors to personal advancement such an education opened.

In Little Havana, the local heroes were the Bay of Pigs veterans, along with the leaders of the Latin American independence struggles. Even today Suarez has some strange heroes by Miami standards. The most important of them, he frequently points out, isn't José Martí or Simón Bolívar. It's a paunchy, balding, middle-aged American named William Donald Schaefer. At the time Schaefer's name was hardly a household word anywhere except up in Baltimore, where he was mayor for many years. But for a whole generation of young American politicians who, like Suarez, came of age in the big northeastern cities during the "urban crisis" of the seventies, Schaefer, who was elected governor of Maryland in 1986, is a living legend. His hands-on style of municipal administration transformed Baltimore from a case study in urban decay into a model of the urban renaissance.

As a teenager Suarez wanted to follow in the footsteps of his Baltimore idol. But realism is the foundation of any successful political career, and in the Northeast Suarez confronted an indisputable reality. Washington, Philadelphia and Boston—the big northern cities where he'd lived and studied—were hardly promising territory for a politically ambitious Cuban-American. So how to make his particular dream come true?

Suarez was in his first year at Harvard Law School; he was driving from Philadelphia to Boston when the inspiration struck him. "I'm going to go to Miami and try my political fortune," he vowed.

So following graduation he bought a used Buick for seventy-five dollars and in 1976, like many other ambitious young people, headed south. The biggest city in the fastest-growing big state in the nation was a propitious place to launch a career, all the more so if you happened to have a Cuban background.

Suarez's plan was not merely ambitious but, by most standards, audacious. First of all, he, unlike some other successful migrant politicians, had no personal fortune. There was also the carpetbagger question. Why should Miami's Cubans vote for a twenty-seven-year-old Harvard graduate from Washington who'd shared in none of their struggles, who hardly spoke their language?

Suarez never did get hold of much money. But he tackled his lack of roots head-on. By the time he got there, many successful Cubans, including Miami's growing fraternity of Cuban politicos, were moving out of Little Havana into those affluent, multiethnic neighborhoods where professional Anglos and Latins live side by side. So Suarez, the outsider, moved into a $135-a-month apartment in the heart of Little Havana. He began to relearn Spanish—and to fill the leadership vacuum he found there. It was a most astute move, and one as carefully calculated as the move to Miami itself.

Yet for nearly ten years, all it produced was equal parts hard work, frustration and defeat. Twice Suarez ran for the city commission; twice he was defeated by saber-rattling, fire-breathing, old-style Cuban candidates who ran against Castro, not him. Finally, in 1983, he got a chance to run, this time for mayor, against a candidate who could not claim to be "more Cuban" than he. But this time Suarez was defeated because American-born voters considered him "too Cuban" and reelected Maurice Ferre instead.

Even when things looked darkest, he never doubted Miami would give him his big chance. In the end Miami delivered—as usual, for a reason no one, not even Suarez himself, could foresee.

Xavier Suarez's greatest asset turned out to be what, at first, had seemed his biggest liability. It was the very fact he wasn't a stereotypical Miami Cuban that gave him the chance to usher in a whole new chapter in the city's political history. For by the time he finally was elected mayor, tens of thousands of Miami Cubans weren't stereotypical Cubans anymore either. They were just as American as he was.

Like Xavier Suarez, Rosario Kennedy is Cuban-born and has a passion for competitive politics. Like more and more Miamians, she's also part of an Anglo-Latin partnership that's both personal and professional. She and her husband, David Kennedy, are real estate partners. In fact her Cuban first name and Irish last name sum up how assimilation works in Miami.

An attractive brunette, Rosario Kennedy bears a noticeable resemblance to Saundra Santiago, one of the supporting actresses on "Miami Vice." But her story is more like those you see on quite another TV series. Her life has contained as many dramatic twists and turns as any episode on "Topacio." "Topacio," which means "topaz" in Spanish, is the city's most popular video melodrama; it even outdraws "Miami Vice."

Consider the scenario: at the age of fifteen, Rosario Arguelles, daughter of a wealthy Cuban landowner, finds her sheltered life as a Havana debutante swept away forever by the Castro revolution. The Arguelles family flees to Miami. As tradition dictates, she is educated at a genteel convent school and then marries a fellow Cuban, a writer named Gustavo Godoy.

But even within Miami's tight-knit Cuban community, the subversive allure of America intrudes. The young woman starts to dream dreams unthinkable in Havana. She divorces; she plunges into community service work, into business and banking, into politics, into the kind of public life that, back in Cuba, only men pursued.

By 1984 the Americanization of Rosario is complete. She is a delegate to the Democratic National Convention, pledged to none other than Gary Hart. That's not all. In her most shocking break with tradition, she marries a divorced Florida politician who just happens to have been Miami's last Anglo mayor. And former mayor David Kennedy, it turns out, is no stranger to melodrama either. An Irish kid from Tampa who fought his way to the top of Miami politics, his political career crashes when he's accused of attempting to bribe a judge to grant a marijuana dealer a retrial. But that's not the end of the story.

Kennedy fights back; the charges against him are dropped and he regains the mayor's office. He remains one of Miami's savviest political operators, but things are never the same again. Some say it's pride, others bitterness, but he never again seeks electoral office. Instead, following their marriage, Kennedy's ambitions more and more seem to be realized through the rising public career of his young Cuban wife.

The first time I met the Kennedys, they turned down my suggestion that we go out for a Cuban dinner. Instead, we went to Monty Trainer's, the steak-and-seafood restaurant that's really the clubhouse for Miami's political power brokers, whether they happen to be Anglo, Latin or black. The discussion at our table centered around politics. This was nearly ten months before Xavier Suarez was elected mayor, but people already were talking about the possibility of a Cuban "takeover." So I couldn't help mentioning to David Kennedy that his fate personified Miami's fate. In fact the symbolism seemed almost too perfect.

Here was Miami's last Anglo mayor married to a Cuban. Both Kennedys laughed and Rosario, in her lightly accented but otherwise perfect English, said, "You don't know half of it. For the first seven years of our marriage, Dave and I, and Dave's kids and my kids, lived with my mother."

"Seven years of *arroz con pollo*," former mayor Kennedy exclaimed, as he stubbed out his cigar and tore into his T-bone. "People forget assimilation is a two-way street."

Maybe, it occurred to me, a single episode of "Topacio" wouldn't be enough. It would take a whole mini-series, "Los Kennedys de Miami," to do justice to the material.

Rosario Kennedy became the first Cuban-American woman to be elected to Miami's city commission at the same time Xavier Suarez was elected mayor. Suarez got much more attention, but in some ways her victory was an even stronger indication of just how American Miami's Cubans have become.

In Miami the office of mayor, although symbolically important, is relatively powerless. Real administrative control is in the hands of an appointed city manager. Even on the city commission, the mayor, like the other commissioners, has only one vote. So if the 1985 election did produce a real Cuban "takeover," it derived from the fact that while previously there had never been more than two Cubans on the five-member commission, now there were three. At the time Suarez and Kennedy were elected, another Cuban, a doctrinaire anti-Communist named Joe Carollo, already held a seat. So now Cuban-Americans had a majority for the first time. Yet no one in Miami spoke of a "takeover" following their victories, and for good reason.

Kennedy's victory, even more than Suarez's, marked a dramatic shift away from violently ideological exile politics toward moderation and consensus. The Cuban "takeover" was a milestone in the city's Americanization.

Had there been a real "takeover," two very different kinds of Cuban candidates would have won. Raul Masvidal, the Bay of Pigs veteran Suarez defeated in the runoff, had parked cars for a living when he first came to Miami. A self-made multimillionaire and widely admired philanthropist, he personified the Bay of Pigs generation's best qualities, including its commitment to social responsibility and hard work. As the *Herald* put it in one of its many glowing endorsements: "He knows what Miami can become: He became it himself. All he needs is the chance."

This authentic son of Little Havana no doubt would have had his chance to be mayor, except for one thing. Miami's *Cuban* voters never really warmed to Masvidal. Instead, in both election and runoff, they overwhelmingly supported that Harvard graduate from Washington, Xavier Suarez.

Masvidal stood for the Cuban community's best traditions; Demetrio Perez, the candidate Rosario Kennedy defeated, epitomized the worst. During his one term as city commissioner, Perez's most notable public service had been a "fact-finding" tour of the *pissoirs* of Paris, conducted during a free junket to Europe. It was in his campaign against Rosario Kennedy, however, that he really stepped into the sewer. One widely distributed circular carried photographs of both Rosario's Cuban first husband and her Anglo second husband. It denounced her, in Spanish, as a "liberated Cuban girl living an exciting public life." His opponent, Perez told Cuban voters, was "too assimilated" to be considered a real Cuban.

Worse still, he alleged, she was part of a conspiracy—hatched by Castro, and supported by Yasir Arafat, Jesse Jackson, Gary Hart and other agents of the worldwide Communist conspiracy—to deny Miami's Cubans their rightful representation on the Miami city commission. In order to avert that catastrophe, Perez urged the city's Cubans to "unite, close ranks and not allow a conspiracy of this type to divide us."

Such tactics weren't limited to the Kennedy-Perez race. Less than a week before the election, Xavier Suarez was also publicly accused of being under the influence of Castro's agents by Joe Carollo, the other Cuban member of the city commission. Carollo wasn't up for reelection, but his motive was clear. In all previous Miami elections, extremist candidates like Perez and Carollo had swept the field. Victories for moderates like Suarez and Kennedy would mark a dramatic rejection of ideological politics by the Cuban community itself.

Perez encouraged such slanders. Masvidal repudiated them, but campaign workers for both men urged Miami's Cubans to vote for the "most Cuban" candidates. Masvidal made it clear just who that was. In an emotional meeting with fellow Bay of Pigs veterans, he declared he was "first and last a Cuban." He also said he would immediately resign as mayor and return to Cuba if Castro were overthrown.

In the face of such tactics, Suarez and Kennedy opted for what until then had been considered political suicide in Miami. Each dared to suggest this was an American, not a Cuban, election and that hatred of Castro and love of Cuba were not, in and of themselves, qualifications for running a big American city. There was a place for the mayor of Miami to take foreign policy positions, Suarez conceded, but that place, he emphasized, was outside City Hall. He then returned to his main campaign theme: Miami needed a mayor who could run Miami, not Havana.

Rosario Kennedy was even more outspoken. "What hurts me most about this campaign is that again we're only talking about irrelevant things, about anti-Communism," she said in one radio debate with Perez. "The minute one talks about a Miami election," she complained, in another unprecedented statement, "the liberation of Cuba comes up." She also ordered that all her campaign literature, even that distributed in Little Havana, be printed exclusively in English.

It was the most pivotal decision Miami's Cubans had faced since the arrival of the Marielitos, and for the same reason. It forced an entire community to take stock of itself and then decide where its real loyalties lay—to the real Miami or to the mythical Havana, to the "most Cuban" candidates or to the best-qualified ones.

Once again, at the pivotal moment, an authentic leader of the Cuban community had the courage to speak out. "It is about time people in this community understand that city of Miami elections have nothing to do with the liberation of Cuba," declared Jorge Mas Canosa, who is chairman of a group called the Cuban American National Foundation.

What made this courageous stand all the more remarkable was that Mas Canosa was a full-time anti-Communist activist. The foundation that he heads is one of the main anti-Castro lobbying groups in the United States. But that hadn't kept him from being outraged at the kinds of accusations Perez and Carollo were making.

Mas Canosa did not endorse any particular candidate. But he called such slanders insults to the intelligence of the voters and concluded with an appeal that, as much as the election results themselves, measured the strides Cubans of all kinds have made since coming to the United States. "Let's keep Cuba out of the elections," he urged. "Elections in Miami have nothing to do with the cause of a free Cuba."

In the final election, Suarez easily defeated Masvidal. Kennedy won by an avalanche. Asked to comment, she gave a reply no one in Miami considered in the slightest overblown.

"It is an historic event," she said.

It wasn't just historic; it was downright inexplicable in terms of the prevailing clichés. Miami supposedly is a city deeply divided along ethnic lines, but Miami's voters had defied each and every ethnic, racial and political stereotype.

Masvidal, the "most Cuban" candidate, didn't get much Cuban support, but he swept the black vote. Marvin Dunn, a black sociologist and educator who was also running for mayor, didn't get much support from blacks, but he did surprisingly well among whites. Suarez, in spite of Carollo's accusations, swept Little Havana and got 75 percent of the Cuban vote. Rosario Kennedy's biggest margins were precisely among non-Cuban voters. But it was within the Cuban community that her campaign produced its most telling results. She got nearly 70 percent of the votes of Cubans under thirty—that is, of those either born or educated in the United States.

The Cubans weren't the only ones to defy the labels. In fact the refusal to be guided by ethnic prejudices was most dramatic of all among blacks. Previously less than one in twenty black voters in Miami had supported a Cuban candidate for mayor. It was the overwhelming majorities black voters gave former mayor Ferre— 97 percent in the previous election—that provided his margins of victory. This time, however, the two Cuban candidates together took about 60 percent of the black vote even though a highly respected black candidate was on the ballot. Ferre got barely 10 percent; it was his repudiation by black voters that ended his long domination of Miami politics.

Ferre's aides were stunned. "How can you go from ninety-seven percent to ten percent in two years?" one of them asked on election night. But as Ferre himself later told me, he lost the black vote and therefore the election for a simple reason. Like many politicians who are used to winning, he'd antagonized his traditional supporters in his last term. In his most serious mistake, he'd outraged black voters through his controversial firing of Howard Gary, the city's black city manager. The incident touched off a bitter political feud that made headlines, and poisoned Miami politics, for months. There was no doubt that most of Ferre's black supporters believed he had betrayed them. Yet Ferre had assumed that no matter what he did, blacks would always prefer an "American" like him to a Cuban candidate for mayor.

But why should they? Miami is supposed to be one of those laid-back life-style Sun Belt cities where old-fashioned City Hall politics simply doesn't matter the way it does in older, northern cities. Nothing could be further from the truth. Habitually beset by tidal waves of drugs, crime and illegal aliens, to say nothing of violent growth and actual hurricanes, Miami is a city where the conduct of local government can make a real difference in people's lives. A banker with a proven commitment both to investing in the black community and to fighting problems like crime and drugs, Masvidal spoke Liberty City's language, even if he spoke it with a Cuban accent. Black support for Masvidal was surprising only if you assumed blacks somehow were oblivious to all the issues that concern Anglos and Hispanics.

But was Masvidal the candidate best qualified to be mayor? Most of Miami's political stereotypes went down to defeat with Ferre in the primary election. The rest of them were blown away in the mayoral runoff. With Suarez leading heavily among Cuban voters, and Masvidal even stronger among blacks, Miami's Anglo voters were expected to vote heavily for Masvidal, who was strongly endorsed by the city's Anglo "establishment," and so assure him victory. Things didn't turn out that way.

While Masvidal campaigned on the admirable but vague platform of ethnic cooperation and civic unity, Suarez bombarded voters with detailed fiscal, administrative and policy proposals that Mayor Schaefer might have envied. This emphasis on the nuts and bolts of city government proved to be decisive.

In the primary Suarez had finished a distant fourth among Anglo voters. Now, in another dramatic voting switch, "real" Americans abandoned Masvidal and voted heavily for Suarez. He picked up a surprising number of black votes, too. Even though Masvidal had outspent Suarez nearly three to one, the final outcome wasn't even close.

The November day Suarez took office, it was gloriously warm and sunny but the city basked in a warm glow that had nothing to do with the weather. Miami's voters were deeply proud that they had given Suarez a mandate for seriousness and intercommunal harmony in the conduct of the city's municipal affairs. Even the losers seemed to sense that this was one election everyone had won. Ferre, in defeat, showed a magnanimity that hadn't been evident during his last years in office. Masvidal promised to support the new mayor enthusiastically. At Suarez's inauguration, one of his supporters shouted out, in Spanish, what people were saying in English, too, "A mayor for us all!" Thanks to the victories of two Cuban candidates, Miami politics was now firmly back in the American mainstream.

There was one even more remarkable feature of this election. Only because black voters had first knocked Ferre out of the race, and only because Anglo voters had then chosen Suarez over Masvidal, had "the former Cuban refugee" been elected.

It was the city's *American-born* voters who had engineered the Cuban "takeover" of Miami.

By that time Xavier Suarez wasn't the only ambitious outsider to make his mark. The Miami Republican party had also been taken over by a newcomer, though there was a big difference.

The new chairman of the Dade County GOP spoke fluent Spanish with a heavy Cuban accent and was a fixture of the political coffeehouses of Little Havana. He was a conservative who emphasized strong family values. In fact he equated the two. "I'm sure my family had something to do with it," he said, when asked about his political philosophy. "I happen to think that the conservative side of the issue is the correct one." When asked why, he replied, "It just is." It almost goes without saying, he was in the real estate business.

When Joel Achenbach of *Tropic* magazine visited the Republican leader at home, he found everyone there speaking Spanish. In fact the man's son—even though he had been born right here in America—spoke no English at all.

"*¡Diablito!* [Little devil!]" the proud father exclaimed as his two-year-old son showed off his first words, which were *agua* (water), *jugo* (juice) and *aquí* (here).

The name of the Republican leader was John Ellis Bush. He is the son of George Bush, vice-president of the United States. How had "Jeb" Bush, an Andover preppie and scion of an old Yankee family, wound up "one of the most important people in Miami's Hispanic community," as the *Herald* described him? The details varied as always, but the plot line was pure Miami.

It all started, Jeb Bush explained, when he met the beautiful daughter of a Mexican real estate salesman named Columba. "I don't know, maybe it was just raw animal magnetism," he told Achenbach. "I just fell in love with her. It's just one of those indescribable things. It's only happened to me once so far. I don't know how to describe it. I can tell you the symptoms. Not being able to sleep. Not having an appetite. She was the first girl I ever felt that way about."

So naturally he converted to Catholicism and learned Spanish. Naturally they married. And needless to say, they packed up their dreams and headed straight for Miami. Where else would a bi-cultural couple with an interest in real estate and politics go?

As I got to know the city's politicians, I discovered a real triumph of American democracy—and not just in politics. Whatever their ideological labels, they proved "E Pluribus Unum" is also an affair of the heart.

Divorce and remarriage, for instance, didn't set Rosario Kennedy apart. Raul Masvidal, the "most Cuban" candidate for mayor, has been divorced twice and married three times. Cross-cultural marriage was also the norm among Miami's politicians. Steve Clark, the "good ole boy" leader of the Dade County government, was married to a Cuban woman and lived in Little Havana. On the other hand, Marvin Dunn, the black sociologist who had run for mayor, was married to a white southern woman and lived in Coconut Grove.

Not even the "most Cuban" politicians were immune from this

process, as I discovered when I met Joe Carollo, the third Cuban member of the city commission. Ideologically, of course, Carollo was one of the least "American" politicians in the city. Unlike Suarez and Kennedy, he could always be counted on to enliven commission proceedings with a good old anti-Castro tirade. Not that Carollo needed to look as far as Cuba to find Reds under beds. It was he, after all, who accused Mayor Suarez of being a tool of the Communist conspiracy, too.

Carollo's detractors call him the George Wallace of Miami. The comparison turned out to be more apt than I could have imagined. At first I thought I must be mistaken as I listened to him denounce "the elitist groups in every community who forget the little people" in the classic Wallace manner. Then Carollo turned to foreign policy. "Ain't a day goes by," he observed, "but Cubans are killed in foreign wars." Why was Castro involved in countries like Mozambique and Angola?

"He's importing blacks from Africa," Carollo explained. "It's easier to use them to sustain Communist rule." Miami blacks, he added, were "guilty of racist tactics." It wasn't just blacks and the liberal elite, however. "Castro has managed to infiltrate every Cuban group in this community," he informed me.

It wasn't what Joe Carollo said that fascinated me; it was the way he said it. I hadn't been mistaken. You could hear George Wallace speaking not just in the words Carollo used, but in the way he pronounced them. The last "real" Cuban on the Miami city commission had a definite southern accent. When I asked Carollo why, Jeb Bush might have been talking.

He'd grown up in an Irish neighborhood in Chicago, but then in 1970 he and his parents had moved south. In Miami he met and married a strawberry blonde from a Deep South family who spoke not one word of Spanish. Soon Carollo was an American success story for a reason as valid as anyone else's in Miami. What better place to cash in on fear? First he'd started a "security" business, supplying guns and guards to protect people from all the phobias that haunt them in Miami. Then he'd expanded his security business into politics—telling lots of voters, not just Cubans, what they wanted to hear: whether it was the loss of Cuba, or the Liberty City riots, or the Marielito thugs, or only that your car got stolen, a liberal, elitist, Communist conspiracy explained it all.

It was impossible at such moments not to be astonished, overwhelmed really, by the force of America. The three most successful "Cuban" politicians in Miami had all started out in the same place. The three of them had all wound up on the city commission. Yet America had transformed Joe Carollo into an Old South demagogue, Xavier Suarez into a northern urbanologist technocrat and Rosario Kennedy into a liberated American woman.

I asked Joe Carollo, as I asked almost everybody, if he'd had any trouble adjusting to life in Miami. "My Spanish has improved since I got here," he said. What about his two sons? "They speak some Spanish," he answered.

What can you say about a city where two of the three "Cuban" members of the city commission, as well as the most recent black candidate for mayor, are married to white Americans from the Deep South?

I would ask you to entertain a truly exotic possibility—that Miami's more like New Hampshire than Casablanca. The similarities are quite striking, starting out with the fact that the prevailing images of both places have very little to do with reality.

Most of us, when we think of New Hampshire, think of WASPs and white steeples, of God-fearing Yankee yeomen out hunting the Thanksgiving turkey. But people up in the Granite State are as likely to be harvesting pot as pumpkins these days. There, as in a lot of other 100 percent American places, the marijuana crop and the underground economy it supports are mainstays of the economy. In New Hampshire the Puritan life-style went out with *Peyton Place* and, ethnically speaking, your average citizen up there is no more likely to be a Son or Daughter of the American Revolution than your average Miamian. According to my *Almanac of American Politics,* only 14 percent of New Hampshire's population is of English descent. Twelve percent descend from French Canadian and 6 percent from Irish forebears. But, like people in Miami, most people in New Hampshire don't much care about ethnic purity when they marry, let alone when they vote, so long as they find the candidate congenial. New Hampshire's archconservative senator Warren Rudman, co-author of the Gramm-Rudman amendment, is Jewish. Its Republican governor, John Sununu, is a Catholic— though that's not his only distinction, as we'll see in a minute.

Besides its political conservatism, New Hampshire has something else in common with Florida. In recent years it's prospered as a low-tax, free-enterprise haven for those who want to escape the constraints of life elsewhere. The results have not been all that different from what you see in Miami. Law and order has become an issue, the environment an even bigger one. Low taxes, people are discovering, don't mean good schools. People up there have learned that getting rich doesn't preserve traditional values. They also have discovered that uncontrolled growth doesn't mean you find happiness, no matter how many state lines you cross to pursue it.

I'm aware that comparing Miami to New Hampshire seems quirky, but I have a particular reason for doing it. Though you don't hear much about exotic New Hampshire, and its marijuana subculture and polyglot population, Miami's not the only place where there's been a Cuban "takeover."

The governor of New Hampshire was born in Havana.

In late 1983, on the twenty-fifth anniversary of the Cuban revolution, the Miami *Herald* published an in-depth opinion poll of the city's Anglos, Cubans and blacks. The survey was supposed to gauge the Cuban impact on Miami. Instead it revealed America's impact on the Cubans.

By large majorities, Anglos, Cubans and blacks all agreed on the need for a balanced federal budget, though blacks actually favored a balanced budget more than Anglos and Cubans did. But all three groups also expressed strong support for women's rights and for greater government spending to help the poor. While these groups, like most Americans, really couldn't be stereotyped either as conservatives or liberals, the poll did reflect traditional American attitudes you never see portrayed on "Miami Vice."

Immense majorities of Anglos, Cubans and blacks declared voting was an important civic responsibility. By overwhelming majorities, they said close family relations were important to them. Large majorities of Anglos, Cubans and blacks also described themselves as optimistic about their city's future even though, at that time, Miami's reputation couldn't have been worse. This faith in Miami's resiliency wasn't blind or unrealistic. There was near-universal agreement that the city's most important problems were crime, lack of jobs and disrespect for the law.

The answers to three of the questions were especially revealing. First those polled were asked whether "people who live in the United States should be fluent enough in English to use that language in their public dealings." They were also asked whether "Cuban criminals who came to the United States in the Mariel boatlift should be returned to Cuba."

Finally they were asked whether "anti-Castro groups are justified in using bombing or other forms of violence." Like the election results two years later, the results of the poll took the measure of a city that, in diversity, had found unity:

	Anglos	Blacks	Cubans
Should Speak English	95	90	81
Should Deport Criminals	93	86	92
Terrorism Unjustified	96	91	76

Another question provided the answer, two years before the election of Suarez and Kennedy, as to why these candidates who defied all the political clichés would prove to be so popular. The intercommunal consensus was astonishing when people were asked whether they agreed or disagreed with the following statement: "Cuban-Americans should spend more time working on local problems and less time talking about Castro."

	Anglos	Blacks	Cubans
Agree with Statement	80	80	75

16

Only in America

The Americanization of people like Xavier Suarez and Rosario Kennedy proves all the rules we learned in our grade-school civics books. But what about the "Latinization" of people like Jeb Bush? David Kennedy was right. Whether the marriage is personal, political or cultural, assimilation is a two-way street.

In an essay on Miami, Professor Barry Levine caught both the complexity and richness of the cultural drama that makes Miami "a city where many Latins look like they shop at Brooks Brothers and many Anglos sport *guayaberas,* where physical appearance is often an unreliable cue [to ethnic identity], and where many people are bilingual. It used to be said," Levine points out,

> that there were two cultures in Miami, the Hispanic and the Anglo. That ignores not only Miami's 280,000 blacks but also the emergence of a culture of the hyphenates. In Miami there are Cuban-Americans as well as Cubans, Colombian-Americans as well Colombians, Latinized-Anglos as well as plain old Anglos.

The same is true of Miami's Jews and Haitians, and its growing community of French Canadians. Within each of these supposedly

well-defined ethnic categories, you encounter a continuum of individual human adaptations ranging from complete alienation to total
integration into American life.

In Miami, as everywhere else, the hyphenates don't stay hyphenates for long. It's taken places like New Hampshire centuries to
become as American as they are. But Miami's Cubans have become
more American than they or anyone else imagined possible in only
twenty-five years.

Their Americanization is happening so fast you have to run to
keep up with it. It isn't just limited to politics. These days a Cuban
woman is as likely to be a working mother as any American-born
woman. The divorce rate among Cubans is now actually higher
than it is among people who were born in the United States. "We
have certainly seen a breakdown of the traditional Latin family,"
Josefina Carbonell, executive vice-president of the Little Havana
Activities and Nutrition Centers, told me when I visited a center
for the elderly near Calle Ocho. "The elderly are increasingly
isolated," said Mrs. Carbonell, who is herself a divorced career
woman. "Their sons and daughters are off at work all day. Their
grandchildren are in college or have moved away. As the families
move to the suburbs, they find there's no room for the old people
anymore. The whole extended family concept is breaking down,
and so these people come here to spend their time."

In a Spanish-language magazine called *Ideal,* there was a cover
photograph of Mayor Suarez, wearing a crimson tie and what
looked like a Brooks Brothers shirt with his Harvard class ring
clearly visible. "El Futuro de Miami Es Magnifico," he announced.

On the last page of the same magazine I encountered another
item that, like Suarez's election, documented a cultural revolution.
It was an ad, in Spanish, for an old folks home in Hialeah. "El Mejor
Cuidado Para Personas Mayores [The Best Care for the Elderly],"
it promised. A line illustration showed two old women, one knit-
ting in an armchair, the other gazing pensively out on the world
from a rocking chair. For them, too, Americanization had worked
with inexorable force, with stunning speed.

All the world now recognizes how the Cubans have changed Miami. But what of the effects on the Cubans of twenty years of color TV, freeways, supermarkets and automobile romances? Middle-generation Cubans have always prided themselves on being different from other Americans. But as the years have worn on, many of them have begun to see that they and their children are really not so different from their Anglo neighbors after all.

If you want to take a look at the future of Miami's Cubans, you don't even have to leave Florida. Just go over to Tampa and drive around Ybor City. Less than thirty years ago, Little Havana wasn't the Cuban capital of the United States. Ybor City was.

Today Ybor City no longer exists. No catastrophe overtook this historic enclave that, going back to the days of Martí, had been the scene of so many dramas. But as the years passed, the Cuban community there gradually disappeared. Hardly realizing it, the Cubans had become Americans. Of course you can still get a Cuban meal in Ybor City and hear Spanish spoken there. But the old parochial school has been abandoned; the churches are mostly empty. The business and residential districts have withered as Tampa's Cubans have moved into skyscraper offices downtown and into houses in the suburbs.

From a thriving, self-contained and self-sufficient ethnic community, Ybor City has been transformed, fittingly enough, into a Florida tourist attraction. The same already is beginning to happen in Little Havana. The famous restaurants there now have branches in the suburbs. And even the veterans of Brigade 2506 hold their reunions downtown or in the suburbs. Few tourists miss the chance to tour exotic Little Havana, but many Miami Cubans now go months without visiting the place.

One result of this fast-paced Americanization is that American English is taking over Cuban Spanish. Even while speaking Spanish, Latins in Miami now order a *rosbif sandwich* or a *coctel*. If it's chilly the evening she's invited out to a *nightclub,* even the woman who can't speak English will decide to wear a *shawl* over her *strapless.* *"Tengan un nice day,"* a Cuban secretary will say to her friends, as she leaves work a little early to do some *shopping.* There's a *gran sale,* she explains.

Miami is often called America's first bicultural city, but I don't think I met one Cuban there who was equally at home in both Spanish and English. The old people speak halting English. Then there are those from forty-five to sixty who have carried three generations of their families from penniless exile to affluence through ceaseless work. They are on top now and, after twenty years, they may speak English well, but still as a foreign language.

What about those who are younger? "When I speak in Spanish, I think in English," Rosario Kennedy, who is in her early forties, once told me, and the same seemed true of most prominent "Cubans" I met. People of Rosario's age are probably the last Cuban-Americans who will speak both languages proficiently without making special efforts to retain their fluency in Spanish. In fact the handwriting is already on the wall, or rather, the blackboard. "Most of the younger generation speak what we call 'Spanglish,'" one young woman told me on one of my first visits there, "as well as perfect English. There were elections at the country club last month, and people would start making speeches in Spanish, find they couldn't, and switch into English."

The Cubans' easy command of English is a source of pride. But as one study points out:

> The relatively limited and poor quality of Spanish [young Cubans] learn may serve as a source of embarrassment for themselves and for their parents. Another problem encountered by some Cuban-American youths who . . . moved to another city is that they have found themselves unable to converse comfortably, or perhaps even at all, with Spanish speakers from other places. To help remedy this situation, there are now Spanish courses being offered at colleges in Miami for native speakers.

This accounts for one dispute that still does deeply divide Miami's Cubans and the city's "real" Americans. The Cubans strongly favor bilingualism in public services, along the lines practiced in New York, San Francisco and other cities. Anglos and blacks strongly oppose it. Perhaps this gap, too, will narrow as both sides develop a better understanding of the other's motivations. Anglos and blacks fear the calls for bilingualism because they see them as a threat to the primacy of English. But fear motivates the Cubans, too. They believe that unless something is done, the Spanish language will be overwhelmed in Miami.

Another sure sign of the future is that, for the first time since the twenties, "Spanish" architecture is enjoying a revival in Miami. One of the most striking examples is located between the downtown business district and Calle Ocho. With its tile roofing, stucco walls, wrought-iron balconies, its open plaza and playing fountains, the place certainly couldn't be more "foreign" in appearance.

This Hispanic fantasyland is called the Metro-Dade Cultural Center. It was designed by Philip Johnson.

Florida architecture has always revealed most what it seeks to conceal. The same continues to be true of the great events in Miami's history. The invasion of the Marielitos and Haitians, far from signifying any defeat for the American dream, signaled its continuing power. This is true also of the "foreign" decor that currently so fascinates the rest of the nation. Miami's incredibly rich cultural hyphenization is truly exotic. But what it indicates is that the drama of Miami's Latinization has already reached its climax. A new and entirely different drama, the Americanization of Miami's Latins, is now in full flood.

The "Miami Generation" of Cuban artists, for example, has produced some work that is every bit as "exotic" as Miami itself. Homage to the Hispanic tradition, variously baroque or surreal, occurs in abundance in these paintings, sculptures and constructions. But these Hispanic references are apt to be self-consciously distant, even nostalgic—and often self-mocking and wry. They

345

show you that artists are looking back over their shoulders at an artistic tradition they are leaving behind. Meanwhile America ceaselessly intrudes into even the most "Cuban" art.

A 1983 painting, called "Findings," by Emilio Falero, sums up what has been happening to Miami's Cubans as accurately as the opinion polls and election results. "Findings" depicts a little girl exactly as Velázquez might have painted her. But this *beaux arts* infant, whom you might expect to find in the Prado, actually stands, in her silk dress, in the middle of a Miami construction site. Behind her a gigantic American bulldozer moves tons of red Florida earth. The foundations of a new shopping mall march toward a tree line. Above the retreating Everglades, Falero has painted in a brooding El Greco sky.

In the paintings of Carlos Macia, Cuban motifs peel off buildings that, beneath their exotic Latin surfaces, prove to be mass-produced American prefabs. Other painters skip this kind of imagery entirely. Some of the most striking renderings of the new Miami skyline have been painted by Luis Vega. His technique— a kind of pastel, hi-tech, magic realism—is about as "American" as you can get, but Vega arrived in 1980 with the Marielitos. He is one of the few "Cuban" artists who was actually trained in the Hispanic tradition.

Probably the "most Cuban" artist in Miami is Cesar Trasobares. In much of his work, not a single American element is present. One of Trasobares's most interesting creations is the kind of jewelry box in which generations of Cuban girls have stored their dreams as well as their trinkets. It has cardboard drawers and a mirrored top that opens to reveal a secret compartment. Costume jewelry spills from the two bottom drawers. But the top compartment is filled with a whole miniature army of eligible suitors in white tuxedos. Like those perfect little grooms you see on the top of wedding cakes, they gaze up adoringly at a traditional Cuban debutante in her white flowing gown. She is haloed, like some rhinestone madonna, with a diamond engagement ring.

"Spaceship to Heaven" was the title Trasobares—who studied art at Miami-Dade Community College, Florida Atlantic University and Florida State University—chose for this work. It makes the same point aesthetically that Rosario Kennedy made politically in her debates with Demetrio Perez: "That's not the way we live now. That's not who we are anymore."

At the very moment the rest of the country is wondering whether Miami is still a part of America, people in Miami are pondering quite a different question. How soon will it be before there are no "real" Cubans left at all?

A consensus already exists. "My grandson will be as American as Johnny Smith," Cesar Odio, the Miami city manager, told me. "Spanish will survive because of its business utility." "My kids will be Americans who like black beans and plantains, the way some other Americans like spaghetti or tacos," Xavier Suarez said when I asked him the same question. "They'll speak Spanish as their second language for the same reasons some other Americans speak French, German or Japanese, partly for cultural reasons, but mostly because, if you want to do well, it's a very useful language to know."

Carlos Luis, who is executive director of the Cuban Museum of Arts and Culture, was even more emphatic. "The Cuban community will die of old age," he told me, "just about the same time I do." When I asked why he was so sure, Luis told me about his own family. His married daughter lived in Queens, New York. One of his sons was married to a South Dakota girl. "They speak Spanish," he said, "but not good Spanish at all."

The Cubans are unlike previous immigrant groups in one striking way. They are *more* American than most of our own immigrant forebears were.

Over the years, as they studied other ethnic groups who have come to America, historians and sociologists discovered something interesting—all immigrants tended to have basically the same experience, whatever their language and national origins. Experts called it the "three generations concept," but what it really meant was that it takes four generations to become totally Americanized.

According to this thesis, the first generation establishes itself in the United States, but the parents, preoccupied with survival in a new homeland, make little progress in becoming culturally assimilated. Then, in the second generation, the children of these immigrants "rapidly abandon the cultural traits of their parents because they were viewed as a handicap toward their upward social mobility in American society."

This doesn't complete the process, however. For fairly obvious reasons, *their* children feel they've lost something in the helter-skelter race to become just as American as the people next door. So there is "a tendency for the third generation to try to recapture some of the elements of the culture of their immigrant grandparents." This is the stage at which, for instance, you find secularized Jews suddenly developing an interest in Talmudic ritual, or Italians who didn't attend parochial schools going on Catholic retreats. So only in the fourth generation do the Irish, say, produce a John F. Kennedy instead of an Al Smith—a figure totally at home both with his ethnic origins and the completeness of his American identity.

Sociologists expected the same thing to happen with the Cubans. Instead, as professors Boswell and Curtis point out in their study, *The Cuban-American Experience,*

> all available evidence seems to indicate the opposite. The
> assimilation momentum built up by the first generation
> and increased by the second should continue to be sus-
> tained during the third and subsequent generations.

Professor Levine calls it "fast-forward" assimilation—a speeded-up "version of what has happened in the United States many times before, indeed has never ceased happening. It is the classic immigration experience, albeit telescoped in time and space." Mayor Suarez has an even simpler name for it. He calls himself and those like him "one and a half generation" Americans. It was left to an outsider, however, to sum up the cultural significance of Suarez's election best.

"It took the Irish 44 years from the time they first came to Boston until they elected their first mayor," a Washington political consultant named Sergio Bendixen observed. "It has now taken the Cubans 25 years to be assured of electing their first mayor. That," he concluded, "should tell you something, either about the Irish or the Cubans."

Actually it tells you something about America at the end of the twentieth century: for all the fears to the contrary, the integrative forces have never been stronger. Once the sweatshop, the tenement and the subway were the pathways to Americanization. Today it's the TV, the computer and the fast car on the open freeway and, if you just look around you in Miami, there's simply no denying it. This new technology has speeded up everything, including assimilation. What will be the end result? The sociologists agree with Carlos Luis, Suarez, Odio and all the rest.

"Eventually, the Cuban element in the United States will become indistinguishable from the rest of the American population," Boswell and Curtis flatly predict.

I would like to suggest a somewhat different, but no less authentically American, result.

These days in Tokyo and Peking—even in Southeast Asia and the Persian Gulf—you run into a kind of American that, recently as ten years ago, you never found in such places. Like previous expatriates, they're highly paid professionals and corporate executives. But unlike their predecessors, they speak the local languages fluently. There is good reason for that. Depending on where you find them, these Americans tend to be Japanese-, Chinese-, Filipino-, even Indian- and Arab-Americans.

These are all people for whom the "three generations concept" worked exactly according to plan. They don't speak Japanese or Mandarin because their parents failed to teach them English. To the contrary, many of them speak these languages much better than their parents or even their immigrant grandparents.

It goes back to what both Suarez and Odio said. For the first time in American history, it has become an asset, not a liability, for immigrants to retain the cultural and linguistic heritage they bring with them to this country. In terms of status and income, it's the difference between working in a Massachusetts shoe factory and scouting the Milan fashion fair for those "Miami Vice" outfits—between harvesting lettuce in California and running the Osaka office of a big U.S. firm. Where once knowledge of an immigrant language was the sign of a failed American, today it's the ticket to the Business Class compartment on the intercontinental 747; it can even get you a seat on the Concorde.

So the best and brightest of Miami's Cubans will stay fluent in Spanish, I predict, for the same reason they learned English so quickly. They will find it enormously profitable to do so. For exactly the same reason, the smartest Anglos in Miami will keep on "Latinizing" themselves, too.

There's another reason why, even on Calle Ocho, Spanish will be spoken for a long time to come. The Cubans in Miami (like the Irish in Boston) may have been the city's first "aliens," but they certainly won't be the last. Already the Colombians and Nicaraguans are following in their footsteps. Many other Spanish-speaking people are not far behind.

What will be the effect of these new migrants on Miami and the rest of the country? Just as the latest "real" Americans always believe the next newcomers can't possibly become as American as they are, so Americans also have always believed something else—that immigrants create problems, rather than solving them.

President Reagan and his Council of Economic Advisers strongly disagree with that view. "For much of the nation's history," the most recent *Economic Report of the President* points out, "U.S. immigration policy has been based on the premise that immigrants" not only improve their own lives, but have "a favorable effect on the overall standard of living" in this country. "Analysis of the effects of recent migrant flows," the report emphasizes, "bears out this premise" too. Today, as in the past, "immigrants come to this country seeking a better life, and their personal investments and hard work provide economic benefits to themselves and to the country as a whole."

One recent finding is that, in some ways, illegal aliens contribute even more to the economy than documented immigrants do. Because they are here illegally, such people tend to work without complaint for lower wages. For the same reason, they tend, contrary to stereotype, to be especially law-abiding: what might only mean a traffic ticket for others can mean deportation for them. Illegal aliens, like everyone else, pay income, payroll, property, Social Security and sales taxes. But unlike the rest of us, they usually aren't entitled to unemployment, welfare, Medicare and retirement benefits. One ironic effect of the "dual economy" illegal immigrants support is that the poorest newcomers to this country wind up subsidizing government services for people who are wealthier, and who have more opportunities than they.

Does this mean we are on the way to becoming a "dual society" in which first-class citizens have privileges a foreign "underclass" does not? One of the darkest truths of American history, which Miami certainly recapitulates, is that in this country we always have marginalized certain categories of people.

U.S. immigration policy has been neither logical nor just. But irrationality and injustice haven't stopped previous migrants from succeeding. Children born in this country are Americans whatever the legal status of their parents. Furthermore, there's simply no direct correlation between the amount of government assistance a particular group gets and how it fares. The Cubans received lavish U.S. assistance and did very well. But the classic immigrants of the nineteenth century got no help from the government.

Many newcomers from Third World countries share important characteristics with the Cubans and other successful immigrant groups. Even most illegal aliens aren't "wetbacks" in the old stereotypical sense. They're students, tourists, businessmen and others who were affluent (and educated) enough to fly into the country on nonimmigrant visas, and then find sufficient work to stay on. Very many of them, nearly half in many categories, are women. And far from being low-skilled agricultural workers, the vast majority of the foreign-born, like the Cubans, are skilled or at least semiskilled workers who live in metropolitan areas. Furthermore, these newcomers tend to have strong entrepreneurial skills. "Market principles," the presidential report concludes, "suggest that immigration in a competitive economy increases output and improves productivity."

It's also a myth that this country is being simply inundated by a tidal wave of poor, unskilled and dark-skinned "aliens." In fact this new wave of immigrants, significant as it is, simply doesn't compare with the massive human tides that swept into this country in the past.

In 1980, for example, the foreign-born proportion of the U.S. population was less than half of what it was in 1910. According to Census Bureau statistics, about 6.2 percent of the people in America are foreign-born, which, as the Council of Economic Advisers points out, is "low by historical standards." This influx of foreigners is also negligible in comparison with that other wave of migration that is also reshaping this country—migration, by native-born Americans, to different parts of the United States. Between 1970 and 1980, for instance, about twenty million Americans migrated across state lines, compared with an overall inflow of about 2.5 million foreigners.

The United States has faced no insuperable problems adjusting to this truly massive internal demographic upheaval, of which Sun Belt shift is only the most dramatic manifestation. It would be illogical to suppose our national life should be threatened by a much smaller inflow of people who happen to be foreign-born. There's another reason not to be alarmed. Even when our government agencies cannot control it, immigration tends to regulate itself, and for a simple reason. Whether they're foreign-born or "real" Americans, people can be counted on to act in their self-interest. They go where the jobs are, not where they aren't. Miami will continue to attract migrants so long as its economy remains diversified and innovative. On the other hand, Houston will be less troubled by "illegal aliens" now that the Texas oil boom has collapsed.

What continuing migration into this country really demonstrates is that the American economy remains the greatest font of wealth and invention the world has ever seen. Since the Cubans arrived, for instance, the U.S. gross national product, in constant dollars, has more than doubled—from $1.7 trillion in 1961 to more than $3.6 trillion today. That is to say, the U.S. *increase* ($1.9 trillion) is considerably greater than the *total* Japanese GNP of $1.2 trillion.

There's no way to quantify it. But the astonishing dynamism of the United States clearly derives, to a very important extent, from the fact that we have never stopped being a nation where the door is always open—to new immigrants, new ideas, new art forms, new inventions.

What would happen if somehow, someday, we were able to slam the door shut and announce that the "Americanization" of America was complete? Miami is an extreme example. But the truth, for most practical purposes, is that without "aliens," Miami, like America itself, would hardly exist at all. Take away the "aliens" and you take away practically everything that makes Miami Miami, from the Calle Ocho festival to Christo's "Surrounded Islands" to the neighborhood sushi bar.

This hardly means native-born Americans don't count anymore. On the contrary, one of the most interesting things about Miami is that the place remains so thoroughly dominated by "real" Americans.

Of Miami's total jobs, for example, about 55 percent are held by whites, 15 percent by blacks and 28 percent by Hispanics, according to the Equal Opportunity Commission. White, native-born Americans hold about three-quarters of all professional, executive, managerial and government jobs; they make up about two-thirds of all technicians and office, clerical, sales and skilled craft workers. Hispanics predominate in only two fields—as unskilled laborers and machine operators. You only have to stand beside Government Cut, the waterway connecting Biscayne Bay with the Atlantic, any Sunday afternoon, and watch the endless armada of sailboats and powerboats go by to realize an important fact. The number of native-born Americans in Miami has never ceased to grow.

In the future the role of "real" Americans, wherever they happen to have been born, will only increase in importance. This is because, in any generation, it takes more than determination and hard work to turn swampland into a city. It takes even more than abundant natural resources and technological innovation.

Rule of law, respect for the individual and a strong commitment to playing by the rules are the truly indispensable foundations of any great, dynamically growing civilization. And it is that American genius for combining spontaneity and order, individualism and responsibility, personal freedom and stable political institutions, that, far more than any other factor, explains Miami's success.

Exactly why has Miami, not Havana, wound up the capital of the Caribbean? The answer seems simple until you consider the fact that, thirty years ago, Havana actually had many advantages Miami did not. It was a natural port. By any measure its social and cultural institutions were far more impressive. It had hundreds of thousands of highly motivated and ambitious people, including lots of Americans with American capital. And no other Latin American city was better positioned to attract more American skills and more American dollars.

One crucial element was missing, however. Cuba lacked the capacity for peaceful reform and orderly political change that, even in the worst of times, somehow always manages to prevail in the United States.

Miami, that redneck town on the other side of the Straits of Florida, had the one resource which Havana, for all its history and sophistication, could not acquire at any price, including war and revolution. What Miami had was more than a political system. It was a whole human culture capable of accommodating the most foreign people, while simultaneously instilling in them those qualities that mark the "real" American, wherever the country of origin. And, as Guarione Diaz points out in his study of how Miami successfully absorbed the Cuban influx,

> In this respect America is unique in the world. It has a seemingly inexhaustible capacity to change its customs and values, preserve its traditions, mix its population, and yet maintain a national character which is continuously regarded as American.

You can see what he means everywhere in Miami these days, from the city desk at the *Herald* to the check-in desk at the Fontainebleau, and from the executive suites in the big skyscrapers to the kitchen at Joe's Stone Crab. Over the past twenty-five years, the Anglo and Jewish names may have changed into Hispanic names. The color of the people may have changed from white and black to that infinite chromatic gradation that lies in between. But whether it's freedom of the press, *habeas corpus,* or simply the right to rent an apartment or eat in the restaurant of your choice, Miami is a lot more American now than it was back when it was a southern town, complete with racial segregation and "Gentiles Only" signs.

What I find all the more impressive about this is that Miami Americanized these newcomers so unconsciously. The subeditors and telephone repairmen and motel managers did not say to themselves, "Well, here comes another wave of migrants. Time to start proving the Melting Pot works again." They just did it the way America always does things best—by not bothering about a person's color or nationality or language; by just saying, "Here is the job. This is the way we do it. If you can do it our way, or do it better, you're in."

They never did get much credit; maybe they never will. But among Miami's true heroes must be counted the clerk in the zoning office and the state employee who gives you your driver's test, along with the public school teacher, the small businessman and the functionary in City Hall.

It can be a newspaper that turns a Cuban "refugee" into an American reporter—and so keeps the First Amendment one of the living forces in American life. It can be an election that turns an "exile" politician into a consensus candidate—and so keeps representative government one of the living forces in American life. Or it can just be the restaurant that turns an "illegal alien" into someone with a job and a future. Whether it's a hardware store or the Harvard Law School, sociologists call them "mediating institutions," and this brings us to the culminating irony of that extraordinary American saga which began with the "loss" of Cuba, and which has wound up with the rediscovery of so many important truths about the United States.

This community which—that sunny December morning, only twenty-five years ago, in the Orange Bowl—imagined its destiny was to "liberate" Cuba today no longer finds itself in the bleachers. Today, thanks to their Americanization, the Cubans now stand where Kennedy stood.

They extend their arms; they orate. And they are hardly more aware of it now than he was—that others are so enthralled not because of what they say, but because of what they are or, more precisely, because of what, thanks to America, they have *become.*

Who couldn't have been thrilled by Kennedy that day? His politics, even the language he spoke, didn't matter. He himself was living proof that even if your ancestors were illiterate peasants, you could have it all—youth, wealth, vigor, power; history itself balanced there in the cup of your outstretched palm, glittering and as full of possibility as the keys to a brand-new car.

Today Miami's Cubans also extend their arms in welcome, whether they realize it or not. A kid in Medellín sees the Grand Prix on TV. And suddenly he realizes: if only he can get to Miami, he can be Ralph Sanchez. A seamstress in Havana hears the story of how some "liberated Cuban girl" actually defeated some *macho* politician in a big election, with all the TV cameras looking at her. And so she decides: If Mariel ever opens again, I will go.

And so the Cubans, like all other "real" Americans before them, in the future will find themselves in a new role. This time they will be giving driving tests. They will be correcting the exams. They will be the ones sitting in the personnel office when the "alien" walks in and asks for a job.

This classic "Only in America" scenario will unfold regardless of what happens in Cuba. In fact that is the most telling sign of the Americanization of the Cubans—that so few of them would leave Miami even if Castro were overthrown.

That's not to say that, even now, it's a question they like you to ask. In fact, in a community both so talkative and so self-assured, it was about the only question that on occasion produced equivocation, even flashes of self-doubt. Still, I felt I had to ask it. What *would* they do if they awoke some morning and found Castro gone?

Predictably, Rosario Kennedy provided one extreme of the Cuban response. "We will *never* go back to the Cuba we left," she told me one day, as we drove around Little Havana. What was unpredictable was that it was so hard to find the other extreme.

Xavier Suarez, for instance, takes much more "Cuban" positions on social issues like abortion. He also strongly supports such policies as U.S. aid to the Nicaraguan *contras*. But when it came to the liberation of Cuba, he seemed to regard the subject basically as a distraction. He told Gael Love of *Interview* magazine:

> I'm a total mainstream politician, an American, but
> . . . I sometimes fight it out with the Miami *Herald* or the
> TV news on this because they make it sound as if I'm a
> knee-jerk anti-communist. I'm not a knee-jerk anything.
> I have lived under communism. I have seen what it looks
> like. It's a high priority for me, for this community and
> for this entire nation to do something about communism
> and its expansion. I spend some of my time advocating

that and working toward that end, but, believe me, the
number of hours I've put into the job of being mayor of
Miami—tending to local concerns and problems—compared to the time I've spent on foreign policy, is 98 to
two percent.

"Foreign policy has no place in what I do," he said on another
occasion. So why did he concern himself at all with "foreign policy"
questions like Cuba?

I think I owe that to the population who elected me. But,
again, as an official who was elected by the people here
in the city of Miami, whose function is to be mayor—the
classic municipal functions—I think I owe it to them to
give them their money's worth in terms of my attention
to local issues and making this city work.

No one in Miami was more in favor of the liberation of Cuba
than Joe Carollo, of course, so that made it all the more interesting:
he agreed with Suarez and Kennedy.

"You can't invade Cuba," he said, astonished that I'd raised the
possibility. Well, I asked, just supposing, somehow, Castro were
overthrown. Would he go back?

"You have to accept things as they are," he said. Later I returned
to the subject of Cuba and he said, not in response to any particular
question, but with impatience, as though I were deliberately missing the point, or even trying to question his loyalties, "I'm a real
American."

In this matter, too, Miami's politicians proved to be truly representative of the people who elected them. In the study of Cuban
migrants that I mentioned in Chapter 14, for example, almost all
those asked initially regarded themselves as "exiles" and said their
ambition was to return to a "free" Cuba. But just six years later,
95.9 percent said they expected to stay in America forever. What
if Castro were overthrown? In 1973, 60 percent had said they

would return to Cuba; by 1979, only 23 percent said they would return to Cuba even if Castro were removed from power.

The same is true of Miami's "Cubans" as a whole. Back in the late sixties, vast majorities said they would go "home" if they had the chance. As late as 1978, about 40 percent of all Cubans still said they would leave the United States if Castro fell. But by 1983 the proportion of those saying they would "move back to Cuba [if] there was a revolution in Cuba and Castro was overthrown" had dwindled to 24 percent.

The proportion today no doubt is even smaller. Yet even those responses underestimate the fundamental reversal of loyalties life in America has produced. The reason is that most of those who say they would leave are elderly retirees who (like many first-generation Poles and Italians) would return to their native villages to live on U.S. Social Security checks, among friends and family they knew in their youth. Among Cuban-Americans under forty, perhaps less than 5 percent would seriously consider returning permanently to Cuba. And, as Cesar Odio remarked to me once, "Seventy percent of those who did return to Havana would be back in Miami within six months."

It's probably the most amazing of all Miami's transformations—all the more so because no one seems even to notice it. In less than one generation, returning to Cuba has been metamorphosed from an obsession into a possibility most people don't even want to consider.

Still, it could happen, because, as Miami proves, anything can happen. In fact it's already happened several times—the news

> exploding from radios and teletype machines: [the dictator] fallen and fleeing: gun-toting rebels storming the streets of Havana. . . . In Miami, the rebel victory touches off horn-honking, flag-waving celebrations among Cu-

359

> bans living here. Three thousand converge on the Miami
> airport. . . . Hundreds more gather in noisy celebration
> at Bayfront Park.

So Charles Whited, twenty-five years later, remembered the "liberation" of Cuba at the end of 1958, though he might also have been describing the celebrations in Ybor City in 1898.

In early 1986 the news once again exploded from radios and Teletypes. Once again, in Miami, the rebel victory touched off horn-honking, flag-waving celebrations. It was one of those wonderful Orange Bowl moments when people laughed and cried and believed that for once, at last, America and its neighbors could have it all. I bought a T-shirt to commemorate this rapturous moment. I bought the T-shirt because it had a slogan on it and the strange inept English of the slogan had that poetic fluency that sometimes only illiteracy can produce. It read:

> *Let Us & U.S. Ring*
> *The Freedom Bell in Haiti*

Until now the Haitians had been the lowest of the low—so black they made the Liberty City crack dealers look white; so poor they made the Marielitos seem like members of the "golden exile." But now the Haitians walked tall. In their churches they gathered by the thousands to sing Magnificats of thanksgiving, and when that music ran up your spine, you threw your shoulders back. You stood proud and tall, with them. The next day a Haitian cabdriver counted out the fare exactly, then handed me back the tip: "Today I'm a free man," he said, "just like you."

What gratified the Haitians, and certainly discomfited some Cubans, was that it was these wretched of the earth, not they in their skyscraper offices, their suburban houses and air-conditioned cars, who'd finally done it! The dollar bills contributed to the resistance, the letters to the congressmen and the president, the protest marches and the clandestine radio broadcasts—the Cubans didn't have a monopoly on the struggle to free a homeland. Miami had turned out to be the capital of the Haitian exile, too. And this, at least, was one group of "refugees" who could go home again.

When the news first reached Miami that Baby Doc had fallen, they poured out into the streets by the thousands. They waved palm fronds in celebration of Haiti's resurrection. They danced. They sang. It seemed the streets were a singing, dancing sea of blue and red, the national colors of Haiti. What made this celebration even more moving was that, in one way, it was like the city elections less than two months earlier.

It wasn't just the Haitians for whom this day was a victory; people from all of Miami's different communities were celebrating, too. Passing motorists waved to the celebrants and blew their horns in support. Cuban, black and Anglo city officials, led by Mayor Suarez, joined demonstrators in a peaceful "liberation" of the Haitian consulate. "We're with them in case something good has happened, and we're with them in case something good has not happened," Suarez explained. In the face of this outpouring of joy, even the Miami riot police were indulgent. "If in fact their liberation is what they're celebrating," said one of them, "I think it's great. Everyone wants to go back to their home country. I wish 'em well."

There was also another old Miami theme running through these revels. The joyous news was false. Duvalier hadn't really been overthrown, not just yet. The Haitians would have to wait another week for their dream to come true.

But, then, finally it was true, and so, as a result, another essential Miami theme reasserted itself. Even after Baby Doc was overthrown, these "refugees" and "exiles" didn't go home. Like the Jews in Miami Beach who thrilled to Israel's every victory, they stayed right where they were, and for the same reason. Miami—America—was now their home.

At one celebration, the parking lot at Notre Dame d'Haiti was filled with big, late-model American cars, and the Haitian families emerged from their cars as if dressed for the Easter Parade. Inside the church they sang of their love of their homeland; they thanked

God for their homeland's liberation. But even as these Haitians sang and prayed, a mural looked mutely down on them. Like that flag that day at the Orange Bowl, it explained, far better than their words, the real significance of this historic event.

In the mural, which was painted by a Miami Haitian artist, Haiti is in the background. Miami is in the foreground. In the mural the land of these people's past is separated from the land of these people's future by an expanse of blue tropical sea. But across these waters, a sailing boat heads toward America. In the sky a jet, carrying more Haitians, flies toward the Land of Opportunity.

The mural depicts the dream, the reality—the process—of America. Perhaps that is the reason the artist also included still another of America's essential themes. As these tempest-tossed huddled masses make their way to these shores, Our Lady of Perpetual Help blesses these latest pilgrims, legitimizing a dream old as the *Mayflower*.

In the mural she gazes down on Miami in a familiar way, her brow haloed with a familiar light. She also has the flowing robes. Of course they're darker. The face is different. She holds an infant, not a torch. All the details aren't exactly the same. Why should they have to be, in this Haitian-American version of the Statue of Liberty?

There is another vital theme in our history that Miami embodies, in addition to immigration. This is the growing importance of cities in American life.

Only ten years ago, even the "experts" were predicting the death of the American city. This notion that cities were un-American—and therefore, like all things un-American, doomed to oblivion—wasn't some by-product of Sun Belt shift. It was a belief, a hope, as old as the United States.

Cities were the "sewer of all depravities," Thomas Jefferson proclaimed, even as he proclaimed the pursuit of happiness America's inalienable right. Jefferson believed that even when Americans became masters of a nation large as Europe, they must remain sylvan, pure, uncomplicated—untainted by the foreign influences many Americans still associate with urban life.

Out of this desire to create an America "separated by nature" from the baneful influences of city life came Jefferson's decision to purchase Louisiana. He saw glimmering there in that immense wilderness what, 150 years later, other Americans saw in the virgin subdivisions of Florida—fulfillment of the dream of "possessing a chosen country, with room enough for our descendants to the hundredth and thousandth generation" to pursue happiness far from all the shadows the tall buildings of the cities cast.

When Jefferson bought Louisiana in 1803, less than 5 percent of all Americans lived in cities and many of those cities "would rank today as rural towns." But as the nation expanded westward, the urban population of the United States soared. Within a few generations, even the farthest reaches of Jefferson's beloved wilderness were speckled "with great cities rivalling those of Europe." As a direct result of his dream of escaping cities, "that dream [had] vanished forever."

Today it's not the city, it's the family farm—last vestige of the old Jeffersonian ideal of rural self-sufficiency—that is almost extinct. Contrary to all predictions, the United States is in the midst of what only can be called an urban renaissance. The *city* has become to the eighties and nineties what the suburb was to the fifties and sixties. Nearly three-quarters of all Americans, 180 million of our 240 million people, now live in metropolitan regions. Five of our ten fastest-growing metropolitan regions are in Florida—which, more even than California, has been built on the urge to escape cities.

Why do some cities flourish and others wither? One of the most interesting things about Miami and Miami Beach is that, in less than thirty years, the positions of the two rival municipalities have become completely reversed. Incontestably in the fifties, and even into the sixties, Miami Beach was the shining jewel,

Miami the tarnished setting, in the necklace of towns and cities, stretching from Boca Raton south to Key Largo, that make up Greater Miami.

Today, however, it is Miami Beach that has fallen from grace. Restoring the beachfront could not restore the old cachet. Miami is now where the action is. It is also where you find the most hope. Meanwhile Miami Beach struggles with a host of problems, the biggest of which is to find a new role for itself now that it is no longer the premier winter resort of the United States.

What accounts for this role reversal? The secret of Miami's success is precisely what once made cities seem so unattractive, even "doomed," to Americans.

Real cities are, inevitably, places where buildings are always burning down and neighborhoods are being abandoned, where desperate people prowl the streets looking for targets of opportunity. But they are also places where new buildings are always rising, where other neighborhoods are coming up—where new Dick Whittingtons never cease to arrive, whether from Hoboken or Havana. And that, more than anything else, explains why Miami was so ideally situated, at the beginning of the 1960s, to exploit the opportunities of sudden, total change that were about to sweep across south Florida.

It was in the tacky subdivisions of Miami, not the chandeliered hotels of Miami Beach, that the Cubans, the Haitians and many others could find housing. It was in Miami's drab business district and in its monotonous warehouse areas—not in Fort Lauderdale and the suburbs of Broward County—that they could find space to start the small businesses that would make Miami the latest incarnation of the American dream.

Miami's total inability ever to be an American paradise singled it out for a greatness its rivals would never achieve.

In 1850 Virginia City, Nevada, was the queen city of the West. San Francisco was only a jumping-off point where those left behind by the Gold Rush decided to settle. Yet today Virginia City, like other ghost towns all over the West, is a necropolis. San Francisco is one of the world's great cities.

Miami Beach, like Virginia City, did what it did all too well. In fact Miami Beach never really learned to do anything else. Specialization—whether the specialization is mining silver, making steel or selling sunshine—is fine, so long as demand for the speciality remains strong. But what happens when times change?

At the very moment Miami Beach's triumph over Miami seemed complete, the omens of failure were there—those "surprisingly" chill winds, those propeller planes flying in formation overhead the night the Fontainebleau opened. Less than five years later, the commercial jets would start flying people off to resorts where it really was warm in January. Miami Beach would be plunged into a crisis from which it has not fully escaped yet.

An untidy, heterodox city like Miami is always ready to exploit —desperate to exploit—new opportunities. But what happens when the whole way we live, not just the way we vacation, changes? Today leafy communities all over the country are in the midst of a veritable "suburban crisis," as the people who settled there in the fifties die or retire elsewhere, their Yuppie children colonize the inner cities, and the urban poor and unemployed, displaced by gentrification, migrate to the inner suburbs.

In the future Miami will go on growing, go on being successful, precisely because it never was, and never will be, the nice, neat, pleasant, homogeneous kind of place Miami Beach and Fort Lauderdale once were.

And Miami Beach, and Miami's other satellite cities, will survive because all the characteristics they once considered contemptible in Miami will more and more come to characterize them. Already, in fact, Hispanic settlers are reviving the dilapidated housing tracts of Broward County, and both Miami Beach and Fort Lauderdale are belatedly trying to attract the kind of people, ranging from Latin tourists to homosexuals, they once were quite content to let Miami monopolize.

The whole key to Miami Beach's survival, in fact, has turned out to be what it once considered its greatest liability—proximity to the city on the other side of Biscayne Bay. Miami Beach is no longer a retirement mecca. But much younger people from Miami are beginning to rejuvenate the old-age ghettos. Never again will Miami Beach be the American ideal of a winter resort. But Miami's new notoriety is attracting visitors to the beach from Europe and South America—as well as international businessmen and corporate conventions. The fashionable shops are long gone from Lincoln Road, but its old storefronts now provide studios for Miami artists, ranging from painters to a ballet company. Young Miami professionals are renovating the old Spanish bungalows of Miami Beach, and the high-rise condos—now so out of fashion with "real" Americans—are attracting Cuban buyers. After many stops and starts, a new residential and recreational complex is rising at the very southern tip of Miami Beach, near Joe's Stone Crab. For the first time in memory, the average age of the population in Miami Beach is declining. Enrollment in Miami Beach public schools is rising as young families, many of them Hispanic, settle there.

Thanks to Miami's success as a city, Miami Beach will face a less haughty but probably more stable future, unless the impulse for the quick fix prevails and gambling is introduced. It will become only one of at least half a dozen peripheral residential and commercial centers—an integral, and by no means dominant, part of the metropolis it once so scorned.

This phenomenon is not limited to south Florida. The "escape" to the Sun Belt and suburbs, sociologists are now beginning to realize, was indeed like the conquest of Jefferson's frontier. This supposed abandonment of urban life has turned out to be merely "a transitional phase between the traditional compact pre-war city" and the creation of vast new regional cities even more immense and inescapable than the cities the suburban and Sun Belt migrants originally fled. And, as two Los Angeles urbanologists, Christopher B. Leinberger and Charles Lockwood, point out, this "dramatic restructuring of America's cities and suburbs" is now sweeping the whole nation. "Not only fast-growing Sun Belt cities like Atlanta and Phoenix but also slow-growing older ones like St. Louis and

Kansas City, and archetypal ones like New York and Baltimore"
are caught up in this new urbanization of American life.

One thing Miami reveals quite clearly is the absurdity of trying
to erect geographical and conceptual barriers—between city and
suburb, between Sun Belt and Frost Belt, between the dream and
reality of America. Successful cities—whether they are Los Angeles
or Boston, Miami or Minneapolis—are successful because they successfully exploit the opportunities around them, not because of
their latitude, architecture, age or climate. And unsuccessful cities
are unsuccessful because they somehow have cut themselves off
from the irrepressible heterodoxy of America, because they have
forgotten that the only constant of survival is constant change. This
is the lesson of Miami Beach and tourism, and of Youngstown,
Ohio, and steel. It is also the lesson of Houston, and its over-
dependence on oil.

In July 1986 Miami celebrated another victory. "Miami Falls to
7th Place in Murders," the headline announced. Actually there was
little real cause for satisfaction. While the murder rate had declined,
violent crime was still increasing. In fact it had risen by nearly 13
percent, the *Herald* reported. Fewer people were being murdered,
but more people than ever were being shot, stabbed and bludgeoned.

Miami Homicide lieutenant Edward Carberry was able to shed
some light on this typical Miami paradox. Rescue techniques developed during the Vietnam war—including airborne paramedic
teams specializing in trauma care—were getting to the victims
much more quickly. "Advances in medicine, the training of the
paramedics and the skill of the trauma teams in many cases turn
what would have been homicide into aggravated assault," he explained to Edna Buchanan.

The big crime news, however, wasn't in Miami. It was up in
Broward County. For at the same time "Miami dropped from third
to seventh place among the nation's most murderous cities . . . a

14.5 percent increase in Fort Lauderdale's murder rate vaulted it from 22nd to 11th, said the FBI's annual summary of national crime statistics.''

Miami's no Casablanca. But it is every bit as frenetic, exciting and dangerous as another fabled metropolis—Prohibition Chicago.

Back in its heyday, the city fathers didn't like to admit it. But Chicago really was speakeasies and bathtub gin, shoot-outs in the street and the national capital of organized crime—just as Miami really is the cocaine and gun-running capital of the United States today.

But Chicago didn't just belong to Al Capone; it belonged to poets like Carl Sandburg and to architects like Frank Lloyd Wright. There were lots of crooked cops in Chicago. But there were also politicians as cunning as the young Richard Daley and leaders as idealistic as the young Adlai Stevenson. Most of all, Chicago belonged to people who, at first, really didn't seem like "real" Americans at all—rednecks from Appalachia, blacks from the South, Slavs from Eastern Europe. They were the ones who made Chicago the pace-setting city of the American industrial revolution, just as today other migrants, from both inside and outside America, are making Miami the pioneer city of the international, postindustrial revolution.

As they watch their sons program computers in English, and their daughters date Anglo boys, and see all their children dress up in the "Miami Vice" gear they first saw on TV, it's a discovery that appalls some Cubans even more than it does some "real" Americans: these days, for both good and ill, Miami *is* America.

Like America, it's fast, big, new, reckless, thoughtless and even kind of scary. But Miami's also got America's saving graces. There's something about the place that engenders cooperation and invention, excites the imagination, and produces hope.

In the years ahead, Miami, no less than the gilded youth of Coconut Grove, will grow older. The ugly, exciting rawness will lose some of its rough edges. However exotic its national image

remains, Miami will go on getting more and more "American"—
and not just because Miami is becoming more and more like the rest
of the country, but because the rest of the country is becoming
more and more like Miami. Other American cities already are
discovering that they, too, have Hispanic voters and that there is
big money to be made in foreign trade. People everywhere else in
America, if they haven't already, will also discover what Miami has
shown. This country will never be Paradise because America's too
big and unpredictable, too open-ended and full of possibility, ever
to conform to anybody's Platonic ideal.

Maurice Ferre lost the election, but even in defeat the oolite
mayor hadn't lost his sense of how things connect. "We're all
Americans, and we're all part of the system," he said the night he
was voted out of office. "Time will show this country is so big it will
absorb all of us."

You have to come to a place like Miami, seemingly so "foreign,"
to appreciate that extraordinary power, that all-pervasive—completely subversive—force of what can only be called American
civilization.

Epilogue:
Good-bye Miami

South of Miami there's an island called Raccoon Key, where a colony of rhesus monkeys lives. The island has a balmy climate, abundant water and vegetation, an absence of the natural enemies of ape and man. To these amenities the island's owners have added artificial ones, including an annual ration of thirty-five tons of Purina Monkey Chow for which the monkeys need neither spin nor toil.

Finding themselves liberated from the law of the jungle, the monkeys have defoliated the mangrove forest, defaced the island's few buildings and made the island uninhabitable for other species. Their feces pollute the adjacent waters. The monkeys quarrel ceaselessly among themselves. But this divisiveness is replaced by militant unity when strangers approach. When some humans in a Boston whaler tried to visit the island, the rhesus monkeys scowled at them; they jumped up and down. They made threatening gestures. They converged on these interlopers, as if beset by a common peril to their way of life.

One day, in Miami Beach, I visited a friend in her twenties who lived in one of those beachfront buildings Morris Lapidus designed.

Her apartment was located on a high floor, but from all its windows you saw only other, identical apartments. However, if you went out onto the balcony and craned your neck to the left, you could see a stretch of sand, a segment of ocean, a patch of sky.

I suggested a walk by the ocean. My friend declined. She wasn't afraid, she explained, though people did sometimes get mugged on the beach. She'd once seen a mugging, right from her balcony, she said. It was just that the excursion would be too complicated and time-consuming. First, we'd have to find the security guard, so he could shut off the electronic alarms and let us out through the iron gate in the twelve-foot-high concrete wall that separated the building from the beach. Then, once out there, we'd have to rush back, because the gate was chained shut for the night at five-thirty.

There was another way, she said. If you went down into the underground garage and back past the incinerator, there was a door that led out into an alley where the sanitation department collected garbage. You could thread your way through trash cans down to the end of the alley, where there was a lower wall. You could then climb over that wall to get to the beach. That, she said, was what she usually did, but there was a problem, she added. Rats lived in that alley.

We calculated how long it took to get from her apartment to the beach below. It took nearly twenty minutes, about the same time it would have taken her to drive to the airport and fly off to some Caribbean resort.

The next afternoon I found that I was not immune from the fear. I was walking along the beach when I sensed the cold shadow overtaking me. I spun around. No one was pursuing me. It was only that the sun, so soon after passing the meridian, had disappeared. The high-rise apartment blocks formed an impenetrable wall, separating the beach from the sun and casting long shadows out into the ocean.

The absence of light made me conscious of the texture of the sand. Even after the beach had eroded, it had been simple enough for the Army Corps of Engineers to replace the sand. But sand doesn't make a beach, any more than buildings make a city. The packed sand was hard as concrete, I noticed, as I walked through the shadows back to my room at the Alexander Hotel. No crabs or other tidal animals burrowed there; hence there were no gulls or other seabirds, only a broad expanse of gravel, lifeless as a parking lot. The beach was like the plastic marlins in the seafood restaurants; the metamorphosis from paradise to imitation of paradise was complete.

As I walked on that beach which was now bereft of sun and life, I tried to understand the fear I felt. It had less to do with the fact that nature had been thwarted than that, in so doing, human beings had thwarted themselves. These buildings, after all, hadn't been built for their own sake. They had been built because so many people wanted to live in the sun, next to the sea. Yet the end result was that people lived lives in these immense warrens of concrete both divorced from nature and cut off from human nature as well. I found myself running back across the beach to the hotel.

Inside, people filled the bar and the restaurant, both of which were dimly lit and air-conditioner cold, so some wore jackets and sweaters. The atmosphere was convivial. But these people might have been in some northern inland city, thousands of miles from the green, warm and thoughtless ocean outside.

I decided I'd had enough of Miami for a while, so a few days later I flew to Paris to visit some friends, and then on (thanks to some journalistic good luck) to assignments in Africa and Asia.

It was late February in Paris and everyone ached to escape winter. Perhaps that's why people pretended it was spring. They would go to dinner without their overcoats and pretend they weren't shivering when they tried to find their cars in the underground parking lot at Les Halles. In a few cafés the Algerian waiters had put tables out on the sidewalks. There, each afternoon for the hour or two when there was direct sunlight, a few shapeless old ladies in cloth coats with squirrel collars, a few kids in blue jeans and Armani jackets, each at their separate tables, would pretend it was April, not February, in Paris.

By five there was no pretending. It would be cold again and dark again, and at my friends' residence we would gather upstairs, in front of the fireplace in the study, with its silver and paintings and books accumulated from half-a-dozen diplomatic posts, mostly in tropical lands. One such dark cold afternoon we had the idea of going to Chartres. The cathedral was a secondary consideration. The goal was to escape winter. As we planned our journey, the sun in our minds grew warmer; buds formed, and leaves sprouted on trees. Only later did I make the connection: it wasn't unique to America, this belief that, by leaving the city, you could find the renewal of life.

Paris gets ugly around the edges the way American cities do, and in February the rest of northern France doesn't get much better. We did not escape winter even when we found Chartres.

"Shall we go inside?" the dear friend who had driven me there asked when we reached the cathedral. It was bone-cold everywhere except inside the car, with the heater on. I didn't tell her I didn't want to visit this old pile of medieval stone, this reliquary built by dead people who piled one stone on top of another to prove you could live forever. It all had been a dreadful mistake, I realized. I should have stayed in Miami, where it was warm.

We left Chartres six hours later, and then only because the light was fading. For all those hours, my teeth clenched in the cold, I'd been unable to take my eyes off Chartres cathedral. If the light hadn't faded, I would have stayed there forever.

It wasn't the stone; it was the light. It was what the light did to the stained-glass windows there. Einstein once said he would be content to spend the rest of his life pondering what light was. But as I watched the light, thin as it was in February in France, transform stained-glass into spiritual rhapsody, I thought of a place even warmer, even gaudier, than Miami. I thought about scuba-diving in the barrier reef off Belize, in Central America. I'd been down for hours, and I couldn't take my eyes off the coral and the fish because the light filtering down from above did to the water what the sunlight did to the stained glass in the windows at Chartres. It animated a world more complex, more unpredictable, more coherent—more beautiful—than any I could either invent or understand.

Was this what they meant by "rapture of the deep"? I only knew I would have been content to explore this foreign world, which I simultaneously felt humbled and exalted to have entered, forever.

But gradually the underwater colors deepened, then darkened. The light was dying, and the approaching darkness filled me with a sad, joyful acceptance of the beauty and transience of life that I did not experience again until that day at Chartres. I felt then what I felt later as we drove back to Paris. If I couldn't stay here forever, it was better to leave.

The more distance I put between me and Miami, the closer Miami got. This wasn't just because, on this earth, you always wind up back where you started if you travel far enough. There was another reason.

Everywhere the world was growing more like Miami. In Cairo, in Bombay, in Hong Kong, skyscraper apartment houses clawed the sky. All over the world people were converging on cities—bringing hopes and dreams, creating wealth and chaos. You could see a whole new world being born.

Who builds worlds? As Miami shows, the real work of history much more resembles the construction, by countless anonymous artisans, of those medieval cathedrals than it does some presidential pronouncement in a football stadium. But history is also like a coral reef, an accumulation of countless lives that stays, even when we go, and so grows into something more immense, of stranger shape, than any of its individual creators could foresee or comprehend.

*

374

The city as cathedral, the city as coral reef—neither the architectural nor the organic metaphor of human civilization is new, of course. They go back beyond Scholastics like Aquinas and St. Augustine, to Plato, Aristotle and classical antiquity. I think these metaphors keep recurring because of what they imply about the nature of human beings, not just the cities people create. Are we like gods? Does our capacity to create Fontainebleaus and TV series and cities bespeak a touch of the divine in human nature? Or are we more like marine insects?

Sometimes Miami suggested more recondite possibilities, like the kinds you find in advanced physics or a Wallace Stevens poem. One winter afternoon, for example, my brother and I were sailing off the Florida coast. It was cloudy, cold and choppy. But a few miles offshore the wind moved the clouds; the sun came out. We turned on the radio. Pachelbel's *Canon* was playing and this music made me feel, as I'd felt at Chartres and Belize, that an underlying unity was expressing itself.

The waves of energy the sun radiated were warming my face, and the waves of air the earth's rotation generated were propelling this graceful sloop through the water, so the boat in turn added its own waves to the infinitely varied cross-hatched waves of the sea. The resonating patterns of the ocean, it seemed to me at that moment, were the same as the resonating patterns of Pachelbel's *Canon.* And I suddenly knew my thoughts and emotions, my physical body, were also composed of waves, as were the condos shimmering on the distant beach and all the debris that lay, unseen, beneath us, on the ocean floor.

Later, as a diversion from writing this book, I took up reading physics textbooks and so discovered that the intuitive notion I had that day is one of the basic principles of quantum mechanics.

According to modern physics, matter does not, on some occasions, act *like* waves. Matter—stones, buildings, cities, us—*is* waves. The behavior of matter waves can be mathematically predicted, through use of formulas like the Schroedinger Equation, and then technologically exploited. Matter waves, for example, made possible the invention of the electron microscope, hence also advances in fields ranging from cancer research to the creation of neutron bombs. This discovery that the most fundamental antithesis in human experience—between the material and immaterial—is only an illusion has allowed scientists to resolve paradoxes, such as the "wave-particle dilemma," which had bedeviled science for centuries. But it has only confronted us with newer, deeper paradoxes.

Are we material, like the Chartres cathedral? Is history organic, like the coral reef at Belize? Or could we and all we create be only resonances, oscillations? These "questions about the underlying structure of the universe" may seem totally irrelevant to daily reality. But as Art Hobson points out in a book called *Physics and Human Affairs,* the conceptual and ethical implications of these discoveries,

> in the opinion of many scientists, have . . . great human
> significance. They may in fact lead our culture toward a
> new understanding, a less materialistic and less object-
> oriented consciousness, of the natural world around us.

The Schroedinger Equation deals with the predictability of waves. In the world of quantum physics, if you have enough white cops kill enough unarmed blacks, you can predict the frequency of race riots. Or if you have enough flight capital flow into enough banks, you can predict the frequency of the new skyscrapers this interference pattern will produce.

No formula, however, can tell you in advance that the skyscraper will have a big hole in it, and that there will be a palm tree and Jacuzzi inside that hole. This is because one of the other discoveries of quantum physics is that the universe is predictable and unpredictable all at the same time.

This discovery, even more than the unity of waves and matter, shook human knowledge to its foundations because, hitherto, a "belief in the predictability of nature" lay at the heart of Western science and all the Faustian powers it conferred. Einstein, among many others, was confounded.

The Heisenberg Uncertainty Principle is to the petty quirkiness of the universe what the Schroedinger Equation is to its grand magisterial order. Again, the paradox is only superficial; in fact it is at this point that human experience and quantum physics converge. For while Heisenberg shows us we live "in a capricious universe, one in which identical causes produce different effects," Schroedinger shows us that in spite of all the capriciousness around us, a

> certain amount of predictability remains. Although individual flashes on the screen are not predictable, the *overall pattern* is predictable. If we allow one billion electrons to hit the screen and if we then repeat the experiment by allowing another billion electrons to hit the screen, we'll find the same overall pattern is formed both times.

Quantum physics rebukes the Chamber of Commerce boosterism of humanity, but it also shows us what our own unscientific, unquantifiable lives do, what Miami does. Those individual flashes may only be electrons or Haitians. But upon close inspection, they exhibit properties which, when we find them in ourselves, we dignify as spontaneity, individualism and free will. In the subatomic world of quantum physics, you can find the comic (Heisenberg slipping on the banana peel). You also encounter the tragic (Schroedinger can't tell us how and when we'll die, only predict with complete accuracy that we will). So while we turn out to be more like subatomic particles than we imagined, there is a consolation. The universe turns out to be more "human" than we could have imagined. If subatomic particles had names like Julia Tuttle or Osceola, rather than being called neutrinos and quarks, we might even say the universe has a soul.

There is another similarity between the subatomic world and Miami. "I can safely say that nobody understands quantum physics," remarks one physicist, in a book called *The Quantum Universe*. In modern physics the discovery of each new particle leads only to another particle, not to any resolution of the fundamental mystery: what *is* going on? Researchers wonder: Are we the new Newtons, or only like Ptolemy, spinning wheel after illusory wheel? In the long run, that may be the most important discovery of quantum physics—the limits of human understanding.

When matter intersects—say, when a bullet hits flesh or a car careens off I-95—a collision occurs, and the objects involved are fundamentally changed. One important way waves differ from matter is that when waves collide, they are not deflected or damaged or changed. They keep going as though nothing had happened. But at the nodal point where waves intersect, there occurs what scientists call an interference pattern and that, I think, gives us an inkling of why practically everything original and worthwhile in Miami was created by more than one person.

Tuttle did not deflect Flagler and Lapidus did not deflect Novack, just as Kennedy did not deflect Castro. But, in keeping with the laws of quantum mechanics, a new little city, a great gaudy hotel, a civilization of hyphenates were created. We generate waves; we also are generated by waves, and if you stop to think for a moment how, in each of us, there converge heredity-waves and environment-waves, and religion- and ethnicity- and education- and love- and ambition- and hate-waves, you have a new way of conceptualizing, and perhaps even understanding, Jeb Bush and Joe Carollo and Miami and yourself.

Whether it's cathedrals or coral reefs, so much of the way we understand ourselves has to do with the use of simile, analogy and metaphor. So I think I can best express the importance of what I felt that day on the boat in the following way: it did not seem to me at that moment that music was *like* sunlight, or that life was transient *as* a passing wave. I was convinced all of them *were* the same thing—the same way a sunrise, a rainstorm, a traffic accident, an eclipse and a lovers' quarrel are parts of the same day.

In a primitive, landlocked society, with no knowledge of marine biology—in Outer Mongolia or Tibet—it would be meaningless to compare a city to a coral reef. But in our technological society, the understandings of quantum physics can help us understand ourselves. It is difficult, of course, to think of the Fontainebleau hotel as a matter-wave that the intersection of Morris Lapidus and Ben Novack created. But what about Michael Mann and Don Johnson and Olmos? They do create material spools of film, but that's only incidental. "Miami Vice" is really an audiovisual resonation.

On sunny mornings it is possible to look at the Fontainebleau and see it as a cathedral, or to look at the apartment houses ranged along Miami Beach and grasp their resemblance to a coral reef. But when afternoon comes, and the hotels and apartment houses begin to cast their shadows over the beach, out into the ocean, you can see the greed-waves and real estate–waves and foolishness-waves, too. Go out to Miami Beach someday when there's a hurricane. Get as close to the interference pattern as you safely can. There you'll get a sense of what Miami *is,* not just what it's *like.*

You don't have to stand by the ocean. At discotheques in Coconut Grove, you can observe the Hispanic-waves and Anglo-waves intersecting. One night the interference pattern will take the form of a fistfight, the next a bicultural romance. It's both capricious and inevitable. Even the laser beams in the discos prove both Schroedinger and Heisenberg were right.

In Ethiopia I saw people starving; in India I saw peasants harvesting massive surpluses of grain. In Hong Kong people were building skyscrapers that made the skyscrapers of Miami seem like toys.

Between the heterodoxy of Asia and the diversity of America, if you follow the Great Circle Route, lies Arctic emptiness. I was flying back toward Miami, looking down on the infinity of Canadian lake and muskeg. That wilderness made me remember: so many memorable moments in south Florida involved animals.

One time, for instance, I was driving around with Andres Viglucci, an Italian–Connecticut–Puerto Rican–American who went to Princeton and writes for the *Miami Herald.* We'd started out at the Jockey Club in northern Miami, driven south along Biscayne

Boulevard for a while, then east across Tuttle Causeway to Miami Beach. We'd had a Jewish-Continental dinner and then a couple of beers at a Marielito-redneck joint.

Our motions were random; they also described a pattern. We were looking for the Helpless Hooker. "She has one of those collapsible wheelchairs," Andres explained. "She's very pretty, even though she can't walk. Like a lot of the prostitutes, she hangs out at bus stops. That way, if the cops question her, she can say she was waiting for the bus. One time," he added, "I saw a big Cadillac stop for her. Her pimp helped her get in the car and fold up the wheelchair."

I played the devil's advocate. Maybe it was just a kindly millionaire, helping the handicapped, I suggested.

"One night, late," he replied, "I was driving home from work. She beckoned to me."

We were at the tollbooth on the Miami side of Venetian Causeway. Andres was driving, and I was reaching for a quarter to feed the toll machine when I saw we were surrounded by tigers.

There were dozens of them—sleeping, stretching, scratching themselves, yawning, staring listlessly at the blinking neon city that reared up in front of them. My eyes met the eyes of one of the tigers.

The eyes of the tiger were expressionless. The tigers no longer questioned their cages. Even when their cages were put on trucks and carted across Venetian Way to the next exhibition of the Ringling Brothers Circus, they found no wonder in the world, not even when all the wonders of Miami rolled past them.

As the plane I'd boarded in Tokyo brought me closer to America, I wondered: Was the lesson of Miami that we are monkeys, or tigers in a cage? Biology, like physics, turned out to offer less predictable, more revealing possibilities, as I discovered when I got back. The *Orlando Sentinel* had run a harrowing series on the Florida environment, so I called up Mike Thomas, one of the reporters who'd helped prepare it. I asked him what he'd learned most from the survey.

"How the human species always likes to think it's special when it's not," he replied. "We always put ourselves in the center, but we're just part of the biological pollution." He described a Florida invisible to most of us—of attacking Australian pines and subversive foreign hyacinths. "Cuban lizards and Muscovy ducks are taking over," he said. Meanwhile even more infinitesimal protagonists reshaped the world in even more gargantuan ways. Fluorocarbons soared skyward from Florida air conditioners toward the ozone layer. By-products of the coca plant reworked the social structure of Liberty City and Brickell Avenue law firms.

I asked Mike Thomas for the latest communiqué from the front. "We're being invaded by walking catfish from South America," he said.

In front of me is a note I wrote to myself more than three years ago. It says, "Don't start with the tigers." But how could I have ended without the tigers?

John Cheever once put together a collection of stories called *Some People, Places and Things That Will Not Appear in My Next Novel.*

Here are some stories and thoughts that have not appeared in this book, preceded by the notes that suggested them. They're nothing but crumpled pieces of paper now. But I think of them as a Miami bouquet—hibiscus harvested from pineapple plants; orange blossoms plucked from avocado trees. The notes, as I mentioned, precede my afterthoughts.

"Marjory Stoneman Douglas and old people in general (Pepper, etc., Barbara Baer Capitman and Opa-locka)."

One day, after listening to some old people complain incessantly about their age, their retirement ghetto, the Social Security system and their last visit to the doctor, I found myself confiding a most illiberal sentiment to my notebook.

"Boring, self-centered, unimaginative young people become boring, self-centered, unimaginative old people," I wrote. I don't retract that statement. Old age may be shipwreck, but one of the most inspiring things about Miami was that you met so many people who didn't let their spirit fail them, even when their bodies did.

In this youth-obsessed city, for example, the most powerful politician wasn't Xavier Suarez. It was Representative Claude Pepper, who was born in 1900, and by 1987 was one of the most powerful, as well as the oldest, man in Congress. He was already fifty, back when he was defeated for reelection to the Senate on the grounds he was "soft" on Communism and civil rights. A lesser man might have "retired" right there and then. But Pepper just let Florida catch up with the youthfulness of his ideas. Now he represented a congressional district that was more than 50 percent Hispanic—and it was clear there would be no Cuban "takeover" here so long as this grand old redneck wished to go on representing Miami in the U.S. House of Representatives.

Barbara Baer Capitman was another Miamian whom neither age nor defeat could stop. She's in her seventies now—and the truth is, her Deco dream never came true. By the end of 1986, to be sure, the often-prophesied revival of South Beach at long last seemed actually to have begun. But savvy real estate developers, not community activists, seemed likely to inherit the Deco district. Capitman's two sons long since had sold out, but in her junky old car, talking a mile a minute, Barbara still pushed on, trying to find it—that perfect past where she could build a perfect future. It was she who dragged me off to Opa-locka that day, and as I sat there in Curtiss's tumbledown old palace, listening to Barbara share her dream with the black city officials, I wondered if it was my youth that made me so priggish.

Have you no sense of history! I wanted to exclaim. These people don't need minarets, they need schools and jobs and antidrug programs. Barbara and the city planner were conferring about the upcoming Arabian Nights Festival. "Maybe it would be better to buy the camel, rather than rent it," she said. "Should we call the zoo?"

And I realized. No, of course, not. Barbara has no sense of history, no sense of being bound by history—that's what makes her, too, one of the greater inventors of Miami.

So here, Barbara, take this, and wear it in your hair. It only looks like a page pulled from a spiral notebook. It's really an orange blossom, and a most special one at that—because it's one of the very orange blossoms that Julia Tuttle sent Henry Flagler. I'm presenting it to you because you're not *like* Tuttle. You are Tuttle—a failure only in the short run. Keep selling camels to the blacks, Barbara! Even the buildings you have managed to preserve someday will crumble. But your crazy idea that, even in Miami, worlds are worth preserving, not just creating, will last a long time, maybe even longer than Miami does.

Another thing dealing with old people in Miami taught me is that I'm prejudiced. Take Marjory Stoneman Douglas. She's on everyone's "must" list. Yet trip after trip would go by, and I wouldn't call her. Oddly enough, it was being able to admit to myself that *some* old people really were selfish and self-pitying that ultimately let me call up Marjory Stoneman Douglas and ask her for a date.

Of course it wasn't a date I had in mind at first, only an interview, Marjory. But then you asked me over for a drink, and the polite thing to do, under such circumstances, was to ask you out—only *pro forma,* of course—to dinner. And suddenly I realized: This ninety-six-year-old icon was ready for a night on the town. On the way over, I had a meeting with the "Cuban" member of the *Herald* editorial board. "Are you in for a treat!" Guillermo Martinez told me. As usual, Martinez was right.

That night after dinner, Marjory, I drove you home and you invited me in for a drink. You were telling me about George Merrick when, suddenly, there was this buzzing sound in your ear. You asked me to change the battery in your hearing aid. My God, I thought, she can't see and she can hardly hear. What keeps her going? And then I noticed: all around you were the tapes of books. And, I realized: so long as those sound waves could intersect with your brain waves, you'd be an egret—beautiful when you soared, beautiful even when your astonishingly graceful intellect was at rest. We talked for nearly an hour more. It was past midnight, but it was still so hot that I was sweating. You said, "I've always enjoyed the heat, I don't mind sweating."

I do. It makes me feel cumbersome, ugly. But I didn't let the sweat stop me. I bent down and kissed you. And, then, having left this big sweaty kiss on your face, this man you'd never seen before left you. I thanked you for the evening, but I didn't thank you for the greatest gift you'd given me, because I hadn't received it yet.

Just before we met, I'd passed my fortieth birthday. So some days in Miami, when I awoke following our date, I bounded out of bed. "The next fifty years are going to be great!" I shouted. That was the gift you gave me—and it was more precious than a barrel of caviar.

"Explain:
(a) why there were tears in the eyes of the immigration cop when he arrested the Haitian;
(b) why the Miami Metrorail doesn't stop at the Orange Bowl;
(c) the relationship between the foundation of Miami and the Challenger disaster;
(d) the relationship between the date of the Calle Ocho festival and the Americanization of the Cubans."

The Haitian had spent his life savings to get to Miami. He was wearing his only suit when he arrived at MIA. Everything life had given him was packed in two cardboard suitcases. And the visa wasn't right. So, after a night in the airport, they'd send him back to Port-au-Prince. What moved the cop so much was what happened when the Haitian reached the X-ray machine. The cop gestured to the Haitian and his baggage, and then to the X-ray machine. The Haitian put one suitcase on the conveyor belt and watched it go through. Then he put the second suitcase on the conveyor belt and watched it go through.

"Then the Haitian climbed on the conveyor belt," the cop said, "and tried to go through. He thought if he could get through the X-ray machine, he would reach America. I really hated to send that guy back," he added. "He made me appreciate how lucky I am to be in Miami."

They spent a billion dollars on the Miami Metrorail system, and, after it was finished, they discovered it didn't go anywhere. It didn't connect anything. It didn't even stop at the Orange Bowl, which is the one place where even Miamians don't want to drive their cars. People asked themselves: How can this be? The answer is simple.

This futuristic construction isn't a transportation system. It's a great piece of Florida architecture, like the Fontainebleau and the Tampa Bay Hotel. In this case it's the actualization of the fantasy that if Miami's going to be a great city, it's got to have a Metro system the way all great cities do. So, at the cost of $1 billion, Miami's notion that if only it spends enough money it can be New York or Paris, not Miami, caused this particular matter-wave to take shape. That doesn't mean the billion dollars was wasted. This is still Florida: it can be turned into a tourist attraction.

As the official report on the *Challenger* disaster pointed out, the booster seals were defective and there also "was a serious flaw in the decision-making process" at NASA. But the O-rings manufactured by the Thiokol Corporation always functioned adequately at temperatures above fifty degrees. They usually functioned at temperatures much lower than that, so nobody at the Florida launch site thought much of the "low temperature enhanced probability" of booster seal erosion.

On January 28, 1986, the date of the *Challenger* disaster, pre-dawn temperatures dropped below freezing at Cape Canaveral. Thirty-mile winds created a wind-chill factor in the teens. Ice formed in water tanks containing antifreeze. Icicles clung to the rocket boosters. At the moment of blast-off, the temperature was thirty-eight degrees. People watching the launch were shivering.

The myth you can escape winter in Florida, which created Miami, was also what killed the astronauts.

As for the relationship between the date of the Calle Ocho festival and the Americanization of the Cubans: traditionally, such Latin festivals are staged just before the pre-Easter Lenten fasting begins. But the Calle Ocho festival, unlike Carnival in Rio and Mardi Gras in New Orleans, is held in the middle of Lent.

No one was able to explain to me why, back in 1977, people in Little Havana decided to hold it during Lent. Some suggested it was because the weather was better then. But even devout Catholics shrugged when I pointed out that the festival occurred at a time when "real" Cubans are supposed to be doing penance, not dancing in the streets. "The Church has pointed it out several times," Msgr. Bryan Walsh told me, when I consulted him about the matter, "that, liturgically speaking, the date is wrong, blasphemous really."

Father Walsh and I were visiting a new Nicaraguan parish in Kendall that Sunday morning. Even though Mass there was celebrated in Spanish, most people you met spoke English, especially the children who attended parochial schools, where classes are conducted exclusively in English. The service was delayed because the public-address system was broken.

As we watched the Nicaraguan altar boys fiddle with the electronic equipment, I remarked that the Catholic Church was one of the most powerful Americanizing forces I'd encountered in Miami. "Yes, that's true," Father Walsh replied. "The Church teaches them English and computers and how to get small business loans and how to register to vote. We help them get mortgages and driver's licenses. Sometimes I wonder what we do to save their souls."

The sound system crackled into life, and the prayers began. They've only been here a few years, I thought, and already they're

Americans. They're already Americans because only Americans believe you need a loudspeaker for God to hear.

It was the same way with the Calle Ocho festival, of course. The very date of this "most Cuban" of all Miami events celebrates the fact that even Little Havana now resonates to the secular, American concept of time.

"End with the Killer Mobile Sculpture (Symmetry of End with Beginning, with the Alligator, even though, as Miami shows, symmetry has its limitations)."

Someday Miami may be less melodramatic, more "typical," even unremarkable—unthinkable as that is now to both those who love Miami and those who hate it. But as the old-timers say, when that happens it won't be "my Miami" anymore, as I realized one day while visiting an immigrant family.

On a computer print-out they looked just like so many of the "illegal aliens" you've heard about. They spoke French; they'd arrived in a boat. For them Miami was a land of opportunity, but they weren't Haitians. Hugues de Rochefort (though he didn't want me to say so) was a French count, and he and the countess were giving me a progress report, over lunch at the Key Biscayne golf club, on how this particular immigrant family was doing.

"We've kept the offices in Germany and France," Rochefort said, referring to his international public relations firm, "but Miami is headquarters for two reasons. It's so centrally located, and we love it."

Like the Haitian boat people, the Rocheforts had no love lost for the immigration service. "It's ridiculous," the count said. "All this talk about controlling illegal migrations, but when we take the yacht out for a sail beyond the twelve-mile limit and return, there's no one there at the port even though the rules we got with our Green Cards say you have to go through immigration. So after we dock, we have to drive over to the airport and check in."

I asked if there were any other disadvantages to building a new life in Miami. "The reputation," I was told. (This was just before Miami became fabulous, became chic.) "All the talk about drugs and crime. It's hard to attract conventional people here, so when I need an executive, I can't advertise in the *Wall Street Journal* or the *New York Times*. We have to seek out the more adventuresome types."

"Actually it's an advantage," the countess interjected. "The kind of person who isn't scared of Miami is just the kind of person we want—someone who knows how to seize an opportunity."

Before driving over to the club in their Bentley, the Rocheforts had shown me their offices. "Here we do with computers in a day what it took us a couple of weeks and a roomful of draftsmen to do in Europe," Rochefort said. "Also here you're at the airport in half an hour, and before you know it, you're in Caracas or Rio. The main difference between Miami and Paris is that everything gets done so much faster."

They hadn't furnished an office. They'd conjured up a world— all high-tech shiny chrome and glass. Every surface glittered. I was going to ask if Windex is tax-deductible, but before I could, Rochefort took me off to show me the pride of his office. It was a modern mobile sculpture—a kind of Arquitectonica fantasy you could hang on a wall. I thought, only in Miami, but he told me it actually had been made in Boston, by a grandson of Henri Matisse.

The thing was as hard to describe as Miami. It was stainless steel glittery and brass glittery, that is to say both scratchy and shiny, stylish and base at the same time. The center part was circular and bright, like the sun. But attached to it were a number of cumbersome weights. The count started the sculpture spinning and as soon as it started spinning, he quickly stood back.

"What I like about it so much," he explained, as we watched it hurtle, "is that once you start it, you can't stop it. The motions are not random, but they are unpredictable. They follow a logic, but it's a logic we can't foresee."

We watched as the center spun and the weights gyrated every which way. Sometimes there seemed no pattern. Then everything would start vibrating in unison. It stopped a couple of times and then, just when you thought it was over, it started again. Several times, for no apparent reason, it reversed direction.

The damn thing was irresistible. I told the count that and asked, "Can I spin it?"

"Okay," he said. "But watch it. If you don't watch it, it'll rip your arm off."

In Miami, that's where some people get off.

It's also where you get on.

Acknowledgments

For more than five years the people of Miami have been helpful beyond my capacity to acknowledge their help adequately.

They have shared their hopes, triumphs, frustrations and insights, also their documents, data and opinions. All without expecting anything in return except a sincere effort to understand their city, they also at various times have fed me, housed me, met me at airports at the oddest hours, driven me to the oddest places and welcomed me into their homes and families.

No writer could have asked for more cooperation; no writer, it sometimes has seemed to me, could have asked for as much cooperation.

It is easy to assemble a list of names. But how to thank the nameless Cuban motorist who spontaneously stops and offers to help change a flat tire? Or the nameless Haitian waiter at Tarks who, at three one morning, spontaneously tells you the story of his adventures in Miami? I did keep the name of David Crawford, the assistant concierge at the Grand Bay Hotel, who literally gave me the jacket off his own back so that I could have dinner there with Marjory Stoneman Douglas. Such encounters, far more than documents or interviews, helped me to understand Miami, and how it works and grows.

390

I offer my deep gratitude to those people and institutions whose names follow. But I also name these names with a sense of trepidation. If I have omitted anyone, it is not out of ingratitude, only because the people who helped me were so numerous as to make any list necessarily incomplete.

Special thanks, first and foremost, to the irrepressible Jere Warren, my companion in the discovery of Miami since 1980. No one better personifies what makes Miami Miami; no one has provided me deeper insights into life there.

Nor did anyone else help so much, unless it was Charles Worthington, whose contributions were beyond telling. Also in this special category are David Smith Soto and Zita Arocha, whose help and friendship were very special gifts.

The debt I owe to my journalist colleagues in Florida is enormous, especially at the *Miami Herald,* which often seemed less a newspaper than a bottomless trove of expertise on every aspect of Miami's life and history. It would be quite impossible to list all those associated in one way or another with the *Herald* who helped. But I must thank by name:

Bea Hines, Guillermo Martinez, Joe Elbert, Andres Viglucci, Geraldine Baum, Anders Gyllenhaal, Barbara Gutierrez, Charles Whited, Fabiola Santiago, John MacMullin, Alvah Chapman and Brian Duffy. Thanks also to John Keasler and Don Wright of the *Miami News* for their encouragement and assistance.

Among those who shared important sociological and economic data with me I want to single out for special thanks Professor Jan Luytjes of Florida International University, whose depth of understanding of Miami may well be unique. Professor Juan M. Clark of Miami-Dade Community College and Guarione M. Diaz of the Cuban National Planning Council also provided me with extremely valuable information. John Motion and the Florida Department of Commerce were a constant source of data, as were a number of other Miami, Dade County and Florida state government agencies. These included Stuart L. Rogel and the Miami Beach Department of Economic Development; Amaury Zuriarrain and the Metro-Dade Aviation Department; Fedy

Vieux-Brierre and the City of Miami Department of Economic Development; the Miami Downtown Development Authority; Woody Graber and the Miami Beach Development Corporation; and the Research Division of the Metro-Dade County Planning Department, among many others.

Sandy Lane and her colleagues at the Greater Miami Chamber of Commerce, including Seth Gordon, were invariably an enthusiastic source of information. I appreciated their help all the more because they realized my purpose was not at all to present some "Chamber of Commerce" view of Miami. The same was true of Allan R. Wolfe and the staff of Al Wolfe Associates, including Jeff Abbaticchio, who were of such enormous help, along with the Miami Metro Department of Tourism.

Florida politicians are a fascinating bunch, and one of the real pleasures of researching this book was getting to know so many of them. Maurice Ferre, of course, tops this exotic list. I am also deeply grateful to former governor Bob Graham; to Rosario Kennedy, to Xavier Suarez and to Joe Carollo, Jack Gordon, Alex Daoud, Ruth Shack, Claude Pepper, Humberto Cortina, Howard Gary, Marvin Dunn, and their staffs and assistants.

Valued sources who became valued friends include Rev. Thomas R. Wenski of the Haitian Catholic Center; Msgr. Bryan Walsh; Sandy Leon; Leo and Mimi Succar; and Barrie Brett. Suzanne B. Spear introduced me to her daughter, Laurinda Spear, and her son-in-law, Bernardo Fort-Brescia, among others at Arquitectonica. But that was only one of her many kindnesses.

The help and kindness of I. B. Singer, Barbara Baer Capitman and Marjory Stoneman Douglas, though obvious throughout the book, were of greater value than I can ever express.

Deep thanks, too, to Irwin Sawitz, Stephen Muss, Helen Muir, Carol Meyers, David Krieff, and to the cast and crew of "Miami Vice." And to: Maria Camila Leiva and the Miami Free Zone Corporation; Brent Eaton, Martin Goren and many others at the Drug Enforcement Agency; to the Immigration and Naturalization Service; to the Roman Catholic Archdiocese of Miami; to past and present Florida state officials, ranging from cops and helicopter pilots to members of the Cabinet, and including Margaret Kempell. And to: countless other officials of the cities of Miami, Miami Beach and Opa-locka, and of Dade County; to Les Brown and the Quest Center; Hank Meyer; Hugues de Rochefort; Lucette E. Fortier and the Florida Department of Law Enforcement; Julie C. Simon; Martin Z. Marguiles; Stuart Bornstein; the Florida Department of Natural Resources; Josefina Carbonell; Bernardo Benes; Jimmy Buffett, Will Jennings and Marshall Chapman; the Florida Marine Patrol; Susana Sori, Arturo Rodriguez, Carlos Luis and the Cuban Museum of Art and Culture; Laura Cerwinske; Ferdie Pacheco; Curtis DeWitz; Cesar Odio; Maryann Haggerty of the Fort Lauderdale *Sun-Sentinel;* Micki Carden of the Miami-Dade Public Library System; and Mitchell Kaplan.

My debt to the historical studies of Arva Moore Parks, Gloria Jahoda and David Nolan, and to the researches of professors Thomas D. Boswell and James R. Curtis, is made clear in the notes, but I wish to emphasize it here.

This book never would have been written or published without the help of people outside Florida. The editors of *Esquire, Harper's* and *GQ* magazines, and above all of the Atlantic Monthly Press supported me generously and enthusiastically in this work. Cate Breslin was a bottomless source of facts, clippings and recondite lore I might otherwise have missed. Minnie Cassatt Hickman, Roger Friedman and Joan Allman helped in countless ways. It was thanks to Bob Anson that I began writing about Miami in the first place.

You haven't really seen Miami unless you have seen it through a windshield, from behind the wheel of a car. So I owe an enormous debt to Donald Cheung, who, during one of his visits to the United States, made an irreplaceable contribution to this book by teaching me to drive like a real American.

Stephen Allman—unsurpassed as sailor, brother and friend—provided another unique perspective in the course of our sails off the Florida coast. In distant Paris, Chantal Curtis had the idea of going to Chartres, and so provided another perspective on Miami I would not otherwise have had. From even farther away, in Hong Kong, Martha Avery and John Stevenson encouraged my amateur interest in quantum physics by sending book after book, and so provided still another way of looking at Miami.

The contributions of all these people were enormous. But immeasurably greater than them all combined was what my friend and editor, Joyce Johnson, did to make this book a reality.

In the course of writing it, I learned even more from her than I did from Miami.

Like Miami, she is irresistible and unique. She was the Julia Tuttle of this book, its essential prime mover.

Notes

The following abbreviations are used in the notes:

APA   Zach, Paul, ed. *Florida.* Hong Kong: APA Productions, 1982.

Herald   *Miami Herald.*

Britannica   *The Encyclopaedia Britannica.* Eleventh edition. Twenty-nine volumes. New York: The Encyclopaedia Britannica Company, 1910–11.

WPA   Federal Writers' Project. *The WPA Guide to Florida: The Federal Writers' Project Guide to 1930s Florida.* New York: Pantheon Books, 1984.

Notes to the Prologue
AN ALEPH OF A METROPOLIS

Page 4. Citations from Wallace Stevens: "Nomad Exquisite," *The Collected Poems* (New York: Vintage Books, 1954), p. 95.

Page 13. Changing media view of Miami: *Wall Street Journal,* 20 May 1982;

House & Garden, June 1983; *Vogue,* October 1984; Joel Achenbach, " 'New' Miami: Redefining Paradise," *Herald,* 14 April 1985.

Page13. "Paradise Lost" view of Miami: *Time*, 23 November 1981.

Page 14. Miami on the "ragged edge of anarchy": *Herald*, 15 June 1985.

Page 15. Proxmire criticisms: Office of Senator William Proxmire, press release, 1 July 1985; *Herald,* 1 July 1985.

Page 15. Hurricane dangers: *Herald,* 28 July 1985; Orrin H. Pilkey, Jr. and others. *Living with the East Florida Shore* (Durham, North Carolina: Duke University Press, 1984), pp. 143–49, 245–54; *Herald,* 17 July 1985; Laura Misch, "Hurricane Hint: Everyone Off Miami Beach," *Herald,* 24 July 1983.

Page 17. Borges quotes: Jorge Luis Borges, *A Personal Anthology* (Secaucus, N.J.: Castle Books, 1972), pp. 138–54.

Notes to Chapter 1
PRIME TIME

Page 22. Details on McDuffie murder and Miami riots: Bruce Porter and Marvin Dunn, *The Miami Riot of 1980: Crossing the Bounds* (Lexington, Massachusetts: Lexington Books, 1984), pp. xiii, 181, 173, 27–47, 50–56; also *Herald,* "The Fire This Time: A Special Issue About the Liberty City Riots," 24 August 1980; interviews with Marvin Dunn, Bea Hines, Maurice Ferre, Kenneth Harms, Jan B. Luytjes and others.

Page 25. Details on Marielitos: "The Boatlift," *Herald,* 11 December 1983, pp. 18M–19M; interviews with Bob Graham, Cesar Odio, David Smith, Guillermo Martinez and others.

Page 30. Details on Miami construction boom: City of Miami. *Miami Business Report: 1983–1984* (Miami: City of Miami Department of Economic Development, 1984), p. 3.

Page 33. Details on Arquitectonica: *Architectural Record,* August 1982; *Progressive Architecture,* February 1983; *House & Garden,* June 1983; *Wall Street Journal,* 7 July 1983; *Time,* 23 July 1984; *Esquire,* December 1984; *Newsweek,* 4 February 1985; interviews with Laurinda Spear and Bernarndo Fort-Brescia; thanks to Suzanne Spear for arranging access to Arquitectonica's buildings, including her own home.

Page 34. Negative comments on Arquitectonica quoted in: L. Erik Calonius, "Architectural Firm Alters Miami's Skyline and Calls National Attention to Its Designs," *Wall Street Journal*, 7 July 1983.

Page 38. Resnick quote: Alexander Cockburn, "The Persecution and Planned Destruction of Old Miami Beach," *Village Voice*, 27 April 1982.

Notes to Chapter 2
IN THE PINK

Page 42. Criticisms of Christo project: Joe Starita, "Red Tape, Red Ink Couldn't Squelch Pink Project," *Herald*, 2 May 1983.

Page 43. Cuban and Haitian participation in the Christo project: Joe Starita, "Dedicated Workers Surround Islands," *Herald*, 2 May 1983; *Herald*, 5 May 1983.

Page 44. Praise for Christo: Jay Maeder, "Hail, Our Surrounded Christo: Often Scorned, He's Smothered With Laurels," *Herald*, 8 May 1983; "Thank You, Christo," *Herald* editorial, 22 May 1983; Joanna Wragg, "Let's Call It 'Biscayne Bay Area,'" *Herald*, 11 May 1983.

Page 44. Christo comments on color pink: *Herald*, 1 May 1983.

Page 46. Details on Regine's and Grand Bay Hotel: Jo Werne, "Grand Artistry on the Bay," *Herald*, 11 December 1983; also *Herald*, 4 December 1983; other information provided by Hank Meyer Associates, Inc.

Page 48. Regine's opening: *Herald*, 7 October 1983; 10 December 1983; *Women's Wear Daily*, 13 December 1983; *Vogue*, January 1986.

Page 48. Regine on Deco: Laura Cerwinske interview, "On Design," December 1983, p. 16.

Page 49. Ralph Sanchez background and quotes: Liz Balmaseda, "Rafael's Prix Destination," *Herald*, 22 February 1983.

Page 55. Miami criticisms of "Miami Vice": Steve Sonsky, "Tonight, America Tunes in to Miami," *Herald*, 16 September 1984.

Page 56. "No earth tones": *Time*, 16 September 1985, p. 60.

Page 56. Comparisons to Casablanca: David Rieff, "Letter from Miami: Virtue and Vice in the Sunbelt," *Vanity Fair,* December 1985; *Time,* 16 September 1985, p. 62; *Washington Post,* 11 March 1984, p. K5.

Page 56. "Paradise Refound": Henri Pierre, "Miami ou le 'paradise retrouve,' " *Le Monde,* 6 June 1986.

Notes to Chapter 3
STAYIN' ALIVE

Page 65. Drugs on everyone's hands: *Herald,* 16 January 1985.

Page 66. Budget figures for "Miami Vice" and Miami vice squad: *Harper's,* October 1985, pp. 15, 76; *Herald,* 11 April 1986, p. 15D.

Page 78. Purses, beepers and smurfs: interviews with Brent Eaton and other drug enforcement officials; John Dorschner, "Welcome to Casablanca," *Tropic,* 15 June 1986.

Page 83. Miami "a military supermarket": *Global Gateway,* June 1985, pp. 134–36, 146–48.

Notes to Chapter 4
SONNY CROCKETT AND THE SUNILAND SHOOT-OUT

Page 86. "Bloodiest shoot-out" and other details: *Washington Post,* 12 April 1986, pp. A1, A6; 20 April 1986, pp. A12–13.

Page 87. "Cops' Theory on Killers"; details on insurance: Martin Merzer, "Cops' Theory on Killers: Each Slew the Other's Wife," *Herald,* 16 April 1986.

Page 88. McNeil and motorist quotes; description of traffic: *People* magazine, April 1986, pp. 112–13.

Page 89. Details on Mireles and other aspects of shoot-out: Brian Duffy, "Death Bathed Sunny Day in Horror: FBI's Plan of Attack Blew Up in Tragedy," *Herald,* 20 April 1986.

Page 92. Details on Platt's life; children's statements; "anything for money": Freedberg article in *Herald,* 24 April 1986.

Page 94. "Up for Grabs": John Rothchild, *Up for Grabs: A Trip Through Time and Space in the Sunshine State* (New York: Viking, 1985).

Page 95. Details on Olmos: Richard Harrington, " 'Vice' and Virtuosity: Edward James Olmos, Along the Cultural Divide," *Washington Post,* 20 December 1985. Deep thanks here to the Cate Breslin clipping service.

Page 97. Details on production of "Miami Vice": Thanks to Carol Meyers for arranging access to the set, and meetings with Don Johnson, Michael Mann, Edward James Olmos and Philip Michael Thomas.

Page 99. Mireles at South Miami Hospital: Richard Wallace, "Agent Checks Out to Hero's Welcome," *Herald,* 25 April 1986.

Page 102. Original idea for "Miami Vice": *Herald,* 16 September 1984.

Page 104. Mailer on Miami Beach: Norman Mailer, *Miami and the Siege of Chicago* (Harmondsworth, England: Penguin, 1968), pp. 12–13.

Notes to Chapter 5
GOLEMS

Page 111. I. B. Singer on Miami: my thanks to Mr. Singer for his constant willingness to discuss Miami, and every other subject conceivable under the sun, during my visits there.

Page 112. Details on Joe's Stone Crab: Thanks to Irwin Sawitz for his insights on both the history of the restaurant and the history of Miami. Additional information was gleaned from: Jack McClintock, "How Stone Crabs Became a Delicacy," published in the *Herald* in January 1975; Janet Chusmir, "Jesse Weiss—'You Go First!' " also published in the *Herald;* and Laura Owens, "Backstage at Joe's," *Herald,* 13 January 1983, and Runyon's column for King Features.

Page 119. Details on Tuttle, Flagler, Miami's foundation and the true story of the orange blossoms: Sidney Walter Martin, *Florida's Flagler* (Athens, Georgia: University of Georgia Press, 1949), p. 154.

Page 124. Other aspects of Miami's early history: Arva Moore Parks, *The Magic City: Miami* (Tulsa: Continental Heritage Press, 1981), pp. 60–64.

Notes to Chapter 6
CARDBOARD WAVES

Page 131. Origins of racial segregation in Miami: Parks, pp. 137, 141; APA, p. 78.

Page 132. Indian skulls given as souvenirs: Barry B. Levine, "Miami: The Capital of Latin America," *Wilson Quarterly,* Winter 1985.

Page 132. Ponce de Leon myth: Marjory Stoneman Douglas, *Florida: The Long Frontier* (New York: Harper & Row, 1967), p. 46; *Britannica,* X, p. 541.

Page 134. Early struggles for control of Florida: Douglas, pp. 62–76, 111, 113.

Page 136. Jackson's outrages in Florida: Gloria Jahoda, *Florida: A Bicentennial History* (New York: W. W. Norton & Company, 1976), pp. 47, 54; Douglas, pp. 129–30; Sidney Lens, *The Forging of the American Empire* (New York: Thomas Y. Crowell, 1971), p. 93.

Page 137. Opposition to U.S. in Florida an early version of the "Red Peril": Thomas A. Bailey, *A Diplomatic History of the American People* (New York: Appleton-Century-Crofts, 1950), pp. 130, 154; Albert K. Weinberg, *Manifest Destiny: A Study of Nationalist Expansion in American History* (Baltimore: The Johns Hopkins Press, 1935), pp. 204–8.

Page 138. Purchase of Florida a myth: Douglas, p. 50; Bailey, p. 173.

Page 139. U.S. principles of liberty excluded blacks and Indians: Jahoda, pp. 47, 54.

Page 139. Details of Osceola's youth: *Britannica,* XX, p. 346.

Page 139. Denigration of Seminoles' valor: *Britannica,* XX, p. 347.

Page 140. Personal description of Osceola: Douglas, p. 146.

Page 141. Osceola's head exhibited as tourist attraction: Douglas, p. 147.

Page 141. Continuing Seminole resistance: R. F. Weigley, *History of the United States Army* (New York: Macmillan, 1967), quoted in Robert B. Asprey, *War in the Shadows: The Guerrilla in History*, two volumes (Garden City, N.Y.: Doubleday & Company, 1975), I, p. 159.

Page 141. Florida population statistics: Jahoda, p. 143; Douglas, p. 38; Jahoda, pp. 158–59; Rand McNally Contemporary World Atlas (New York: Rand McNally & Company, 1978), p. 102.

Page 142. Harney attacks on Seminoles: Parks, p. 33.

Page 143. Jackson "The Devil": Jahoda, p. 47.

Page 143. Invention of air conditioning scorned: Douglas, p. 152.

Page 144. Miami "not a good city in which to be black": Andrew Neil, "America's Latin Beat: A Survey of South Florida," *Economist,* 16 October 1982.

Page 144. Leasing of black convicts: *Britannica,* X, p. 543.

Page 147. Blacks banned from Palm Beach: WPA, p. 229.

Page 147. 1964 Civil Rights Act finally ended civil war: Jahoda, p. 78.

Page 147. Northern adoption of southern racial attitudes: Douglas, pp. 11–12.

Page 148. Mizner's "Spanish" architecture: WPA, pp. 229–30; David Nolan, *Fifty Feet in Paradise: The Booming of Florida* (New York: Harcourt Brace Jovanovich, 1984), p. 33.

Page 149. Mythical antiquity of St. Augustine: Nolan, pp. 60–61; WPA, pp. 250–57; APA, p. 234.

Page 150. "Cardboard waves" extravaganza of false history at Pueblo Feliz: Parks, p. 121.

Page 150. Seminole War names on modern road maps of Florida: WPA, p. 228; Asprey, I, p. 160; Parks, pp. 28–29.

Page 152. Disney World castle copied from Ludwig the Mad: APA, p. 109.

Page 152. "Double bar-sinister" in American life: Walt W. Rostow, *Politics and the Stages of Growth* (Cambridge: Cambridge University Press, 1971), pp. 184–86.

Page 153. Coachoochee statement on liberty: John T. Sprague, *The Origin, Progress and Conclusion of the Florida War* (New York: D. Appleton Co., 1848), p. 260. Quoted in Jahoda, p. 64.

Page 154. Sixteen million dollars for the Seminoles: APA, p. 67.

Page 154. "History of white Florida . . . began with violation," and American forgetfulness of historical truth: Jahoda, pp. 19, 10.

Notes to Chapter 7
ELSEWHERE DESTINIES

Page 156. Flagler conquest of Florida: WPA, p. 227; Martin, pp. 185–87; Nolan, p. 136.

Page 158. Henry Plant and the Tampa Bay Hotel: Jahoda, pp. 92–93; Henry James, *The American Scene* (Bloomington: Indiana University Press, 1968), p. 450; WPA, p. 228; Douglas, pp. 244–45.

Page 160. "Horrible excesses in Havana": *Britannica,* VII, p. 604.

Page 160. Early Cuban impact on Key West: WPA, p. 60.

Page 161. Cuban casualties in struggle against Spanish: Asprey, I, p. 173.

Page 162. José Martí speeches in the United States: Jorge Manach, *Martí* (New York: Devin-Adair, 1950), p. 276. Cited in Jahoda, p. 97; Asprey, I, p. 174.

Page 162. McKinley and Roosevelt on war with Spain: Robert W. Leopold, *The Growth of American Foreign Policy* (New York: Knopf, 1965); Theodore Roosevelt, *The Rough Riders* (New York: Charles Scribner's Sons, 1906), p. 1. Cited in Jahoda, p. 98.

Page 163. Growth of Florida railroads: Nolan, p. 79.

Page 164. U.S. decision to declare war on Spain: Bailey, p. 509; Asprey, I, p. 172.

Page 164. Convergence on Tampa Bay Hotel: Jahoda, pp. 97–98; Bailey, p. 511; Jahoda, p. 99; Nolan, p. 127.

Page 165. Racial prejudice against Cubans: Asprey, I, p. 176; II, p. 935.

Page 165. Spanish capitulation before war was declared: Walter Karp, *The Politics of War* (New York: Harper & Row, 1979), pp. 91–92.

Page 165. Bismarck on the U.S.: Samuel Eliot Morison and Henry Steele Commager, *The Growth of the American Republic* (New York: Oxford University Press, 1954), II, p. 332.

Page 167. U.S. "liberation" denied the Cubans the right to liberate themselves: Thomas D. Boswell and James R. Curtis, *The Cuban-American Experience: Culture, Images, and Perspectives* (Totowa, N.J.: Rowman & Allanheld, 1983), p. 16.

Page 168. U.S. domination of Cuba and abuse of other Latin neighbors: Asprey, II, pp. 935–36; John Gunther, *Inside Latin America* (New York: Harper & Brothers, 1941), p. 464; Walter LaFeber, *The Panama Canal: The Crisis in Historical Perspective* (New York: Oxford University Press, 1978), p. 53.

Page 168. Theodore Roosevelt "accused of seduction" and proved "guilty of rape": David McCullough, *The Path Between the Seas: The Creation of the Panama Canal 1870–1914* (New York: Simon and Schuster, 1977), p. 383.

Page 169. Tampa's growth as a result of the Spanish-American War: Jahoda, p. 93.

Page 169. Miami's early travails and resourcefulness: Parks, pp. 73–78, 59; Nolan, p. 126; Martin, p. 67.

Page 171. No white soldiers punished for attacks on blacks: Porter and Dunn, p. 3.

Notes to Chapter 8
OOLITE

Page 174. Flagler's cautions on Tuttle's debts: Nolan, p. 125.

Page 174. Background information on Stephen Muss, Maurice Ferre and Marjory Stoneman Douglas: Thanks to all three for their time and cooperation, also to Barrie Brett for arranging the meetings with Stephen Muss.

Page 183. Background on Mel Fisher: Thanks to Bob Graham, Jimmy Buffett, Will Jennings and Marshall Chapman for their help in Key West; Susan Ornstein, "Midas Man Fisher Wins Admiration of Conchs," *Herald,* 28 July, 1985; Patty Shillington, "Treasure Hunters Hit Jackpot Off Key West," *Herald,* 21 July 1985.

Page 184. Bob Dubois and the Haitian boy: Russell Banks, *Continental Drift* (New York: Harper & Row, 1985), pp. 312, 346–47.

Notes to Chapter 9
CIRCUMSPICE

Page 186. Background on Carl Fisher: Nolan, pp. 157–58.

Page 186. Environmental conflict built into Miami geography: Parks, p. 87.

Page 187. Denunciations of Broward's drainage schemes and early environmental efforts: Douglas, pp. 254, 7; Parks, p. 87.

Page 188. Cuban relief effort biggest in U.S. history: Boswell and Curtis, p. 3.

Page 189. Early automobile history of Miami: WPA, p. 406; Parks, p. 95; Douglas, p. 8.

Page 190. Early aviation and commercial history: Parks, pp. 95, 130, 188, 202, 180, 183.

Page 191. Description of Firestone mansion: WPA, pp. 220–21.

Page 191. William Jennings Bryan in Miami: *Britannica,* IV, p. 697; Douglas, p. 17; Parks, p. 116.

Page 191. President-elect Harding in Miami: Nolan, pp. 170–71.

Page 192. Background on George Merrick: Nolan, pp. 161, 176; APA, p. 184.

Page 195. Details on Hialeah, Opa-locka and Glenn Curtiss: WPA, p. 220; James Nelson, "A Tale of Twin Cities and How They Parted," *Herald,* 9 September 1985; Michael J. Maxwell, "Opa-Locka: The Baghdad of Dade," *Preservation Today,* 1985; *Opa-locka Times,* 12 January 1927. Quoted in James J.

McKnight, "The Tale of Opa-Locka," *Miami Sunday News,* 4 July 1951; Nolan, p. 199; *Opa-Locka Times,* 23 February 1927.

Page 199. Blacks unwelcome at City Hall: City of Opa-locka, Public Affairs Department. Taped oral history interview with Freeman Collins, Sr. (undated transcript).

Page 199. Nineteen-eighty arson in Opa-locka: Porter and Dunn, pp. 19–20, 66.

Page 208. "Mom and Pop" incorporation of cities in Florida: Parks, p. 93; Edward Sofen, *The Miami Metropolitan Experiment: A Metropolitan Action Study* (Garden City, New York: Doubleday, 1966), pp. 267, 13.

Page 209. Larkins renamed South Miami: WPA, p. 324.

Notes to Chapter 10
THE CITY OF TOMORROW

Page 211. Florida population boom in the twenties: WPA, p. 61.

Page 211. Moorish skyscrapers: Parks, p. 119.

Page 212. Immense newspaper advertising: Frederick Lewis Allen, *Only Yesterday: An Informal History of the 1920's* (New York: Harper & Row, 1959), p. 232.

Page 212. Construction boom: WPA, p. 213.

Page 215. Mosquitoes and Miami: Parks, pp. 16, 34, 71, 83; Mike Capuzzo, "Seems Like Old Times," *Herald,* 4 April 1984.

Page 217. Cold of Miami winter: Douglas, p. 13.

Page 218. Florida as panacea, and writers who praised it: Nolan, p. 31; Douglas, p. 216.

Page 219. Henry James on Florida: James, pp. 411, 423–60; Leon Edel, *Henry James: A Life* (New York: Harper & Row, 1985), pp. 608–9.

Page 220. Will Rogers on Fisher and Sunshine State: Nolan, p. 156.

Page 220. Twenties Miami a "world of speculative make-believe": John Kenneth Galbraith, *The Great Crash: 1929* (Boston: Houghton Mifflin Company, 1954), pp. 8–9.

Page 221. Miami Beach as Fisher created it: WPA, pp. 210–11.

Page 222. Money in Miami banks: Allen, p. 234.

Page 223. Miami only place where breakfast lie is true by evening: *Herald*, 8 April 1984.

Page 223. "Soothing Tropic Wind": Allen, p. 232.

Page 224. Impact of hurricane of 1926: P. W. Harlem, *Aerial Photographic Interpretation of the Historical Changes in Northern Biscayne Bay, Florida: 1925 to 1976* (University of Miami Sea Grant Technical Bulletin 40, 1976). Quoted in Pilkey, pp. 248–49; Pilkey, pp. 139, 248.

Page 224. Hurricane's effect on Hialeah: *Herald*, 24 July 1983.

Page 224. Aftermath of hurricane: Nolan, p. 222; Pilkey, p. 245; *Herald*, 21 August 1983; Parks, pp. 126–27.

Page 224. Miami still the "Riviera of America," other PR efforts to deny effects of hurricane, and real damage: Galbraith, p. 11; Pilkey, p. 249.

Page 225. Collapse of banking and real estate: Allen, p. 234; Nolan, p. 229.

Page 226. Fate of George Merrick: Parks, p. 129; discussion with Marjory Stoneman Douglas.

Page 226. "Malevolent Providence": Allen, p. 233.

Page 226. Hurricanes of 1928 and 1935: WPA, pp. 61, 330; Parks, p. 88; Nolan, p. 297.

Page 228. Development of Deco architecture: Paul A. Rothman, ed., *Miami Beach Art Deco District: Time Future* (Miami: Community Action and Research, 1982), p. 4; Laura Cerwinske, *Tropical Deco: The Architecture and Design of Old Miami Beach* (New York: Rizzoli, 1981), pp. 12, 41, 13.

Page 229. Capone in Miami: Nolan, pp. 236–37; Allen, p. 216; WPA, p. 221.

Page 230. Higher murder rate in Miami in the twenties than now: *Herald,* 8 April 1984.

Page 231. Miami recovering from Depression: Parks, p. 133.

Page 232. Miami thriving in the late thirties: WPA, pp. 208–9.

Page 233. The "real McCoy": *Herald,* 8 April 1984.

Page 234. Escape the secret of Miami's continuing appeal: Allen, pp. 227–28.

Page 236. Castro in Miami: John Dorschner, "The Castro Story: The Evolution of an Enigmatic Leader," *Herald,* 11 December 1983.

Page 236. Denials Miami will become drug center: *Herald,* 8 April 1984.

Page 236. Tuttle arrival and her predictions Miami will become center of South American trade: Parks, pp. 63, 151.

Notes to Chapter 11
THE MOUSE, THE MOON AND THE TOILET SEAT

Page 240. Miami problems following World War II: Nolan, pp. 259–61.

Page 243. Disney World and creation of water: Nolan, p. 269; *Harper's,* March 1986, p. 56.

Page 243. Impact of Disney World on central Florida: APA, p. 106; Nolan, pp. 264–66.

Page 247. Details on Busch Gardens: APA, pp. 141–42.

Page 250. Exclusion of Jews from Broward County: Michael Barone and Grant Ujifusa, *The Almanac of American Politics 1984* (Washington, D.C.: National Journal, 1983), p. 261.

Page 252. Genesis of Fontainebleau hotel, and Lapidus-Novack feud: Mike Capuzzo, "The Sand Castle," *Herald,* 19 February 1984.

Page 253. Statistics on Fontainebleau: Julie C. Simon, " 'One Great Name Behind Another': A Short History of the Fontainebleau Hotel" (Fontainebleau Hilton, undated press release); "Did You Know That the Fontainebleau Hilton Is . . ." (Fontainebleau Hilton, undated press release).

Page 253. Fontainebleau visitors, including presidents and elephant: *Herald,* 19 February 1984; Theodore H. White, *The Making of the President 1968* (New York: Pocket Books, 1970), pp. 295, 303.

Page 254. Napoleon's embellishment of the original Fontainebleau: *Britannica,* X, pp. 606–7.

Page 259. "Are Cities Un-American?": William H. Whyte, Jr. and others, *The Exploding Metropolis* (Garden City, N.Y.: Doubleday Anchor Books, 1958), p. 1.

Page 262. "ARE ALL BIG CITIES DOOMED?": *U.S. News & World Report,* 13 April 1976.

Page 262. "O Florida, Venereal Soil": Stevens, p. 47.

Notes to Chapter 12
THE SHARK IN THE WATER

Page 266. U.S. citizens unwilling to risk war for Cuba: Jean Wardlow, "North Americans Differ on Tribute: Called 'Least He Could Do,' " *Herald,* 30 December 1962.

Page 267. Details of Kennedy at the Orange Bowl: *Herald,* 30 December 1962.

Page 268. Bay of Pigs ransom: Parks, p. 154.

Page 268, 275. Kennedy hand extended, and "E Pluribus Unum" in president's flag: thanks to Humberto Cortina for his memories, photographs and documents about the Kennedy speech at the Orange Bowl.

Page 274. The shark in the water: Associated Press, "Sharks Halt Kennedy Swim," 29 December 1962.

Notes to Chapter 13
YEARS OF DESTINY

Page 276. Kennedy on Cuba and Alliance for Progress: *Public Papers of the Presidents, 1961* (Washington: U.S. Government Printing Office, 1962), pp. 17, 306.

Page 276. Growing Latin American debt: Frederico G. Gil, *Latin American-United States Relations* (New York: Harcourt Brace Jovanovich, 1971), pp. 3, 268; United Nations, *Second United Nations Development Decade: Latin America's Foreign Trade Policy* (Lima: Economic and Social Council, Economic Commission for Latin America, 1969), p. 86; Sam Dillon and Andres Oppenheimer, "U.S. Watches Latin Debt Crisis Grow," *Herald,* 5 September 1985.

Page 277. Destruction of democracy under Alliance: Claude Julien, *America's Empire* (New York: Pantheon Books, 1971), p. 253.

Page 277. Latin protests: *New York Times,* 16 June 1969.

Page 278. "So far from God and so close to the United States": George Pendle, *A History of Latin America* (Harmondsworth, England: Penguin, 1971), p. 164. Pendle credits Mexican dictator Porfirio Díaz with coining the phrase.

Page 279. "Accident" of Cuban revolution: Levine, p. 69.

Page 280. Details on Cuban diaspora: Guarione M. Diaz, "The Changing Cuban Community," unpublished research paper, Miami, 1981; Sergio Diaz Briquets and Lisandro Perez, *Cuba: The Demography of Revolution* (Washington: Population Reference Bureau, 1981), p. 26. Cited in Boswell and Curtis, p. 42; Boswell and Curtis, pp. 1, 40.

Page 281. Few "fled" Cuba: Clark Fact Sheet, p. 1.

Page 282. Other causes than Castro for leaving: Boswell and Curtis, p. 38; Msgr. Bryan Walsh, "Castro or No Castro, Miami Would Be Hispanic," *Herald,* 18 December 1983.

Page 284. Cuban migrants not an elite group: Boswell and Curtis, p. 1; Richard R. Fagen, Richard A. Brody and Thomas J. O'Leary, *Cubans in Exile: Disaffection and the Revolution* (Stanford: Stanford University Press, 1968), p. 19. Cited in Boswell and Curtis, p. 46; Diaz, p. 4; Strategy Research Corporation, *The 1983 Dade County Latin Market* (Miami: Strategy Research Corporation, 1983), p. 27.

Page 286. U.S. government aid for Cubans, and Cuban dependence on government welfare programs: Jan B. Luytjes and others, *Economic Impact of Refugees in Dade County* (Miami: Florida International University, 1982), p. 2; George Stein, "Cubans Gain Economically, But Many Are Left Behind," *Herald,* 18 December 1983; Tom Alexander, "Those Amazing Cuban Emigres," *Fortune,* October 1966.

Page 288. Cuban gains at expense of blacks: Luytjes, p. 2.

Page 288. Problems Great Society created for blacks: Parks, pp. 157–59.

Page 290. Gradual rise in Miami Cuban population: Strategy Research Corporation, 1983, p. 8.

Page 293. Successful Cubans all over the United States: "Cuban Emigres Who Made Their Mark," *Herald,* 18 December 1983.

Page 295. Official U.S. effort to force Cubans to settle outside Florida: Boswell and Curtis, p. 64.

Page 297. Castro's sister in Miami: Jay Ducassi, "Brother Fidel Betrayed Everyone, His Sister Says," *Herald,* 11 December 1983.

Notes to Chapter 14
FANTASY'S CHILD

Page 306. Kennedy on the "self-indulgent" being swept away: *Public Papers of the Presidents, 1961,* p. 306.

Page 310. "Anti-Castro" terrorism in Miami: *Herald,* 18 December 1983.

Page 313. Rise in Cuban incomes: Luytjes, p. 20; *Herald,* 18 December 1983; Boswell and Curtis, p. 3.

Page 314. Cuban consumption of American fast food, and other signs of assimilation: Strategy Research Corporation, pp. 35–44.

Page 315. Cuban migrants' optimism about themselves and Miami: Alejandro Portes, Juan M. Clark and Manuel M. Lopez, "Six Years Later, the Process of Incorporation of Cuban Exiles in the United States: 1973–1979," *Cuban Studies/Estudios Cubanos,* January 1982, pp. 10–13.

Page 316. Cubans' refusal to make either/or cultural choices: Strategy Research Corporation, pp. 52–54.

Page 317. Migrants' optimism and high evaluations of themselves, their English and of Miami: Portes and others, pp. 6–7.

Page 318. Details on Calle Ocho festival: Lourdes Meluza, "Calle Ocho: Little Havana Is Throwing a Giant Street Party, and You're Invited," *Herald*, 7 March 1986.

Page 320. Miami Cuban response to the Marielitos: Carlos J. Arboleya, "Cuban Influx: Miami's Explosive Blessing," *Herald*, 8 June 1980.

Notes to Chapter 15
THE AMERICANIZATION OF ROSARIO

Page 322. "Cuban Refugee Elected Mayor": *New York Times*, 13 November 1985.

Page 323. "Mayor of 'North Cuba' ": *Time*, 11 November 1985.

Page 323. Xavier Suarez background: Thanks to Xavier Suarez for his time and help both before and after becoming mayor. Other details are taken from: Neil Brown, "Suarez Engineers a Careful Campaign," *Herald*, 15 October 1985; Tom Fiedler and Rick Hirsch, "In Mayor's Race, Choice Could Be Matter of Style," *Herald*, 10 November 1985; Gael Love, "Politics: Mayor Over Miami—Xavier Suarez," *Interview* magazine, September 1986, pp. 50–51; Guy Gugliotta, "The Importance of Being Xavier Or, Why the First Cuban Mayor of Miami Is from Washington," *Herald*, 28 September 1986.

Page 324. Cuban migration from the North: Boswell and Curtis, pp. 66–67.

Page 332. Analysis of 1985 Miami election: Thanks to Marvin Dunn, Maurice Ferre, Howard Gary, David Kennedy, Rosario Kennedy, Guillermo Martinez and Xavier Suarez, among many others, for their time and comments. Direct quotes and other facts were also taken from: Luis Fieldstein Soto, "Commission Foes Aggressively Court Cuban Vote," *Herald*, 11 November 1985; Tom Fiedler, "Miami Race Shakes Up Ethnic Myths," *Herald*, 6 November 1985; "Long-Sought Win Brings Formidable Tasks," *Herald*, 13 November 1985; Guillermo Martinez, "At Last, a Cuba-Less Miami Election," *Herald*, 8 November 1985; Luis Feldstein Soto, "Kennedy Handily Knocks Off Perez," *Herald*, 13 November 1986; Marc Fisher, "Consensus Candidates Popular With Voters," *Herald*, 7 November 1985; Neil Brown, "Suarez Engineers a Careful Campaign," *Herald*, 13 October 1985, and other press reports.

Page 334. Details on Jeb Bush: Joel Achenbach, "The Family's Business," *Tropic* magazine, 1 January 1986.

Page 336. Details on Joe Carollo: Thanks to Joe Carollo and his staff for their time and help; Marilyn A. Moore, "A Puzzle Called Joe Carollo," *Miami News,* 20 October 1984.

Page 337. Political details on New Hampshire: Barone and Ujifusa, pp. 712–19.

Page 338. Intercommunal consensus in Miami: Richard Morin, "A Survey of Miami's Attitudes: Conflict Is on the Decline"; "Full Survey—Questions, Responses," *Herald,* 18 December 1983. The survey covered the whole of Dade County. Some other responses were as follows:

	Anglos	Blacks	Cubans
Favor Balanced Budget	86	87	76
Favor Women's Rights	87	90	83
Favor Help for Poor	66	91	78
Close Family Relations	91	93	94
Satisfied with Miami	66	76	82
Will Stay in Miami	67	78	90
Crime a Problem	97	95	98
Lack of Jobs	74	93	90
Disrespect for Law	86	87	77

Notes to Chapter 16
ONLY IN AMERICA

Page 341. "A culture of the hyphenates": Levine, pp. 68–69.

Page 342. Cuban retirement homes: *Ideal,* no. 239, 1986, p. 64.

Page 344. Americanization of Cuban Spanish: Boswell and Curtis, pp. 122–23.

Page 345. Analysis of Cuban-American art: Thanks to Susana Sori, Arturo Rodriguez, Carlos Luis and the Cuban Museum of Arts and Culture; Cuban Museum of Arts and Culture, *The Miami Generation: Nine Cuban-American Artists* (Miami: Cuban Museum of Arts and Culture, 1983).

Page 349. Similar Irish and Cuban experiences in America: Tom Fiedler, "Miami Race Shakes Up Ethnic Myths," *Herald,* 6 November 1985.

Page 349. Cubans becoming "indistinguishable" from other Americans: Boswell and Curtis, p. 102.

Page 350. Positive contributions of immigrants: Council of Economic Advisers, *Economic Report of the President* (Washington, D.C.: U.S. Government Printing Office, 1986), pp. 213–34, 254.

Page 355. America "unique" in its ability to simultaneously change and stay American: Guarione Diaz, "The New Cuban Exodus," undated mimeographed report provided by the Cuban American Planning Council, p. 5.

Page 358. Decreasing Cuban desire to return to Cuba: Portes and others, p. 10; Richard Morin, "The Desire to Return to Cuba Is Dwindling," *Herald,* 18 December 1983.

Page 359. Miami Cubans celebrating Castro's victory: Charles Whited, "Miami Then: Peak of Nightlife Era," *Herald,* 11 December 1983.

Page 361. Celebrations in Little Haiti following overthrow of Baby Doc: Thanks to Rev. Thomas Wenski of the Pierre Toussaint Catholic Haitian Center for his help. Other details are taken from articles in the *Washington Post* published on 1, 8 and 10 February 1986.

Page 362. Jeffersonian desire to escape cities: Morison and Commager, I, p. 384.

Page 363. Urbanization of the frontier: Constance McLaughlin Green, *American Cities in the Growth of the Nation* (New York: Harper Colophon, 1965), p. 1.

Page 366. Growth of new regional cities: Christopher B. Leinberger and Charles Lockwood, "How Business Is Reshaping America," *Atlantic,* October 1986, p. 43.

Page 367. Converging crime rates in Miami and Fort Lauderdale: Edna Buchanan, "Murder Rate Declined in Dade in '85," *Herald,* 5 January 1986; "Miami Falls to 7th Place in Murders," *Herald,* 27 July 1986; Christopher Wellisz, "Crime Rises 12 Percent in County," *Herald,* 14 March 1986.

Notes to the Epilogue
GOOD-BYE MIAMI

Page 376. Insights of quantum physics: Art Hobson, *Physics and Human Affairs* (New York: John Wiley & Sons, 1982), pp. 245–76.

NOTES

Page 377. "Nobody understands quantum physics": Richard Feynman, quoted in Tony Hey and Patrick Walters, *The Quantum Universe* (Cambridge, England: Cambridge University Press, 1986). Statement cited in *New York Times Book Review,* 5 October 1986, p. 55.

Page 381. The walking catfish invasion: Thanks to Mike Thomas for his insights; Leslie Kemp and James C. Clark, "Florida's Shame: What Price Progress—A Paradise Lost?," *Orlando Sentinel,* 15 April 1984; Mike Thomas and others, "Florida's Shame: We're a Water Wonderland Drowning in a Tide of Growth," *Sentinel,* 21 April 1985.

Page 384. The X-ray machine and the Haitian: Thanks to Amaury Zuriarrain, of the Metro-Dade Aviation Department, for telling me this story, and for the other information on Miami International Airport that he provided.

Page 386. Winter and the *Challenger* disaster: *Time,* 9 June 1986, pp. 14–25; 23 June 1986, p. 32.

Index

415